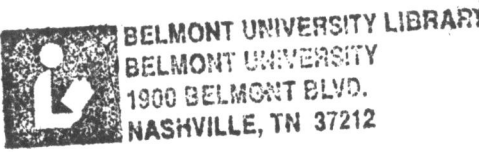
BELMONT UNIVERSITY LIBRARY
BELMONT UNIVERSITY
1900 BELMONT BLVD.
NASHVILLE, TN 37212

On Records

Delaware Indians, Colonists, and
the Media of History and Memory

ANDREW NEWMAN

University of Nebraska Press : Lincoln and London

© 2012 by the Board of Regents of the University of Nebraska
Material from chapter 1 was previously published as
"The Walam Olum: An Indigenous Apocrypha and Its Readers,"
American Literary History 22, no. 1 (2010): 26–56. A version of chapter 2 was
originally published as "Mapping a Native Account of European Land Fraud," in
Early American Cartographies, edited by Martin Brückner, 248–75. Published for the
Omohundro Institute of Early American History and Culture. Copyright © 2011 by
the University of North Carolina Press.
Used by permission of the publisher.

All rights reserved
Manufactured in the United States of America

Library of Congress Cataloging-in-Publication Data
Newman, Andrew.
On records: Delaware Indians, colonists, and the media of history and memory /
Andrew Newman.
p. cm.
Includes bibliographical references and index.
ISBN 978-0-8032-3986-9 (cloth: alk. paper)
1. Delaware Indians—Historiography. 2. Delaware Indians—Colonization.
3. Indians of North America—First contact with Europeans—Delaware.
4. Indians of North America—History—Colonial period, ca. 1600–1775.
5. Delaware—History—Colonial period, ca. 1600–1775. I. Title.
E99.D2N49 2012
974.004'97345—dc23
2012012436

Set in Quadraat by Kim Essman.
Designed by Ashley Muehlbauer.

For Mira and Reuben. And Levi.

Royalties from the sale of this book will be
donated to the Lenape Native American Foundation.

CONTENTS

List of Illustrations ix
Acknowledgments xi
Introduction 1
1. Lenape Annals................... 25
2. An Account of a Tradition.......... 55
3. The Most Valuable Record 95
4. Writings and Deeds.............. 133
   Afterword: A Chain of Memory 185
   Notes 197
   Bibliography 239
   Index 271

::::::::::: ILLUSTRATIONS :::::::::::

1. Glyphs 20–26, Book 3, from the
   "Wallam Olum" 37
2. Dido Cutting the Ox-Hide 85
3. Queen Dido founding Carthage 90
4. Hicks's *Penn's Treaty with the Indians* 98
5. West's *William Penn's Treaty with the Indians* 100
6. Penn's Tree, with the City and Port of Philadelphia 106
7. Treaty Belt 124
8. Lenape wampum belts 126
9. Map presented to the Delawares 148
10. Historical map of the Walking Purchase 157
11. "Teedyuscung's Speech" 173
12. Advertisement from the *Pennsylvania Gazette* 182

MAPS

1. Occurrences of "Deceptive Land Purchase:
   Ox Hide Measure" 74
2. Lehigh River and Tohickon and
   Neshaminy Creeks 135

ACKNOWLEDGMENTS

I have been looking forward to writing these for years. It is a pleasure to express my appreciation for the people and institutions that have helped me to write this book.

For grant support, I thank the University of California at Irvine, the Huntington Library, the Andrew W. Mellon Foundation, the Library Company of Philadelphia and Historical Society of Pennsylvania, the Faculty of Arts, Humanities and Social Sciences at Stony Brook University, and United University Professionals.

At Irvine, I had the guidance of a wonderful dissertation committee, chaired by Michael Clark, with Sharon Block and Brook Thomas as readers. I am grateful to the department of English at the University of Southern California, especially Joseph Boone, for hosting me through a year-long postdoctoral fellowship. I deeply appreciate the colleagues who have provided support and friendship at Stony Brook University. In my department, these include Peter Manning, Stacey Olster, Joaquín Martinez Pizarro, and Stephen Spector, as well as the brilliant and kind members of my reading group, Helen Choi, Douglas Pfeiffer, Ayesha Ramachandran, and Jeffrey Santa Ana. Susan Scheckel deserves special mention. Thanks also to Margaret Hanley, Lizabeth Rehn, and Martha Smith. My students Matthew Kremer and Michael Pesin provided valuable research assistance. Beyond the department, I am particularly grateful to Ned Landsman, the mentor who has become a collaborator. Thanks also to Donna Rilling, as well as the members of my interdisciplinary Long Island Railroad cohort, especially Daniel Levy and Paul Gootenberg, who invited me to present at their Initiative for the Historical Social Sciences and have generously shared their expertise.

I owe thanks to many scholars in early American studies and related fields. Among those I have gotten to know through the collegial meetings of the Society of Early Americanists, I'm indebted to Ralph Bauer, Matt Cohen, Dennis Moore, Gordon Sayre, Teresa Toulouse, Hilary Wyss, and especially Kristina Bross, whose comments helped me to understand my book's priorities. My thanks to participants in the colloquium series at the Omohundro Institute for Early American History and Culture, the McNeil Center for Early American Studies, and Columbia University. I am very grateful to Fredrika Teute for her generous commentary on early and late versions of this project. Daniel Richter provided helpful feedback on drafts of two chapters. Further thanks to Roger Abrahams, Michele Currie, Evan Haefeli, Sean Harvey, Jaap Jacobs, Michael LaCombe, Mark Meuwese, James Spady, and Dennis Tedlock.

I am grateful to Gordon Hutner, Ed White, and an anonymous reader for *American Literary History*, which published research that appears in different form in my first chapter, and to Martin Brückner and the readers for his edited collection *Early American Cartographies*, which includes a version of my second chapter. Thanks to Oxford University Press and the University of North Carolina Press, respectively, for permission to reprint.

James Rementer has responded to dozens of my e-mailed queries about the history and language of the Delaware Indians, and he generously read through my manuscript. Thanks also to correspondents he put me in touch with, Deborah Nichols-Ledermann and Ray Whritenour.

I could not ask for a more intellectually engaged and supportive editor than Matt Bokovoy of the University of Nebraska Press; he really got what I was trying to do. So did the editorial readers, Amy Schutt and Laura Stevens, and they helped to make it better. My thanks to Elisabeth Chretien, Lona Dearmont, and everyone at the University of Nebraska Press who was involved in the production of this book.

Throughout this process, I have had the unconditional support of two extended families, with the added benefit of expert advice. Alexander and Mieke Gelley provided a nurturing environment for my young family during our years in Irvine, and they continue to inspire me through their intellectual and artistic devotion. Ora Gelley and I have been sharing in each other's challenges and accomplishments for years. My parents, Robert and Ruth, and my brother Richard formed a loving household that fostered intellectual curiosity and creativity, and my eldest brother, Michael, has been a role model and advisor. My life has been enriched by the expansion of this family to include Bette Alexander, Gabriela, Ariel, and Pauline Newman, and Francisco Ordoñez, brother and colleague.

This book is dedicated to Mira, Reuben, and the new addition to our family, Levi. *On Records* is partly about the limitations and the possibilities of language; I have never experienced either so fully as when I try to find words that can express what Mira, Reuben, and Levi mean to me. I find: no words.

On Records

INTRODUCTION

In 1819 John Heckewelder, a member of the Christian sect known as the Unitas Fratrum (United Brotherhood), or the Moravians, published *An Account of the History, Manners, and Customs of the Indian Nations that Once Inhabited Pennsylvania and the Neighboring States*. Heckewelder's *History*, informed by three decades of missionary work among the Delaware (otherwise known as Lenape) Indians and related groups in Western Pennsylvania and the Ohio Country, immediately became the primary channel for the transmission of information from the traditional cultures of these displaced persons to nineteenth-century American men of letters.[1] For example, it was the "sourcebook" for the representation of Indians in James Fenimore Cooper's *Leatherstocking Tales* (1823–1841).[2] Almost two centuries later, it is still qualified as "the basic source on the Delaware."[3]

The first part of the *History* represents the Indians' accounts of their own history. According to Heckewelder, the Delawares told him:

- that "many hundred years ago" they had lived "in a very distant country in the western part of the American continent" and after an epic migration had settled in the region on the Atlantic seaboard spanning the Hudson and Delaware Rivers;[4]
- that their ancestors had been among the first natives to welcome Europeans to North America, and that the first Dutch colonists had asked for as much land as "the hide of a bullock could cover or encompass" and then had cut that hide into strips and claimed all the land they could encircle;[5]

- that Pennsylvania had been "'a last, delightful asylum'" where they had welcomed William Penn, "'the great and good MIQUON,'" who came bearing "'words of peace and good will'";⁶ and
- that before long their "'joy was turned into sorrow,'" for Penn's successors "'now only strove to get all our land from us by fraud or by force.'"⁷

These stories are the topics of the four chapters of this book: the Delawares' origins, their first contacts and land transaction with the Dutch, their first treaty with William Penn, and the "infamous" 1737 Walking Purchase land fraud.⁸ Heckewelder gives a good idea of how the Delawares' history can come to exemplify what has been grossly summed up as "the American Indian experience."⁹ The accounts he presents pertain to the vexed question of the peopling of the continent, and epitomize the highs and lows of colonial transactions. "Often I have listened to these descriptions of their hard sufferings," he wrote, "until I felt ashamed of being a *white man*."¹⁰ Yet these are not simply Lenape stories; the Delawares' history is also American history. The account of the Indians' migration had a complex bearing on the alleged right of the colonists to supplant them, and the stories of dispossession, whether "peaceable" or fraudulent, correspond to the founding stories of the settlers in the mid-Atlantic region. They were alluded to or represented in popular traditions and in works by the painters Benjamin West and Edward Hicks and the writers Voltaire, Charles Brockden Brown, Washington Irving, and Cooper, among others.

While the Delawares' exemplarity and their prominence in cultural works make their early history relevant well beyond its regional scope, this book's claim to significance beyond even early American and Native American Studies lies in its conceptual explorations. Each of the episodes in this history is controversial, and the controversies hinge on questions about the media of history and memory: can the spoken word be a reliable record of past events? If so, how many links can the chain of communication sustain, as it reaches back through generations? What authority do certain material forms, such as wampum (Algonquian or Iroquoian shell beads), or landmarks, or relics, contribute to spoken recollections? Is alphabetic writing a reliable repository for memory, or does it distort memory by alienating it from a necessary interpretive context? Can the intent behind Native American utterances be communicated across the hazards of translation and transcription, even assuming good-faith efforts to do so? As abstract formulations, these questions may be the province of philosophers of language and literacy theorists. As methodological problems, they challenge colonialist scholars. They were also matters of immediate, practical concern to cross-cultural negotiators who were framing agreements of lasting consequence, as well as to members of succeeding generations who were seeking to understand or construe past intentions and occurrences.

RECORDS AND REPRESENTATIONS

This book examines the relations between records, or the "documentation or recording of facts, events, etc.," and representations—depictions, portrayals, symbolic substitutions.[11] In legal contexts, records are considered neutral and objective, while representations are subjective. In current scholarly practice, it is now generally recognized that historical records are partial, biased, incomplete, and necessarily and sometimes deliberately distorted; in other words, all records are actually representations. Nevertheless, there remains an operative distinction between the two terms, which may be ranged along a spectrum from complete objectivity (however ideal and unrealizable) to absolute subjectivity and unreliability. Other concepts sometimes demarcate this spectrum, including past and present, writing and speech, history and memory. The closer the act of writing is to the occurrence of the event it depicts, and the less apparently artful or biased its composition, the more likely it is to be qualified as a record. Outside the domain of art, representations of events typically aspire for such qualification. For example, the literary critic Louis Montrose observes that Sir Walter Ralegh, "in his attempt to represent" his *Discovery of Guiana* (1595) "as the transparent record of his discovery . . . must seek to deprecate its style"; that is, Ralegh must minimize the extent to which his writing is shaped by literary conventions rather than observation and experience.[12]

It is Montrose who coined the neat "chiastic" slogan for the loosely defined school of criticism that emerged in the 1980s as the "New Historicism": the New Historicists' "reciprocal concern" with "the historicity of texts and the textuality of history" has had a formative influence on the burgeoning field of early Americanist literary scholarship.[13] As some New Historicists turned from the European Renaissance to contemporary writings about the New World encounters, the intervention they posed toward colonialist historians was the argument that supposed documentary sources were in fact *Representations* (the title of their journal of record). "We can be certain only," writes Stephen Greenblatt, the leading figure associated with the New Historicism, "that European representations of the New World tell us something about the European practice of representation."[14]

There is good reason why representations of New World encounters have proven so fascinating and theoretically productive for cultural critics. These representations are driven by practical and ideological agendas, informed by ancient prejudices, and draw upon extremely limited resources of language and knowledge. The indigenous peoples they depict stand at the cusp of unmapped continents and unfathomable precolonial pasts, and their own historical representations are either mediated by European ones or are even more opaque. Thus the topic presents profound epistemological challenges. Greenblatt's caveat, however, actually backs away from these challenges, and may be less commonsensical than it appears. Interpreting "European representations of the New World" without some empirical knowledge of that world is like interpreting a supposed portrait without any independent knowledge of its subject. We might arrive at a host of plausible and interesting inferences about the "practices" involved, but nothing "certain."

The imputation that historians naively approach documentary sources as transparent records depends on an intellectual straw man, or at least an obsolete model of historiography. The field of ethnohistory, conceived in the mid-twentieth-century judicial context of the Indian Claims Commission, both expanded the archive for the study of Native American cultures and developed a pragmatic skepticism toward documents.[15] Francis Jennings brought that perspective to the history of Pennsylvania-Indian relations, and his impassioned scholarship helped make this book possible.[16] Another invaluable resource has been the work of the historian James Merrell. Merrell has disavowed the label "ethnohistorian," arguing that the field's self-definition effectively sectioned off the history of Native Americans from mainstream colonial historiography. Yet in 1989 he claimed that "students of early America"—perhaps owing to European influences such as the Annales school—"are now doing what ethnohistory's champions have been pushing them to do: borrow freely from other disciplines and examine all sorts of evidence to give voice to the historically silent."[17]

However, Merrell's easy metaphorical conception of the historian's task—"to give voice"—positions the historian as the last in the chain of "mediators" who carry the voice of historical Native Americans to the reader.[18] It belies the conceptual, methodological, and even political complexities that his scholarship has helped to bring to light. In an analysis of the representations of speeches by the Delaware leader Teedyuscung that appear in various and conflicting versions of the minutes from a series of 1756 treaty council meetings, Merrell observes that such sources are compromised by the fallible processes of translation and transcription and legitimate questions about the competence and good faith of the persons who carry these out. "Nevertheless," he writes, "most scholars (myself included) find these sources too rich, too abundant, too available, and altogether too tempting to linger long on their faults or avoid them completely." He concludes, perhaps optimistically but hardly naively, that it is indeed possible to hear "genuine echoes of a long-forgotten native voice" in the treaty council minutes. But what would it mean to "listen to" that voice?[19]

To formulate a chiasmus of my own, it is one thing to consider European representations as records of Native American statements, and still another to consider those represented statements as statements of record. Merrell's question is, primarily, whether the treaty minutes record Teedyuscung's intent, and secondarily, whether Teedyuscung, as a spokesman or medium for other Indians, reliably conveyed the intent underlying the messages he was entrusted with. But his observation that the colonists' faith in the superiority of writing over "oral tradition" was misplaced suggests the compounded problem of one unreliable medium being represented through another. When the erratic, volatile, often (allegedly) inebriated Teedyuscung, in 1756, accused the Pennsylvania Proprietors of having committed "fraud" a generation earlier, he was presenting an oral tradition—a representation of a "message" from the previous generation, which in turn was linked to a message from the generation before that.[20] Heckewelder represents "historical traditions" that purport to reach back much further into the past, ostensibly told to him by Indians who were many miles and generations removed from the places and events they describe. To what extent might we consider written representations of Native American oral forms as records not only of spoken language but also of the sometimes distant historical events that were spoken of?

The history of the Delawares and their relations with colonists reveals a variety of tendencies in the handling of such hybrid, doubly extenuated sources. Colonial officials typically considered their own written renditions of Native American oral performances to be authoritative records of Indian speech, and those produced outside their supervision to be misleading representations. The colonists felt that written records automatically trumped "memory," but when it suited their interests, one of which was to exclude the Indians from having direct access to writing, they were perfectly willing to allow "that the Indians have good Memories, and can remember what was transacted twenty years ago, as if Yesterday."[21] In subsequent generations, popular historians were invested in local oral traditions and open to alternative accounts, and they therefore reached different conclusions about events such as the Great

Treaty and the Walking Purchase than did some credentialed scholars who confided in official records.

As for representations of native and popular oral traditions, many writers in the nineteenth century and later, while implicitly expressing faith in their chosen medium of expression, were expedient in their judgments. They accepted represented traditions as historical records when their content was useful for their scientific or cultural agendas. Academic scholars, according to their conventional practices, have been more rigorous. Historians and cultural critics such as literary scholars, folklorists, and art historians have largely concurred in qualifying oral traditions as purely subjective representations. The resulting division of labor allows scholars to operate within their disciplinary comfort zones. Historians can exclude representations of oral traditions from their data, while cultural critics can interpret them within the historical context in which they are told and recorded. But the opposing ends of the spectrum offer a false sense of security: the fixed certainty of a documented fact; the liberating confines of an interpretive context "stitched together" by the very interpreter.[22] On the one hand, the fallacy is that an interpretation that excludes unverifiable but possibly significant evidence is less speculative than one that does not. On the other, it is that a representation's basis in fact is less than crucial to understanding its meaning. Scholars who have pulled away from the record-representation poles have produced some of the most innovative recent work in colonial studies.[23] As James Wilkinson observes, while the recent proliferation of forms of evidence that have become subject to historical analysis still leaves us without a foundational basis for interpretations, that "the whole truth cannot be known does not mean that partial truths are unattainable."[24] I would only amend his phrase: not "partial" but *possible* truths.

LANGUAGE IDEOLOGY AND THE GREAT DIVIDE

As a study of communications between cultures and across generations, this book taps into the multidisciplinary fields devoted to the concepts of collective memory and language ideology.[25] I discuss collective memory (or social or cultural memory; these terms sometimes are used interchangeably and sometimes entail conceptual distinctions) in the succeeding section. Language ideology is less established as a keyword designating a field of inquiry. As defined by Kathryn A. Woolard, it designates "[r]epresentations, whether explicit or implicit, that construe the intersection of language and human beings in a social world."[26] The relevant scholarship, with contributions from several social scientific and humanistic disciplines, develops the insight that linguistic practices, including forms of speech and writing, are attended by value judgments and implications for the social order. The view that speech is a more (or less) trustworthy medium than writing, or doubts about "the copiousness" of Native American languages, are relevant examples of ideologies of language.[27] Woolard notes that some "of the most provocative recent work on linguistic ideology, clearly tracing the links among linguistic, ideological, and social forms, comes from studies of colonialism."[28]

In recent decades, colonialist scholars have increasingly complicated the familiar "great divide" between native orality and European literacy.[29] Some have focused on how Native Americans adopted and adapted alphabetic writing for their own purposes, and have pointed out that neither the cultures of the indigenous Americas nor those of early modern Europe can be simply categorized on the basis of their use of a single communicative medium.[30] Others, more polemically, have insisted that the notion that the Indians did not write is itself ideological, and depends on a definition of writing that arbitrarily excludes a variety of communicative media, including pictography, the Incan knotted cords known as khipu, and wampum.[31] This intervention in the definition of writing proposes to correct the fallacy that "people without writing" are "people without history" by eliminating its premise—that there are or were "people without writing."[32] My own argument is that while history, like language, is a cultural universal, writing is not, and does not need to be redefined as one. It makes more sense to challenge the automatic link between writing and historical consciousness than it does to reaffirm it by straining to attribute writing, however defined, to all native peoples.[33]

What then *is* writing? It's an impossible question. When I refer to writing in what follows, I refer primarily to uses of alphabetic script. But definitions are contingent on context, and like all communicative interactions and determinations, they are subject to conditions of power, whether institutional or military. Heckewelder nicely illustrates this point in an anecdote in his chapter on Indian "Signs and Hieroglyphics." After explaining that Indians do not possess our "Art of Writing," which he defines as the use of "alphabets, or any mode of representing to the eye the sounds of words spoken," he describes an incident in which a "white man in Indian country" accused a Shawnee Indian of having stolen his horse. Unable to convince the white man of his innocence, the Indian drew "two striking figures" in charcoal: "the one representing the white man taking the horse, and the other, himself, in the act of scalping him; then he coolly asked the trembling claimant 'whether he could read this Indian writing?'"[34] The legibility of this "Indian writing" stands in counterpoint to the illegibility of the documents invoked by colonial grantees. In both cases, though, it is the threat of violence that speaks clearly.

COMMUNITIES OF HISTORY AND MEMORY

Language ideology and collective memory fundamentally converge with the observation by Maurice Halbwachs, an influential progenitor of the contemporary field of memory studies, that it "is language, and the whole system of social conventions attached to it, that allows us at every moment to reconstruct our past."[35] "Mnemonic communities," or communities of memory, "socialize us to what should be remembered and what should be forgotten."[36] This process supports the continuity of group identity—whether that identity is familial, regional, ethnic, religious, or as in many studies of collective memory, national. Importantly, mnemonic communities are also "discourse communities," which is a term that is more narrowly applied in studies of academic literacy. That is, they share not only content but also forms, including "participatory mechanisms," genres, and languages.[37] Thus they are defined not only by their collective memories but also by the ways in which they transmit them. Memories are shared through media, including spoken and written language, images, relics, and monuments. The uses of these different forms entail different attitudes and truth claims. They also, importantly, observe conventions that are specific to the groups that employ them. This book analyzes the interactions among several such memory/discourse communities, including the colonial Delawares and their descendants, the colonists and their descendants, and contemporary scholars in several fields, and their predecessors.

The name Delaware applies to more peoples retroactively than it did contemporaneously during the colonial era. The colonial English labeled the Algonquian bands inhabiting the central Delaware valley after the river that flows into the bay they had named for the Virginian governor, Thomas West, the third Lord De La Warr. These peoples designated themselves using variants of the now-standardized ethnonym *Lenape*, which is usually translated as "the people," or "the original people."[38] When the Delawares/Lenapes migrated westward, ceding their ancestral territory to colonists, they mingled with Indians from neighboring areas who "shared linguistic and other cultural patterns."[39] The names Delaware and Lenape came to be applied to the indigenous inhabitants of these areas as well. As a geopolitical entity, *Lenapehoking*, the Delaware homeland, may exist only in retrospect, and the term itself is of recent coinage.[40] Nevertheless, while usages vary, peoples living during the onset of European colonization in what are now Delaware, New Jersey, Eastern Pennsylvania, New York City, Long Island, and the Hudson Valley as far north as the Catskills have all been called Delawares or Lenapes.[41]

Some of the descendants of these peoples still inhabit these regions, but the largest communities are in Oklahoma.[42] They use both ethnonyms. Although "Delaware" may be the more appropriate usage in communications with outsiders, according to a folk etymology it is not entirely exogenous. It derives not from an English nobleman but from an early colonial interaction: a white man, after asking an Indian what tribe he belonged to, had difficulty pronouncing "Lenape"; when he finally got it right, the Indian said: "'Nal në ndëluwèn! Nal në ndëluwèn!' ('That's what I said, That's what I said!')." They were henceforth called Delawares.[43] According to a version of this story told by Leona Parton in a 1937 interview for the Works Progress Administration, the Indian's interlocutor was William Penn himself. "When making the treaty Penn kept asking over what the Indian said and they used the word Delaware so much that they were called Delaware, though there is another name that is the true name. I can't pronounce it nor spell it for we always go by the name of Delaware."[44]

In the colonial period, the Delawares and the colonists had competing as well as collaborative representations of their interactions with one another. Both sides, of course, maintained and communicated memories through the spoken word. Additionally, the Delawares, like some of their Algonquian and Iroquoian neighbors, used strings and belts made from shell beads, or wampum. Wampum was a "mnemonic device," and more.[45] Its exchanges structured treaty meetings (including land sales); it "embodied" the terms of an agreement; it had a contractual function and, like the colonists' written instruments, it also served as a form of record.[46] Accordingly, wampum has often been compared to alphabetic writing, and sometimes classified as a form of writing. I will discuss this comparison further in chapters 3 and 4.

Like other Native Americans, and like the colonists, the Delawares carried memories out of the colonial era through traditions. Traditions, as defined by the Africanist Jan Vansina's influential *Oral Tradition as History*, are "verbal messages which are reported statements from the past beyond the present generation."[47] They are transmitted through "a chain of iterations" beyond the period in which they supposedly originated.[48] Tradition is distinct, then, from oral history, which refers to accounts told by an event's participants and witnesses. While different Native American groups have used a variety of sign systems, including wampum, the primary medium for their traditions is speech. However, for most scholars, and increasingly for Indians as well, the only, necessarily partial, access to these traditions is through recorded (and translated) speech. Peter Nabokov, in his important study of Native American philosophies and media of history, points out that when scholars hold up oral traditions against the "written record," they are typically found wanting: "keen disappointment can ensue when the facts of these stories don't add up or seem 'softer' than hard facts should be. This attitude can mushroom into blanket repudiation, as with anthropologist Robert Lowie's notorious pronouncement in 1915, 'I cannot attach to oral traditions any historical value whatsoever under any conditions whatsoever.'"[49] As Nabokov suggests, when oral traditions are recognized as a dynamic, porous medium, their "historical value" can become more ascertainable.

The opposition between Native American and Western memory practices can easily be overstated. Anglo-American communities, too, have oral histories and traditions, and they have served much the same functions as Native American ones. The adjective most often used to designate these is "popular." Popular traditions have also been subjected to "blanket repudiation." The primary repository—in effect, a medium—for both native and popular traditions is aged persons—the ideal transmission is not between consecutive generations but between the very old and the young. This book, accordingly, mentions many septuagenarians and octogenarians. The aim was to minimize the number of links in a chain of memory by maximizing their length: a single interlocking set could span a century and a half. In the nineteenth century, the task of preserving memories from before the War of Independence was taken up by popular or local historians, who gathered in local historical societies, compared accounts in dedicated "olden time" columns in local newspapers, placed monuments, and compiled sometimes monumental volumes. The paradigmatic work in this genre is John Fanning Watson's *Annals of Philadelphia*, which was originally published in 1830 and was reissued in 1844 in a two-volume expanded edition with the title *Annals of Philadelphia and Pennsylvania, in the olden time; being a collection of memoirs, anecdotes, and incidents of the city and its inhabitants, and of the earliest settlements of the inland part of Pennsylvania, from the days of the founders* (1830).[50]

A sense in which such memory work can be contrasted with that of Native American tradition-bearers is with regard to place.[51] While Native American refugees strove to maintain a sense of cultural continuity on behalf of a deracinated people, historians like Watson attempted to imbue an exogenous community with a sense of rootedness. This mission was shared, sometimes from an ironic, or even physical, distance by visual artists like Benjamin West and John Trumbull, and writers like James Fenimore Cooper and Washington Irving, whose commendation was included in Watson's second edition: "he is doing an important service to his country, by multiplying the local associations of ideas, and the strong but invisible ties of the mind and of the heart which bind the native to the paternal soil."[52]

Popular historians sought not only to discover and preserve "traditional and other testimony" but also to restore or substantiate it through archival research.[53] They were not always insensible to the opinions of the practitioners of what Edward Shils calls "scientific or critical historiography."[54] Often, the local historians and antiquarians were men of means and prestige, like Roberts Vaux, a founding member of the Historical Society of Pennsylvania (HSP) in Philadelphia, and William W. H. Davis, founder of the Bucks County Historical Society; they wished to be recognized as serious amateurs. While they were unwilling to concede the disinterested pursuit of truth to professional scholars, they were more avowedly motivated by the love of their regions.[55]

While academic historians and other professional students of the past also manifestly participate in discourse communities, characterized by highly specialized generic forms and, above all, an emphasis on documentation, these scholarly disciplines are not typically considered as mnemonic communities. Yet as Astrid Erll writes, "history is but yet another mode of cultural memory, and historiography its specific medium."[56] Many of the theoretical generalizations about collective memory can be applied to the corpus of scholarship surrounding a given field of academic inquiry. For example, it can be divided into a "canon" of standard texts and a vast repository, or "archive"; it is characterized by a large "floating gap" separating a scant few decades—generations?—of current and recent scholarship from foundational texts and figures.[57] In their orientation toward the past, historical fields, like historical memory, also have a "dynamic" relation with present political and cultural concerns.

Thinking of academic historians and other professional scholars as participants in communities of memory is one way to move beyond the opposition between lifeless history and living memory that was a tenet of the early scholarship in the field of memory studies.[58] Instead of opposing history to memory, we can consider the interactions, sometimes conflictive, between discourse communities. Yet the conceptual distinction between history and memory remains useful.[59] I retain the word *history* in my subtitle because the interaction between memory and language ideologies in relations between Native Americans and colonists was historically significant. In many instances, the media of memory were also the media of land transactions and treaties. Moreover, memory itself was a factor in diplomacy, as the parties invoked supposed precedents or called for the renewal of former terms.

MEMORIES OF ENCOUNTERS, ENCOUNTERS OF MEMORIES

For the descendants of the Native Americans and the colonists, the diffusion and deterioration of the community of memory as such was one of the prompts to the production of memory work, in the forms of commemoration, retrospection, and, importantly, research. Yet as each community has a different experience of the discontinuity of the present with the past, they can also come to depend on one another. For example, as I will discuss in chapter 3, when commissioned to corroborate the popular tradition that a Great Treaty took place between William Penn and the Lenapes under the Elm Tree at Shackamaxon soon after Penn's landing in 1682, Peter Stephen Du Ponceau and Joshua Francis

Fisher invoked the authority of Native American memory. They drew from Heckewelder's description of the Delawares' commemoration of the Great Treaty, noting that the Indians' use of wampum, "with the aid of tradition," enabled their memories of Penn to survive "the lapse of one hundred years."[60]

Similarly, Indians increasingly consulted the work of non-Indian scholars for information about their history. They came to depend on extrinsic archives and the scholars who accessed and interpreted them because, until they began to create their own written records, they had no "passive storing memory" of their own.[61] For example, Richard Calmit Adams, a Delaware Indian who tirelessly served his people as a legal advocate during the period of the Dawes Act (1887–1934), also attempted to restore their history.[62] In *A Brief History of the Delaware Indians* he clearly articulated the relation between his legal advocacy and history writing: "my effort is only to produce a brief and accurate sketch of the history of my people, at the time when the last bond uniting them in tribal relations is being severed by the action of the General Government in segregating their lands, allotting them in severalty, and thereby rendering them in all respects citizens of the United States."[63] Adams was attempting to counter this centrifugal force through history writing, yet his dependence on the writings of non-Indians itself attests to the ongoing disintegration of Delaware community and memory, and the challenges facing a historian of a people who had been radically uprooted from their ancestral territory.

If Adams's rhetorical purpose for his written history was to establish Delaware peoplehood to outsiders, the purpose usually attributed to collective memory is the establishment and maintenance of in-group identity, at levels ranging to families and small social cliques to nations. Theories of memory correlate to the spectrum between subjective representation and objective record discussed above. The central question has been whether the "present is predominantly shaped by the past or vice-versa."[64] For Halbwachs, the present is both a filter and a lens for the past; groups select, forget, amplify, minimize, and perhaps otherwise distort elements from their past according to their present needs and circumstances.⁶⁵ The more tendentious "presentist" or "invention of tradition" approach posits a top-down construction of memory "as a means of exercising power, to establish or legitimize institutions, to symbolize social cohesion and to socialize individuals to the existing social order."⁶⁶ The current, more nuanced view posits that collective memory always involves "a fluid negotiation between the desires of the present and the legacies of the past."⁶⁷

An implication of this "dynamic" view is that traditions might present something of a sedimentary record of their passage through time, including their inception.⁶⁸ However, the tendency of memory studies is "to study the existence of tradition in the present without searching for what is beneath it and without asking whether such memories are authentic."⁶⁹ The difference for this study is that the receptions of the stories of the Delawares' and colonists' pasts were precisely concerned with issues of truth and authenticity—the validity of the represented memories as historical records. These controversies involved language ideologies, judgments about which media were the most reliable conduits for communication between the past and the present. Importantly, the concern was at both ends; treaties and land transactions involved prospective efforts to relay their results to future generations, and therefore should fit within the purview of a colonialist mnemohistory. Similarly, acts of remembrance were also communications to the future, like switches in a telegraph; there is no easy distinction between retrospective and prospective memory. "Your Leagues with your Father *William Penn*, and with his Governours," Governor Patrick Gordon declared to delegations of Conestoga, Brandywine Delawares, Conoy, and Shawnee Indians in May 1728, "are in Writing on Record, that our Children and our Childrens Children, may have them in everlasting Remembrance: And we know that you preserve the Memory of these Things amongst you, by telling them to your Children, and they again to the next Generation, so that they remain stamp'd on your Minds never to be forgot."⁷⁰

Gordon's speech had been prepared in writing in council, thus we can have relative confidence that the words that appear in the minutes are indicative of the ones he pronounced on the occasion of a treaty meeting to settle the peace after an outbreak of murders and retaliations. The written representation of the spoken response of the Indian spokesman, interpreted by a colonist, John Scull, is much more mediated.[71] Nevertheless, it might remind us that the dynamic process of the transmission and construction of memory, perhaps especially in situations of conflict, could involve deliberate suppression as well as retention: "presenting a Belt of Wampum of Eight Rows, they say: They would not have the Governour grieve too much for the rash inconsiderate Actions that of late have been committed; they must be buried & forgot." Somewhat paradoxically, the wampum belt may have functioned as a contract to remember to forget the immediate past and to fixate on the more distant one: "they are extreamely glad & satisfied with what the Governour said to them yesterday, it greatly rejoiced their Hearts that they have no such Speech made to them since the time that the Great William Penn was amongst them, all was good and nothing was amiss."[72]

The distinction Gordon makes between "Writing on Record" and unwritten "Memory" is central to the four chapters that follow. Far from a simple binary opposition, though, what emerges is a complicated and layered interrelationship, involving, for example, written representations of unwritten memories of written records. The first chapter is on representations of the Delawares' accounts of their own origins, and therefore might be expected to observe the familiar fault line between prehistory and the advent of written history with the arrival of the colonists. In the early national United States, the view that Indians were unwilling and unable to learn to read and write, the notion "that history contains no records of a Red or of a Black nation, which has rivaled the Whites, in the high attainments of genius and knowledge," was a basis for skepticism about the possibility of civilizing the Indians and therefore an argument for their removal to lands west of the Mississippi.[73] I argue that the well-meaning opposition to this racial prejudice can help explain the reception, and even the existence, of the *Walam Olum*. This elaborate, ideographic version of the migration tradition recorded by John Heckewelder is the "one native record" from "what is now the United States," according to the 1921 *Cambridge History of American Literature*, that "could be called, in our fashion, a book."[74] The *Walam Olum* first appeared as a manuscript, an alleged copy made by the naturalist Constantine Rafinesque of a set of etched cedar sticks that he never brought forward. The authenticity controversy illustrates the interrelationship between media and between communities of memory: one of the evidences against the authenticity of the *Walam Olum* is the lack of attestation for it in the written representations of Delaware oral traditions composed by Heckewelder and his Moravian colleagues and in subsequent ethnographic research. "For a document purporting to contain the most important record of North American Indian origins," writes David M. Oestreicher, the principal debunker of the *Walam Olum* "hoax," "the silence in the record is baffling and astonishing."[75]

While in the case of the *Walam Olum* the absence of collaboration in recorded oral traditions is negative evidence against the authenticity of a document, it is more typical for an absence of corroboration in the so-called documentary record to be cited as evidence against the historicity of an oral tradition. The question is not so much whether the traditional account of an event is an authentic product of a given culture, but rather whether it has any value as a record of that event. The two issues overlap, however; the determination that a given tradition does not issue from the event it purports to represent, or that that event never occurred, contradicts the tradition's implicit explanation of its own provenance and attributes to it a sort of artificiality. In the case of Heckewelder's rendition of the "Indian Account of the First Arrival of the Dutch at New York Island," the represented tradition contains either a record of an implausible event or evidence of European cultural influence. For the most part, as some historians have suggested, the tradition is plausibly congruent, or at least compatible, with Robert Juet's journal of Hudson's third voyage in 1609. But the conclusion of the traditional account diverges sharply from any colonial sources, presenting a parallel, instead, to the classical tale of Queen Dido's acquisition of the site for her citadel at Carthage.

According to this tale, Dido asked King Hiarbas for as much land as an oxhide could cover, and then cut it into strips, laid it out in a circle, and claimed all that it enclosed. How do we explain the appearance of the "Dido motif" in a native tradition?

I argue that what might seem to be the obvious explanation, that the Indians learned the story from Europeans and incorporated it into a historical tradition as a metaphorical representation of "colonial trickery," depends on questionable assumptions about the transmission of stories, both between peoples and across time.[76] This explanation struggles to account for what appears to be a widespread discursive phenomenon—the appearance of the Dido motif in multiple non-European accounts of the founding of early modern European maritime imperial outposts. My goal in the second chapter is not to demonstrate that, in any particular instance, colonists asked for as much land as a bullock's hide could cover, and then cut the hide into strips to claim land as the site of the fort (as the multiple instances maintain). I do hope to demonstrate that this explanation for the inception of the tradition is at least as likely as the alternative, and therefore, that the near universal refusal in existing scholarship to consider the possibility that Dutch colonists might have employed Dido's ruse is a product of language ideology—of preconceptions about verisimilitude, word-of-mouth transmission, and the reliability of oral traditions vis-à-vis the documentary record. Language ideologies are not necessarily wrong, but they are worth examining.

Adducing the *absence* of a written record as negative evidence against a tradition is perhaps the ultimate expression of the ideology of language that has been called "archival positivism," the dependence on the primary source document as the "vehicle of historical truth."[77] In the nineteenth century, popular historians felt that positivism threatened the tradition that William Penn had met with Delaware leaders, especially the famous Tammany (Tamanend) under a Great Elm tree at the Indian village of Shackamaxon in 1682. Thanks largely to reproductions and adaptations of Benjamin West's historical tableau *William Penn's Treaty with the Indians When He Founded the Province of Pennsylvania in North America* (1771–72), the story had become more widely diffused, colorful, and detailed than ever. It was Pennsylvania's civic myth.[78] The treaty was, according to a florid encomium published on its supposed bicentennial, "part of our first inheritance of freedom; a part of the Christianity of the world." Yet there were those who "questioned the precious story," who subjected it to their "narrower scrutinies" and determined that "humanity in its credulity and dependence upon such noble examples, had created out of its own imagination this story of 'The Man and the Sorrowless Tree.'"[79] Skeptics pointed to the unlikelihood or impossibility of some of the accumulated details of the tradition, especially the 1682 date, and especially to the lack of "positive proof."[80]

Art historians indirectly espouse such positivism in their tendency to reduce the treaty tradition to its most prominent expression in West's "Penn's Treaty."[81] That is, the absence of a treaty document is conducive to treating not only the painting but the tradition as a reflection of the political situation in 1771–72 rather than a historical record of an event at the founding of Pennsylvania. Actually, however, there are documentary indications that Penn did hold a significant treaty meeting with the Delawares during his first year in Pennsylvania, and nothing to contradict its location under the Elm Tree at Shackamaxon. Chapter 3 focuses on the response of proponents of the tradition to positivist "doubts," and to the threatened rupture of the "chain of memory," especially with the fall of the Great Tree in an 1810 storm.[82] The most fascinating aspect of this response is the recourse to Delaware memories, as represented by Heckewelder, and as supposedly embodied by the Treaty Belt, a wampum belt passed down through the Penn family until Granville John Penn donated it to the Historical Society of Pennsylvania in 1857.

Missing records figure prominently in this book: the etched cedar sticks of the *Walam Olum*; a colonial document corroborating the tradition about the bullock's hide; the parchment containing the articles of the Great Treaty; and the 1686 deed in which Delaware sachems (leaders) agree to transfer to William Penn a tract of land to be measured by a day and a half's walk. This missing deed, represented by a doubtful copy, was the basis for the 1737 Walking Purchase, an act of optimization in which the Pennsylvania Proprietors stuck closely to the letter of the purported agreement, but interpreted it unilaterally, hiring athletic men as the walkers and pushing them beyond their physical limits (only one was able to complete it). Through the so-called Indian Walk, the Proprietors took in approximately five hundred thousand acres, including the Forks of Delaware region they coveted.[83]

While the historiography on the Walking Purchase has focused on the questions of whether and how the Proprietors cheated the Delawares, I examine the controversy as a clash of mnemonic communities. The 1737 Indian Walk and the negotiations that preceded it pitted the erudite provincial secretary James Logan, with his equivocal written record, against the Forks sachem Nutimus, and the "Indian Way" of communicating and remembering land transactions.[84] After the Walking Purchase, the Forks Indians attempted to intervene in the written record and to get redress for their grievances. During the period of the French and Indian War, following Nutimus's nephew Teedyuscung's allegation of fraud in 1756, the Proprietors, their Quaker political opponents, and the Delawares contended over what had happened during the 1730s. To an extraordinary extent the dispute became embroiled in matters of communicative protocol, over who should have access to the existing documentary record and control over the production of the ongoing one. Afterward, the debate among historians depended largely on whose archives of represented memories they consulted, and on their approaches to reading them; the Walking Purchase was either a legitimate grievance or a retroactive "casus belli" for Delaware raids and a scandal engineered by the Quakers to deflect the blame for their pacifist refusal to fund the defense of the frontier onto the Proprietors for their handling of Indian affairs.[85]

The Walking Purchase archives provide evidence of the other side of the methodological problem facing colonialist scholars who listen for the "voices" of Native Americans through written records. The Indians were unequal participants in "literacy events," a term used by the sociolinguist Shirley Brice Heath to signify "any event in which a piece of writing is integral to the nature of the participants' interactions or their interpretive processes," or "any action sequence, involving one or more persons, in which the production and/or comprehension of print plays a role."[86] In these scenes of translation and transcription, of reading aloud, brandishing documents, and composing depositions and affidavits, the challenge facing the Indians was to make their voices heard. They found themselves trapped in the same orality-literacy dialectic that has since preoccupied literary critics.[87] On the one hand, an oral utterance might be authentic, but as Walter Ong wrote, it "exists only when it is going out of existence."[88] It might be unheeded or misconstrued; it cannot simply pass into the written record, but it must be represented. In the process of translation and transcription, the spoken word is unavoidably, and perhaps deliberately and egregiously, distorted. There is no necessary relationship between speech and represented speech; colonial scribes can put words in the mouths of Indian orators almost as novelists can attribute speech to their characters. On the other hand, when the Indians attempted to communicate through writing, their statements were subject to critique: their words were inappropriate; the words in writing could not possibly *be* their own words; someone has misrepresented their intentions in putting their words to paper. Part of what makes Nutimus and Teedyuscung such compelling figures is that they sought more control over the destiny of their words than the British were willing to allow.

I have arranged the chapters that follow in a straightforward chronological sequence, roughly from the period before colonization to the mid-eighteenth century. The contrived nature of this organization becomes apparent in view of the various "moments" in the life of a history or memory. Here I am borrowing Brook Thomas's schema for the analysis of a historical novel. He examines "three historical moments: its moment of representation, its moment of production, and its many moments of reception, from the time it was produced until today."[89] With *The Scarlet Letter*, for instance, these moments are the mid-seventeenth century, the mid-nineteenth century, and the period from 1850 to the present. (A complication with memories is that reception and production overlap, although the same might be said of the "construction" of texts.[90]) Thus the moments of representation for the stories I discuss line up sequentially, but the other moments do not. The media of memory become the central issue when the memory becomes exposed to doubt: with the treaty tradition, this moment occurred in the early nineteenth century, especially after the fall of the Great Elm in 1810; with the Walking Purchase, it was almost immediate. Thus the temporal emphases of my chapters vary. Another way to conceptualize the order of the chapters is that the spans between the moment of representation and the moments of reception become progressively narrower: the stories of origin in chapter 1 look back as far as Creation, while the Walking Purchase controversy during the French and Indian War was over events from the 1680s and the 1730s, as well as ones unfolding in that past present.

I
Lenape Annals

"For their *original*," wrote William Penn of the Delawares in 1683, "I am ready to believe them of the Jewish race."[1] Penn was adding his opinion to a voluminous body of literature concerning the origin of the Native Americans. Consulting the Bible and classical sources, and correlating those with physical and cultural characteristics and geography, Europeans identified the Indians' ancestors variously as Carthaginians, Atlanteans, Phoenicians, Tartars, Scythians, and the Lost Tribes of Israel.[2] Each conclusion had different implications for the possibility of converting and civilizing the Indians.[3] The question of origin was, therefore, a profoundly political one.

What information might the Indians themselves have to contribute to this subject? This question, too, was political, because it concerned the compatibility of their beliefs with Christianity, their status with regard to divine revelation, and especially their capacity to retain knowledge of their distant past, which was itself a key criterion in qualifying them as barbaric or civilized. The Delawares, whose oral traditions furnished the written records with two conflicting accounts of their origins, feature prominently in this discussion.

Like many peoples, the Delawares had a story of autochthonous origin: the first man and woman, their ancestors, had sprouted from a tree that grew from the back of the primordial turtle or tortoise that was their world. This account first appears in the 1679 journal of the Dutch Pietist Jasper Danckaerts, who presents it as evidence of how misguided the Indians are without the benefit of scriptural revelation.[4] However, regardless of the factual accuracy of the tradition, its existence indicates that they had occupied their territory since time immemorial. It therefore was consistent with indigenous land rights and constituted evidence against the authenticity of the second tradition—that the Delawares had migrated to their homeland within the scope of historical time.

The migration tradition, in its reception and permutations, is the focus of this chapter. First transcribed and translated by John Heckewelder in the late eighteenth century and published in his *History, Manners, and Customs of the Indian Nations Who Once Inhabited Pennsylvania and the Neighboring States* (1819), it relates how the Lenapes came from "a very distant country in the western part of the American continent." On their journey eastward, they carried out an epic war with a mysterious Mississippi valley people known as the "Talligewi," or "Alligewi," while their duplicitous rivals, the "Mengwe," or Iroquois, hung back and let them absorb the casualties. The tradition concludes with the founding of Lenapehoking: the Lenapes "settled on the four great rivers (which we call Delaware, Hudson, Susquehannah, and Potomack) making the Delaware, to which they gave the name of 'Lenapewihittuck,' (the river or stream of the Lenape) the centre of their possessions."[5]

The tradition recorded by Heckewelder enabled contemporary proponents of Indian Removal to construe the Indians as "latecomers," in Vine Deloria's phrase, "who had barely unpacked before Columbus came knocking at the door."[6] The so-called romantic archeologists adduced it in support of their theory that the Indians were descendants of a barbarous Asiatic people like the Scythians, who had flooded across the Bering Strait in hordes, destroying the preexisting civilization that had constructed the impressive mounds in the interior of the continent.[7] Thus any effort to bring Indians to civility and Christianity was hopeless, and their aboriginal claim to the continent was tenuous at best.

The problem with invoking the Indians' own traditions in support of removal, however, was that doing so contradicted the view that the Indians were a "barbarous people," void of historical sensibility and the possibility of improving through cumulative knowledge: "The past and the future being alike disregarded, the present only employs their thoughts."[8] The romantic archeologists, not overly concerned with logical consistency, touched only lightly on this paradox, but it is central to James Fenimore Cooper's representation of the Heckewelder tradition in The Last of the Mohicans (1826). While he uses this account of the onset of the "time of the red men" to lend an aspect of mournful inevitability to their demise, he also vindicates native traditions and repudiates dependence on "black marks" on paper as an assertion of "mental independence" from Europe.[9]

The most intriguing adaptation of the Heckewelder tradition first appeared as a manuscript titled:

> Wallam Olum
> First and Second Parts of the
> Painted and engraved traditions
> of the Linnilinapi

The bottom of a title page reads:

> translated word for word by means of Zeisberger
> and Linapi Dictionary—with explanations &c
> By C. S. Rafinesque—1833.

Constantine Samuel Rafinesque was an eccentric and prolific antiquarian and naturalist with a checkered reputation. His *Walam Olum* represented an ontogeny and an epic migration, corresponding to the tradition recorded by Heckewelder, through 183 pictographs, a supposed transcription of a Lenape recitation that accompanied the pictographs, and Rafinesque's supposed translation. Despite recurrent doubts about its provenance and its contents, the *Walam Olum* has been repeatedly brought back from the brink of obscurity, retranslated, and republished. The ideological significance of indigenous writing was certainly a factor in this long, controversial reception history, raising the stakes in what might otherwise have been an easily resolved question of authenticity.

"THE PRAIRIES"

The narrative account of the Lenapes' migration appears in the first chapter of John Heckewelder's History, entitled "Historical Traditions of the Indians." For Heckewelder, "Historical Traditions" are distinct from "Indian Mythology," which he presents in a later chapter; they are representations of the human past. He is noncommittal regarding the factual accuracy of these representations (he indicates that he is merely presenting what the Delawares have told him), but he vouches for their authenticity: they were "handed down," like an heirloom, "by their ancestors."[10]

The historicity of this account is unverifiable and perhaps also irrefutable. Herbert Kraft's objection that archeological evidence contradicts the idea of "a new people suddenly appearing on the scene at a particular time" is addressed to the *Walam Olum*, but the Heckewelder account, as is typical of oral traditions concerning the distant past, does not offer a precise and therefore falsifiable chronology.[11] It suggests that the Lenapes first gathered in the Midwest and gradually found their way eastward after some initial exploration: "they began to emigrate thither, as yet but in small bodies."[12] It is certainly possible, a recent example from Africa suggests, for a people to retain memories of a remote origin through oral tradition.[13] David Oestreicher, whose research on the *Walam Olum* I discuss below, argues that the battle recounted in the Heckewelder tradition refers to "an incident that occurred in approximately the year 1700" in which "a group of Cherokee . . . were conquered by the Delaware after the introduction of firearms."[14] A comparison of Heckewelder's account to his Moravian colleague David Zeisberger's account of the Cherokee battle supports this conclusion.[15] A reference to the Delawares' conquest of "the Nation Dallagae" in a 1776 speech by White Eyes is more ambiguous.[16] It is possible that the tradition conflates one or more events from different periods, an instance of the social-memory phenomenon of "keying."[17]

Whatever the locations of the tradition's moments of representation, its bearing on its late-eighteenth-century moment of production and reception, when it was told and represented in written English by Heckewelder, is more apparent. "Every traditional message," as Jan Vansina observes, "has a particular purpose and fulfills a particular function, otherwise it would not survive."[18] The migration account recorded by Heckewelder charters the Delawares' claim to Lenapehoking in the same way that Genesis and Exodus charter the Jewish claim to Israel: it was "the country destined for them by the Great Spirit."[19] The tradition displays "in-group favoritism," validating the Delawares' character over and against that of their rivals, the Iroquois, who craftily hung back during the war with the Alligewi while the Lenapes absorbed the casualties.[20] "Mr Heckewelder's naivete is really amusing," wrote Lewis Cass, the Michigan territorial governor, ethnographer, and eventually, as Andrew Jackson's secretary of war, a primary agent of Indian Removal. "It appears never to have occurred to him, that these traditional stories, orally repeated from generation to generation, may have finally borne very little resemblance to the events they commemorate, nor that a Delaware could sacrifice the love of truth to the love of his tribe."[21]

In a long digression in an anonymous 1826 essay in the *North American Review*, Cass objected especially to the migration account: "Of all sources of information these legendary tales are the most uncertain," he noted, likening it to the "many accounts" Indians had told about "the former existence of the mammoth." (Cass was mistakenly confident that humans and mammoths had never coexisted on the continent.) He lamented the widespread "effect of Mr Heckwelder's work," which has "furnished materials for the writers of periodical works, and even of *history*; and in one of those beautiful delineations of American scenery, incidents, and manners, for which we are indebted to the taste and talent of our eminent novelist, 'the last of the Mohegans' is an Indian of the school of Mr. Heckewelder, and not of the school of nature." It was perhaps especially galling to Cass that the villain of *The Last of the Mohicans*, Magua, was a Huron, or Wyandot.[22] In an 1824 letter, Cass cautioned the historian Joseph W. Moulton "against placing too much confidence in

Heckewelder's historical account of the Delawares," arguing that the migration tradition was singular and uncorroborated, even by other Delawares, and that Heckewelder conveyed a false impression of Delaware preeminence. According to Cass, it was his own informants, the Wyandots, who were "the first tribe in rank as well as in information among all our Indians."[23]

If the "Delaware tribe was the first and the last object of [Heckewelder's] hopes," as Cass maintained, the uses that nineteenth-century scholars made of the migration tradition he recorded would have been entirely contrary to his wishes.[24] When Heckewelder's *History* was published, in 1819, Anglo-Americans were undertaking the removal of the Indians to the west of the great river. The migration tradition lent itself to an interpretation that supported the cause of Indian Removal. It allowed scholars to portray the Indians not as autochthones but as arrivistes. It suggested that their territorial claim was based not in aboriginal land rights, which were theoretically inalienable except through purchase, but in conquest, which could be superseded by another conquest. More specifically, the Heckewelder account was taken up by a school of thought whose adherents Robert Silverberg has characterized as "romantic archeologists," who theorized that middle America had been formerly inhabited by a white race, the mound builders, that had been overrun by savage hordes from the far side of the Bering Strait. For romantic archeologists like Moulton, coauthor of *History of the State of New-York: Including Its Aboriginal and Colonial Annals*, and Josiah Priest, author of *American Antiquities and Discoveries in the West* (1833), the Talligewi or Alligewi seemed to correspond to the mound builders.[25]

The view that the first Americans had composed a populous, industrious, agrarian civilization, and that the Indians were savage interlopers rather than natives, had obvious attractions during the early nineteenth century. The archeological writings drew widespread interest and directly informed literary culture. Among the numerous literary expressions of the mound builder thesis, the best known today is William Cullen Bryant's poem "The Prairies" (1832). The poem's speaker, looking westward and contemplating the mysterious mounds, looks also into the past and imagines the "roaming hunter tribes" attacking the "disciplined and populous" farmers, who had harnessed bison to plows. Back in the present moment,

> . . . All is gone;
> All—save the piles of earth that hold their bones,
> The platforms where they worshipped unknown gods,
> The barriers which they builded from the soil
> To keep the foe at bay—till o'er the walls
> The wild beleaguerers broke, and, one by one,
> The strongholds of the plain were forced, and heaped
> With corpses.[26]

The myth thus cast the European settlers then streaming into the Midwest as the harbingers of the return of culture to the site where it had once thrived, the end of the American Dark Ages. The Heckewelder migration legend, accordingly, was put to the service of the American adaptation of the Renaissance story of the movement of civilization (*translatio imperii e studii*) from the Middle East to Rome to western Europe—to America. The Indians, unlike the supposedly white Alligewi, came from the wrong direction. As Priest puts it, "the Tartars, Scythians, and descendants of the ten lost tribes, came across the Straits of Bhering."[27] It was as if the spiked tail of prehistory snapped back against the course of historical progress—Priest even speculates that one of the formations in Ohio might have been the ruins of a Roman fort. Thus the story becomes doubly disqualifying to the Indians' land rights—not only are the Indians migrants rather than natives, but their migration was a violation of the providential design for the peopling of the continent.

Although the notion that the mound builders had been non-Indians had long had liberal dissenters, such as the ethnologist Henry Rowe Schoolcraft, it was not until 1894 that Cyrus Thomas, working for the Bureau of American Ethnology, excavated the mounds and debunked the myth. This was one year after Frederick Jackson Turner famously announced "the closing of a great historic movement . . . the advance of American settlement westward."[28] As Randall McGuire has argued, the archeological data demonstrating the Native American origin of the mounds had long existed, but "[s]ince the deed was done, the data could now carry the field in the academic debate over the past."[29] In other words, science could afford its ideal of disinterestedness once there was little or nothing at stake politically.

The nationalist archeologists' use of Indian legends as part of the "data" is consistent with their ideologically driven practice. Certainly, they cherry-picked their evidence; they disregarded the many traditions of in situ origins. In a sense, however, the use of native traditions at all was at cross-purposes with the colonialist agenda. The American savages were supposedly descended from Asiatic savages; at the same time, in order to demonstrate this descent, early archeological writers had to validate the Indians' historical consciousness, which was a criterion of civilization. For example, Benjamin Smith Barton, in *New Views of the Origin of the Tribes and Nations of America* (1798), claimed that "their traditions inform us that they came from the west; that they crossed the Mississippi, and that they gradually traveled towards the east." Barton argued that "notwithstanding the rude condition of most of these tribes, their traditions are often preserved for a long time in considerable purity, as I have discovered by much attention to their history. Besides, it is certainly an easy matter for nations, however ignorant of arts, to preserve, through a series of several generations, the great features of their history."[30] Thus the Indians are uncultivated ("ignorant of arts") yet capable of bearing historical witness against themselves.

The archeologists' use of native traditions, however, was not simply intellectual expedience but also an expression of their romanticism. It was consonant with Europe's own abiding sentimental interest in its tribal, pre-scriptural past, which was fueled and indulged most famously by James MacPherson's controversial Ossian poems (1760–65). The oft-noted difference for the new United States was that their supposed antiquity had to be borrowed from sources even more culturally remote than the Celtic traditions represented by MacPherson were to the English, and there was no available counterpart to Thomas Percy's *Reliques of Ancient English Poetry* (1765), which afforded to the English a sense of a deep-rooted cultural presence in their native land. Thus early Americans, even as they uprooted the Indians, sought to retain the roots; they repeatedly attempted the sort of cultural graft exemplified by Henry Wadsworth Longfellow's *Song of Hiawatha* (1855), which embellishes material from Schoolcraft's *Algic Researches* with elements from Norse and Greek mythology, and positions the narrator—along with the readers—as the keeper of the fading oral traditions of a receding race.

> In those days said Hiawatha,
> "Lo! How all things fade and perish!
> From the memory of the old men
> Fade away the great traditions,
> The achievements of the warriors,
> The adventures of the hunters . . ."[31]

Longfellow's Hiawatha is a transitional figure, auguring the coming of the white man both literally, through prophecy ("Let us welcome, then, the strangers, / Hail them as our friends and brothers") but also by creating a precursor to the European technology of writing through his invention of "picture writing."[32] The white men complete the evolution and preserve the supposed native traditions for future generations—of Anglo-Americans.

While *Hiawatha* contributed to the incorporation of the Iroquois as representatives of the American prehistory, the Delawares were already in place as iconic Indians in American popular culture. This process began locally in the Philadelphia area, through the Tammany Societies, which apotheosized the Delaware sachem Tamanend—a party to early land transactions with William Penn—as their patron saint, and therefore the sanctioner of their ownership of the land. It was furthered through Benjamin West's painting *Penn's Treaty* (1771–72), which, as I discuss in chapter 3, became the most popular image of early Pennsylvania.

This fictional transfer of land and culture was amplified especially by James Fenimore Cooper's *Leatherstocking Tales*, especially *The Last of the Mohicans* (1826), which appropriated material from Heckewelder's *History* much as Longfellow later used Schoolcraft. Cooper did not invent the last of the race motif, but he helped to make it "the dominant motif" for the popular representation of Native Americans.[33] While the Mohicans—Heckewelder's Mahicans, or Mahicanni—were not strictly Delaware, Cooper, following Heckewelder, represented them as an associated tribe, animating his one-dimensional characters with metaphorical expressions, customs, and historical traditions lifted directly from Heckewelder. "Tamenund" (Tamanend), whom Heckewelder describes as "an ancient Delaware chief who never had his equal," pronounces Cooper's closing oration: "In the morning I saw the sons of Unâmis happy and strong; and yet, before the night has come, have I lived to see the last warrior of the wise race of the Mohicans!"[34]

BLACK MARKS

The third chapter of *The Last of the Mohicans* stages a contest between representatives of competing communities of memory. The frontiersman Natty Bumppo, or Hawkeye, as he is called in that installment of *The Leatherstocking Tales*, and his best friend Chingachgook are "lingering on the banks of a small but rapid stream," debating the justice of the British colonization of North America. "'Even your traditions make the case in my favor, Chingachgook,'" declares Bumppo: "'Your fathers came from the setting sun, crossed the big river, fought the people of the country, and took the land; and mine came from the red sky of the morning, over the salt lake, and did their work much after the fashion that had been set them by yours; then let God judge the matter between us, and friends spare their words!'"[35]

In a footnote to the 1831 edition, Cooper explains that Bumppo "alludes to a tradition which is very popular among the tribes of the Atlantic states." He suggests that "[e]vidence of their Asiatic origin is deduced from the circumstance, though great uncertainty hangs over the whole history of the Indians." Bumppo cites the tradition as evidence that the Indians held their lands by right of conquest rather than indigenous status, and suggests that the Europeans had equal right to dispossess them. Chingachgook raises two objections. First, he questions whether the European conquest, compared to the Lenape conquest, can be construed as a fair fight: "'Is there no difference, Hawk-eye, between the stone-headed arrow of the warrior, and the leaden bullet with which you kill?'" Second, he questions whether the Europeans were greeted with hostility by his ancestors, as his ancestors were by the Alligewi: "'What say your old men? do they tell the young warriors, that the pale-faces met the red men, painted for war and armed with the stone hatchet or wooden gun?'" Bumppo attempts a rejoinder to the first point, but he has to concede the second, because he admits to not knowing about the early encounter between Europeans and Indians, because the only English records of the early encounters were in writing. He laments that it is one of his people's ignoble "'customs to write in books what they have done and seen, instead of telling them in their villages, where the lie can be given to the face of a cowardly boaster, and the brave soldier can call on his comrades to witness for the truth of his words.'"[36]

Bumppo loses the argument because he must concede that his race's preferred medium—"'black marks on paper'"—is falsifying, ignoble, unmanly. By contrast, Chingachgook asks for, and receives, corroboration of the reliability of oral traditions, by soliciting Bumppo's eyewitness confirmation of his received knowledge that as the Hudson nears its mouth, "'its waters grow salt, and the current flows upward!'" Bumppo assures him that "'The Holy Bible is not more true, and that is the truest thing in nature.'" This discussion serves the ancillary function of binding the language to the landscape, through the ubiquitous figure of flowing water. Explaining the phenomenon of the tides, Bumppo declares, using stock phrases of the Romantic aesthetic of the sublime: "'You might as well expect the river to lie still on the brink of those black rocks a mile above us, though your own ears tell you that it is tumbling over them at this very moment!'"[37]

Cooper thus transformed the record of the migration tradition he found in Heckewelder into a fictional representation of an authentic living memory, pronounced in part by a white character—"'a warrior of the wilderness, though a man without a cross'"—who had become habituated to Native America.[38] This adaptation was consonant with an aesthetic and political agenda—shared by other writers in the United States and other former settler colonies—of achieving "mental independence" from the mother country.[39] These writers attempted to establish a rhetorical distance from the written word and to imbue their own writing with the authenticity and accountability of oral tradition, of language grounded in community and, importantly, in the local landscape.

Having proven to himself and Bumppo that his traditions are indeed accurate, Chingachgook proceeds to elaborate on the migration legend, the Lenapes' war with the Alligewi, and their claim to all the land from "'the place where the water runs up no longer'" on the Hudson down to "'a river twenty suns' journey toward the summer'" (the Delaware). "'All this I have heard and believe,'" Bumppo responds, "'but it was long before the English came into the country.'"[40] Chingachgook follows with material from Heckewelder's second chapter, "Indian Account of the First Arrival of the Dutch at New York Island," explaining how the Dutch settlers plied the Indians with "'the fire-water'" and incrementally dispossessed them of their land. Thus Cooper draws from Heckewelder to suggest that the Indians gained their land through conquest and lost it through European—but not English—subterfuge. The Indians retain their valor and integrity, and the Anglo-Americans get the land and the traditions that root them in it.

THE *WALAM OLUM* AND ITS READERS

The *Walam Olum* is a different sort of appropriation; it takes the conventional, compromised form of the Native American oral tradition, transcribed and translated by the ethnographer, and renders it both strange and familiar. Strange, because its 183 pictographs, or glyphs,

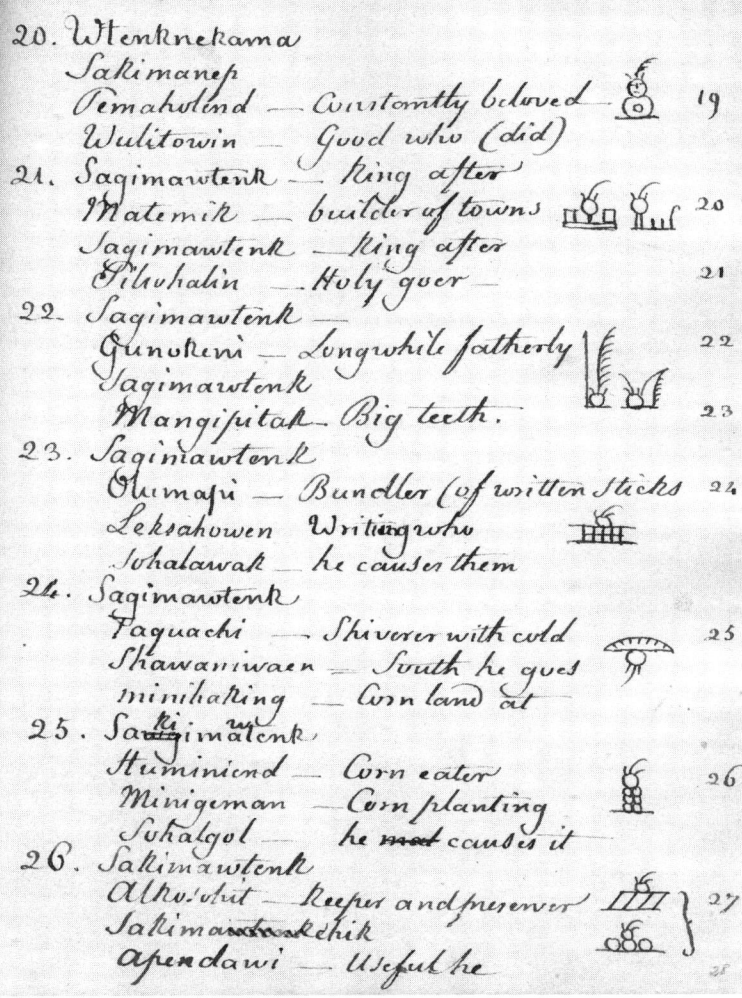

1. Glyphs 20–26, Book 3, from the "Wallam Olum: First and Second Parts of the Painted and Engraved Traditions of the Linnilinape" by C. S. Rafinesque. MS 1833 [1834?]. Courtesy of the Rare Book and Manuscript Library, University of Pennsylvania.

seem indicative of a storage capacity not typically associated with Native North American memory; familiar, because they seem more comparable to Western memory media. Thus the 1917 *Cambridge History of American Literature* deems it the "one native record" from what is now the United States "that could be called, in our fashion, a book." Otherwise, "the record of the Amerind soul was committed to the mind and heart."[41]

The *Walam Olum* first appeared as an unbound manuscript, dated 1833, produced by Constantine Samuel Rafinesque-Schmaltz (1783–1840), a Turkish-born, French-educated polymath who was better known for his prolificity than his rigor. Rafinesque published (often at his own expense) in botany, linguistics, archeology, anthropology, and other fields, but he spent his career as an outsider striving for recognition in the scholarly community.[42] The occasion for his production of the *Walam Olum* manuscript may have been his participation in a contest held by the Royal Institute of France for the best essay on Algonquian languages. In a supplement to his original submission, Rafinesque offered to send the *Walam Olum* as supporting evidence; the institute showed no interest, and typically for Rafinesque, the essay prize went to an established expert, Peter Stephen Du Ponceau.[43]

The manuscript included the pictographs, which Rafinesque claimed to have copied from etched cedar sticks that were presented to him in 1822 by a certain "late Dr. Ward of Indiana."[44] Rafinesque also furnished a key to the pictographs—an accompanying chant that he claimed to have received from an unidentified individual and to have translated after a "deep study of the Linapi" language.[45] The manuscript also included a supplementary "Fragment," without pictographs, that Rafinesque purportedly received in translation from a man named "John Burns."[46] The *Walam Olum* extended the narrative thread of the migration account in Heckewelder backward and forward. It prefaced it with a representation of creation and a flood (like Genesis), and placed the Lenapes' point of departure not "in the western part of the American continent" but rather in the continent to the west, depicting the crossing of the Bering ice bridge ("frozen sea").⁴⁷ It neatly brought the narrative up to the recorded history of European colonization, concluding with the arrival of strangers from the east: "Friendly they / big ships or birds / Who are they?"⁴⁸ The "Fragment" then serves as an epilogue, relating postcontact injustices and depredations, and the forced reverse migration of the Delawares. Rafinesque published the *Walam Olum*, without pictographs, in his *American Nations* in 1836, but he never produced the wooden originals. Thus it had doubters from the start. Yet beginning in 1849, it was repeatedly translated and reissued in editions and anthologies.

In 1994 a PhD student in anthropology at Rutgers University, David M. Oestreicher, published an essay based on his dissertation research in the *Bulletin of the Archeological Society of New Jersey* that thoroughly debunked the *Walam Olum*, attributing it to Rafinesque himself. Oestreicher persuasively argues that Rafinesque fabricated the pictographs, the supposed chant, and the narrative itself using available materials. For instance, Oestreicher shows the seams where, apparently, Rafinesque inexpertly patched together "broken stems" from words he culled from Lenape language materials compiled by the Moravian missionaries Zeisberger and Heckewelder. According to Oestreicher, these grammars and word lists were, as Rafinesque claimed, his translation aids, except they helped him not to decipher the *Walam Olum* but rather to render his English original into an otherwise unaccountably aberrant approximation of Lenape.⁴⁹ For example, even the title *Walam Olum*, translated by Rafinesque as "painted record," is a grammatically impossible combination of a root incorrectly broken off from the place-name Wallamâning, "the place where paint is," and a root incorrectly broken off from the name of a chief, Olumapi, which the author of the *Walam Olum*, helped along by a typo in Heckewelder's published word list, "translates" erroneously as "'Bundler of written sticks.'"⁵⁰ The alleged Lenape pictograph that accompanies the name Olumapi in the *Walam Olum* is based on a *Chinese* symbol for writing; other glyphs are demonstrably composites of Chinese, Egyptian, Mexican, and Native American pictographs that were available to Rafinesque from published sources. Finally, the plot of the *Walam Olum* is a pastiche of traditions recorded by Heckewelder and elements of world mythology.[51]

I do not add to Oestreicher's meticulous philological expositions of the apocryphal nature of the *Walam Olum* and of the compounding series of errors and oversights made by the preceding investigators into the *Walam Olum*, although I do analyze a significant reproduction of the *Walam Olum* that postdates his debunking. My principal contribution to the now considerable body of research on the *Walam Olum* is to illuminate the political and ideological tendencies underlying its creation and reception. Oestreicher's comprehensive research makes apparent just how motivated the reception of the *Walam Olum* had to be in order to sustain belief in its authenticity. That is, its proponents neglected the easy and obvious explanation for the *Walam Olum*'s existence and instead devoted their efforts to vindicating Rafinesque's dubious reputation, substantiating his fishy story about his acquisition of the document, and in some sense tampering with the evidence: as Oestreicher demonstrates, its translators corrected perceived errors that were actually clues that the *Walam Olum* was created by someone lacking basic competency in Lenape. There were two interrelated motives to go to such lengths. The first was regional and national pride, coupled with the well-known Anglo-American inferiority complex: the *Walam Olum* was a potential prize for the United States' antiquity, which otherwise failed to measure up to those of Europe and Mesoamerica. The second was a desire to credit Native Americans with a degree of cultural achievement that otherwise, by Western standards, they had failed to demonstrate. The emphasis shifted over time, from claiming the *Walam Olum* on behalf of the United States, to claiming it on behalf of Native Americans. I argue that the suspension of critical judgment regarding the *Walam Olum* was a misguided response to an age-old colonial chauvinism: the claim that the possession of writing entails a cultural superiority. The ideological investments in the existence of an indigenous "book" from what is now the United States have magnified and complicated what might have been a simple and easily settled question of authenticity, altogether typical of its nineteenth-century cultural moment.[52]

As for Rafinesque's motives in creating the *Walam Olum*, Oestreicher's qualification of the *Walam Olum* as a "hoax" may not capture the spirit in which he brought it forward. Indeed, Charles Boewe, whom Oestreicher himself considers to be "the premier Rafinesque scholar," attests to the prime suspect's basic honesty and humorlessness.[53] Boewe does not dispute that the *Walam Olum* is apocryphal. Indeed, he accepts "some of the onus for revealing this blot on Rafinesque's character," having abetted Oestreicher in his "brilliant detective work," which "has made three generations of scholars look foolish."[54] Where Boewe contests Oestreicher is in his identification of Rafinesque as the creator of the *Walam Olum*: "of course there was a hoaxer, but it is even more likely that gullible, credulous C. S. Rafinesque was his victim." Boewe points to the eagerness of scientific contemporaries, whether famous (e.g., John James Audubon) or anonymous, to "twit Rafinesque's pretensions to scholarship."[55] While Boewe raises credible objections to Oestreicher's "Byzantine" philological demonstration, I remain persuaded by his attribution.[56]

In the absence of another identified author, Rafinesque's own claim to have practiced "Historical Palingenesy or the restoration of ancient nations and languages presumed lost" through a process analogous to the work of Georges "Cuvier and the modern Paleontologists, who restore extinct animals by the fragments of their bones" would seem to confirm that he carried out just such a reconstruction as Oestreicher describes.[57] The *Walam Olum* may have been less a "hoax" than the product of a wishful and overzealous application of a sincere but flawed and naive (apparently, apt descriptors of Rafinesque himself) theory. Rafinesque may have imagined that the scientific community owed him appreciation for his reconstruction of a lost masterpiece.

Oestreicher seems too indignant at Rafinesque's "hoax" to credit him with any altruism; he points to his "mercenary motives," especially the Prix Volney essay contest. Not coincidentally, as Oestreicher argues, the

Walam Olum supported the theory that Rafinesque had espoused a decade earlier, in his *Annals of Kentucky* (1824), that the Indians had migrated to America over the Bering Strait.[58] Yet the *Walam Olum* also had political significance. Rafinesque was a critic of Indian Removal, and the *Walam Olum* supported his stance through its content and especially its form. The *Walam Olum*, if authentic, would demonstrate that the Algonquian peoples of the eastern United States shared a common humanity and cultural heritage with the white Christians who wished to dispossess them, and also that they had achieved a level of cultural development that was inconsistent with their characterization as refractory primitives. These implications do not vindicate Rafinesque's fabrication of the *Walam Olum*, but they may help to explain it; they certainly help to explain its reception.

Oestreicher thoroughly examines the bearing of the early European and American intellectual climates on the production of the *Walam Olum*, including not only the important debates about the origins of the Native Americans but also the evident precedents of James MacPherson's *Songs of Ossian* and Joseph Smith's *Book of Mormon*.[59] However, it is the legacy of removal, more than the intellectual questions of Rafinesque's day, to which the *Walam Olum* owes its relative longevity and popularity. Rafinesque, who pronounced himself "a great friend to the native Tribes of America," actually prefaces the first publication of the *Walam Olum*, or "Linapi Annals," with this issue.[60] In his *American Nations* he decried the United States' treatment of "the reduced tribes": "They compel them to remove, to emigrate, disperse, sell their lands and homes, at one tenth of the value; and this is called fair dealing!"[61]

The *Walam Olum* expressed opposition to removal by documenting the Delawares' ancient claim to their new territories in Ohio and Indiana by right of conquest, and the manifestly anti-imperial "Fragment" even reminds readers of the claim to land "beyond the Masispek (muddy water, or Mississippi) near to our ancient seat."[62] More importantly, the existence of a *Walam Olum* contradicted the prejudices that supported removal. It showed that the Indians were hardly uncivilizable heathens:

their religion shared a common heritage with Christianity, and importantly, they practiced writing.

True, Indians north of Mexico used pictographs (whose components Rafinesque assimilated into his own system), but the instances were relatively sparse and limited in application. For instance, the Delaware pictographs observed by the missionaries memorialized specific battles or warriors' deeds, preserving their memory for only a few generations—not long enough, according to some commentators, to indicate a true historical sensibility.[63] In Rafinesque's presentation, by contrast, the *Walam Olum* put the Delawares on a level with the great civilizations of the Ancient World and Mesoamerica; moreover, he extends the evidentiary claim—that the Indians had writing—to most of the indigenous hemisphere. Rafinesque's references to the "American graphic systems of Apalacha, Amahuac, Otolum, Peru," and a "high civilization" that was "scattered from the Apalachis and Nachez of Florida to the Chilians south of Peru, filling the whole intermediate space" misleadingly suggest that the *Walam Olum* was more typical than otherwise.[64]

In an 1840 essay on "The Graphic Systems of the *Ancient American and Chinese Nations*" (emphasis original), Rafinesque, anticipating subsequent scholars, self-referentially cited the *Walam Olum* as evidence of native North American literacy. Referring his largely imaginary readership to his 1836 publication, Rafinesque claimed that the *Walam Olum* exhibited seventy-four of the "over 200 simple signs" once "used by the nations deemed *Savages* (although they were half civilized Hunters at their discovery)."[65] With such claims and with the production of the *Walam Olum* Rafinesque addressed by fiat the challenge facing those who would even out the ledger by asserting that the Native North Americans, too, had literacy and its prerogatives—historical and legal legitimacy. A hundred and thirty years later, C. A. Weslager, who argued for the authenticity of the *Walam Olum*, suggested that the colonists were mistaken to consider the Delawares as "illiterate heathens emerging from the Stone Age": "In retrospect, it is apparent that in contrast to the primitive life of the Paleo-Indians, the ascendancy of the Delawares to the level of cultural development they reached when the first Dutch explorers sailed into Delaware Bay"—that is, the endpoint of the *Walam Olum* proper—"was an example of remarkable progress."[66]

Such views suggest how the *Walam Olum*'s doubters were thus taking a politically unsavory position, especially in recent decades. They were also contradicting some of the foundational figures in American anthropology. The first "translation" of the *Walam Olum* was by published in 1849 by Ephraim George Squier, who has the dubious distinction of having recovered Rafinesque's manuscript from oblivion.[67] Schoolcraft responded skeptically, lamenting to Squier "that the elements of such a document should have fallen into the hands of Rafinesque, who spoiled, *historically* and *scientifically*, everything he touched."[68] He noted that there was no precedent for the discovery of a record with the "extent and continuity" of the *Walam Olum* from America north of Mexico. Nevertheless, in 1884 Daniel G. Brinton followed Squier by featuring his own translation of the *Walam Olum* in his *Lenâpé and Their Legends*. "Not without hesitation do I send forth this volume to the learned world," he wrote in the preface. "Regarded as an authentic memorial, the original text of the *Walam Olum* will require a much more accurate rendering than I have been able to give it; while the possibility that a more searching criticism will demonstrate it to have been a fabrication may condemn as labor lost pains that I have bestowed upon it."[69]

Among the validators and popularizers of the *Walam Olum* was M. L. Harrington, whose 1938 ethnohistorical novel *Dickon among the Lenape Indians*, intended as "the most complete and accurate account of this interesting people that has yet appeared," constructs an imaginative context for the "Wa'lum O'loom."[70] The young hero, as a "rare privilege," attends a Big House ceremony at which the itinerant bard, "Talking Wood," reads from the tablets in "a sort of swing like poetry." Later, Dickon sneaks a peek: "A strange thing about the figures was that very few of them seemed to be pictures of anything; they were merely signs, which no one could understand unless previously instructed."[71] (In other words, they were not pictures but ideographic writing.) For Harrington, the *Walam Olum* represents an essential mystery at the core of the otherwise transparent ethnographic data he imports from scholars and from living informants. Dickon's exposure to the *Walam Olum* is the climax of his initiation; it appears in the chapter "A Full-Fledged Lenape" as a preliminary to his adoption. Yet the *Walam Olum*'s aura of mystery and inscrutability is attributable not to its sanctified place at the heart of Lenape ceremonial culture but rather to its contrived connection to that culture.

The *Walam Olum*'s proponents misconstrued the evidence of its inauthenticity as symptoms of the discontinuity of Delaware cultural traditions. Its highly aberrant language was a lost dialect; the absence of "a single reference to the *Walam Olum*" in the voluminous ethnographic records on the Lenape, as well as in the Lenapes' oral traditions, could only mean that the Lenapes themselves had lost track of it.[72] By contrast, science—anthropology, linguistics—and the technology of writing implicitly gave non-Indian scholars a privileged access to what was lost to the descendants of the supposed creators of the *Walam Olum*. For example, Brinton envisioned himself as an intermediary between the Lenape past and present, serving the natives by preserving their culture for posterity. In a footnote, he indicates that he meant to pay off "a debt of gratitude" to the nation who had succored his settler ancestors by gathering

> its legends, its language, and its memoirs, so that they
> in books recorded
> May, like hoarded
> Household words, no more depart![73]

While his allusion is to Longfellow's poem "Seaweed," in publishing his version of the *Walam Olum* Brinton has reprised the role of the narrator of the *Song of Hiawatha*. As the fictional transcriber of the songs of the Indian bard, the narrator occupies a higher stage of literacy than Hiawatha, the supposed inventor of Indian "Picture-Writing."

The *Walam Olum* actually emerges from much the same cultural milieu as Longfellow's 1855 epic poem, sharing its intercourse with the emergent field of anthropology, the romantic fascination with recovered bardic traditions, and, of course, with picture writing. Yet it was many years before someone took on the relatively simple task of demonstrating that it has no more relation to the historical Delawares than the *Song of Hiawatha* does to either the Ojibwas described in Longfellow's source text, Schoolcraft's *Algic Researches*, or the historical Iroquois. Instead, investigators chose the far more difficult challenges of rationalizing away the obvious explanation for the *Walam Olum*'s existence, explicating its artificial and incoherent sign system, and constructing a plausible scenario for its ceremonial use. This task was undertaken by the Indiana Historical Society, among others. The IHS carried out a twenty-year study of the relic, commissioned by the pharmaceutical tycoon and antiquarian Eli Lilly, who suggested "an exalted comparison": the Delaware pictographic history was of tantamount "historical value" to "the Homeric epics."[74] This comparison implies that the *Walam Olum* was a credit not merely to the Native Americans who produced it but to the United States and especially to the region in which it was supposedly found. The IHS study produced a ponderous gilt edition (1954), complete with scholarly essays and annotations—a magnificent example of "labor lost."

Perhaps like some of the laboratory research undertaken for Eli Lilly's chemical and pharmaceutical company, the findings of the *Walam Olum* study may reflect sponsorship bias.[75] In their efforts to corroborate the authenticity of Lilly's "Hoosier Iliad," the researchers knew what to look for—even if they could not find it—and what not to look for.[76] Jim Rementer, the director of the Lenape Language Project for the Delaware Tribe of Indians in Bartlesville, Oklahoma, finds it "puzzling" that C. F. Voegelin, the lead investigator, neglected to consult living Lenape speakers who might have contested the *Walam Olum*'s authenticity.[77] He points out that Voegelin disregarded a 1951 letter from an attorney in nearby Dewey, who wrote: "So far as I know they all think it a white man's story."[78] The search for supporting archeological evidence, however, and for the identities of Dr. Ward and John Burns, was necessarily unsuccessful. The authenticity became a matter of faith: "The authors believe wholeheartedly that some day discovery of additional facts will further vindicate our faith in the genuineness and value of the *Walam Olum*."[79] Pending that "discovery," they were ready to pronounce the *Walam Olum* "probably the most important and the most interesting recorded tradition derived from any American aboriginal source north of Mexico."[80]

The description of the *Walam Olum* as a "recorded tradition" is in some ways suitable to the parallel with Homer, but it is also more modest than some later characterizations. The IHS study perhaps reflects a 1950s scholarly consensus that pictographs do not constitute writing, exactly. Voegelin corrects what he believes to be Rafinesque's mistaken rendering of the verse accompanying the crucial twenty-third pictograph in book 3: "'Olumapi' is no longer the 'Bundler of written sticks / Writing who / he causes them' but 'Red Paint Person, the one who originated drawing.'"[81] While Voegelin translates the name of a later chief, "Lekhihitin," as "one who writes," it seems that neither chief is precisely a writer but one who "writes, makes pictures," or at the very least, keeps "records." A gloss on glyph 5 in book 5 by the ethnographer Erminie Voegelin suggests that the *Walam Olum* marks the apparent apogee of Lenape cultural development, the threshold of a cultural evolutionary transition: "A settled mode of life, in which there was some opportunity for specialization on the part of talented individuals, plus contacts with southerly tribes possessed of more complex cultures than the northern groups, would put the Delawares in a position to elaborate on such nonessential arts as record keeping."[82]

Arguably, it wasn't until the multiculturalist late twentieth century that the *Walam Olum* found its ideal readership. This period saw an increasing emphasis on the *Walam Olum* as writing, not legend or tradition but history and literature. The text's appeal to a New Age sensibility is illustrated by the small press edition by the poet Joe Napora (1992), and by the publication of the artist David McCutchen's translation *The Red Record = The Walam Olum* by the Avery Publishing Group, a press specializing in self-help, healing, and spirituality (1993). The cover of Napora's edition hails it as "A North American 'Dead Sea Scrolls' of sorts."[83] McCutchen's jacket copy declares it the "Oldest Written Account of a Native North American People." He accuses skeptics of ethnocentrism: "It was more convenient for Americans to believe that this continent was empty before the colonists came, or, at most, inhabited by people incompetent to record their history." He attributes William Newcomb's plausible speculation that the *Walam Olum* was a product of native revivalism to an unwillingness to accord Indians the intellectual capacity to maintain "a written history of ancient times."[84]

"Such statements may be 'politically correct,'" writes Oestreicher, "but as the evidence now demonstrates, they are simply not correct." According to Oestreicher, when he presented Joe Napora with his evidence, Napora recanted, "dismayed that the writers upon whom he relied had been so negligent in their investigations of the document, and that the hoax should have continued as long as it has."[85] Oestreicher seems especially incensed by McCutchen. Yet McCutchen's translation was endorsed by a resolution of the Delaware Nation in Anadarko, Oklahoma, and includes a preface by Linda Poolaw, then grand chief of the Delaware Nation Grand Council of North America: "It is an old song," she writes, "by an ancient people. I believe it was sung by the Grandfathers. I believe it was sung many, many times for many, many centuries. I believe it was sung by my ancestors, as they traveled thousands of miles in search of that place where the Sun wakes up. I pray that this song of the Lenape will be heard. Listen."[86]

Poolaw must speak in terms of belief, because the Delawares had no cultural memory of a *Walam Olum*. The receptiveness of some was indeed an indication of the faltering transmission of their cultural heritage, caused by territorial dispossession and the associated pressures to adapt to the majority culture. Thus Richard Calmit Adams, the author of *A Brief History of the Delaware Indians* (1906), had to rely on Heckewelder for his information about his people's "legendary period"; he excerpted long passages from Heckewelder's "Historical Traditions" chapter.[87] Perhaps cautiously, he relegates his discussion of the *Walam Olum* itself to a long footnote in his appendix, where he pronounces it "a most interesting and instructive legend of the Lenni Lenapi." He refers readers to Brinton and expresses gratitude to Rafinesque for "the preservation and first translation of a document that presents the traditions of the Delawares in regard to the Creation and Ontogeny, of the Deluge, of the passage to America, arrival in America, settlement in Ohio, from Ohio to the Atlantic States, and back to Missouri." In other words, to the native historian as well as the non-Indian ethnohistorian, the *Walam Olum* is a tantalizing representation of cultural continuity. Adams gestures subtly at an authenticity controversy, declaring that "[w]hatever its origin, the Walam Olum is a most ingenious work, consistent with itself, and its principal statements supported from other sources."[88] Since Rafinesque apparently used the these "sources"—especially Heckewelder—as material for the *Walam Olum*, this corroboration was circular.

As in the academic community, however, among Delawares the *Walam Olum* had its doubters. According to Jay Miller, who reviewed McCutchen's *Red Record* for the *American Indian Culture and Research Journal*, Poolaw's preface is not indicative of general opinion. "All of my elders agreed," writes Miller, "when I asked about the authenticity of the Wallam Olum, that it was '*nuchkway*, worthless and of no account.'" The idea that the Delawares were migrants, instead of autochthones, was potentially offensive. "The Delaware know only too well that they have always lived on this land, this back of the turtle."[89] Oestreicher drew the same response from his older informants, and reports that even Linda Poolaw's mother, Winnie, in an interview taped years before Linda Poolaw's endorsement of the *Red Record*, "denies ever having heard of it."[90] Oestreicher notes that many of the younger Lenapes, less versed in their language and traditions, "eagerly seized upon" the *Walam Olum* "as a glorious remnant of their culture."[91] It was especially appealing to Christians, who saw it as evidence of a proto-Christian heritage, a restored sacred text. When Oestreicher presented his findings in 1996, "some Lenape were deeply disappointed."[92]

This disappointment, and the refusal of Oestreicher's evidence, is not surprising in light of the significance accorded to the *Walam Olum* by some non-Indians. In *The Book of the Fourth World*, Gordon Brotherston, perhaps the most recognized interpreter of indigenous texts, opines that if authenticated, the *Walam Olum* would have to be considered as one of the indigenous Americas "major classics." He suggests that the skepticism was politically motivated: "Like Algonkin texts assuredly genuine, in defending Ohio as a prime focus in ancient and modern Turtle Island it has upset yet again the official U.S. doctrine of 'American' prehistory and history, touching the particularly raw nerve of the Ohio."[93] In a previous publication, Brotherston was less cautious regarding the *Walam Olum*'s authenticity: "It is the very time-scale and historical precision of the *Walam Olum* which have made it so unwelcome and problematic. In official US historiography it has been depoliticized like the Indian history in Cooper's *Leatherstocking Tales* or Longfellow's *Hiawatha*." He complains that even where the *Walam Olum* is accepted as authentic, as by Brinton and Weslager, it is not taken seriously as a historical record, only as a record of a tradition. For Brotherston, the *Walam Olum*, including the "Fragment" (which he calls the "Mattanikum chapter," after the first chief mentioned) stands as a most important extant text of Native America north of Mexico, a key component of "a corpus of native chronological works" that are "a cultural constant of the first order."[94] Such indigenous writing has long been disregarded, he writes in his *Image of the New World* (1979). "The neglect stemmed in part, perhaps, from the blank disbelief that American Indians were ever capable of writing anything down themselves."[95]

Similarly, Dennis Tedlock, in the headnote for the *Walam Olum* in the *Multilingual Anthology of American Literature*, edited by Marc Shell and Werner Sollors, apparently suspected that doubt about the *Walam Olum* was motivated by a broader skepticism about native literacy—a disbelief that a native document could be what it appeared to be, writing. He therefore made a deliberate effort to move beyond the controversy, and focused on "normalizing the document," showing how it might have been used in its native context by comparing it to apparently related forms such as the Ojibwa Midewin Birchbark scrolls.[96] Tedlock approached the *Walam Olum* through his particular expertise as a Mayanist—interestingly, this field is one in which Rafinesque has received some posthumous recognition, with accompanying credibility, because he made insightful observations about Mayan writing: specifically, that it had phonetic elements and was related to modern Mayan languages.[97] Tedlock apparently equated the suspicions directed against the *Walam Olum* to the reluctance he has observed among scholars to recognize the discovery that Mayan script is indeed largely phonetic, and therefore is *writing* in the most widely accepted sense of the word.[98]

It seems likely that at least some of the animus against the *Walam Olum* has indeed been motivated by Eurocentric views of Native American communication systems. That the skeptics have been vindicated does not prove otherwise. However, the many promoters of the *Walam Olum* have also applied a Western system of values to native cultures. What this overview of the reception of the *Walam Olum* suggests is that it was invested with too much significance. This significance—a great burden of representativeness—is based on the notion that the possession of writing, and especially a written history, is a key aspect, even a defining factor, of civilization. However, if the *Walam Olum* is celebrated as a cultural credential, one that contradicts the persistent popular characterization of Native Americans as savages, then where does that leave the many Native American groups without such a document to their credit? Where does that leave the Delawares once the *Walam Olum* is debunked? What would it even mean, had the *Walam Olum* been authentic? According to the ethnographic speculations described above, it would mean that, among the Delawares, a small group of specialists (the successors of "Olumapi" and "Lekhihitin") maintained a form of record-keeping that was somewhat analogous to European writing.[99] Making this practice an exhibit in the argument that the Delawares should not have been dispossessed of their land, or insisting, as some colonialist scholars have recently done, that all Native American forms of record-keeping should be validated as "writing," only substantiates the ideological connection between writing and political and cultural legitimacy.

The *Walam Olum*'s inclusion as the longest selection in *The Multilingual Anthology* is probably the capstone of its reception history.[100] The anthology presents works in their original language with "facing page" English translations. The *Walam Olum*'s "red paint" pictographs appear on the cover, superimposed upon the 1752 "Petition from the Indians at Mashpee to the Massachusetts General Court" to form a digitally composed palimpsest. Inside, the frontispiece is the "Christian Covenanting Confession," a bilingual Massachuset-English devotional by the seventeenth-century English missionary John Eliot. The three works seem to form a hierarchy of perceived cultural purity—indigenous writing, a transculturative use of European writing by Indians, and a translation and transcription by a European missionary. Together they suggest that the volume's agenda of recovery and canon revision is strongly identified with Native America—it seems that the editors are among those, in Sollors's phrase, "for whom 'American multilingualism' signifies foremost Native American languages."[101]

The *Walam Olum* is both anomalous and curiously representative of the anthology. In his afterword, Marc Shell describes three kinds of implied readers. The first "knows the language" of the original work and therefore has no need for the English translation. The second "does not know the language of the particular original work" but has enough familiarity with linguistic plurality to "be reminded" by the incomprehensible "facing page original" of "what she is missing." The "third hypothetical reader," like humans before the Tower of Babel, "knows all languages."[102] Unlike the other "facing page originals," the *Walam Olum* has two components, the pictographs and the pseudo-Lenape transcription. The pictographs convey no information to most readers, who rely on the English. Instead, they contribute an "authenticity effect."[103] Perhaps more than the other, authentic originals in the anthology, the pictographs may remind the readers of what they are "missing," not only the "inessential content" in Walter Benjamin's phrase, that may be lost through linguistic translation, but also, as Tedlock's headnote (and Harrington's fictive reconstruction) reminds us, a performative context, a living world that is critical to their intelligibility.[104] The pseudo-Lenape transcription was Rafinesque's partly successful contrivance to confine the ambiguity of the pictographs, which otherwise would have been subject to wildly varied and speculative readings. Yet if the pictographs elicit the perspective of Shell's multilingual second reader, they also intimate that of the omnilingual third. They are, in theory, supralinguistic—independent of language.[105] Rafinesque, who claimed proficiency in more than forty languages, was also a romantic who yearned for the time before Babel, when the entire world, he thought, shared a single, universally intelligible script.[106] Even as Shell requires us to relinquish the monolingual illusion, he maintains this romantic yearning throughout the afterword; ironically, no entry speaks to it so well as the *Walam Olum*.

While an authentic *Walam Olum* would be an important and compelling artifact, the proof that it is inauthentic does not mean that the Delaware Indians, or Native Americans in what is now the United States, did not have a history or a sense of historical time, or that their culture was inferior to that of the European colonists. Nor does the fact of inauthenticity mean, certainly, that the *Walam Olum* should no longer be taught and studied: on the contrary, it is an intriguing document with a fascinating history. This history, in part, is that of a desire. It is a desire to have the native peoples who were ravaged by the violent European invasion speak to us fully, without mediation, to circumvent the processes of negotiation involved in reading for the "real" Native Americans in writings by non-Indians. Unlike, for example, John Neihardt's *Black Elk Speaks*, for which so much of the criticism has focused on problems of mediation, the *Walam Olum* conveyed a simulacrum of the voice of the precolonial Indians, intact, to the postcolonial United States, packaged into a recognizable form, a "book." It was not, to use Rafinesque's paleontology conceit, an obscure fragment of bone but the foundation narrative of a major tribe, the whole story, "stretching from the beginning of the world to the arrival of the Europeans."[107]

The fantasy of the *Walam Olum* is sustained by writing's metaphysical illusion: it brings the past to the present, like the "eternal lines" of Shakespeare's sonnets.[108] Shakespeare's contemporary Samuel Purchas, the chronicler of colonialism, also boasted that "by writing Man seemes immortall, conferreth and consulteth with the Patriarkes, Prophets, Apostles, Fathers, Philosophers, Historians, and learnes the wisdome of the Sages which have been in all times before him."[109] For its various readers, the *Walam Olum* thus seemed to close the distance between "prehistory" and history, or between the eastward migrants and the westward refugees, or between the ancestors of the victims and the remorseful legatees of the victimizers. More reliably, however, the *Walam Olum* illustrates the proximity of Constantine Rafinesque and the audiences who shared and sustained his fantasy.

The next chapter picks up where the pictographic narrative leaves off—"Friendly they / big ships or birds / Who are they?"[110] Here were the Europeans, with their writing implements, paper, and alphabet. Yet their written record of first contact with Native Americans would not tell the whole story either.

2

An Account of a Tradition

A Delaware oral tradition about the arrival of the first colonists in the New York region includes the curious detail that they asked for as much land as the hide of a bullock (or cow) could cover, and then claimed as much land as that hide, cut into strips, could encircle. They used the land they gained as the site for a fort.

To be sure, there is no mention of a ruse with a bullock's hide in the European primary source documents concerning the founding of the colony of New Netherland. This detail is, however, a common feature in recorded traditions relating the establishment of other outposts of early modern European maritime empires in the Indian and Pacific Oceans. These accounts of Europeans employing an oxhide to measure land are also uncorroborated by the colonists' own records, although at least a couple colonial writers allude to the legend of the Phoenician Queen Dido (or Elisa), the founder of the colony of Carthage: "For 'tis believed *Dido* purchased no more ground then might be compassed with the hide of a Bull or Ox, which being cut out into very slender thongs contained a larger space, then the sellers did imagine, and it was sufficient whereon to Erect a Castle, which from thence is thought to be called *Byrsa*."[1] (*Byrsa* means animal hide in Greek and resembles the Phoenician word for citadel.) This story expressed a Roman characterization of the Carthaginians as "treacherous, perfidious," as encapsulated in the phrase "Punic faith."

How does a classical motif come to appear in a Native American tradition? This question is tied to others, such as, how potentially useful are oral traditions as historical sources?

This chapter's argument is as follows: (1) Except for the "Dido motif," the Delaware account of the arrival of the whites bears an intriguing correlation with Robert Juet's journal of Henry Hudson's 1609 voyage. However, by ignoring the oxhide, scholarship on the founding of New Netherland has neglected the element in this narrative account that has the most to teach us. (2) As Washington Irving demonstrates in his *Knickerbocker's History of New York*, the oxhide cut into strips is an apt metaphor for colonial transactions; as such, it was taken up as an exemplary story by Native American groups without ancestral ties to the New York region. This use and this pattern of distribution, however, do not exclude the possibility that the tradition records information about an actual historical event. (3) On the contrary, despite the motif's apparent lack of verisimilitude, the notion that it is merely a "simple tale" incorporated by either the performers or the recorders of native traditions struggles to account for its global pattern of distribution.[2] (4) A better, if still flawed, explanation is that the colonists themselves emulated a ruse from classical antiquity, and that the various parallel traditions record this act. Thus the traditions furnish new information about the colonists' interactions with native peoples vis-à-vis their own cultural traditions.

It is an elaborate argument, certainly, and to some it will seem farfetched. But I plan to demonstrate that the prevailing omission of the oxhide from the history of New Netherland and early modern imperialism more generally is at least equally farfetched, and depends on questionable assumptions about oral traditions.

FIRST IMPRESSIONS

The first phase of contact, Daniel Richter tells us, is especially challenging to scholars. "All we have to go on are oral traditions of Indians who lived generations after the events described, written accounts by

European explorers who misunderstood much of what happened in brief face-to-face meetings with Native people, and mute archeological artifacts that raise more questions than they answer."[3] As Richter suggests, each mode of historical evidence has its attendant shortcomings. Yet these problems are not commensurate, perhaps especially when we shift from Richter's perspective, "facing east," and instead imagine an overhead view of a colonial encounter. Compared with documentary evidence, oral traditions are generally less datable, less attributable, less stable in content, and less susceptible to cross-referencing and independent corroboration. "Unlike information drawn from radiometric dating, stratigraphy, or seriational analysis," writes the archeologist Ronald J. Mason, "methods that have global legitimacy and are based on known physical laws or firmly grounded cultural principles, and that are themselves testable by independent means, most of the contents of oral traditions are of an entirely different nature and should not be treated in the same way."[4]

The question underlying the debate over the "historical value" of native traditions is not whether they carry information about the past, but rather whether this information is of any use when it is not verifiable or falsifiable. In *Oral Tradition as History*, the Africanist Jan Vansina describes the evidence from oral traditions as "'on probation'"; however, it is only in exceptional cases subject to proof.[5] One's approach to oral traditions, therefore, may depend on one's self-conception as a practitioner of a scientific or humanistic discipline. For the former, oral traditions may be of little to no value because the information they convey is inadmissible unless it can be corroborated by other means, and if it can be corroborated it is "superfluous," providing no new information, except perhaps about the people that tell the story.[6] Yet the a priori exclusion of evidence from oral traditions is itself predicated on uncertainty, or at least a questionable logic—a presumption that historical truth is scalable, that is, that an analysis that does not take into account possibly significant evidence does not risk being therefore less true. Especially when we consider that the documentary record is not only patchy but also sometimes simply dishonest—that, especially in circumstances of oppression or exploitation, the omissions and distortions can be purposeful, it seems mistaken to ignore whatever oral traditions may retain of opposing perspectives on events.

Those scholars who do consider the recorded native traditions about the first encounters in New York Harbor generally correlate them with the documentary record, beginning with Robert Juet's journal of Henry Hudson's 1609 voyage to North America. The datelines of that journal seem as close as possible to objective statements of record. They mark events—most reductively, the composition of journal entries (although, as the controversies surrounding the *Walam Olum* manuscript and the supposed copy of the supposedly missing Walking Purchase deed suggest, even ascribed dates of composition can be questionable). With relative confidence, we can construe the journal as a record of participation in a momentous series of events and therefore as an authoritative representation of first contact: "a fairly detailed picture of what happened, at least through European eyes."[7] Juet's journal is fixed in its connection to Hudson's voyage, and it comes to us from that moment in the past.

By contrast, the events recorded by the dates associated with Native American traditions about the arrival of Europeans in the lower Hudson—among them 1650, 1801, 1824, 1849, and 1939—are acts of transcription, translation, and publication.[8] These may be the only moments in the past to which these oral traditions can be authoritatively fixed.[9] Any necessarily speculative argument that a given tradition also preserves the memories of eyewitnesses to or participants in the encounters it purports to depict must address a series of questions and challenges: To what extent is the account compatible with the documentary record? (The more compatible, the more persuasive the dating.) How consistent does its content seem with our (also speculative) ethnographic understanding of the indigenous culture and worldview at the time of the encounter? (Again, the more consistent it is, the more plausible.) To what extent does the tradition seem to relate to subsequent events and experiences? (The more it seems to relate to the present and recent past, the less convincingly it belongs to the more remote past.)

The first brief European representation of the Indian tradition about the arrival of the Dutch, published by Adriaen van der Donck in 1650, is self-serving in its use of the tradition to corroborate the Netherlands' claims of colonial precedence in the region, but there is nothing in the Indians' supposed initial wonderment as to whether the ship "might be a rare fish or a sea monster, and those on board devils or humans" that is inconsistent with the notion that the tradition records the 1609 arrival of Hudson's *De Halve Maen*. Furthermore, the tradition cited by van der Donck gives a plausible account of its own inception in the "strange reports of the event" that were "current in the country at the time and caused great despondency among the Indians."[10] Such a remarkable event, whose occurrence was broadcast from neighbor to neighbor, would likely also be carried forward as an oral tradition.[11] It is certainly plausible that this "momentous event" would be committed to cultural memory. There is a relevant parallel in the Hopi tradition about the coming of the Spanish and the Pueblo revolt—a tradition that had an even longer span between documentation and the events it recounts, and has been corroborated in some of its details.[12]

As Vansina emphasizes, instead of generalizing about the traits of oral traditions, it is important to identify the genre to which the specific tradition belongs. The "Indian account of the first arrival of Europeans at York Island" is evidently a "narrative account"; unlike a "tale," it was not likely considered permissible to improvise new details in individual performances. It was undoubtedly subject to accidental alteration, but the intent would have been to convey its "message" intact, from the original event down through the generations. However, as Vansina also points out, "the notion of 'truth' is itself culture bound and cannot be assumed to correspond to the 'historical truth' familiar to an academic scholar."[13] In his presentation, accordingly, Heckewelder is at pains to be true to the narrative of the tradition but reticent about its factual accuracy.

In an 1801 letter to the historian Samuel Miller he presents the account "verbatim as was related to me by Aged & respected Delawares; Monseys & Mahicanni . . . near 40 years ago."[14] He later published it, without substantial changes, as the second chapter of his *An Account of the History, Manners, and Customs of the Indian Nations Who Once Inhabited Pennsylvania and the Neighboring States* (1819). Here he specifies that it "was taken down many years since from the mouth of an intelligent Delaware Indian, and may be considered as a correct account of the tradition existing among them of this momentous event. I give it as much as possible in their own language."[15] Heckewelder had good reason to attest to the accuracy of his ethnography and the authority of his informant(s), as well as to hedge as to the truthfulness of the story; the account is at least somewhat unbelievable in its details. Thus he presents not an account of an event but "an account of a tradition." He implies that the traditional account may not be "correct," but his account of it is.

The first part of the account recounts the astonishing appearance in the harbor of a "wonderful object" that the people assembling on the shore eventually realized was "a large house of various colours . . . full of human beings, of quite a different colour from that of the Indians, and dressed differently from them; that in particular one of them was dressed entirely in red, who must be the Mannitto himself." The Mannitto—supernatural being—and others landed in a small boat, and a circle of chiefs greeted him. He passed around a cup with a "strange liquor," first drinking from it himself. The chiefs passed it from one to another without daring to sample it, but one among them, fearful of offending the Mannitto, drank the whole cup. He collapsed, fell asleep, and then awoke to say he "has enjoyed the most delicious sensations, and that he never before felt himself so happy as after he had drunk the cup. He asks for more, his wish is granted; the whole assembly then imitate him, and all become intoxicated." The "man with the red clothes" then distributed presents "consisting of beads, axes, hoes, and stockings such as the white people wear." Then the strange men—"the Dutch"—departed, explaining through signs that they would return again next year, at which time they proposed to stay a while, for which purpose "they should want a little land of them to sow seeds, in order to raise herbs and vegetables to put into their broth."[16]

So far, so good. Except for the mention of the upcoming request for land, which anticipates the implausible conclusion to the tradition, there is nothing exceptional in the account of first contact. Therefore, perhaps, most historians either ignore it or give it slight notice.[17] Milton Hamilton's *Henry Hudson and the Dutch in New York*, Edwin G. Burrows and Mike Wallace's *Gotham: A History of New York City to 1898*, and Russell Shorto's popular *The Island at the Center of the World* all give one-paragraph summaries of the part of the tradition about the first encounter, comparing it to the account by Juet. They differ as to whether it "gibes" with or "does not correspond to Juet's more explicit account."[18] They apparently concur in determining that the tradition can furnish no substantive information, although Shorto suggests that the description of the captain's "red coat all glittering with gold lace" is a "nice and by no means incongruous addition to the portrait of Hudson."[19] None of these writers so much as refers to the story about the hide trick.

Although they also omit mention of the Dido motif, Paul Otto and Evan Haefeli furnish more extensive and innovative discussions of the account of first contact. Whether the tradition "vaguely corresponds" or displays "remarkable congruencies" with Juet's account, it offers insights into the Native Americans' experience of first encounters and provides grounds for the reinterpretation of the European documentary sources.[20] For Otto, it allows an understanding of the welcomes and the hostilities described by Juet in terms of the Munsees' "concern with maintaining social reciprocity."[21] For Haefeli, it presents a corrective for the ubiquitous European claims of "apotheosis": that the natives mistook the Europeans, with their wondrous paraphernalia, for deities. Heckewelder's transcription of the Algonquian term *Manitou* suggests a more nuanced understanding of the Lenapes' actions and perceptions: "They were bargaining with power."[22]

Reading the tradition as evidence of the native actors' subjective worldview relieves the pressure to demonstrate its objective historical accuracy. Thus Otto allows that the tradition "may not even refer to Hudson's visit."[23] The authors of *Gotham*, more dismissively, observe that neither Hudson nor Juet mention a landing on Manhattan, and that the Indians they met were evidently already aware of the existence of Europeans. They opine that the tradition "if authentic . . . almost certainly alludes to events that occurred before Hudson arrived."[24] An irony of this suggestion is that Adriaen van der Donck provided the earliest extant reference to the Delaware tradition, according to Haefeli, "to bolster the Dutch claim to the region by right of discovery."[25]

To check oral traditions against the documentary record for inconsistencies is to hold them to an unrealistic standard. It is certainly possible that the tradition recorded by Heckewelder refers to an encounter with Verrazano or another of Hudson's predecessors, and it is also possible that it refers to a meeting with Hudson's crew that took place somewhere in lower New York Harbor, where Juet does describe a landing, and that it eventually drifted, in the telling, to the more recognizable setting of Manhattan.[26] The story of the clever use of a bullock's hide to secure the site for a fort similarly may have accounted not for the founding of Fort Amsterdam, but for its smaller predecessor on Governors (Nooten or Nut) Island—the 1625 "Instructions for Willem Verhulst Director of New Netherland" refer to an earlier fort there.[27] The much-noted fallibilities of memory and verbal transmission shift, conflate, confuse, exaggerate, embellish, and erase some details and circumstances. These distortions may be an effect of the necessarily warped lens shaped by a society's present concerns and points of reference.[28] But oral traditions can also preserve details—especially remarkable or, in a word, memorable ones. In this regard, in those instances where the traditions and documents overlap, the correspondences do more to substantiate the traditions than the discrepancies do to disqualify them.

When approached more flexibly, in light of the vagaries and the relative porousness of the medium, then Juet's journal and the account recorded by Heckewelder show some intriguing correspondences. One is with "the red coat all glittering with gold lace"; Juet records that on September 9, 1609, having already had some skirmishes, Hudson's crew took as prisoners two Indians who were visiting their ships "and put red Coates on them."[29] As to whether some of the crew also wore red coats, or whether they gave some to other Indians, Juet does not say, but either possibility seems likely, as it does that memories would fix on the distinctive color. Cognitive studies suggest, first, that red is an especially memorable color; they allow the inference that it would function as such not only in the memory of the event but also in the visualizations that would accompany subsequent recountings. Second, red is a nearly universal color category, so that if the coat in the tradition did originate with Hudson's ship, Juet and the Indians would have had equivalent terms for the color of the coat, which would again emerge as "red" when the tradition was translated into English.[30] The color, if not the coat, may be preserved in Bessie Snake's 1978 version of the account, in which the whites give the natives a red flag.[31]

    The scene of intoxication also has an especially close parallel in Juet, albeit on a visit with Mahicans upriver rather than with Munsees on Manhattan. In his 1801 letter Heckewelder listed both Mahicans and Munsees as informants for the tradition, and although in the published version he seems to collapse the multiple informants into a single "intelligent Delaware Indian," he also notes that "the Mahicani or Mohicans, who then inhabited the banks of the Hudson," probably shared with the Lenapes "the honour" of being the first natives to welcome Europeans to the mid-Atlantic region.[32] Thus Heckewelder's account appears to be a composite from different sources, or perhaps the different strands of oral tradition had already comingled before his coming. In any case, while the tradition represents an episode of drinking as taking place on land, in Juet's account Master Hudson "and his Mate" (Juet) invited "some of the chiefe men of the Country" into the ship's cabin to determine "whether they had any treacherie in them" by making them drunk. They gave them "much Wine and *Aqua vitæ*, that they were all merrie."[33]

As in the scene in the oral tradition, Juet observes that the Indians were ignorant of alcohol and its effects. In both scenes, a single man passes out, and his companions express anxiety. In both, "he falls into a sound sleep."[34]

Noting these parallels takes us about as far as discussions of oral tradition generally go: the comparison to documentary sources supports the idea that the traditions do indeed preserve memories about the past, while the traditions themselves contribute at least an intimation of the natives' perspectives on interactions that we already know about through the written record. To go further, we need to consider events described in native traditions that are not attested to by the colonists themselves.

The second part of the tradition, the return visit, is the part most emphasized in the subsequent retellings.[35] This part contains two "counterintuitive concepts"—elements that may have contributed to the preservation of the account over many generations.[36] The first is the Indians' inappropriate use of the colonists' gifts. The Dutch found the Indians wearing the axes and hoes as ornaments and using the stockings as tobacco pouches. They "laughed at the Indians," who, after learning the proper uses of the objects, good-naturedly laughed at themselves. The second is the colonists' inappropriate use of an animal hide to measure land. Here I will quote the conclusion of Heckewelder's chapter "Indian Account of the First Arrival of the Dutch at New York Island" in its entirety:

> As the whites became daily more familiar with the Indians, they at last proposed to stay with them, and asked only for so much ground for a garden spot as, they said, the hide of a bullock would cover or encompass, which hide was spread before them. The Indians readily granted this apparently reasonable request; but the whites then took a knife and beginning at one end of the hide, cut it up to a long rope, not thicker than a child's finger, so that by the time the whole was cut up, it made a great heap; they then took the rope at one end, and drew it gently along, carefully avoiding its breaking.

It was drawn out into a circular form, and being closed at its ends, encompassed a large piece of ground. The Indians were surprised at the superior wit of the whites, but did not wish to contend with them about a little land, as they had still enough themselves. The white and red men lived contentedly together for a long time, though the former from time to time asked for more land, which was readily obtained, and thus they gradually proceeded higher up the *Mahicanittuck*, until the Indians began to believe that they would soon want all their country, which in the end proved true.[37]

The French Canadian colonialist Denys Delâge, the only historian who discusses the Heckewelder account in its entirety, observes that the finale has a parallel in Virgil, and deduces that the hide "metaphor" must be an import and an add-on. He suggests that the ethnic authenticity of a tale should not be a criterion in "judging its validity as a representation of reality"; he argues that Indians borrowed it in order to relate ("rendre compte") their own history ("leur proper histoire"). That is, the story can have an authentic relation to its moments of production and reception without truly pertaining to its moment of representation. Might it actually originate with the founding of New Netherland? Might there actually have been a hide trick? "Certainly not; it is a metaphor, as we just indicated."[38]

A COLONIAL EPITOME

The "metaphor of the bull's hide transformed into strands" is indeed wonderfully suggestive.[39] The best analysis of it is by Washington Irving, who humorously demonstrates its figural logic in his *Knickerbocker's History of New York* (1809), for which he consulted Heckewelder's manuscript in the New-York Historical Society. Irving's authorial persona Diedrich Knickerbocker brings forward the most obvious explanation for the appearance of a classical motif in a native tradition: that "the learned Dominie Heckwelder" [sic] himself imported the "old fable . . . from antiquity." With typical irony, he has Knickerbocker offer an even more farfetched account of what happened in the founding of the first Dutch settlement in Manhattan. According to the "true version," the deal was for "just so much land as a man could cover with his nether garments." For the measurement, the Dutch brought forward "Mynheer Ten Breeches," and the "simple savages, whose ideas of a man's nether garments had never expanded beyond the dimensions of a breech clout, stared with astonishment and dismay as they beheld this bulbous-bottomed burgher peeled like an onion, and breeches after breeches spread forth over the land until they covered the actual site of this venerable city."[40]

Irving recognized the folkloric formula in the bull's hide story and adapted it to his satire. He simply replaces the cutting up of the bull's hide with the unfurling of Mynheer Ten Breeches' underwear. The Dutch colonists exploit the discrepancies inherent in cultural translation: the incommensurability of the Dutch and Delaware ideas of underwear. Having obtained the agreement through the grantors' understanding, they implement it with the grantees' understanding, cashing in the difference. By having Knickerbocker note "that Mynheer Ten Breeches, for his services on this memorable occasion, was elevated to the office of land measurer," Irving suggests that the folkloric formula is indicative of the approach colonial officials brought to land transactions with natives. Again with heavy irony, Irving implies that such operations typify colonial history: "The land being thus fairly purchased of the Indians, a circumstance very unusual in the history of colonization, and strongly illustrative of the honesty of our Dutch progenitors, a stockade fort and trading house were forthwith erected on an eminence in front of the place."[41]

Irving imbricates his parody with details from the archives—as the "Provisional Regulations for the Colonists" issued by the West India Company in 1624 make clear, fortification and trade were immediate priorities: "They shall take up their permanent residence at the place to be assigned to them by the Commander and his Council and use all diligence to fortify the same by common effort, likewise erecting in common the necessary public buildings and establishing trade relations as far as possible."[42] Thus while Irving ridicules the historical accuracy of the story, he also emphasizes its historical relevance.

In Irving's presentation, the bullock's hide, or the underwear, serves as an apt figure for equivocation, the capitalization on linguistic ambiguity by imposing one understanding in place of another. Equivocation depends on a threefold language ideology that today we might qualify as legalistic: the first precept, that agreements must be kept, was codified as a tenet of natural law: *pacta sunt servanda*.[43] The second precept, however, is that the agreement is constituted not by mutual understandings but by its terms. Third, the grantee can remove the letter of the agreement—whether spoken or written—from its dialogic context and interpret it unilaterally: the transaction is limited not by what the grantor understood but by what the language allows. That is, it depends on the successful communication of an understanding that is different from the one the grantee intends to act upon. The implementation of the agreement, then, is an act of optimization, in which the grantee works within, or *at*, the semantic limits of the wording, taking advantage of any ambiguity or lack of specification in order to maximize the capacity of the means of measurement, whether human, animal, or material, like the bull's hide or Mynheer Ten Breeches' underwear.

In the Delawares' telling, the act with the bullock's hide is generalizable, in the sense that it is characteristic of the colonists' approach to language and agreements. In a second version of the tradition Heckewelder includes in his *History*, the speaker complains: "'The great man wanted only a little, little land, on which to raise greens for his soup, just as much as a bullock's hide would cover. Here we might first have observed their deceitful spirit. The bullock's hide was cut up into little strips, and did not cover, indeed, but encircled a very large piece of land, which we foolishly granted to them.'"[44] Here the diction would seem to support Irving's implication that the source for this motif was Heckewelder himself: the distinction between "cover" and "encircle" corresponds to commentary on the relevant passage in Virgil's *Aeneid*, while it seems unlikely that the Delawares would have used a Lenape equivalent to the English word "bullock." By contrast, the version told by Bessie Snake in Lenape in 1978 more simply expresses a memory of bewilderment:

> Na hùnd luwe, "He yu kmilaneyo maxkelahitikàn." Luwe hùnd, "Tëta saki kulhatuneyo tàngitìch ta haki kmilihëna èlkikwi wèshëmwis knihëlawëna xu na pxinan nàn." Na mayay hùnd mata ènda paxkihëlak në xès mayay tàngiti kwishkshawòò. Na hùnd pihpënaneyo. Na èt ma na xingwi pàke hàking yuk kènu Lënapeyok ènda lòmwe kikayuyëmënaninga ènda milahtit.
>
> Then he said, "I will give you this red flag." He said, "As long as you keep this you give us a little piece of land as much as a cow we will kill and then skin him." Then they did not take the hide off but cut it into very small pieces. Then they looked good at it. It was a big piece of land our Lenape ancestors of long ago gave to them.[45]

The most treacherous term is one that is implied but unstated. The deceit hinges on the grantors' commonsense assumption that the hide will remain whole and the grantees' deliberate omission of a specification to the contrary. In a Yuchi version, the grantors complain: "they had not understood it was to be done that way . . . they answered that they had taken just as much land as one cow hide; very much land they had taken indeed."[46]

The proliferation of the motif in North America and beyond expresses a common experience of European colonization. This general representative value leads to the conclusion that the tradition is not directly connected to any particular event. Thus Marius Barbeau, describing a Huron instance as a "parable" without specific reference to "historical facts," argues that "it seems to characterize in a symbolic manner the whole problem of the spoliation of the Indian's rights by the white invader."[47] The legal scholar Stuart Banner, in *How the Indians Lost Their Land*, cites the Yuchi tradition as evidence that events such as the Walking Purchase gave rise to "Indian tales of colonial trickery."⁴⁸ In *Yuchi Ceremonial Life*, Jason Baird Jackson suggests the classical story "comes to symbolize the entire history of Indian-European relations from the Yuchi perspective."⁴⁹ He helpfully classifies it, borrowing a term from Raymond Fogelson, as an "'epitomizing event.'"⁵⁰ According to Fogelson, "Epitomizing events are narratives that condense, encapsulate, and dramatize longer-term historical processes."⁵¹ The parallel instances from across the globe have inspired like-minded reasoning: for example, Sanjay Subrahmanyam, commenting on an instance from Malayasia, suggests that the "use of the classical myth of the animal's hide as a device for territorial aggrandizement" implies "that contracts between strangers, and the ambiguities inherent in the letter thereof, are often apt to be exploited by one or the other party; this *was* indeed the case at times in Portuguese relations with Asian rulers."⁵²

While proliferation of the story would seem to argue against the notion that the Delaware instance represented an actual event experienced by the indigenous inhabitants of New York Harbor, a closer look at the North American distribution actually undermines the basic premise of the folkloric explanations for the global distribution: that one people, hearing the story of something that happened to others, would easily adapt it as something that happened to themselves. Actually, the various versions of the Native American "cowhide purchase" story would provide a fascinating subject for a study on the changeability and consistency of oral traditions. A comparison suggests that the story did originate with the Delawares and closely related groups—the ancestors of Heckewelder's informants—and was transmitted with relative integrity to other tribes.

The Wyandots are actually quite clear in identifying "the Delawares" as the native grantors, in effect blaming them for the breach in the native sovereignty of North America. In the telling, the story is indeed presented as an epitomizing event: "'So it is, and so shall it always be! The white fellow shall always undermine the Indian until he has taken away from him his last thing.' This was a kind of prediction."⁵³ In the Yuchi version, the transaction takes place between "the red people" and "pale faced White people" on an "island"—Manhattan?—"somewhere under the rising sun."[54] The Creek versions recorded by John R. Swanton are less specific, but one of them contains a detail about drunkenness and capture that is reminiscent of the scene in Heckewelder's version (and in Juet's account) as well as a promise "that they would treat the Indians right as long as the streams ran and water lasted"—phrasing that sounds a lot like the traditions about Penn's Treaty.[55] As with other instances, the Wyandot tradition recorded by Henry Rowe Schoolcraft presents a series of "figures of speech" to exemplify the "cession of territory and its renewal at other epochs": an uncaned chair, "a bull's hide," and "a man walking." Schoolcraft's informant identified the original grantors as the "Lenapees [sic], alluding to the cognate branches of this stock, who were anciently settled at the harbour of New York, and that vicinity."[56]

The Delawares' history, then, supplied a number of "epitomizing events," not only the hide purchase but also Penn's Treaty and the Walking Purchase (this epitomization is partly the occasion for this book). They would have shared these stories with other Indians throughout their westward migration and dispersal; their paths intersected with the Wyandots in Ohio, Indiana, Ontario, and again in Oklahoma, where they continue to participate in "a broader system of Woodland ceremonialism" that includes the Creeks and the Yuchis.[57] Thus the pattern of distribution of the Dido motif in Native American traditions—unlike the global pattern—is consistent with a single point of introduction.

Among the peoples who have told of the Europeans' use of the oxhide, the Delawares are perhaps unique in having a documented event in their history that bears such a close resemblance to the ancient ruse. One classicist, even without apparent awareness of the Delawares' tradition, noted the Dido story's relevance to their history: "In like manner was the poor untutored Indian often made the dupe of many a wily government agent and fraudulent bargain through which he lost much of his land. A somewhat amusing, though to the Indian humiliating and exasperating, deal, practised upon the Indian in the East, was the 'Walking Purchase' of 1737."[58]

That the Delawares themselves made the connection between their version of the hide story and their memory of the Walking Purchase does not mean that one was figurative and one was literal. Rather, the linking is understandable as an instance of "keying," a phenomenon in collective memory that "transforms the meaning of activities understood in terms of one event by comparing them with activities understood in terms of another."[59] (For example, in the news media the United States' foreign interventions are commonly keyed to the Vietnam War.) Keying does not mean that a given precedent is understood exclusively as a metaphor; the comparison entails distinguishing between events and insisting on the historicity of both.

When the Delawares told the story of the hide, they referred not only to their initial contact with the Dutch but to the course of their relations with "the white man."[60] In a version told by the Delaware Captain Pipe to C. C. Trowbridge in 1824, the trick with the bullock's hide was followed by another trick involving a chair seat: "the bottom of the chair, which was composed of small cords, was taken out and like the hide, stretched around the lands." According to Captain Pipe, "this second deception determined them to give no more lands without fixing some boundary understood by both parties distinctly."[61] (This clause especially seems to refer to the Walking Purchase.) In 1849, similarly, the Munsees reminded President Taylor not only of the hide trick but of a second transaction, for "as much land as a middling sized lad could travel around a tract of land in one day's journey."[62] Bessie Snake relates that the Lenapes immediately protested the hide trick: "Then he [white man] said, 'Now you have already finished signing this paper!' Now that is where our money now comes from that we receive, and we are still fighting it."[63] Thus the hide becomes a figure for the entire history of dispossession the Delawares suffered at the hands of European colonists and American settlers.

By the late eighteenth century, when Heckewelder first recorded the tradition, the Delawares were already in the Ohio Country and interacting with other Indian nations. The transmission of the story to other Native American communities of memory involves a plausible model of "information flows."⁶⁴ The inception of the tradition among the Delawares, however, remains a question. Swanton, referring to the Creek instance, points out that the motif "dates back as far at least as Virgil" and supposes that it was "reinjected into Indian thought, apparently from a modern schoolbook."⁶⁵ At least some Indians may have been exposed to Livy and Virgil by Swanton's time, but not in Heckewelder's.⁶⁶ Another explanation is necessary—one that might account for the story's dissemination not only in North America but throughout the world.

THE DIDO MOTIF

Virgil's *Aeneid*, the most-cited source for the Punic story, does not so much recount as refer to the Phoenician Queen Dido's use of an oxhide to cozen King Hiarbas and found the North African colony:

> mercatique solum, facti de nominee Byrsam,
> taurino quantum possent circumdare tergo (I.367–68)

A literal translation would be: "They bought the land called by the name 'Byrsa,' and made it as great as one could encircle with the ox's hide." According to the fourth-century commentator Servius, Virgil's use of *circumdare* (encircle) instead of *tegere* (cover) indicates that the hide has been cut up into a thong.⁶⁷ That readers brought this understanding to the text is evidenced by John Dryden's celebrated 1697 translation:

> At last they landed, where from far your eyes
> May view the turrets of new Carthage rise;
> There bought a space of ground, which (Byrsa call'd,
> From the bull's hide) they first inclos'd, and walled."⁶⁸

As Hans-Jörg Uther notes in *Types of International Folktales*, the motif with the bullock's hide "is often part of legends of the founding of cities."⁶⁹ Along with the Delaware tradition, the Dido story belongs to a widespread folkloric motif (K185.1, "Deceptive land purchase: ox-hide measure") and tale type (927C).⁷⁰ Folklorists have catalogued numerous variants of the motif in stories throughout Europe and Asia. Among these instances, several belong to what I argue should be treated as a distinct subset: stories about Europeans establishing imperial outposts. Stories attribute the hide trick to the Portuguese in Ceylon, Malaysia, India, Cambodia, and Burma; the Spaniards in Manila; and the Dutch in Jakarta, Cambodia, Taiwan, South Africa, and New York.[71] The correlation between these stories and the progress of early modern maritime imperialism produces a fascinating distribution map. According to Charles Lemire, because of the Portuguese use of "the ruse of Dido's companions" to acquire land for a Catholic mission in Cambodia (he dates it to 1553), the natives gave Europeans the epithet "the people from the country of the stretched-out hide."[72]

The classification of these accounts as "folktales" entails implicit premises: that the story spread by word of mouth and that the individual instances of it do not record actual events. Folklorists have collected many instances of the motif, yet they have been surprisingly incurious about the story's pattern of distribution and its relation to colonial history. For example, among the six stories of "Hide-Measured Lands" listed by Sir James Frazer, three—from South Africa, Cambodia, and Bali, all sites where the Dutch established colonies or trading stations—attribute the hide trick to Dutch colonists securing land to build forts.[73] Yet Frazer does not speculate about the relationship of the story to the Dutch maritime empire.

Frazer's logic is typical of the understanding of the transmission of folklore: stories, perhaps preserving a vestigial relationship to a distant reality, beget stories, perhaps presenting a figurative relationship to current events. The appearance of the Dido motif at disparate sites of colonization, however, challenges this conventional understanding. For example, the eminent historian of Southeast Asia Anthony Reid observes that natives used the hide story to explain how the Dutch and Portuguese gained "enough ground to build a great fort" in founding their colonies at Jakarta (which the Dutch named Batavia, in Java) and Melaka (Malaysia), respectively. The story may have helped to explain

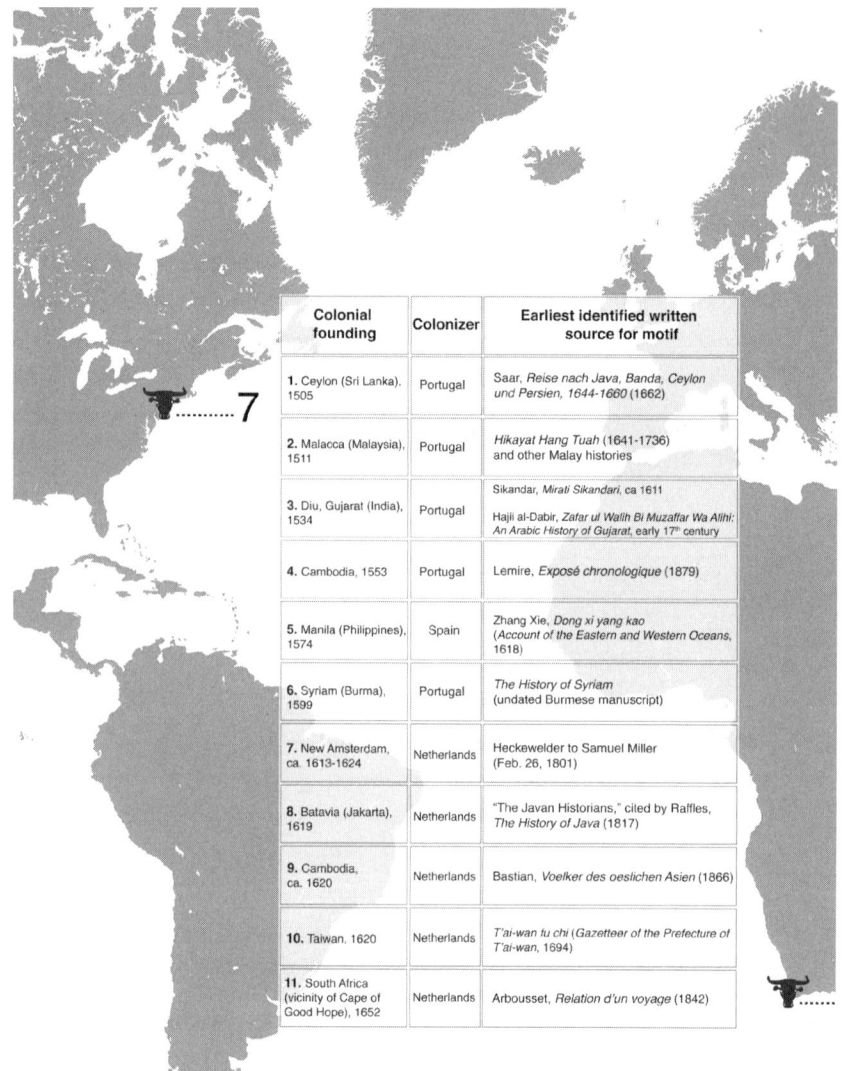

1. Location of occurrences of "Deceptive Land Purchase: Ox Hide Measure" (Motif K185.1 in Stith Thompson's Motif-Index of Folk-Literature) in association with European imperialism. Image by Mira Gelley, background map by VectorWorldMap.com, submitted to the public domain.

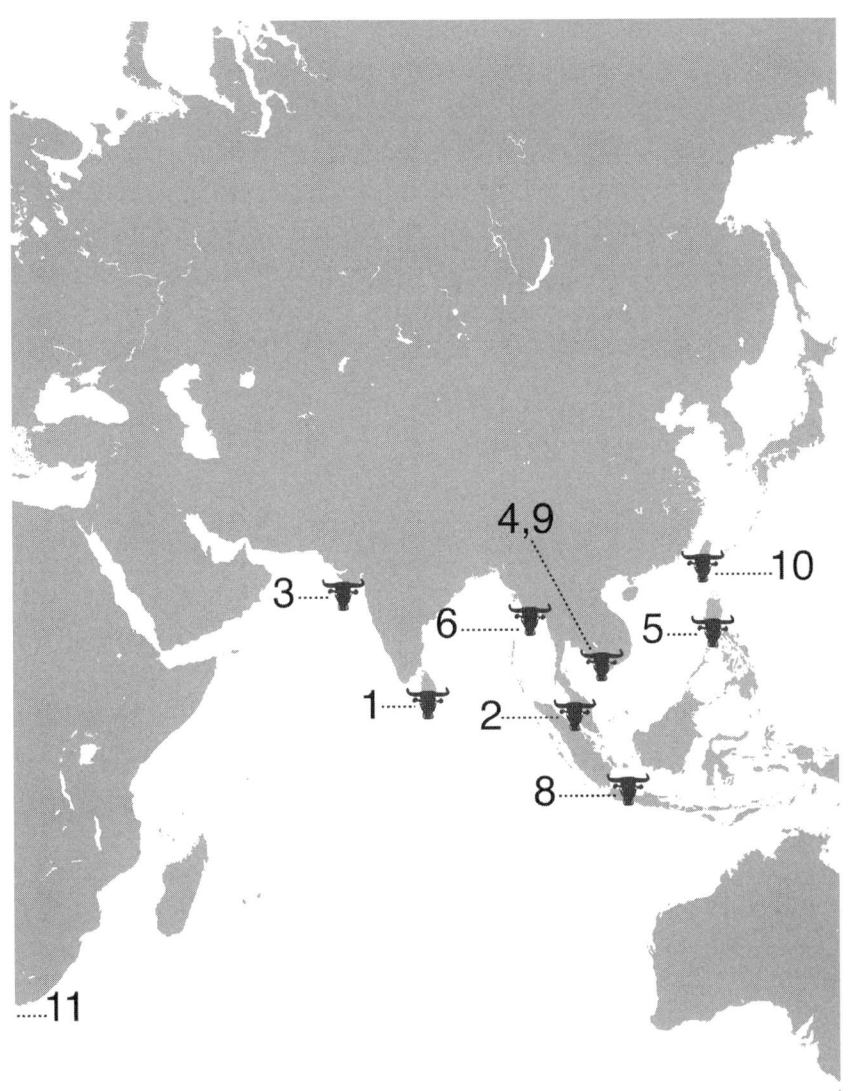

"how a handful of people coming from the other side of the world, ostensibly to trade, could have ended by making themselves impregnable and strangely powerful." Reid finds the "borrowing of stories" between Java and Malaysia to be likely enough, but he has "no explanation" for how the "exact same story" might appear in Burma, where the hide trick is attributed to the Portuguese adventurer Felipe de Brito. He speculates that the tale might have spread from the West through "the long-established Middle Eastern connection," or that it might have been brought to Southeast Asia by the Portuguese.[74] Yet if it is "surprising" that the story has traveled as far as Burma, how about South Africa? Or America?

The sinologist Berthold Laufer, who presents an appendix on "The Dido Story in Asia" in his "The Relations of the Chinese to the Philippine Islands" (1907), suggests that the story is an aberrant instance of the upstream migration of folklore: "it affords one of the few examples of a Western tale spreading to the extreme East, while as a rule the stream of folk-lore flowed from east to west in the old world." According to Laufer, the story is also unusual in that "it shows that the transmission of folk-lore still goes on, even in recent times, by mere oral accounts." Unlike European stories with Asian origins, there is no "written testimony for the legend of Dido in any Asiatic literature to which, as a starting-point, all the current versions could be reduced." Laufer theorizes that the motif's "occurrence in southern and eastern Asia is due to the oral stories of European sailors and merchants, who had probably imbibed it during their school-days, while its propagation in Siberia seems to have emanated from the mouths of vagrant Russian adventurers."[75] Reid and Laufer agree that the distribution of the story demands some sort of explanation, but they limit their speculations to establishing the possible channels for word-of-mouth transmission.

Laufer ridicules a historian who accepts the story about the Dutch using the hide trick to found Fort Zealand in Formosa (Taiwan) as "an actual historical event." He writes: "It is certainly far from this. In the Dutch sources regarding the history of Formosa, nothing of the kind is found. We have here nothing more than a simple tale, which has spread over almost the entire continent of Asia, and it is most curious to note that in nearly all cases the Asiatic peoples with whom the story is found make the tricksters some European nation who were then invading their country."[76]

What makes Laufer, and most other commentators, so confident that the story is not historical? The two principle objections are the lack of documentation by the colonists themselves and the lack of verisimilitude.

That there is no extant written agreement or firsthand account referring to the use of an oxhide to measure land does not mean that no such document ever existed. The Dutch, for example, kept copious records, but a large proportion of the East and West India Company archives were dispersed and destroyed.[77] Moreover, it is difficult to assign a value to such negative evidence: the colonists had motives not to document any bad-faith transactions. They were concerned with establishing the legality of their actions, even as they themselves defined the terms of that legality. Nevertheless, the absence of documentary evidence is grounds for skepticism.

The tradition, by contrast, is quite well documented, and by cross-referencing we can clear Heckewelder from Knickerbocker's imputation of having taken poetic license by arguing that even those traditions that weren't recorded until the nineteenth century, like the one attributing the hide trick to the Dutch in South Africa, had their inception during the early modern period. For instance, in 1662 Johann Jacob Saar, in his service for the Dutch East India Company learned of the "fraudulent pretext" ('betrüglichen Prætext") the Portuguese had employed in securing the site for the "Black Fort" they raised in Ceylon. They asked the so-called King of Candi to "grant them as much land as could be comprised within the limits of a cow's or bullock's hide" and then "cut up a bullock's hide into small strings, and fastening them together, enclosed a space large enough to build a fort."[78] A Sinhalese war poem from the late seventeenth century also attributes the hide trick to the Portuguese in Ceylon, this time in founding the fort in Colombo, about seventy-five miles north of the site of the Black Fort in Galle.[79] It seems implausible that the Portuguese would be able to perpetrate an already unlikely ruse twice within a short span of years and miles, but the original site of an event is just the sort of detail that can mutate through the transmission of a tradition. There has been, for example, controversy over whether the Portuguese first landed in Galle or Colombo.[80]

If the cultural, temporal, and geographic diversity of the writers who recorded the traditions is evidence against the notion that the motif was a simple literary embellishment, the short interval between some records and the supposed event argues against the theory, espoused by one would-be debunker in the eighteenth century, that the tradition must have been "set on foot long after the time," after the Dido story was introduced by Europeans.[81] The writer's reference is to Alexander Hamilton's observation in 1744, over two centuries after the Portuguese established their fort in Diu, of "a Tradition, that the *Portugueze* circumvented the King of *Guzarat*, as Dido did the *Afrikanus*."[82] However, the Guzarati tradition had also been recorded by non-European authors within a generation or two of the Portuguese acquisition of Diu from the Sultan Bahadur in 1535.

These authors, however, also expressed skepticism. One of the variant manuscripts of the early seventeenth-century *Mirati Sikandari*, or *The Mirror of Sikandar*, pronounced it "manifestly improbable that the Firangís should only have asked for so much land as a cow's hide could cover," or that "the Sultán should have been so foolish as to believe these enemies of his state and faith."[83] Hajji al-Dabir, the author of the *Arabic History of Gujarat*, raised a different objection: he had consulted with persons who would have known of the transaction, had it occurred, and "the demand of a place in proportion to the ox-hide is not mentioned by any one from among the old persons who were with Bahādur at Dīv." He claimed that the story of the Portuguese and the oxhide did not pertain to Diu and the Sultan Bahadur, but to "the ruler of Hormuz."[84] While Hajji al-Dabir did not apparently find the story itself unbelievable, his inquiries among potential witnesses to the transaction did not turn up corroborating testimony, which was strong negative evidence against its factuality.

The Gujarati instance is important because it is the only one with written sources from both sides of the initial land transaction; neither attests to the use of the hide trick. The terms of the 1535 agreement negotiated by Martim Afonso de Sousa and Simão Ferreira with the Sultan Bahadur, according to the version reproduced in Fernão Lopes de Castanheda's *História do descobrimento e conquista da Índia pelos portugueses* (1551), specified that "the Coltão Badur is pleased to cede to the King of Portugal a fortress in Diu at any spot that the governor Nuno da Cunha desires, on the side of the bulwarks facing the sea or the land, of the size that he finds acceptable, and also the sea-bulwark."[85] The Sultan Bahadur himself wrote to the governor, Nuno da Cunha, to affirm his grant of "What you had desired and not received for years, that is a place for some of the people of Portugal to reside."[86] He subsequently wrote two letters to the king of Portugal. The first reviews his conferral of several forts in his territories and hints that the governor had overstepped "the stipulated agreement."[87] The second explicitly complains that the governor "wrote down that which should not have been written and excluded that which should in fact have been put down" and that he "has transgressed the limits and is still doing so in this matter."[88] For his part, in a single clause Castanheda describes how the governor took possession of a site for the fort "that had been demarcated with flags with the Portuguese arms."[89]

While these sources do not foreclose the possibility that a measurement with an oxhide took place at Diu, the absence of any mention of one constitutes negative evidence. Bahadur's letter does demonstrate the potential aptness of the oxhide as a figure; the tradition expressed the sentiment that the Portuguese overreached their agreement and characteristically acted in Punic faith, culminating in the treacherous shipboard murder of the Sultan Bahadur in 1537.[90] Considering this particular instance in isolation, in the absence of positive proof, the idea that the natives of Diu heard the story of the oxhide and used it to account for their experience of the Portuguese seems plausible. However, it doesn't fully explain the inception of a tradition that two different writers, Hajji al-Dabir and Sikandar, encountered as a relation of fact within a generation or two of the event it purported to describe.

The *Dong xi yang kao* (Account of the Eastern and Western Oceans), by the Chinese official Zhang Xie, may be the most authoritative early record affirming the occurrence of the ruse. It first appeared in 1618, forty-four years after the founding of the Spanish colony in Manila, and it may have been composed earlier. According to that account, the Franks (Spaniards) determined that the island of Luzon was vulnerable, plied the local king with gold, and

> sought land the size of a buffalo hide, in order to build houses. The king was trusting and allowed this. The *Franks* then took the buffalo hide and cut it into strips, joining them together, which they then extended as a perimeter around a piece of land and they asked for the land to be given as promised. The king was in a dilemma, but did not want to lose the trust of the distant foreigners. He thus eventually gave them the land, with a monthly tax levied in accordance with the laws of their tribe. The *Franks* obtained the land, built walls and barracks and arrayed their cannons and weapons in abundance. After a time, they surrounded Luzon, killed the king, drove him into the hills and Luzon gradually came to be controlled by the *Franks*.[91]

The existence of such sources has done little to persuade scholars. Laufer is unimpressed by the reports in the *T'ai-wan fu chi* (Gazetteer of the Prefecture of Taiwan) and the *Ming Annals* (which were probably informed by the *Dong xi yang kao*): These early records only serve as evidence "of a comparably recent story-migration, which is further evidenced by its absence in any Asiatic literary records of an earlier date."[92] The most he is willing to concede is that a comparison between the account in the *Ming shi* and Antonio de Morga's chronicle *Sucesos de las Islas Filipinas* shows that the former "is not quite without foundation in some details."[93] Morga's account has the Spaniards entering the land through force of arms, and then establishing terms of "peace, friendship, and obedience"; the local leader Rajamora donated to the Governor Miguel López de Legazpi the land on which to build his city, and the conquistador, preserving the native name Manila, "took as much land as he needed for the city."[94] As with the account of the possession of Diu in Castanheda's *História*, Morga does not specify the means by which the land was measured.

While Laufer seems to feel that the *Ming Annals* should be tested against the Spanish chronicle and not vice versa, earlier scholars were more blatantly ethnocentric in their dismissals of non-Western histories. "That is the way they invent history in India," writes Joseph Gerson Cunha in *Notes on the History and Antiquities of Chaul and Bassein* (1876), "and that is, moreover, the credulous silliness with which it is recorded in the papers in my possession. We know better; the cession of Revadanda [Chaul] to the Portuguese had nothing to do with cow-hides." He continues: "The tradition does not stop here; it goes on to assert that these facts are recorded on the foundation-stone of the fort of Chaul."[95]

In the *History of the Decline and Fall of the Roman Empire* (1776), Edward Gibbon was similarly dismissive of an account in the "Turkish Annals" that "revived the foolish tale of the ox's hide, and Dido's stratagem," in attributing the hide trick to Mahomet II in his conquest of Constantinople: "The annals (unless we are swayed by an antichristian prejudice) are far less valuable than the Greek historians."[96] Gibbon was evidently imputing such a "prejudice" to his secondary source, the Romanian historian Dimitrie Cantemir's *History of the Growth and Decay of the Othman Empire* (1734), which was based on Turkish "Materials."[97] Cantemir speculated that Mahomet II "imitated Eliza Queen of *Carthage*," pointing out that he was reputed "to have been studious of Antiquity, and particularly delighted with reading the Expeditions of ancient Kings and Generals."[98]

From a judiciously skeptical perspective, the probability that a particular instance of the Dido motif records an actual event may seem weak when measured against alternative explanations. My question is what happens when such a perspective is applied to the whole set of hide stories relating the use of the oxhide ruse by European colonists founding forts. How does the possibility (factoring in the absence of primary source evidence) that the ruse was a systematic feature of Portuguese, Dutch, and (in at least one instance) Spanish colonization measure against the one that all these unrelated writers, including Heckewelder, the British colonial official writing about the Dutch colonization of Java, the French missionary writing about the Dutch colonization of South Africa, the Sinhalese author of the *Maha Katana*, and the Chinese author of the *Dong xi yang kao* all decided to surreptitiously embellish native traditions in precisely the same way? Or that European colonizers systematically decided to recount the story of an ancient colonial ruse to native peoples? How possible is it that in each case the story would have crossed the cultural barrier relatively intact, and that in each case, even within the space of a generation, native storytellers, from the Atlantic coast of North America to the Indian Ocean, grafted the motif into their traditional narrative accounts as an event that had occurred to their ancestors, perpetrated, perhaps, by predecessors of the very people who had told them the story?

Indeed, the assumption that the story could only have spread by word of mouth relies on a false distinction between discourse and event that diminishes the status of storytelling as an event—in this case, an unlikely and undocumented one. As far as I know, there is no documentary record of colonists recounting to bemused natives the story of Dido's founding of Carthage. Thus there is also negative evidence against the prevalent explanation for the distribution of the Dido motif. Moreover, the notion that the natives then considered the Dido story as something that happened to them is contrary to research on collective memory, which finds that memories typically have a factual basis, however much those facts may be distorted.[99] A single instance of such an artificial tradition would be highly unusual; multiple, independent parallel instances are unaccountable.

Yet the hide trick does seem more appropriate to folklore than to history. Indeed, the account of the Dutch use of the trick in their founding of Taiwan appears not only in an official Chinese history but also in a collection of fantastical tales compiled in the mid–seventeenth century by Pu Songling, the *Liaozhai zhiyi*. In that version, the Dutch use a very stretchable carpet instead of a hide.[100] While the Dido motif appears in otherwise conventional and plausible accounts of first contact, highly compatible with European histories, it seems like one of those moments in Native American accounts of colonial contact in which the narrative veers sharply away from verisimilitude. Is the Dido motif one of those characteristic features of oral traditions, in Robert Lowie's phrase, that exceed the limits of "physical possibility"?[101]

This question is the mathematical "Dido's Problem," and it is one occasionally addressed by high school students, who may cut a sheet of paper into strips and lay them out in a room, or cut up a bedsheet and lay it out on a football field.[102] The solution to the isoperimetric problem of which shape takes in the greatest area is a circle; even better is a semicircle, in which one boundary is not the cord but a body of water. (For this reason, mathematicians typically recall Dido laying out the thong in a semicircle on the beach, although there is no indication of this shape in the classical sources.) Stefan Hildebrandt and Anthony Tromba, in *The Parsimonious Universe*, suggest that the length of Dido's thong (and therefore the circumference of the circle) might have been "between 1,000 and 2,000 yards if we assume that the width of the strips was as small as 1/10 inch."[103]

Two thousand yards would not be capacious enough to enclose the legendary proportions of the site for the Byrsa at Carthage, which Servius reports at twenty-two stadia, or approximately 4,450 yards.[104] Such a thong would be more than sufficient, however, to encompass an impressive colonial fort: the instructions for Fort Amsterdam sent to Cryn Fredericksz specify a "circular circumference" of 3,150 Dutch feet, or about 975 yards.[105] It may be, however, that the length of the hypothetical thong proposed by Hildebrandt and Tromba is exaggerated. Given an intact hide with an area of forty square feet (the size of a large cowhide rug) cut into strips "not thicker than a child's finger" (the width specified in Heckewelder's version of the Lenape account), Frank Morgan,

An Account of a Tradition ::: 83

an expert on questions of optimization, suggests a width for the thong of one-third of an inch and a length of 1,600 feet, or about 533 yards.[106] This length would still have been more than sufficient to encompass the sites for forts less ambitious than Fort Amsterdam—the provisional strongholds the colonists established in the initial expeditions described in the native accounts.[107]

A STORY OF EMPIRE

In 1980, at a symposium at the State University of New York at Purchase, the Delaware elder Nora Thompson Dean (Touching Leaves Woman) recounted the tradition about the Dutch use of the hide in the founding of New Amsterdam.[108] Also in attendance were Herbert Kraft, the archeologist and prolific author on the Lenape, the anthropologist David Oestreicher, whose research would debunk the *Walam Olum*, and Jim Rementer, now the director of the Lenape Language Preservation Project for the Delaware Tribe of Indians. According to Rementer, during the question-and-answer time, a literature professor "got up and said in a smart-aleck way that was the same old Queen Dido story and what did she think about that. Her reply was, 'Nothing.'"[109] She was insulted by the challenge to her cultural memory.

As Vansina suggests, a traditional account "forms a hypothesis that should be tested first, before any other hypothesis is considered. A body of tradition thus becomes an agenda for research."[110] The hypothesis of the Delaware tradition was that the Dutch colonists employed the ruse with a hide to procure the site for their fort. Apparently, few scholars have considered this hypothesis worthy of consideration. Moreover, when put to the usual test for the factual accuracy of oral traditions, it fails: "In the Dutch sources," as Laufer writes of the Taiwanese instance, "nothing of the kind is found." Yet scholars who dismiss the Delaware hypothesis (including those who pass over it without comment[111]) have not felt it necessary to test their assumptions, either. In this chapter I have argued that seemingly more plausible explanations for the appearance of this

2. *Dido Cutting the Ox-Hide*, woodcut by Tobias Stimmer, in Titus Livius and Lucius Florus, *Von Ankunfft unnd Ursprung des Romischen Reichs . . .* Straszburg, 1575, fol. 220. Courtesy of Houghton Library, Harvard University. [OLC.L765.En575]

classical motif in a Native American tradition may be less so than they appear, while the hide trick itself may be less incredible. I would hardly claim to have cinched my case; it will remain leaky.

The Delaware hypothesis requires further explanation. Here is mine: the Dutch, who "initially borrowed all their means to overseas empire from the Portuguese," adopted a "ceremony of possession" that the Portuguese had modeled on Dido's legendary foundation of Carthage.[112] I am not the first to suggest that the colonists may have been emulating classical history: Heckewelder himself, in a footnote, speculated that the "Dutchmen were probably acquainted with what is related of Queen Dido in ancient history, and thus turned their classical knowledge to a good account."[113] The nineteenth-century historian Franz Kottenkamp, discussing the Delaware instance, wonders if "a white exploited in such a way the tradition of Dido which he had learned in school, by transforming poetry into prose and serious reality."[114] At the symposium in 1980, Herbert Kraft responded to the literature professor's question by pointing out this possibility. It can work as an explanation of the Delaware tradition, and it can also stretch to become a systematic explanation for the dissemination of the Dido motif.

Its virtue is in its model of "information flows."[115] Although the Dido motif is extrinsic to the bodies of tradition in which it appears, the classical sources for the Dido story, especially Livy and Virgil, were canonical within the culture of early modern European imperialism. Similarly, the channels that may have carried the hide trick from the Portuguese to the Spanish and the Dutch are well established. The three powers were intimately and antagonistically related throughout the period in which the Dido motif is set, with active commercial and political ties. Portugal was brought under the Spanish Habsburg umbrella in 1580, ten years after the Dutch Republic began its long struggle to get out from under it. Finally, the degree of parallelism between the recorded traditions may be better accounted for as the outcome of a common experience than as the result of the multiple transmission of a story by word of mouth across linguistic and cultural barriers.

The chronology suggests that the Portuguese began to employ the hide trick in the early sixteenth century, that the Spaniards borrowed it for the taking of Manila in 1574, and that the Dutch took it up in the seventeenth century. The French, English, and other colonists also engaged in transactions that would have been appropriate referents for the oxhide as metaphor, but it is not specifically associated with them in native accounts. It is an English colonist, however, who makes the most explicit mention of the story in a colonial context: William Strachey's *True Reportory of the Wrack and Redemption of Sir Thomas Gates, Knight* (1610), a source for Shakespeare's *Tempest*, describes the potential site for a fort near Jamestown: "A low levell of ground about halfe an Acre, or (so much as Queene Dido might buy of King Hyarbas, which she compassed about with the thongs cut out of one Bull hide, and therein built her Castle of Byrza)."[116]

Of course, the notion that Europeans were emulating a ruse from classical antiquity cannot account for all the instances of folklore motif K185.1. For example, it cannot explain the attribution of the hide trick to a "divine virgin" in the founding of a temple in Nepal, or to a female slave in the founding of a city in Burma.[117] The story may be associated etymologically with Moscow and Calcutta, just as the Dido story itself explains the name Byrsa. By definition, such stories come into existence as explanations of the way things came about, not as accounts of events.[118] What folkloric explanations overlook, however, is the ambivalent exchange between stories and history. Stories can be descriptive and/or prescriptive. They can represent events that happened—or did not happen—and they can also become precedents or models for future events, which in turn can inspire stories. The Dido motif may have originated in folklore, and it definitely participates in it, but its appearance in the *Aeneid* and related texts, founding documents of Western civilization, positioned it to be a historical factor.[119] With the landings of Europeans on the coasts of Africa, Asia, and the Americas in the fifteenth, sixteenth, and seventeenth centuries, the story came full circle.

More so than we do today, early modern Europeans experienced the interaction between story and history. Famously, the English Puritans walked in the steps of Old Testament figures as they founded the New Jerusalem in New England. Similarly, the Portuguese, Spaniards, and Dutch sailed through the discursive milieu of imperial Rome as they established their rival far-flung empires. They compared their exploits, sometimes favorably, to classical heroes and compared the peoples and civilizations they encountered to ones of the Ancient World.[120] The story of the foundation of Rome by the Trojan Aeneas especially served, in sociological terms, as a "primary framework" for conceptualizing contemporary imperialism.[121] It was construed not as myth but as history, and the European adventurers and colonists were acting in the same story line as it unfolded in a different time and place.

As noted above, the story of Dido's foundation of the Byrsa, as part of the backstory to the episode recounting Aeneas's sojourn in Carthage, was only alluded to in the *Aeneid*. It was part of the lost "Second Decade" of Livy's *Roman History* (*Ab urbe condita*), but it was restored in vernacular translations, which were informed by alternative sources such as Justinius. These translations were part of the project of *translatio imperii et studii*: the establishment of the rival European powers as legitimate political and cultural successors to Rome.[122] Thus João de Barros (1496–1570), the "Portuguese Livy," wrote a prose account of Portuguese expansion in Asia modeled on Livy's *Roman History* (or *Ab urbe condita*), while Luis de Camões (1524–1580), the "Portuguese Virgil," modeled his verse epic on the *Aeneid*.[123] In canto 9 of *The Lusiads*, Venus spoke to Cupid of the Portuguese:

> And because they copy so uncannily
> The deeds of my old Romans, I propose
> To show them every kindness, be benign
> To the limits of our powers, yours and mine.[124]

The narrator cites a precedent: Venus had Cupid soften the heart of Dido so that Aeneas and his crew might be received "in that meadow where Dido's subtlety / Bought Carthage with a bull's hide."[125]

References to Virgil and Livy are also profuse in the seventeenth-century theoretical writings on international law that provided the rationales for the conquest of foreign peoples and the competing claims of rival powers. For example, in the *Freedom of the Seas* the Dutch jurist Hugo Grotius, who became directly involved in policy development on behalf of the Dutch East India Company (VOC), cites the *Aeneid* to support his assertion of a "law of hospitality," a universal right to land and engage in commerce on foreign shores:

> What men, what monsters, what inhuman race,
> What laws, what barbarous customs of the place,
> Shut up a desert shore to drowning men,
> And drive us to the cruel seas again.[126]

Aeneid I:539–40 is part of an episode that begins with the arrival of the Trojans in Carthage and includes the story of the city's founding. The quotation, apparently something of a commonplace in the emerging discourse of international law, is from a speech by Ilioneus, who invokes "hospitable rights" and "human laws" to urge Dido to make an exception to common practice and afford the Trojans safe harbor:

> Permit our ships a shelter on your shores,
> Refitted from your woods with planks and oars,
> That, if our prince be safe, we may renew
> Our destin'd course, and Italy pursue.[127]

Some of the native traditions involve similar appeals to the hospitality of the grantors. According to James Davidson, the Dutch captain shipwrecked off Taiwan in 1620, "no doubt with intention of turning the mishaps which had befallen him to some advantage," asked the Japanese who had colonized the island for as much land as an ox skin would cover, on which to build "a sort of depot." Then the "wily Dutchman with an old trick in mind proceeded to cut the ox-skin in very long narrow strips."[128] A year earlier, according to British East India Company official Thomas Stamford Raffles, a Dutch captain scuttled his own vessel at Jakarta to supply a pretext to impose on the hospitality of a local prince. He then employed the hide trick to obtain the site for a fort.[129]

Both Aeneas and Dido may be patterns for this sequence. Niccolò Machiavelli, in his *Discourses on Livy*, offers "Aeneas, Dido, [and] the Massilienses," the founders of Rome, Carthage, and Marseilles, respectively, as examples of refugees who "are obliged to occupy some location with cunning and, once it has been occupied, to maintain themselves there by means of allies and confederations."[130] The Portuguese, Spaniards, and Dutch may have aspired to be Romans, but the Portuguese and Netherlandic empires, especially, more resembled the Punic than the Roman model: in contrast to Rome, which established its dominion over land, ancient Carthage was devoted to commerce and "successfully established, taxed, and defended colonies in far-flung maritime outposts

3. *Queen Dido founding Carthage* by Matthäus Merian, 1630. From Johann Ludwig Gottfried, *Historische Chronica*, Frankfurt a.M., 1657. By permission of the Rare Books Division, New York Public Library, Astor, Lenox, and Tilden Foundations.

for hundreds of years."[131] It became a "favorite model for builders of modern sea empires," and was accordingly showcased in histories of the Ancient World.[132]

Thus as meaningful as the ox's hide cut into strips became to native peoples looking back at their history of colonization, it was even more specifically significant to colonizers establishing imperial outposts. They hoped to do as Dido, according to Justinius, had done: she "made overtures of friendship to the natives, who were themselves happy at the arrival of these foreigners with whom they could conduct trade by barter." She then employed the hide trick to take "possession of a greater area than she had apparently bargained for," and raised the Byrsa, a citadel into which "neighboring peoples flooded." Subsequently, "successful enterprises brought material prosperity to Carthage."[133]

As illustrated by the 1608 orders to Admiral Willem Pieterzoon Verhoef of the VOC, befriending the natives and erecting forts were part of the basic colonization formula: "In the principal places where you conclude friendships and alliances, we recommend that you establish fortresses with the consent of the Indians, in order that we may secure these places and defend them as our possessions, keeping their trade for ourselves alone and excluding the Portuguese and all others."[134]

These same priorities are reflected across the board in the native accounts, which complete the correspondence to the Dido story by recounting how the colonists employed the hide to obtain more land than they "had apparently bargained for."

In New Netherland, colonists were instructed in 1624 to "take especial care, whether in trading or in other matters, faithfully to fulfill their promises to the Indians or other neighbors and not to give them any offense without cause as regards their persons, or property, on pain of being rigorously punished therefore."[135] This injunction was seconded the following year in orders to company director Willem Verhulst, who was told that the Indians should be "shown honesty, faithfulness, and sincerity in all contracts, dealings and intercourse, without being deceived by shortage of measure, weight, or number."[136] They were to conduct land transactions without "craft or fraud." Such instructions may suggest, as one scholar argues, that the West India Company "sincerely and programmatically" intended to do right by the Indians.[137] However, that would make the Dutch colonists, in Irving's phrase, "very unusual in the history of colonization." Rather, the instructions may constitute a tacit acknowledgment of an existing state of affairs—that the beginnings of New Netherland were hardly characterized by scrupulous dealings. The use of the word "craft" is especially suggestive of a gray area between forthrightness and fraud—one in which "Punic ingenuity" would have room to operate.

When the Dido motif is understood as having only a figurative relation to history, then the Delawares' account of their first land transaction with Europeans is simply teleological—they retroactively construe it as "the beginning of their end."[138] However, when it is accepted as a literal account, then it has implications for the understanding of the initial phase of Dutch colonization. For example, it would make little sense to consider the first settlers as an "alongshore people" who intended to touch down lightly, but by expanding and encroaching "betrayed themselves—their ideals and values—and the indigenous people."[139] Instead, the Dutch may have initiated their presence in North America with a remarkable gesture of bad, or Punic, faith. Moreover, if it happened in the founding of New Netherland, it happened elsewhere, where non-European accounts have told the same story. The gesture was not a singular act—carried out, say, by a rogue landing party—but a programmatic element of early modern European maritime imperialism, implemented by Europeans at numerous colonial beachheads around the world.

Moreover, the question of the historicity of the Delaware tradition is important because it concerns the possibility that oral traditions can furnish information not only about the subjective experiences of the peoples who share them, but also about the actors and actions they depict. In this case, the apparent lack of corroboration by colonial documents—a principal objection to be raised against the tradition's historicity—is what makes it potentially valuable. This story might tell us something the colonists themselves do not, about their relations with native peoples, and with their classical heritage.

Most previous readers of the Delaware tradition regarding the bullock's hide were presumably unaware of its counterparts from Asia and Africa and of the relationship of the classical histories containing the story of the foundation of Carthage to Dutch imperialism. This chapter has shown that, as a story, it is very relevant to the moment in which it is set, as well as the moments in which it was later told. In a sense, it is the story of colonial land transactions, not only in North America but also around the world, and not only during the golden age of Portuguese, Spanish, and Dutch imperialism but also, as we shall see, during the Anglo-American eighteenth century. That is, the story has both historical and allegorical significances—as history generally does. Even if we treat the native accounts skeptically, and construe them as stories borrowed from European colonists by many otherwise unrelated native peoples and subsequently taken down in writing by many otherwise unrelated ethnographers and travel writers (as well as by seventeenth-century Asian historians), we might still consider all these separate tellings, borrowings, retellings, translations, and transcriptions as revelatory of a fascinating aspect of early modern colonial encounters and their aftermath: one that only comes to our attention through non-European sources. However, the idea that the story is a literal representation of an actual colonial practice is more in accordance with the logical principle of Occam's razor: it is simpler and leaves less (though still quite a lot) to account for. This happenstance might lead us to question our assumptions about oral traditions that have no such parallels: to be open to the capacity of native histories to shed new light on the colonial period.

The subject of the next chapter is a popular tradition about the arrival among the Delawares of colonists with a profounder directive to bring practice in line with policy: a change from Punic faith to the Quaker faith. While the Delaware hide story bears a thematic resemblance to the Walking Purchase, its reception resembles that of the story of the Great Treaty between William Penn and the Indians, another "undocumented" tradition about a colonial encounter.

3

The Most Valuable Record

"All human greatness has its apogee and every great career has its climax," wrote the historian Augustus C. Buell in 1904. "And this moment or measure is regulated by the schoolbooks. The average schoolboy knows Washington best as the author of the Farewell Address; Franklin best as flying his kite to catch the lightning; and William Penn best under the 'Treaty Elm' at Shackamaxon."[1]

The persistence of this schoolbook image represents a small victory for popular tradition over professional historiography.[2] Citing the absence of a specific written record, historians since the colonial era have raised doubts about the longstanding popular tradition that Penn met the Lenapes in 1682 under the "Treaty Elm" in the former Lenape village of Shackamaxon, in the present-day Philadelphia neighborhood of Fishtown, where memorials to the "legendary treaty" now stand within a city park.[3] "No topic connected with the History of Pennsylvania has been more thoroughly investigated," declared an editor for the Historical Society of Pennsylvania (HSP) in 1864.[4] Yet these investigations—their claims notwithstanding—have failed to either debunk or corroborate the tradition, rendering it inadmissible as historical evidence but leaving it fully viable as a source of civic or even national pride.

From the standpoint of contemporary colonial history and ethnohistory, the questions of when and where and even whether the treaty occurred are trivial. William Penn and his agents had several meetings with

Indian groups in the area of the colony, and the records and references to these provide ample grounds to speculate about what the contents of an original treaty document would be, if it existed. Its discovery would contribute little if anything to the academic understanding of early Pennsylvania Indian relations. Yet it might shed light on the factual basis for a tradition that idealizes those relations.

The reason these details matter is because the ideal of the Great Treaty became so important. During the colonial era, the Indians and colonists (and competing factions among the colonists) increasingly invoked this ideal as they lapsed into conflict. Tensions over land transactions and encroachment, epitomized by the 1737 Walking Purchase, erupted into open warfare in the 1750s. Benjamin West created the ubiquitous image of the treaty—his famous painting *William Penn's Treaty with the Indians When He Founded the Province of Pennsylvania in North America* (1771–72)—at a moment of escalating conflict with the mother country. Thereafter, the treaty stood for the virtues of the colonial founding—a development that parallels the invention of the "pilgrims" and the appearance of an associated iconography in New England.[5]

As the Great Treaty became increasingly significant, it increasingly incurred the problems of remembrance and the controversy that are the subject of this chapter. In the nineteenth century, the treaty represented the best of the colonial past at a time of increasing estrangement from that past; it was a tradition to be cherished, even as cultural and demographic changes threatened to rupture the chain of memory. It became a test case—to question the details of the treaty tradition was to question tradition itself. Paradoxical efforts to vindicate the treaty tradition through research, however, were counterproductive. In the absence of immediate documentation—a record—of the treaty itself, the historians who attempted to substantiate the tradition depended on alternative media such as West's historical painting, on the "silent witness" of the "Treaty Tree," and on documentation of the "testimony of tradition" in the form of memories of old-timers.[6] Eventually, when the sought-after "record" did turn up, its form was one that challenged Western conceptions of documentation, and its content, arguably, challenged the popular understanding of the Great Treaty.[7]

"PENN'S TREATY"

The story of the Quaker founder William Penn, the Delaware chief Tamanend, and their respective entourages meeting under an enormous elm tree to frame an eternal treaty of peace and friendship is Pennsylvania's "civic myth"—a historical tradition pertaining to social and political origins.[8] Its development was roughly contemporaneous with those of other regional myths of colonial origin during the early national period: thus a sandstone relief of *William Penn's Treaty with the Indians* (1827) above the north door of the U.S. Capitol rotunda completes a set with the *Landing of the Pilgrims* (east door), the *Preservation of Captain Smith by Pocahontas* (west), and the *Conflict of Daniel Boone and the Indians* (south). The Jamestown story may have been compromised from the beginning by greed and factionalism, and the Plymouth story by religious extremism and intolerance; both supposedly auspicious foundings soured within a generation, lapsing into the sort of violence that characterized Boone's opening of the western wilderness from its beginning.[9] Only Penn, according to the myth, laid a durable "foundation" for a lasting peace and a tolerant society. Thus the caption under the folk artist Edward Hicks's painting: "Penns Treaty with the Indians, made 1681 without an Oath, and never broken. The foundation of Religious and Civil Liberty in the U.S. of America."

Hicks's painting cites two sources that had elevated the local tradition of the Great Treaty to the status of civic myth, and thereby set the stage for a historiographic controversy. If, as traditionalist historians in the nineteenth century would claim, it had once been common knowledge that Penn and the Delawares had convened beneath the Great Elm Tree in 1682 (Hicks uses the 1681 date of the Pennsylvania Charter), a commendation by Voltaire and the representation by Benjamin West

4. *Penn's Treaty with the Indians* by Edward Hicks, c. 1830.
Gift of Edgar William and Bernice Chrysler Garbisch. Image courtesy of the National Gallery of Art, Washington.

invested these facts with a great importance and provided an impulse that perpetuated this memory beyond what might have been its natural lifespan of eighty years or less, thereby putting proponents of the treaty tradition in the position of having to prove it.[10]

Fifty-one years after the supposed Great Treaty, and four years before the Walking Purchase would seemingly invalidate his statement, Voltaire's *Lettres philosophiques sur les Anglais* (1733) described Penn's accord as "the only treaty between those people and the Christians that was not ratified by an oath, and was never infring'd."[11] Voltaire's specific reference was to the Quaker proscription on oaths; for Quakers, the idea of telling the whole truth or considering a promise binding only when under oath suggested a lessened obligation to be honest and faithful when not under oath; they were to be honest and honor-bound always.[12] Voltaire's acclaim, echoed by the Abbé Reynal in 1770, helped to establish the Great Treaty's American and international reputation, and made Penn a perhaps unlikely inspiration for French Republicanism.[13] Voltaire's "made without an oath and never broken" became one of the stock phrases of the treaty tradition, sometimes appearing in a condensed form—"Unbroken Faith"—as in an 1827 monument in Kensington marking "the Scite of the Great Elm Tree." The art historian Charles Coleman Sellers goes so far as to claim that Voltaire's comment preceded and inspired the details of the treaty tradition, instead of vice versa. Philadelphians "responded to Voltaire's acclaim" by "fixing upon the exact spot at which the memorable event had taken place. The old elm by the wide river would henceforth be held in reverence by the city and the world alike."[14]

Whereas Hicks cites Voltaire in the caption, he adapts the image of *Penn's Treaty* from the famous painting that Benjamin West, a Pennsylvania expatriate living in London, composed in response to a commission from the late William Penn's elderly son, Thomas. Almost definitively a representation, rather than a record, of historical fact, a question is whether West's *Penn's Treaty* is in part a record of a cultural fact, namely, the existence of a popular tradition. If so, then West's embellishments and inaccuracies jeopardized the very tradition he recorded and amplified.

West's "tremendous anachronistic canvas" was first exhibited in the Royal Academy in 1772 and was disseminated through prints made from an engraving produced in London in 1775 by John Hall for John Boydell.[15] The *Penn's Treaty* image enjoyed an enormous mainstream popularity in Pennsylvania during the first part of the nineteenth century and became a customary gift at Quaker weddings. It became the ubiquitous embodiment of the commonwealth's civic myth.[16] In 1976 Governor Milton J. Shapp summed up a long tradition of what might be called Pennsylvania exceptionalism in welcoming the American bicentennial exhibition *Symbols of Peace: William Penn's Treaty with the Indians*: "Benjamin West's painting of Penn's Treaty with the Indians symbolizes the history of

5. *William Penn's Treaty with the Indians When He Founded the Province of Pennsylvania in North America* by Benjamin West, 1771–72. Courtesy of the Pennsylvania Academy of the Fine Arts, Philadelphia. Gift of Mrs. Sarah Harrison (Joseph Harrison Jr. Collection).

Pennsylvania from its earliest attempts to organize a small democratic society to its current efforts to insure the rights of all its citizens, however strange and unpopular their views."[17]

Penn's Treaty was not only the ubiquitous popular image of Pennsylvania's founding, but it also became an almost unavoidable threshold for historical inquiries. An early commentator described West's technique in *Penn's Treaty* as "narrative painting," but its effect was to substitute a tableau for a historical narrative, exercising the power of a composed image over a verbal account that was, to use a visual metaphor, sketchy.[18] This transformation is evident in a before-and-after comparison of historical accounts of the Great Treaty. For example, what is often described as the first reference to the Great Treaty appears in John Oldmixon's *The British Empire in America* (1708). Oldmixon, who was informed by Penn himself, reports that as "soon as [Penn] arrived he took the Government into his own Hands, and enter'd upon Treaties with the Indian Kings, for purchasing his Patent-Lands and others."[19] About ninety years later, Robert Proud's *History of Pennsylvania* (1797), which was composed during the Revolutionary War, before West's image became widely disseminated, provided a paragraph-long account emphasizing the promises exchanged and the rhetorical figure of "a *chain of friendship* and covenant indelible, never never to be broken, so long as the sun and moon endure" (emphasis original).[20] (His use of "covenant" conflates Delaware with Iroquois relations.[21]) Proud's apparent sources are the diplomatic records of subsequent treaties, which refer to an original precedent. He fixes its date in 1682, the year of Penn's arrival, and makes no mention of the setting.

By contrast, the accounts of the treaty in biographies of Penn by Thomas Clarkson (1813) and Mason Weems (1819) seem like instances of *ekfrasis* —written descriptions of visual art. "It is much to be regretted," wrote Clarkson, "when we have accounts of minor Treaties between William Penn and the Indians, that in no historian I can find an account of [the Great Treaty], though so many mention it, and though all concur in considering it as the most glorious of any in the annals of the world. There are, however, relations in Indian speeches, and traditions in Quaker families descended from those who were present on the occasion, from which we may learn something concerning it." He explains that Penn wore his "usual clothes," adorned only by "a sky-blue sash around his waist." He refers to the "roll of parchment, containing the Confirmation of the Treaty of Purchase and Amity" that Penn held in his hand, and the "various articles of merchandize," and notices that the chief sachem wore "a kind of chaplet, in which appeared a small horn."[22] Weems, apparently borrowing from Clarkson, emphasized "the theatre of that memorable event"—on "the western banks of the great river Delaware ... a fine green near the pleasant villages of Shackamaxon and Coaquanoc." Both writers give particular notice to the "elm tree of prodigious size," which "from its giant arms threw far and wide a refreshing shade over many a grassy acre."[23] Clarkson had the blue sash (now at the HSP) in his possession, but he acknowledged to Joshua Francis Fisher, the coauthor with Peter Stephen Du Ponceau of an 1836 report on the Great Treaty for the HSP, that his Pennsylvania informant on the treaty tradition was none other than Benjamin West, whose grandparents on both sides had been early settlers.[24] Fisher and Du Ponceau's comment on Clarkson's prose would apply equally to that of Weems: it "savour[s] something more of the brush of the painter than the pen of the historian."[25]

The predominance of the visual image based on West has induced even such document-based colonialist historians as Francis Jennings and James Merrell to make forays into art criticism.[26] Historians who question "the historicity of a single great treaty under the legendary elm at Shackamaxon" need only do so because that legend was so dramatically reified by West's picture; otherwise, there would be no visualization to set aside.[27] Meanwhile, interpreters of *Penn's Treaty* have seemed pleased with the idea that the painting is a translation without an original, "an apocryphal legend," and that "there had never been a 'Great Treaty.'"[28] The placard by the painting in the Pennsylvania Academy of the Fine Arts resolutely declares that "the scene is allegorical rather than historical." Several critics refer to the speculation that the legend of the undocumented Great Treaty coalesced out of the memory of a "series" of several minor, documented treaty meetings.[29]

The now considerable body of criticism on *Penn's Treaty* dwells on the painting's anachronisms and inaccuracies. The Quaker garments, the architecture, and even Penn's figure belong to periods well after the 1680s; the depicted buildings arose in Philadelphia, not Kensington, and the Indian accoutrements represent various groups. Such "disjunctions" are conducive to historicist readings that emphasize the painting's 1771–72 moment of production instead of its "ostensible" seventeenth-century moment of representation.[30] On the one hand, scholars have interpreted *Penn's Treaty* in light of its immediate colonial past, focusing on Thomas Penn's troubled reputation with regard to Indian relations and land speculation, which were focal points of his political conflict with his nemesis Benjamin Franklin and the antiproprietary Quakers. In this view, Thomas Penn commissioned the painting to vindicate himself from accusations of malfeasance stemming from the Walking Purchase, the 1756 Albany Conference, and the 1768 Treaty of Fort Stanwix by invoking the honorable reputation of his father.[31] On the other hand, scholars have interpreted the painting in relation to the transatlantic "crisis of 1771."[32] According to Anne Cannon Palumbo, *Penn's Treaty* illustrates the mutual benefits of the mercantile relationship between colony and mother country: "the nostalgia it reflects is not for an earlier century but rather the good old days before 1763."[33] In this view, William Penn becomes a figure for England, and the Native Americans figures for America.

The scholarship on *Penn's Treaty* has an intriguing correspondence to the "presentist memory approach" within social memory studies, epitomized by the influential 1983 collection by Eric Hobsbawm and Terrence Ranger, *The Invention of Tradition*. Scholars who subscribe to this view "assimilate collective memory to manipulation and deception, a mere tool in the arsenal of power."[34] While the interpretations of *Penn's Treaty* have been almost uniformly presentist, within memory studies this approach has been supplanted by a "dynamics of memory" approach, which allows that "many groups use the past for instrumental reasons" but "denies the past as purely a construction and insists that it has an inherent continuity."[35] It suggests a continuous process in which memories are shaped through a "fluid negotiation" between present needs and past realities.[36]

A dynamic interpretation would not contradict the understanding of *Penn's Treaty* as an "allegory of Colonial America."[37] Nor would it discount the basis for that allegory's primary level of signification in a historical tradition that was part of the heritage of the West and especially the Penn families, and that was also part of the context for the image's reception, especially in Philadelphia.[38] West's own, retrospective statement of intent, from an 1807 letter to W. Darton, was that the "great object I had in forming that composition, was to express savages brought into harmony and piece [sic] by justice and benevolence, by not withholding from them what was their right, and giving to them what they were in want of, and as well as a wish to give by that art a conquest that was made over native people without sward or Dagder [sic]."[39] A quick dismissal of the historicity of the painting frees critics to interpret it as pure representation, not as a visual expression of an oral tradition that records a seventeenth-century "conquest" that was supposedly different from others in its recognition of aboriginal land rights and its pacifism.[40] A dynamic interpretation would consider the painting as a critical juncture in the history of that tradition, in which the memory of the first treaty meeting, or meetings, between Penn and the Indians was shaped by present concerns and repackaged for popular consumption. Above all, a dynamic interpretation would take seriously the notion that the memory, conditioned by successive presents, also drew its impetus from the past. Indeed, the painting, with its marked anachronisms, might be read as a visual allegory for the medium of oral tradition, flattening time by making the past simultaneous with the present.

THE SILENT WITNESS

Paradoxically, some of the notorious "inaccuracies" of *Penn's Treaty* may be attributed to West's zeal for a different kind of accuracy—"likeness"—combined with a family pride. In effect, West sacrificed consistency for similitude. As he explains in the same letter to Darton, he made "every enquire . . . to obtain portraits of those who accompanied" Penn "into the wilderness of North America; but without effect." The only portrait he was able to obtain was that of William Penn himself, in a peace medallion made by Silvinius Bevan, which represented the founder in late middle age. Accompanying the figure of Penn, West painted his own "honoured Father" and his "half Brother." These were unrealistic interpolations into the scene, certainly, but they were true-to-life portraits. "I have taken the liberty to introduce the likeness of our Father, and Brother of Reading, into the picture in the group of Friends that accompany Wm. Penn," West wrote to his brother William. "[T]hat is the likeness of our Brother that stands immediately behind Penn, resting on his cane. I need not point out the figure of our Father. I believe you will find some likeness of him in the print though they have all lost something of that when compeared [sic] with the original picture." In depicting the Indians, too, West prioritized likeness over historical accuracy. As he wrote Darton, "by possessing the real dresses of the Indians I was able to give that truth in representing their costumes which is so evident in the picture of the Treaty." If his collection was eclectic, at least its items were authentic.[41] But one key icon in the tradition did not have a "likeness" in the painting at all: the tree.

If everything else in West's *Penn's Treaty*—the buildings, the clothing, Penn's waistline—seems like it has been captured in fast-forward, as with time-lapse photography, only the tree seems to belong to a period *before* 1682—if indeed it is represented in the painting at all. As several critics have noted, West "slights the tree."[42] According to the prolific popular historian John Fanning Watson's *Annals of Pennsylvania*, when the tree fell in the 1810 storm, it had a girth of twenty-four feet, and a cross-section revealed an impressive 283 annual rings; in 1682 it would have been 155 years old. A close look at the painting reveals, in the right background, a pair of mature trees, but neither is the tree of "prodigious size" referred to by Clarkson, nor the "recognizable elm" with the "wide-spreading" branches characteristic of *Ulmus americana*.[43]

The tree in the painting can hardly be said to be a "likeness" of the one that West himself recalled was "held in the highest veneration by the original inhabitants of my native country, by the first settlers, and by their descendants."[44] Perhaps West was trying to avoid interference from cross-currents of contemporary visual rhetoric, to eschew, rather than invite, certain presentist interpretations. In 1770 a gathering of American savages around a tree was a potentially provocative allegorical image.[45] In any case, it is a testament to the independence of the tradition from the painting—or that the painting was assimilated into the tradition, instead of vice versa—that the elm "of extraordinary size" remained the central feature of the treaty scene in the verbal or visual adaptations of

6. *Penn's Tree, with the City and Port of Philadelphia, on the River Delaware from Kensington, 1800* by William Russell Birch. Philadelphia: William Birch and Son, 1800. Courtesy of the Library Company of Philadelphia.

West's painting by Clarkson, Weems, Hicks, and others.[46] The comments on *Penn's Treaty* by nineteenth- and twentieth-century critics show that they also knew to look for it, and at least one recent interpreter somehow decries a "massive elm tree" in the right background.[47]

The tree flourished, too, in the popular memory of residents in and around Philadelphia. Until its demise it stood as "silent witness" to the legendary transaction. A poem in *Watson's Annals* apostrophizes:

> But thou, broad Elm! Canst thou tell us nought
> Of forest Chieftains, and their vanish'd tribes?
> —Hast thou no record left

> Of perish'd generations, o'er whose heads
> Thy foliage droop'd?—thou who shadowed once
> The rever'd Founders of our honour'd State.

As Watson notes, "other cities in our Union have had their consecrated trees."[48] He probably had in mind not only the Liberty Tree in Boston but also the Connecticut "Charter Oak" and the "Liberty Tree of Annapolis," which was celebrated as the site of the first treaty between the English and the Susquehannocks. Several of the local traditions roughly parallel that of the Treaty Elm: before the arrival of Europeans, the trees had been landmarks, or more especially "council trees," for the Native Americans; the Europeans (and later, Americans) were brought into council, and the trees thus became revered as "treaty trees." Subsequently, as a result of the traditions, the trees became civic centers, the sites for club meetings and other community events.[49] If the traditions are true, then it is more plausible that the choice of the elm as the site of the Great Treaty was attributable to the Delawares' customs, rather than Penn's discernment, as Watson supposes. For Watson, "lofty and silent grandeur" is especially conducive to "the enlargement of conception and thought," making great trees not only suitable venues for great actions but also appropriate memorials to them. "There long stood the stately witness of the solemn covenant—a lasting emblem of the unbroken faith, 'pledged without an oath, and never broken!'"[50]

After a storm in 1810, however, the tree was no longer a living memorial. "In a squall of wind last night," the merchant Thomas Cope recorded in his journal entry for March 6, the "venerable & large Elm tree at Kensington, under which it is said Wm. Penn held his first treaty with the Aborigines, was blown down. It has been on the decline for some years, previously to which it was a princely tree, its branches extending sixty feet from the trunk on every side, forming a shade impenetrable to the sun."[51] Watson dates the fall of the tree to March 3: "it fell on Saturday night, and on Sunday many hundreds of people visited it." The tree had germinated long before the arrival of Europeans in the region, and it had survived the original Dutch, Swedish, and English settlers, and several succeeding generations. By 1810 the demise of Americans with firsthand memories of the colonial era was at least within view.[52]

Thus with the loss of the Great Elm, the tradition was in a precarious position. If an oral tradition is a memory of an event carried beyond the death of its participants and witnesses, the Great Treaty tradition was now at a point where those who had firsthand contact with those who had had firsthand contact with members of the founding generation were dying off. The fall of the elm, "the only mark by which the locality was designated," was only one of the rapid environmental changes that jeopardized memory.[53] Unlike the Delawares, whose historical traditions were shorn of geographic referents as a result of their territorial displacements, the descendants of the colonial Philadelphians found their "fast-growing, industrializing, uproarious, and splintering city" moving away from them.[54] In an 1825 address to the HSP, of which he was a prominent founder, the jurist and philanthropist Roberts Vaux worried "that the lapse of time, with other concurring circumstances may hereafter render the fact [of the treaty's taking place at Kensington] equivocal, and perhaps, cast over it the veil of oblivion, should the evidence which remains pass away uncollected and unrecorded."[55]

This evidence, such as it was, consisted mostly of early attestations of the existence of the tradition. Vaux was not quite able to reach back far enough to show documentation of the tradition as an oral history. He presented testimony from Deborah Logan, the elderly widow of James Logan's grandson. He also cites Benjamin West's comments about the tree, and discusses the painting. Although Vaux complains about West's misrepresentation of Penn's person and the period costume, he commits a key interpretive and historical error of his own: "One of the five dignified individuals, who were present with the Proprietary at that Treaty, was the grandfather of West; and the painter has given a likeness of his own ancestor, in the imposing group of Patriarchs." As discussed, West painted the likenesses of his father and half-brother; his grandfather was an early immigrant but not part of Penn's cadre. Nevertheless,

Vaux, unable to anticipate twentieth-century art historians, held "this circumstance to be of great authority; because West had an opportunity of being intimately acquainted with all the particulars of the treaty, and it will not be questioned that he intended to perpetuate a faithful narrative upon his canvas."[56]

As Watson conceded a few years later, the "fact of the treaty being held under the Elm, depends more upon the general tenor of tradition, than upon any direct facts in our possession. When all men knew it to be so, they felt little occasion to lay up evidences for posterity."[57] Thus both Vaux and Watson cite an 1825 letter from the eighty-one-year-old Judge Richard Peters, who recounted a recent conversation he had had with his still older friend David H. Conyngham about "olden times." Peters and Conyngham remembered the elm tree; they had bathed by the site of the treaty and had always known the history. "No person then disputed the fact, that this was the tree under which Penn's treaty was held." Moreover, Conyngham remembered "distinctly" being instructed by the "eccentric" old Quaker Benjamin Lay, who had arrived in Pennsylvania in 1731 and therefore "must have known some of the contemporaries of William Penn." Lay, "[a]fter dilating on the worth and virtues of that good man, and particularly as they applied to his treatment of the natives," would "call on the boys, point to the Elm-tree; and enjoin them to bear in mind, and tell it to their children, that under the tree Penn's treaty was held; and they should respect it accordingly."[58]

The passing of the tree, then, not only signaled a loss of the memories of William Penn but also threatened a further lapse in the values associated with him. It also marked a transition from the investment of memories in living witnesses to "olden times" to relics, artificial monuments, historians . . . and poets. Judge Peters urged Pennsylvanians to "each take a relic from that hallowed tree, / Which like Penn, whom it shaded, immortal shall be." For Peters, due reverence for the tree—and for elms in general—ensured the continuity of the "sage lessons it witnessed." He hoped "our trustworthy statesmen, when called to the helm, / Ne'er forget the wise treaty held under the elm."[59] Neighbors did indeed make the wood into relics, including boxes, frames, and at least two armchairs. Many years after the fall of the tree, perhaps in the twentieth-century—the manuscript in the HSP is undated—Rosalie Vallance Tiers Jackson narrated to her nephew Clarence Van Dyke Tiers a "family tradition" that the tree, which grew on the property of a Mr. Van Dusen, fell on that of her ancestor Franklin Eyre, who agreed to saw it up and share the lumber. "This was done and from those boards this box was made." According to Jackson, when they dug up the root of the tree "it was found to have an Indian vase imbedded in it, but this crumbled upon exposure to the air." The HSP collection holds several fragments of this root, as well as boxes—perhaps the one Jackson referred to—and a bust of William Penn made from wood from the Treaty Tree.[60]

The tree was survived, of course, by its offspring, "silent witnesses to the memory of the Great Treaty."[61] Watson lamented the demise of a "sucker" from the Treaty Tree that for a time "flourished" on the grounds of the Pennsylvania Hospital. He had envisioned having it transplanted it to the treaty site, where "it would have been an appropriate shade to the marble monument, since erected near the site of the original tree to perpetuate its memory." In 1838 Watson himself had two elm saplings, of less noble pedigree, planted at the Town Hall in Kensington, which also housed one of the chairs constructed of "relic woods" from the Treaty Tree (Benjamin Rush owned the other). "Long may it be preserved as a memento of the past," Watson implored, "and long may the trees, so planted, endure to link one generation with another,—to stand like living monuments speaking forth their solemn and soothing lessons, as from fathers to sons and the sons of sons."[62]

THE EMPTY ENVELOPE

"No transaction connected with the settlement of Pennsylvania has higher claims on the respect of those who are interested in her early annals," Vaux declared in his 1825 address to the historical society, "than the First Treaty which was concluded between the pacific Founder and the Indian natives, in 1682." The purpose of his presentation was to quell "doubts" that had "been recently suggested, which are calculated to unsettle the long-received opinion, that Kensington was the scene of the memorable negotiation." Vaux never identifies the doubters. After presenting his evidence—mainly a demonstration that the "opinion" was indeed "long received"—he concluded by proposing that "measures be put in train for erecting a plain and substantial *Obelisk of granite*, near where the *Tree* formerly stood at Kensington; with appropriate inscriptions."[63]

Philadelphia's "first public monument" was erected by the Penn Society, of which Vaux was also a founder, in 1827, "to mark the Scite of the Great Elm Tree," as the inscriptions on one panel indicate.[64] Other panels give the date of Pennsylvania's founding, 1681 ("By deeds of Peace") and of William Penn's lifespan, 1644–1718. The key one reads:

> TREATY GROUND
> of
> WILLIAM PENN
> and the
> INDIAN NATIVES
> 1682
> UNBROKEN FAITH

While Vaux was successful in getting his obelisk in place, Edward Armstrong observed in an editorial footnote accompanying the 1864 reprinting of Vaux's treatise in the HSP *Memoirs* that "neither the question of the Site, nor the nature of the Treaty, had been settled beyond controversy." He concluded that the "question of the Site of the Treaty still remains a matter of tradition; no positive proof has been afforded, and perhaps can never be presented."[65] In 1882 Frederick Stone conceded that the "evidence is not convincing" regarding the site of the treaty, yet, observing that "a skepticism has grown up which questions if such an event ever occurred," he claimed to have at hand "enough evidence" to "prove that just such a treaty as the early traditions point to was held."[66]

Stone's exhibits included correspondence from William Penn that *refers* to a treaty meeting. In a 1681 letter, Penn looks forward to holding one with the Indians, and in a 1683 letter he looks back on one he had held. Penn arrived in Newcastle on October 28, 1682. In 1681 he had written a letter "To the Kings of the Indians" in which he professed his "great love and regard toward you," and his intentions to "gain your love and friendship by a kind, just, and peaceable life." He proposed a system of settling grievances between the Indians and the settlers through juries ("an equal number of honest men on both sides") and announced that he would "shortly come to you myself, at which time we may more largely and freely confer and discourse of these matters. In the meantime, I have sent my commissioners to treat with you about land and a firm league of peace." In a separate letter, Penn instructed his deputy, William Markham, "to act all in my name as proprietary and governor" and to "treat speedily with the Indians for land before they are furnished with things that please them."[67]

Penn first thought that the owners of the land on the west bank of the Delaware were the Susquehannocks, but Markham, who was in-country, must have learned otherwise. On July 15, 1682, Markham formalized Penn's first land transaction with the Delawares. An addendum, dated August 1, records a follow-up meeting at which the goods that composed the purchase price for the land were specified. It lists seven articles of agreement concerning the political relations between the Delawares and the colonists—a treaty, in the specific sense of the word. (Because the Proprietors had an exclusive prerogative to purchase land, land transaction agreements were also political agreements, and were considered treaties.) These articles anticipate the ones recalled in later references to the initial treaty. This meeting was at "the house of Capt. Lasse Cock," the Swedish interpreter, but it is not apparent which house. Cock had lived at Shackamaxon, and had remaining relatives and property there, but by 1678 he had established his "home plantation" to the southwest at Passyunk, and he also had property upriver at Matinicum (Burlington) Island.[68] Markham's meetings that summer, in which William Penn was present in name but not in body, might be the historical basis for the treaty tradition.[69]

In his 1681 letter to the Indians Penn had also promised to appear in person to expand on the preliminary discussion with his agents. One of the articles in the agreement between the Delawares and Markham was that "there be a meeting once every year to read the articles over."[70] In August 1683 Penn wrote a letter to the Free Society of Traders in which he describes a meeting at which land, trade goods, and pledges of eternal friendship and fairness were exchanged. It seems likely enough that he was referring to the treaty meeting that took place during a few days around June 23–25, approximately a year after the preliminary meetings with Markham. During these days Penn received six deeds, four of them signed by his celebrated counterpart Tamanend, the Indian most associated with the tradition, as either grantor or witness. All but the last of these deeds (which was executed on the twenty-fifth) were witnessed by Lasse Cock and his Swedish neighbors.[71] Thus the historical basis for the tradition might be these 1683 meetings between William Penn and the Delawares, possibly conflated with the 1682 meetings with Markham.

These records seem to indicate that within a year of his arrival in Pennsylvania, William Penn and the Delawares held a political treaty from which no explicit treaty document has survived. There is no evidence to falsify the tradition's specificity in locating the treaty meeting at Shackamaxon. Why has there been any controversy at all? The answer may lie in way the memory of the treaty waxed in importance, insisting on the preeminence of one of several broadly similar treaty meetings with Native American groups. Also, the tradition fixed on certain details, such as the tree and the words exchanged, that were not verifiable, and others that were falsifiable, such as the participants depicted by Benjamin West, and especially the date. The retroactive impulse to make the treaty Penn's first order of business after his October arrival became an invitation to skeptics to dismiss the whole story.

Actually, within the historiography on Penn's treaty, a subsidiary tradition emerged about the former existence of a document that would have specified the date and vindicated the treaty tradition. Thus Watson, in his *Annals of Philadelphia*, notes that an exhaustive search of the Pennsylvania State Archives in Harrisburg produced nothing more than "one paper" which "barely mentions that, 'after the treaty was held, William Penn and the Friends went into the house of Lacy Cock.'" However, Watson reports that "Mr. Gordon, the author of the late *History of Pennsylvania*, informed me that he could only find at Harrisburg the original envelope relating to the treaty papers; on which was endorsed 'Papers relative to the Indian treaty under the great Elm.'"[72] Like much else in Watson's *Annals*, however, this sighting seems to have been secondhand; in an appendix to his *History of Pennsylvania* (1829) Thomas Francis Gordon observes that Redmond Conyngham (the son of the aforementioned David H. Conyngham) had told him of the discovery of this empty envelope "in a bundle of papers there, relating to the Shawanese Indians, with the following endorsement: 'Minutes of the Indian conference in relation to the great treaty made with William Penn, at the Big Tree, Shackamaxon, on the fourteenth of the tenth month, 1682.'"[73] Conyngham himself, in "Some Extracts from the Papers in the Office of the Secretary of the Commonwealth, at Harrisburg, and from Other Documents," which he presented to the HSP in 1826, apparently used the endorsed envelope as a primary source: "William Penn held his most important interview with the Indian chiefs under the shade of the great elm, on the 14th of October, 1682."[74]

Conyngham's date is obviously impossible, since Penn had not yet landed. It is surprising that a Pennsylvania antiquarian would make such an obvious error concerning the Old Style calendar—the "tenth month" was not October but December. Gordon made this correction silently. "It has been doubted," he complained, "whether the conference between William Penn and the Indians, of the fourteenth of December, 1682, was holden under the Great Elm, at Shackamaxon, and whether it was accompanied by a formal treaty." Yet the place and date were "confirmed by uncontradicted tradition for near a century and a half." If we "doubt of these facts," Gordon declared, "historical tradition is unworthy of acceptance, and little credit can be given to ordinary historical testimony." For Gordon and his contemporaries, these stakes were not simply methodological—doubts about the treaty were aspersions against the credibility of their ancestors.[75]

Yet "little credit" can be given to this December date. There was no room for such a meeting in Penn's busy schedule. Nearly "every day of Penn's time" after the December 4 meeting of the Legislature at Upland "can be shown to have been otherwise occupied."[76] Perhaps for that reason, variants of the tradition move the meeting somewhat earlier: "Here is the site of the Great Treaty of Amity Between William Penn and the Indians," reads a plaque by the cluster of monuments in Penn Treaty Park in Fishtown, "which was held in November, 1682." Yet November, too, is highly unlikely. As J. Thomas Scharf and Thompson Westcott observe in *The History of Philadelphia, 1609–1884*, Penn's correspondence provides a lot of detail about his busy November in 1682, including mention of visits to "'New York, Long Island, East Jersey, and Maryland,'" with nary "a syllable about the Shackamaxon treaty." Skeptics have a very good case in supposing that if Penn had met with the Indians in that month, there would be some evidence of it.[77] The November 1682 date, however, was probably not furnished by memory, but by "memory transformed by its passage through history."[78] Benjamin West, for example, evidently had no such date in mind: one of the supposed inaccuracies of his painting is that the "fuzzy umbrage" in the background is "altogether too well leafed for a November conference (also too cold a season for his half-clad natives)."[79] Instead, the painting seems to depict a summer meeting.

An ethnohistorical perspective provides a stronger argument than the negative evidence against the 1682 dating: Penn's arrival was too late in the year for the Indians to convene. Late fall was the Delawares' "principle season" for hunting, and they spent the winter dispersed into small groups.[80] On September 10, 1683, for example, Kekelappan sold William Penn half his land and promised "to sell unto him at ye next Spring, on my return from hunting, ye other half."[81] The Delaware leaders were not plenipotentiaries; they required communal assent before making decisions and entering agreements that affected others in the community. On October 10, 1728, Sassoonan delivered a response to a speech Governor Patrick Gordon had made the previous spring, apologizing for the scant representation of other Indians but indicating that he was the appointed spokesman: "at this time of year they connot [sic] conveniently come; that nevertheless, he now speaks in the Name & Behalf of them all."[82] In mid-August 1731 he told Gordon not to expect a formal reply to his address "till he has discours'd [with] the rest of their people, that these are scatter'd into many places of ye Countrey & cannot all meet before next Spring[;] that then they will come & treat further."[83] Thus, the spring of 1683 would have been the first opportunity for a formal meeting between Penn and the Delawares.

In "Penn's Treaty with the Indians: Did It Take Place in 1682 or 1683?" (published in 1882, the bicentennial of the quasi-traditional date), Frederick Stone points out that the many references in early eighteenth-century treaty meetings to a precedent that took place "when the Great *William Penn*, the Father of this Country . . . first brought his People with him over the broad Sea" are vague enough that they might as easily refer to 1683, when the Proprietor had documented land transactions with the Delawares, as 1682, when he did not.[84] As Stone points out, traditionalist historians eager to establish the treaty as Penn's earliest priority, rationalized the absence of a document by characterizing the aims of the meeting as "friendship only": "It was a great meeting of *verbal* conference and pledge," wrote Watson, "popularly called the Treaty,—in which civilities were exchanged, and reciprocal promises of friendship and good will severally made. To this fact, the testimony of tradition has been unceasing and unchanging. It has been told and believed from the beginning—or from a time, as the civilians say, 'in which the memory of man runneth not to the contrary.'"[85]

Watson's insistence on an unwritten treaty, unsullied by any pecuniary transactions, is of a kind with his romantic valorization of oral traditions. An "unceasing and unchanging" tradition implies a sort of ideological continuity that the simple survival of an archival record does not, and the notion that both the Quaker founder and his Delaware counterparts would consider their reciprocal verbal pledges to be perpetually binding is consistent with the idealized memories of both. Penn himself, in his 1683 "Letter to the Free Society of Traders," described the Indians as natural embodiments of the ideals of primitive Quakerism; they had no need of the forms that characterize the covetous, legalistic European culture: "They are not disquieted with *Bills of Lading* and *Exchange* nor perplexed with *Chancery-Suits* and *Exchequer-Reckonings*."[86] Watson asked Pennsylvanians to reciprocate this language ideology from a nineteenth-century vantage point: to demand a written record was to be of little faith.

Yet what about that mysterious empty envelope in the Pennsylvania State Archives? "Unfortunately," wrote Thomas Gordon, "the valuable papers which the envelope contained are no longer to be found."[87] Had such papers, or even the envelope, ever existed? Stone argues that it is unlikely that a legal arrangement such as the arbitration of disputes by six men from each side, as recounted in the "Letter to the Free Society of Traders," would not have been put into an instrument of writing. At least one such record of a "political treaty" survives, from a 1701 council with the Susquehannocks in Philadelphia, and it is at least possible that a 1683 written treaty with the Delawares had been a precedent. The 1701 treaty provides evidence that diplomatic protocol could involve giving copies of such records to the Indians themselves; in 1720 the Conestoga Captain Civility (Taquatarensaly) told the governor that the Conoys "have no writing to show their League of Friendship as the others have and therefore desire they may be favored with one."[88] There is no solid indication, however, that the Delawares ever had such a document. Gordon writes that "the Indians, in 1722, at a conference held with governor Keith, exhibited the roll of parchment containing the treaty," and he speculates that it had been "carefully preserved at least forty years before its exhibition to governor Keith, and may now be in the possession of their descendants." However, the 1722 meeting he refers to involved Susquehannock, not Delaware, Indians, and so the "parchment" was probably the 1701 document.[89] Poignantly, another reference to this document appears in 1763, in an inventory of the remains from the fiery massacre of Susquehannock converts at Conestoga.[90]

If the Delawares never presented a treaty document, the numerous references to an original treaty in the diplomatic records, coupled with the references in Penn's correspondence, invalidate the notion that West's *Penn's Treaty* painting is "the earliest known document of any sort indicating that such an event took place at all."[91] Even West's visual "iconography of peace" had visual precedents in diplomatic medals. The Quaker Friendly Association struck the Richardson Medal in 1757 to remind Indians that at least one faction of Pennsylvanians remained true to "the Peaceable Principle."[92] The obverse depicts a Quaker sitting beneath a tree extending a peace pipe across a council fire to an Indian. The reverse of the William Penn Medal (1720) supplied West with the "likeness" of Penn as a stout older man, and the obverse, which depicts a Quaker grasping the hand of a classically posed Indian warrior, supplied the tradition with the phrase "By Deeds of Peace" (repeated on the Penn Society obelisk). If it is not quite an explicit reference to a treaty with the Delawares, this medal does anticipate the civic myth by suggesting that Pennsylvania was founded through Indian diplomacy. The verbal references in treaty minutes are more specific. In 1731 Governor Gordon recounted to a group of Delawares that on William Penn's first arrival in the country, he "immediately" convened a meeting with "the Chiefs of the Indians," declaring that "his people and ye Indians should be the same"; "he made a strong chain of Friendship with them which has been kept bright to this day." The Delaware leader Sassoonan responded that "he understands every word that has been said he remembers when W Penn first came into the Countrey he himself was then a little lad."[93]

The basis of doubts about the treaty tradition on the absence of a treaty document is an example of the language ideology known as "archival positivism"—the belief in the stability and ultimate authority of archival records, especially official documents, "at the expense of other media," such as recorded oral traditions.[94] Stone observes that the absence of a written treaty should be unsurprising to "any one who is acquainted with the carelessness to which the archives of this State have been exposed."⁹⁵ Francis Jennings, who depended on the very archival records he sought to debunk, suggests more cynically that Penn's successors may have "destroyed the document that would have exposed their breach of faith."⁹⁶ Given their subsequent references to the original treaty, including through West's painting, this claim is implausible. Nevertheless, the absence of a treaty document is a questionable basis on which to dispute whether the Great Treaty took place under the Elm Tree, or whether "it happened at all."⁹⁷ Of course, the tradition hardly constitutes proof that the treaty with the Delawares at Shackamaxon, "Great" or otherwise, did take place, but as Stone asserts, "nothing can be brought against it but the charge that it *is* a tradition, and upon the whole we think that there is as much reason to believe that Penn's Treaty was held at Shackamaxon as that the Pilgrims first set foot on Plymouth Rock."⁹⁸

His analogy is apt. The rock, like the tree, was not only an icon of a colonial founding but an embodiment of object permanence in the midst of historical change. In principle, these objects were "unceasing and unchanging," like the "testimony of tradition"—but the tree died (only to be regenerated) and the rock cracked and chipped (to be partially repaired); pieces of both were made into relics. If the supposed fact that the tree had lent its shade to the Great Treaty "has been told and believed from the beginning—or from a time, as the civilians would say, 'in which the memory of man runneth not to the contrary,'" the tradition about the rock had parallel claims to aboriginality, yet it was first recorded in 1741, when the ninety-four-year-old Thomas Faunce, the longtime "keeper of the Plymouth records," who had known the "Old Comers" in his childhood, insisted that Plymouth Rock was the place where they had landed, and that it should not be subsumed into the foundation of a wharf.⁹⁹ The rock's status as the Pilgrims' landing place "is generally insisted upon by Plymouth antiquarians and tour guides but refuted or ignored by historians."¹⁰⁰ It was assuredly *not* where the Pilgrims first set foot, since there were exploratory landing parties from the *Mayflower* before the settlement at Plymouth. But the doubt that it figured in the general disembarkation at Plymouth, as the historian Samuel Eliot Morison once conjectured, is also speculative.[101] It rests, again, on the absence of contemporary documentation: the supposition that "had a convenient natural pier been provided," the Pilgrims' "contemporary journals, filled with instances of providential aid, would have made some mention of it."[102] Such reasoning allows a facile pivot to the view that "our national memory has created our past, not the other way around."[103]

THE MAN ON THE LEFT

If the providential rock is a significant omission from the Pilgrims' journals, Edward Armstrong, in his comment of Vaux's "Memoir on the Locality of the Great Treaty," finds it equally unlikely that there would be no mention of the Great Elm in the Indian "conferences . . . with which our annals are filled." How is it possible that "a race so strong in their feelings of association, in their fondness for designating places and streams the most insignificant, so apt to draw their illustrations from material objects,—should not, in speaking of their great father, Penn, and his great Treaty with them, have pointed to this Tree as the living embodiment and proof of an event on which they so much love to dwell"?[104]

Armstrong's critique is reflective of the most fascinating aspect of the nineteenth-century historiography on the Great Treaty, which is its appeal to the greater authority of Native American memory-keeping and oral traditions. While documentary evidence always trumped oral tradition, whether popular or Native American, in the absence of "positive proof," at least so long as the conclusions they supported were desirable, the Native Americans' traditions were more authoritative than those of the Euro-Americans because they were practiced in the art of perpetuating memory. They had not alienated their capacity for memory by coming to depend on writing, "this invention," as Socrates described it in Plato's *Phaedrus*, that "will produce forgetfulness in the souls of those who have learned it."[105]

Du Ponceau and Fisher, who were commissioned to inquire into the question of the locality, broadened the scope of their investigation to the "whole history of the great Treaty, which they found involved in much doubt and obscurity, principally from the want of contemporary records"; they promise to present a thorough investigation and apply the "torch of criticism" so as to dispel the "popular notions" that had "crept in amidst the various traditions that have been received from our ancestors" and to correct the "erroneous notions" and "false inferences" introduced by previous researchers.[106] Yet they admit of no doubt as to the historicity of "this important transaction, which, to Pennsylvania and her illustrious Founder, is a crown of glory that will last to the end of time." They support their case by referring to the Indians' traditions, which they find are more reliable conduits for undocumented memories: "through successive generations until their final disappearance from our soil," the Indians "never could nor did forget" their "gratitude" to William Penn, "to the last moment kept alive in their memories."[107] Their primary exhibit was a passage from Heckewelder's *History*.

According to Heckewelder, the treaty meetings (as opposed to a singular Great Treaty) with Penn were a particular "subject of pleasing remembrance." To commemorate, the Delawares "frequently assembled together in the woods, in some shady spot as nearly as possible similar to those where they used to meet their brother Miquon, and there lay all his 'words' or speeches, with those of his descendants, on a blanket or clean piece of bark, and with great satisfaction go successively over the whole. This practice (which I have repeatedly witnessed) continued until the year 1780, when the disturbances which then took place put an end to it, probably for ever."[108] (Heckewelder's closing reference is to the persecutions the Moravians suffered during the American Revolutionary War, culminating in the massacre of ninety-six converts by American militia at Gnadenhütten, Ohio.) The "words" they laid out would have included writings they had received from the English—perhaps including an original Great Treaty document—as well as "strings and belts of wampum."[109]

There is a considerable body of scholarship, in ethnohistory, anthropology, and, most recently, literary studies, on wampum, the white and purple ("black") beads made from whelk and quahog shells, respectively. After contact with Europeans, the production and trade of wampum increased dramatically. It developed as a New World currency in the fur trade with the Dutch. It also served an important function in Eastern Woodlands diplomacy, in protocols that originated among the Iroquois but were also adopted (and adapted) by Algonquian peoples, including Delawares, and by Europeans in treaty council meetings. Wampum strings and belts "embodied" messages and terms of agreement that were formulated in tribal council, memorized, and pronounced by spokesmen at treaties.[110] Accepting the wampum meant accepting the agreement; it was "the Indians' method of signing, sealing, and delivering an agreement."[111] The strings and belts then served as records; not simply as contracts to be kept on file for reference, if necessary, but as scripts to be actively reviewed and periodically renewed by the contracting parties.

According to the ethnohistorian William N. Fenton, Heckewelder's is the "best contemporaneous account of reading the wampum."[112] Heckewelder explains that when he was among the Delawares during the late eighteenth century, the "chiefs," using wampum, could "relate very minutely, what had passed between William Penn and their forefathers, at their first meeting and afterwards, and also the transactions which took place with the governors who succeeded him." He describes how, for "the purpose of refreshing their own memories, and of instructing one or more of their most capable and promising young men in these matters," the Indians would hold annual or biannual assemblies at which they would lay out all "the documents" on "a large piece of bark on a blanket" in "such order, that they can at once distinguish each particular speech, the same as we know the principal contents of an instrument of writing by the endorsement on it." They would have "some trusty white man (if such can be had)" read the European writing to them. A skillful speaker, reading the wampum, "in an audible voice delivers, with the gravity that the subject requires, the contents, sentence after sentence, until he has finished the whole on one subject."[113]

As Fenton notes, scholars disagree about the cogency of the analogy between reading wampum and reading alphabetic script. Heckewelder, pressing the analogy, describes the practice of "the turning of the belt," explaining that when it "is done properly, it may be as well known by it how far the speaker has advanced in his speech, as with us on taking a glance at the pages of a book or pamphlet while reading; and a good speaker will be able to point out the exact place on a belt which is to answer to each particular sentence, the same as we can point out a passage in a book."[114] The question is whether the function of wampum is simply mnemonic, assisting in the commitment of a speech to memory and enabling its reproduction, or whether it stores information that can be extracted by someone who has been trained in the communicative practice (wampum literacy) but is not versed about the specific event with which the wampum is associated. The answer seems to be that while wampum belts did employ recognizable communicative conventions, the sort of verbatim reproduction of speech events described by Heckewelder was impossible without the content having been committed to memory in association with the wampum.

Like other commentators on indigenous media, Du Ponceau and Fisher considered wampum a form of "artificial memory"—they compared it to "the *Quipos*," or knotted cords, employed by the Incas.[115] The Moravian missionary George Henry Loskiel explained that "[e]verything of moment transacted at solemn councils, either between the Indians themselves or with the Europeans, is ratified, and made valid by strings and belts of wampum. . . . These strings and belts of wampum are also documents, by which the Indians remember the chief articles of the treaties made either between themselves, or with the white people. They refer to them as to public records, carefully preserving them in a chest made for that purpose." Like Heckewelder, Loskiel described gatherings at which they would open these boxes, pass around the strings and belts one at a time, and "repeat the words pronounced on its delivery in their

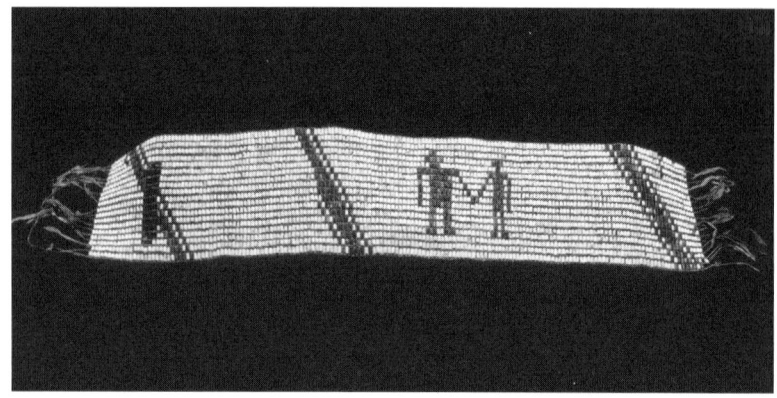

7. Treaty Belt. Courtesy of the Philadelphia History Museum at the Atwater Kent, Historical Society of Pennsylvania Collection.

whole connexion." Because "it is their custom to admit even the young boys, who are related to the chiefs, to these assemblies, they become early acquainted with all the affairs of the state; and thus the contents of their documents are transmitted to posterity, and cannot easily be forgotten."[116]

In 1857 Granville John Penn referred to this passage in Loskiel in an address to the HSP upon the presentation of a "document" that had passed down through his family. Penn understood the so-called Penn Wampum Belt to have been given to his great-grandfather on the occasion of the Great Treaty in 1682. "That such is the case there can exist no doubt," he maintained, "as (though it has come down to us without any documentary evidence) it plainly tells its own story." Penn observed that the belt's width, of eighteen rows, was a clear indication that it signified "some very important negotiation." The central figures "of an Indian grasping with the hand of friendship the hand of a man evidently intended to be represented in the European costume, wearing a hat . . . can only be interpreted as having reference to the treaty of peace and friendship which was then concluded between William Penn and the Indians, and recorded by them in their own simple but descriptive mode of expressing their meaning, by the employment of hieroglyphics." Penn also invoked "the fact of its having been preserved in the family of the Founder from that period to the present time." He compared it to another family heirloom, the medal presented by Parliament to Admiral Penn, the First Proprietor's father, which "descended amongst the family archives unaccompanied by any written document but is recorded on the journals of the House of Commons." Therefore, "equal authenticity may be claimed for the Wampum Belt confirmatory of the Treaty made by his son with the Indians; which event is recorded on the page of history, though, like the older relic, it has been unaccompanied in its descent by any document in writing."[117] Thus the Wampum Belt may have been a "document," but it was not quite a self-authenticating one, bearing an "endorsement"—a descriptive label on its back—such as referred to by Heckewelder.

The HSP officers received the belt with enthusiasm. Charles Miner, first vice president, although prevented by "extreme age" from attending the presentation, wrote to say that the "emblem of acknowledged justice—pledge of assured peace—is worthy of special regard. If sufficient of the old Treaty Elm remains, a casket for it should be carved for its safe keeping."[118] Henry Gilpin, the vice president and a trustee, composed the reply to Penn, thanking him "for now placing among our archives the most valuable record that exists of the most interesting incident in the early story of Pennsylvania." Citing Voltaire—"'not sworn to and never broken'" he proclaimed the Great Treaty "the beacon-spot in the history of Pennsylvania."[119] Never abrogated nor formally revoked through the return of the belt, the treaty was, instead, a contract that had become obsolete; the Indian parties to the agreement were gone, and Pennsylvania had progressed into a different age. Gilpin gratefully received the belt "on behalf of the people of Pennsylvania, to whom it so appropriately belongs; not, indeed, as the pledge of a compact they can now be called on to fulfil [sic], but as evidence and symbol of the Christian spirit in which their institutions were laid at the first, and of

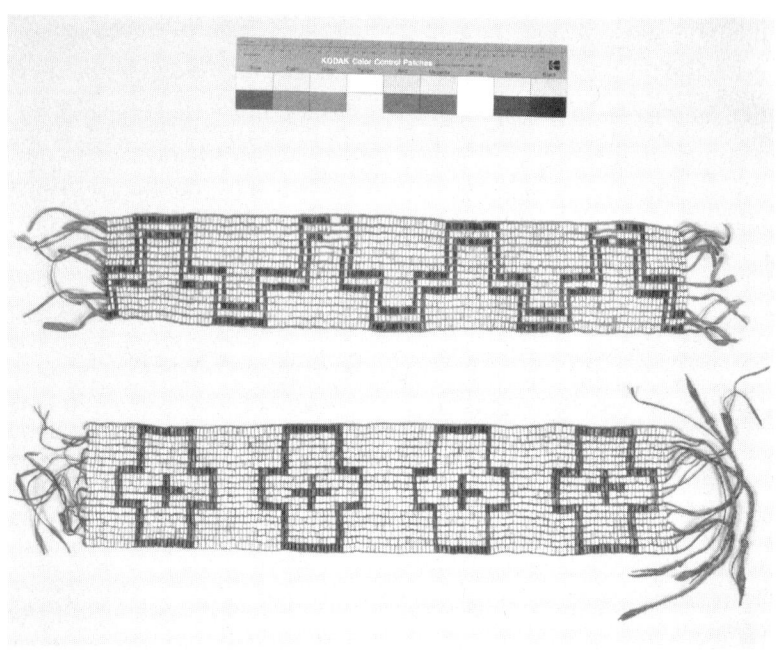

8. Lenape wampum belts at the National Museum of the American Indian, Smithsonian Institution (record numbers 5/3150 and 5/3151).

the enduring obligations of benevolence and justice which they have inherited with them."[120]

The Penn family had two other wampum belts. Granville John Penn may not have been aware of them, or he may not have wanted to diminish the magnanimity of his donation by revealing that he was withholding two related artifacts. In 1887 they became the property of J. Merrick Head when he bought the Penn estate, and in July 1916 they were auctioned by Christie's of London. They sold for $430 and $350, respectively, prices that were lower than those fetched by some Penn family paintings and books but more than the $100 obtained for a lock of William Penn's hair.[121] The notice of the sale brought the belts to the attention of the Museum of the American Indian, Heye Foundation, which soon purchased them and brought them to New York.[122]

In 1925 the anthropologist Frank Speck undertook the study of the three "Penn Wampum Belts." Speck accepted that the belts came from the same source but considered them "memorials undocumented in history." They were relics "torn" from their "ceremonial setting," with "no documentary grounds" upon which to reliably link them to "any known event" and therefore no possibility of correlating them with speeches recorded in the colonial annals that would restore to them their specific significance. The best Speck could hope to do was to gain insight by exhibiting them to people who were familiar with the symbolic conventions of diplomatic wampum, and he found a surviving bastion of such expertise among the Six Nations in Ontario, who "have retained in their possession a number of wampum belts, and have laudably kept alive the tradition of their decipherment in the inner recesses of their esoteric life."[123]

Speck exhibited photographs of the Heye belts and a print of the HSP belt (the "Treaty Belt") to his informants, the Onondoga chief David Sky and the Cayuga chief Seneca Hill. He took their "depositions" separately so that they might independently corroborate one another's statements. They both agreed that the white background of the belts "represented 'parchment,'" that is, the belts were conceived as equivalents or counterparts to written contracts. The first belt Speck labeled the "Freedom" belt because of Chief Sky's interpretation of the lines as signifying the "freedom of the Indian" to traverse the land they had released. Chief Hill interpreted the same lines as "'paths in territories which had been sold.'" Speck found these essentially compatible interpretations to be plausible, because the "privilege of free passage" often became a sticking point in colonial land sales.[124] It is surprising, though, that he did not then go back to compare these readings to the colonial archives. Markham's "Memorandum" concerning the first purchase of land from the Delawares, on July 15, 1782, lists an article of agreement "[t]hat we may freely pass through any of their lands, as well that which is not purchased as that which is, without molestation as they do quietly amongst us."[125] One of the nine items Governor Patrick Gordon listed in 1728 in a renewal of the "strong League and Chain of Friendship" with the Delaware, Conestoga and Shawnee Indians who had joined with William Penn "when he first brought his People with him over the broad sea" was "[t]hat all Paths should be open and free to both *Christians* and *Indians*."[126] Thus there were plausible rhetorical occasions for the presentation of the "Freedom Belt."

The paths on the Freedom Belt may have been metaphorical as well as literal, representing the diplomatic channels that must be kept free from obstructions in order to ensure continuing amity. The Pennsylvania archives present several occasions at which one or more of the Penn Treaty belts might have been exchanged: they might have referred to an earlier treaty without having been presented at it. Thus at a conference on July 6, 1694, Tamanend told Penn's representative, William Markham, "Wee have had a continued friendship with all the Christians & old Inhabitants of this river, since I was a young man, & are desirous to Continue the same as long as wee live," and he gave him a "belt of Wampum." Then he continued: "Wee and the Christians of this river Have allwayes had a free rode way to one another, & tho' sometimes a tree has fallen across the rode yet wee have still removed it again & kept the path clean, and wee design to Continue the old friendship that has been between us and you," and he gave another "Belt of Wampum."[127] In 1715, at a council held in Philadelphia with "Chiefs of Delaware & Schuylkil Indians," Sassoonan gave Deputy Governor Charles Gookin three belts, each attending an expression of hope for present and future amity, including: "that they and wee [the English] should Joyn hand in hand so firmly that nothing, even ye greatest tree, should be able to divide them a sunder."[128] This rhetorical occasion, with the reference to joining hands, would have been suitable, certainly, for the presentation of the Treaty Belt.[129]

As for the second of the Penn Wampum Belts, Speck felt that his informants' "reserve" in offering speculations as to the significance of the "cruciform figures" lent credibility to whatever comments they did offer on the three belts. Chief Hill did "offer his opinion that the four enclosures represented territories to which the belt had reference."[130]

The idea that the belt attended the transfer of four territories is consistent with Anthony Wallace's research on Delaware land tenure and social structure; he argues that the multiple Delaware sachems listed as parties to land sales in deeds were actually transferring their individual ownership rights to adjacent territories. Thus, for example, the belt could have been handed to William Penn on June 23 or July 14, 1683, both days on which Penn received deeds conveying land from four different sachems.[131]

Regarding the Treaty Belt, the chiefs gave differing interpretations of the three "oblique bars"—one thought they were "'stamps' or 'seals' of validity," and the other thought they designated different territories. They concurred, however, in supporting the seemingly self-evident significance of the pair of figures clasping hands as indicating a pact of friendship between Europeans and Indians. They also concurred in an interpretation that stands in "absolute contradiction" to the understanding of the belt by white "readers," at least from Granville John Penn onward: the chiefs stated independently that the "projection of two dark beads" on the head of the man on the left was not representative of a European's hat but an Indian's "'feather.'" The disparity in size between the two figures was indicative of a power differential: "at the time the belt was made the Indian would have been the stronger, and the white man the recipient of his hospitality and protection."[132]

"One is strongly inclined," wrote Speck, "after giving the conflicting opinions due consideration, to regard the latter interpretation as being more valid."[133] The idea that the man on the left is an Indian is certainly in keeping with a "Facing East" revision of our Eurocentric readings of colonial relations, perhaps even literally—in the array of figures from left to right. Why would an early Native American representation of the Treaty of Amity represent the same paternalistic understanding of the agreement that has passed down through the Anglo-American oral tradition? The revised understanding suggested by Speck's informants is more consistent with Indian memories of a time when, as the Ojibwa Peau de Chat said in an 1848 speech, "the red man had the power to crush, [but] he had the humanity to save and protect the white man, who became his brother."[134] It seems plausible that each party understood the alliance differently, and construed itself as taking the superior part.[135] Instead of "William Penn's Treaty with the Indians," then, the Delawares might have thought of the pact as the "Lenapes' Treaty with Miquon."[136]

A recent study of historical memory from a distant context illustrates how the Delawares and colonists may have had different understandings not only of the terms of their initial relationship but also of their respective adherence to those terms, their faithfulness to mutual promises. Pennsylvania has a close parallel in New Zealand, where the 1840 Treaty of Waitangi, "conceived as a partnership between indigenous peoples and Europeans," is popularly viewed as "the foundation of the nation's sovereignty and its key historical event." Yet a team of researchers led by the social psychologist James H. Liu found that Maoris and Pakehas (European descendants) have discrepant views of both the probity of the framers of the treaty and the parts played by the different ethnicities in honoring the treaty. Maoris generally attributed "more fairmindedness and less malice" to the Maori framers and felt their ancestors had "honoured the Treaty better than the Pakeha." The Pakeha attitudes depended in part on their level of education. College students agreed with the Maoris, although they attributed less differential to the two parties in their adherence to the treaty, while Pakehas in the general population rated the two parties' original intentions and subsequent observance of the treaty about equal.[137]

Pennsylvania is similar to New Zealand, and unique among the United States in its celebration of a treaty with native peoples as a founding moment. Yet the natives apparently remembered the treaty as a pact entered into on good faith by both sides but upheld only by one. In *The Traditions of the Delawares* (1845) Chief Waubuno, or John Wampum, explained that, when his "great grandfather was chief of the Delaware Tribe," they were "the first to welcome William Penn on shore. The two made a treaty . . . still unbroken on the Indians side."[138] Similarly, each time Heckewelder, or his informants, mentions William Penn, it is to evoke the contrast with more recent times. In his characteristic first-person plural ethnographic voice, Heckewelder's Delawares recount that "Great and good Miquon came and brought us words of peace and good will. We believed his words, and his memory is still held in veneration among us. But it was not long before our joy was turned to sorrow." The "strangers" who succeeded Penn "no longer spoke to us of sitting down by the side of each other as brothers of one family, they forgot that friendship which their great man had established with us, and was to last to the end of time." Their complaint alludes specifically to the Walking Purchase—"they now only strove to get all our land from us by fraud or by force"—and to the 1742 treaty meeting at which the Onondaga ("Mengwe") spokesman Canassatego ceremonially took the remaining Delawares "by the hair of our heads" and evicted them from the Forks territory.[139] In 1978 Bessie Snake, speaking in Lenape, looked back at Penn's "words" with bitterness. She recalled the Great Treaty as the precedent to the hide trick. "This one when he was first here, he wanted to fool us, our elder brother. They said, 'We will treat you good for as long as the creek flows and our uncle, the sun, moves and as long as the grass grows every spring, for that long I will take care of you people and I will be friends with you people,' he said. He just wanted to fool us, and it seems that he is still fooling us."[140]

The Delawares within Pennsylvania's civic myth sanctioned the beginning of an exceptionally virtuous and just society, but contemporary Delawares could hardly be expected to look back through the prism of removal, massacre, and land fraud and to confirm this memory. According to James Rementer, the night before she was to speak at a William Penn Day event, the Lenape elder Nora Thompson Dean (1907–1984) "stayed awake many hours trying to decide whether to tell what she had been told or to tell the audience what they would want to hear." The next day, she spoke to the celebrants: "'I have been asked to come here today and tell what my Delaware people thought about William Penn,'" she said. "'My people thought he was a scoundrel.'"

There was a "pregnant pause," according to Rementer, during which "the man dressed as Penn left the room, and perhaps did not hear her add, 'but we found out in more recent times that he was not the one who tricked us but it was some of his heirs.'"[141]

As far back as 1825, when the civic myth was still taking shape, one of its primary proponents seemed to realize that the claim of "unbroken faith" was exaggerated. For Roberts Vaux, the "compact was not more distinguished for its justice and generosity, than for the fidelity with which it was observed by the contracting parties, and their descendants, for upwards of half a century after its ratification." A half century from 1682 or 1683 would only bring us into the 1730s; Vaux was too diligent a historian not to recognize that the date of his address to the HSP—September 19—was the eighty-eighth anniversary of the Walking Purchase.[142] Unlike the Great Treaty, the Walking Purchase was precisely datable, with ample contemporary documentation. Nevertheless, the intense controversy that surrounded it was a contest over records—not over whether and when or where it had taken place, but over authenticity, interpretation, and access. It was a colonial diplomatic and political controversy, rather than a postcolonial historical one, so there was a great deal more at stake for the participants.

4

Writings and Deeds

Like the controversy over the *Walam Olum*, the one over the 1737 Walking Purchase involves a disputed "copy" of a supposedly missing original.¹ Like the trick with the bullock's hide attributed to the Dutch by native traditions, the Walking Purchase involves an optimization of folkloric proportions. Its foil, at least for some mnemonic communities, has been the Great Treaty, as celebrated for its fairness as the Walking Purchase is "infamous" for its fraudulence.

When Delawares from Ohio and Western Pennsylvania and other erstwhile allies of Pennsylvania attacked frontier settlements in 1755, the Quakers in the Pennsylvania Assembly stood accused of having left the backwoods vulnerable and exposed through their refusal to appropriate defense funding.² In 1756 the Delaware leader Teedyuscung cited the Walking Purchase as a cause for their hostility, blaming the Proprietors for practicing fraud and the Six Nations for abetting them. These charges "would rock the provincial and imperial world for several years," according to James Merrell, "as they have engaged the scholarly world since."³

In the fraught political context of the French and Indian War, the Walking Purchase became the subject of an intense diplomatic dispute involving the rival Quaker and Proprietary political factions, different contingents of Delawares, and Iroquois. The principal questions at issue were: Had the Proprietors committed fraud? If not, were the Delawares, and especially their spokesman Teedyuscung, sincere plaintiffs, or were they puppets of the Proprietors' Quaker political opponents? This political controversy, which was officially decided in favor of the Proprietors, generated overlapping, conflicting archives. These have been the source material for historians, who have continued to dispute the initial questions.

Their conclusions may have been determined, at least in part, by which archives they consulted. As might be expected, scholars who hearkened to the "countermemory," represented by the Quaker archives and local popular traditions, have been more inclined to inculpate the Proprietors than those who depended on "official proprietary records that distance the Penns and their agents from blame."[4] Yet revisionist historians may have exaggerated the prevalence of the interpretation they were overturning. Even Francis Parkman, whose triumphal seven-volume epic *France and England in North America* (1865–1892) was credited by Francis Jennings as the negative inspiration for his almost equally monumental revisionist history, had sided with the Indians on this one.[5] Parkman bases his account in *The Conspiracy of Pontiac* on Charles Thomson's compilation of the Quaker case against the Proprietors, *Enquiry into the Causes of Alienation of the Delaware and Shawanese Indians from the British Interest*. Parkman provides a fascinating footnote in which he refers to a copy of the Thomson's pamphlet that had belonged to the Proprietary ally and former Pennsylvania governor James Hamilton, noting that while Hamilton in his margin comments "cavils at several unimportant points of the relation, he suffers the essential matter to pass unchallenged."[6]

The scholars Jennings describes as the "Penns' apologists" would include Julian C. Boyd, who introduced that magnificent compendium of official records, *Indian Treaties Printed by Benjamin Franklin* (1938), by dissenting from the "generally accepted conclusion" that the Walking Purchase was a fraud, and William Hunter, who complained that "in accounts of the 'Walking Purchase' passing moral judgment often takes precedence over ascertainment of facts."[7] They saw themselves as being

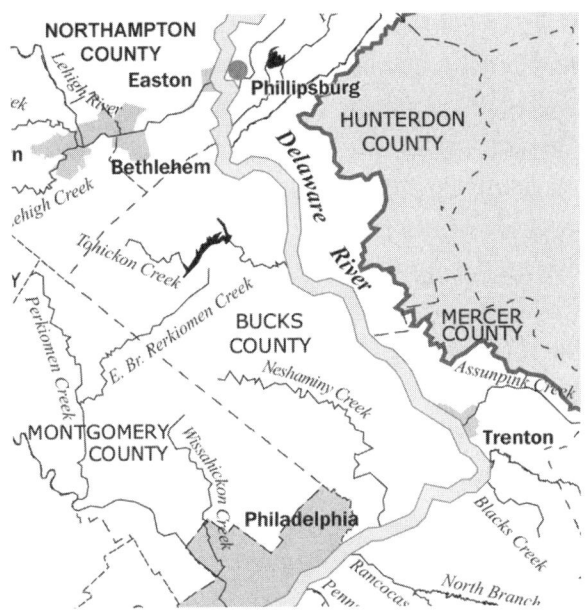

2. Detail of Pennsylvania from a modern map, showing the Lehigh River and Tohickon and Neshaminy Creeks. Source: Delaware River Basin Commission.

in the minority. Today there is effectively only one scholar who challenges the understanding that the Proprietors cheated the Delawares of their territory above and below the "Forks" where the Lehigh River meets the Delaware River. The anthropologist Marshall Becker maintains that the Forks Indians themselves were "squatters" from New Jersey pressing a "specious, if not fraudulent claim" to a previously uninhabited "buffer zone."[8] With the exception of Becker, the Walking Purchase is now "universally reckoned" as the "archetypical Indian land fraud."[9] In contemporary academic and popular discussions, it is nearly always labeled the "infamous" Walking Purchase.[10]

The Walking Purchase may be "archetypical," but it is not necessarily typical. With its "flagrant scale" and its multigenerational controversy, it had few counterparts among colonial land grabs.[11] Its distinguishing feature was that it was a contest not simply over the terms of the agreement but especially over the interpretation of those terms: the meaning of the phrase "as far as a man can goe in a day and a half." The "Indian Walk" was an interpretation through implementation, a historical instance of the folkloric "crafty bargain," and it became an epitome of colonial bad faith.[12] Thus its particular infamy.

Instead of attempting to reopen the case against the Proprietors, and to decide it yet again in favor of the Delaware plaintiffs, this chapter subjects the colonial controversy itself to a different sort of analysis. The Walking Purchase archive, as a whole, is unique for the insights it affords on the conflicting perspectives of the grantees and grantors in colonial land transactions. It is even more remarkable for its theoretical and practical preoccupation with records: the respective validities of the English way and the "Indian way" of recording land transactions, and the problems of how to interpret records from the past, how to gain or control access to the written record, and how to record the dispute over records for future generations.[13] As much as the Walking Purchase controversy was over the rightful ownership of the "very ground" beneath the disputants' feet, it was over communication and memory.[14]

This chapter is organized according to phases in the Walking Purchase controversy, their key figures, and corresponding issues. The first section is on the years from 1735, when provincial secretary James Logan and Thomas Penn presented the Delaware sachem Nutimus with a dubious record of an 1686 land transaction, to 1742, when Logan orchestrated the eviction of Nutimus's band by representatives of the Six Nations from territory the Proprietors had claimed through the Walking Purchase. The contest between Logan and Nutimus instantiates an age-old philosophical dispute over the value of writing as a medium of memory. The second section is on the political and diplomatic controversy during the French and Indian War, beginning with Teedyuscung's allegation of fraud in 1756 and ending with his retraction in 1762. In records of the controversy, the questions as to what had happened in 1735 and 1737 are superseded by challenges to Teedyuscung's sincerity and authority, as well as doubts about the reliability of the records themselves; at the same time, they attest to Teedyuscung's struggle to access documents pertaining to the Walking Purchase and to participate in the production of the records of his own words. Finally, a 2004 lawsuit revisited the Walking Purchase from the distance of two and a half centuries. Its central figure was the eighteenth-century Delaware interpreter Moses Tatamy, who had achieved a measure of success in negotiating the English system of record-keeping and property ownership.

This chapter organization is artificial because, for example, most of the representations of what took place during the 1730s were generated in the 1750s. What Jennings presents as a "straightforward readable account of events"—which he created by sifting through, collating, and cross-referencing the "deeds and documents" of the Walking Purchase, is as much a constructed narrative as any of the competing ones.[15] There is no point where it is possible to separate event from representation, or past from memory, or to establish a simple two-step sequence. A deed of sale is a prescription for an event and also an attempt to condition the memory of that event for future generations; the so-called confirmation deed of 1737 contained within it the (possibly apocryphal) text of the anterior deed from 1686. The negotiations in the 1730s were simultaneously interpretations of the relations and transactions from the previous generation and an establishment of terms for the next. The issues at controversy are subjective matters: intentions, motives, understandings, good or bad faith. Such issues are necessarily determined through interpretation—in this case, through the interpretation of an archive containing competing treaty minutes, reports, depositions, affidavits, maps, letters, the occasional "remonstrance," and even some poetry: "O change the rash sentence, and listen, ye youth, / Their Hell is on Earth, who are Strangers to Truth."[16] The case of the Walking Purchase can help exemplify the precept, more often acknowledged than observed, that objective truth in history is an impossible ideal.[17]

NUTIMUS-LOGAN DEBATE, 1735–42
The "Ancient Deed"

James Logan's career in public office spanned the proprietorships of William Penn and his sons; he was arguably "the most important and most influential public figure in the Proprietary province of Pennsylvania during the first half of the eighteenth century," an "under-secretary for all affairs."[18] He was also the leading intellectual of his day in Pennsylvania and perhaps in British America: an arrogant "mighty Schollard," the "foremost scientist," whose book collection became "the greatest single intellectual monument to colonial America that has survived."[19] The scholarship on Logan has tended to observe a strict separation between these spheres of activity: the real world of practical engagements and the disinterested realm of the Republic of Letters. For example, Edwin Wolf II, introducing the annotated catalog of the magnificent Loganian Library, delimited a safe zone of intellectual inquiry: "His career as appointed and elected official, judge, agent of the Penn family, land speculator, trader and negotiator with the Indians and merchant does not concern us here."[20]

This kind of exclusion is an irresistible challenge to a reader of Edward Said's *Culture and Imperialism*; surely it is not a simple coincidence that the "Quaker Imperialist" was also early Pennsylvania's most prominent exponent of the Enlightenment. Yet it is not easy to draw connections. For example, Logan's books, with his marginalia, much of it in Latin, provide few discernable tie-ins to his worldly affairs. It is especially surprising that this Lockean philosopher, so interested in the nature of man, should evince so little intellectual interest in Locke's Americans.[21] While Logan's "mind range[d] the whole of the universe," as a scholar he apparently overlooked the Indians who were often literally camped in his yard.[22] Nevertheless, the most notorious incident in Logan's administration of Indian affairs can be productively approached through the domain of philosophy—as a conflict over memory and meaning.

"There is a turbulent fellow one Nootamis from Jersey," Logan explained to the Indian agent Conrad Weiser. "This man while he lived in Jersey pretended that a Relation of his on this side of Delaware left him his lands by will & accordingly he came over & claimed a great Quantity of Land to wch the other had no right & made himself very troublesome."[23] Although he was not giving Weiser the entire picture, he did seem to feel that this "vile" band of Delawares was without legitimate property rights to the Forks region.[24] Yet the land was practically worthless to speculators while there were Indian claims on it, and as Jennings and others have pointed out, the Penns' excessive debt gave them a pressing need to sell land. The Walking Purchase was a scheme to extinguish the Forks Indians' claims without compensation.

Thomas Penn, Logan, and other Proprietary representatives put this scheme into action at a 1735 meeting with Nutimus, Lappawinzoe, and other Delawares in Pennsbury. The minutes of this meeting are missing, somewhat suspiciously, but there are several references to it in subsequent treaty minutes, as well as opposing retroactive accounts in the form of depositions taken during the midcentury political controversy from the Proprietary ally William Allen and the Delaware interpreter Moses Tatamy. Penn and Logan showed the Indians a document that they claimed constituted proof that William Penn had purchased a tract above the first documented Penn land purchase in 1682: an "Antient Copy" of a supposedly lost original deed from 1686.[25] They produced aged witnesses who claimed to recall seeing Delaware grantees sign the deed and receive merchandise in payment. According to the agreement, the southern boundary of the tract, Neshaminy Creek, was fixed by the 1682 purchase; the eastern boundary was the Delaware River, and the western boundary was set by the reach of Neshaminy. The northward extent was indefinite: the tract "doth extend itself back into the Woods as far as a Man can goe in one Day and a half."[26] Unbeknownst to the Indians, the Proprietors' men had already conducted a "trial-walk," enduring "extraordinary fatigue and hazard," to determine "how far that day and half Traveling will reach up the Country."[27] It carried all the way to "the mountain"—the Kittatinny or Blue Mountain ridge—well beyond the Forks. Thus Logan and Penn had in mind an optimization of the day and a half's walk: the most advantageous route, the maximum pace, and the fullest exploitation of the window of time.

As Richard Peters and Benjamin Chew, acting as lawyers for Penn's sons, later explained, it "occasioned the Proprietaries much trouble to prove the Reality of this [1686] purchase, and the Truth of a Copy of that Deed produced . . . in support of their Right to the Lands in Controversy."[28] In 1762 William Johnson became convinced of the legitimacy of the 1686 deed by "sundry Extracts from ancient Letters mentioning at that time a Treaty to be on foot for purchasing Lands above the Forks of Delaware from the Indians," and by other written evidence, including "an acct. of goods paid," apparently in exchange for the land.[29] He found especially persuasive an affidavit by then Chief Justice William Allen, who recalled that at the 1735 treaty meeting at Pennsbury his predecessor James Logan brought forward aged witnesses—"Joseph Wood (who was an Anabaptist Minister) and William Biles Esquire"—who had attended the treaty conference in 1686 and "saw the purchase fairly made."[30]

The Allen deposition is a complex variant of a typical hybrid form—the documented oral history. Specifically, it is a documented memory of a memory of a document. Wood and Biles were typical purveyors of oral history. At ages seventy-five and sixty-four, respectively, they were senior Bucks County community members—both former justices of the peace—living links to a previous era.[31] According to minutes from 1737, Wood had signed the 1686 deed as a witness, while Biles had been merely "present"—presumably alongside his father, also named William Biles—"and remembers well all that then passed."[32] In his deposition, Allen also invoked the overheard testimony of a Delaware contemporary of Wood and Biles. During a break from the proceedings, he had taken a stroll "on the Banks of the River Delaware," where he witnessed "an ancient inhabitant of the said Province" approach Tischucunck, an elderly Delaware, and, "after taking him by the Hand," declare that "he was present in the year 1686, when the said Purchase of the said Lands was made of the Delawares, and saw part of the Goods delivered to them, and the said elderly Man, further addressing himself to Tischucunck, said 'I saw you there present.' On which the said Tischucunck laughingly acknowledged it to be true, but said 'tho' I am satisfied about it, there are others who are not but desire further Time to consider about it.'"[33]

Johnson and the Proprietors effectively conflated the questions of whether negotiations had taken place in 1686 and whether the copy of "antient deed" was valid. "Does the remembering that there was a Treaty prove the Execution of a Deed at that Treaty?" Thomson later demanded.[34] The Indians did not deny that there had been a treaty meeting. Indeed, according to Moses Tatamy's recorded testimony from 1756, there had actually been a walk in 1686; the transaction had been called off when the Proprietary party insisted on crossing Tohickon Creek, which the Delawares insisted was the boundary of the tract.[35] The supposed "copy" of the deed, however, was a mere "paper," according to Jennings, that may have been at best "a preliminary draft of a deed": in "an English court . . . [n]o judge would have looked at this paper a second time."[36]

The "Indian Way"

In a 1736 letter to Weiser, Logan described the presentation of "a Deed with witnesses yet living" (he elided the point that the original was supposedly lost) as a master stroke that left "Nootamis & his associates . . . baffled and greatly disappointed."[37] Yet Tatamy offers a different perspective on their encounter, according to which Nutimus answered Logan point for point. Logan demanded to know "how he came to have any Right on this Side the River as he was born in the Jerseys." Nutimus explained that his mother came from the west side of the river, "& besides the Indians did not consider the River as any Boundary for those of the same Nations lived on both Sides of it.—As Nutimus thought this a trifling Question, he in banter asked him how he came to have a Right here as he was not born in this Country? There was a good deal more said to the same Purpose."[38]

This response can also be addressed to Marshall Becker's argument that the "Forks of Delaware was largely an uninhabited buffer area" until about 1730, when the Jersey Indians migrated there. Becker claims that Teedyuscung's "allegations appear to have become the basis for the myth that the 'Walking Purchase' was a land fraud perpetrated by the colonials, when the reverse is more nearly the case."[39] Yet there is considerable evidence of fraud on the part of the Proprietors, while the only basis on which to impugn the "basic honesty" of Nutimus and his cohort is that they had migrated to the Forks from east of the river.[40] It is unclear why, in response to colonial encroachments and the westward departure of the Susquehannocks, the Delawares might not legitimately redesignate what had formerly been a "shared resource area" for settlement, nor why Nutimus's claim to a matrilineal inheritance of the territory should be discounted.[41] Becker, concurring with Logan's position, applies Western conceptions of boundaries (the river) and property ownership to his evaluation of the Forks Indians' property claims. According to Tatamy, Nutimus had inherited the land between Tohickon Creek and the Lehigh River from his maternal grandfather, Tishhexkam (Tashiowycam); when he had "come over, his Grandfather being dead," the area "from Tohicon and all between the Forks was full of Indians." Nutimus explained to Logan that Penn's 1686 negotiations had been with "Unami Indians," who "never claimed a Right to any Land" above Tohickon Creek, an area that "belonged to the Unalimi or up River Indians of which he was Chief."[42]

When Logan "ask'd Nutimus how he came to know what the Bargain was or how much Land was sold as he was very young at the time & the Indians had no Writings," Nutimus responded with an explanation of the "Indian Way" of communicating and recording land transactions:

> Nutimus said, he had it from his Fathers. Besides from the Indian Way of selling Land he could not but know. For the Indians who posses'd Lands had it bounded by Rivers, Creeks & Mountains & when they sold, the Chief always with the Leave of the others undertook to sell & when he had agreed he called together the Heads of the Families who had any Right in the Land sold, & divided

among them the Goods he got for the Land, telling them for what they receiv'd those Goods. Then the heads of the Families again divide their Portion among the young People of their Families & inform them of the Sales & thus every individual, who have any Right must be fully acquainted with the matter.[43]

Nutimus further explained how the grantor also gives "a Share of the Goods" to the "Chiefs of the Neighboring Tribes" so that "no Land can be sold without all the Indians round being made acquainted with the matter."[44] His entire account of gift distribution is anticipated by William Penn's ethnographic description in his "Letter to the Free Society of Traders"; however, Penn did not recognize that the economic transaction—"Wealth circulates like the blood"—was also a communicative one.[45] The systemic allotment of goods disseminated and preserved information by extending the context rather than removing the information from it. By contrast, Nutimus and Tatamy saw the English use of writing as treacherous, because it allowed the text of the agreement to be removed from its original context and given a new one: "and this we think a way to have it better known than you take, for when you have got a Writing from us you lock it up in your Chest & nobody knows what you have bought or what you paid for it."[46]

Such decontextualization was hardly what Penn envisioned for the role of writing in Indian land transactions. Penn, whose Delaware and Iroquois titles (Miquon and Onas) signified pen, or quill, playing on the homophonic significance of his name, considered writing as a neutral space of publication, a safeguard against underhanded dealings. In an early injunction concerning land transactions to the commissioners of West New Jersey, Penn required first that they announce their "intention" to settle an area before proceeding to survey it, and then that they "give the Natives what present they shall agree upon for their good will or consent and take a grant of the same in writing under their hands and seales or some other publick way used in those parts of the world which grant is to be Registered in the publick register allowing alsoe Natives (if they please) a coppie thereof."⁴⁷ The imagined oral communication suffers no hazards—no difficult negotiation of translation and cultural difference. But Penn was sensitive to the temptation to craft and deceit. The safeguard is writing, which is not a treacherous arrogation of the language of an agreement but a publication. Writing is the equivalent of the open air of the "public market" where Penn wished trade with the Indians to be conducted, so that measurements and valuations could be carried out in plain sight and the presence of disinterested third parties would discourage cheating.⁴⁸

Penn's emphasis on the "publick" naively idealizes the potential for linguistic meaning to become communal. The willingness to give the Indians copies of deeds was significant; decades later the officials responded diffidently to Teedyuscung's request to see all writings pertaining to the Walking Purchase. However, in Penn's case it was more a gesture indicating candor than an actual sharing of information. It was consistent with his instructions to his commissioners in Pennsylvania to announce to the Indians, as a hallmark of the colonial regime change, the new policy of justness: "Let my letter and conditions with my purchasers about just dealing with them be read in their tongue, that they may see we have their good in our eye, equal with our own interest."⁴⁹ Penn's "model of linguistic communication," to use Jurgen Habermas's rubric, depends on the validity claim of "rightness": if the Indians allow this claim then there is no reason to look for fine print.⁵⁰ But the illusion of Penn's ideal of publication is that language can stand between communicants as an independent object, like the scale in the marketplace. Penn also, naively, ignores the hazards of translation. In practice, the Indians had little means to intervene in the interpretation of the written deeds, which was a process controlled by the English "interpretive communities," or interpretive cliques, that had created them or inherited them.⁵¹

In taking a more skeptical view of writing, and asserting the supremacy of oral communication and local knowledge, Nutimus was unwittingly taking a position in a longstanding debate in Western philosophy about the value of writing as medium of record. Versions of the dispute between Nutimus and Logan had also taken place, repeatedly, in medieval Europe, as the use of written records became increasingly prevalent but the development of conventions of authentication and authority lagged.[52] The opposition between memory and written records was also a topic of classical philosophy; Nutimus's position was Platonic. In Plato's *Phaedrus*, Socrates declares that "once a thing is put in writing, it rolls about all over the place." Writing is a mnemonic device masquerading as a complete communication, nothing more than "a reminder to a man, already conversant with the subject, of the material with which the writing is concerned." Once the writing is detached from such knowledge, it becomes treacherous. One cannot ask "written words" for an "explanation": "they go on telling you the same thing, over and over forever."[53] What the 1686 "copy" kept on saying was "as far as a Man can goe in one day and a half."[54] It did not explain what sort of "man," or the trajectory of the journey, or what was meant by "go," or the angle at which a line was to be surveyed from the endpoint of the journey back to the Delaware River.

Another word that the agreement dated 1686 kept repeating was "hereby." More than a simple statement, the text was worded, as a contract, to perform an action: it was a "speech act." In principle, "written utterances," despite the apparent oxymoron, are classifiable as speech acts.[55] However, the application of speech-act theory to writing has been tentative and controversial, owing to the Platonic notion, articulated by J. L. Austin in *How to Do Things with Words*, that "written utterances are not tethered to their origin in the way spoken ones are."[56] In a famous critique, Jacques Derrida argued that no utterances are "tethered" to anything at all, and therefore all utterances, in his sense, are "writing." His ensuing debate with Austin's disciple John Searle hinged on the distinction between "iterability" and "permanence." The former was Derrida's term for the fundamental property of all "texts," insofar as they consist of conventional "marks" (whether phonic or graphic) to be instantiated in context after context, with no such context ever being wholly definable. The latter was Searle's term for the capacity of writing to subsist as a verbatim record of utterances. Each philosopher accused the other of confusing "iterability" with "permanence."[57]

If Nutimus may have been an accidental Platonist, Logan was hardly a Derridean. Instead, avowedly, he was Lockean. Yet the belief that the relation between words and things was arbitrary and conventional was hardly his negotiating position with Nutimus and the Forks sachems; his position, rather, was that the supposed 1686 deed, and by extension written records in general, was comprehensive, authoritative, and self-evident. Logan was deeply invested in the domain of letters and the authority of writing. His view, consistent with the conception of writing as the key component of civilization, was that human memory was "short and weak"; writing enabled the accumulation rather than alienation of knowledge. It helped set Europeans above the rest of humanity, and helped set him in particular "above thousands of others who are a no less noble part of the bodily Creation yet are unhappily strangers to the great Ends of it."[58] The erudite Logan might have assumed that he had the upper hand once his debate with Nutimus shifted to epistemology: from *what* had taken place in the 1680s to *how* Nutimus could possibly know.

Yet Logan did not secure the Forks Indians' confirmation by persuading them of the validity of their ostensible written record, but rather through a manipulation of power and a blatant misrepresentation. Upon learning, in 1736, that Nutimus intended to appeal to the Six Nations (Iroquois) to intervene on his behalf, Logan preempted him.[59] He instructed Weiser to carry a wampum belt to the Six Nations, calling them "honest, wise, discreet & understanding men," in contrast to the "weak & too often knavish Delawares (such as Civility—Pesquetomen—Nootamis & the like)," and to ask them to sign a deed releasing their claim to all lands "as far Eastwd as Delaware." He pointed out that they lost nothing in so doing: they only "release & quit all their claims there & as they make none, it is in reality nothing & yet may prevent disputes hereafter."[60]

Weiser, with apparent hesitation, did as he was instructed. "They have signed the large deed after they had it in consideration from morning to night," Weiser reported to Logan. "It went very hard about signing over their Right upon Delaware because they said they had nothing to do there about the Land & they were afraid they should do anything amiss to their Cousins the Delaware."[61] The Iroquois were reluctant because the deed was the equivalent of a false promise; their release was an inappropriate speech act because it did not have the condition of a preexisting ownership. Accepting Logan's belt of wampum, therefore, was acceding to a specious premise. In 1756 the Six Nations spokesmen told Weiser that they had "intended nothing by this Release" or by their eviction of the Delawares from the Forks in 1742; these acts were "simply an acknowledgement that they were convinced we [the Proprietors] had fairly bought them from the Indians."[62] The release served Logan's purpose of giving the Delawares no recourse in challenging the authority of the supposed 1686 deed.

An "Equivocal Project"

Jennings has likened the Proprietary agents' other stratagem, which they implemented at the August 1737 negotiations at which Nutimus and the others placed their marks on the confirmation deed, to a "carnival swindler's shell game."[63] The Penn family legal counsel Andrew Hamilton drew up a map that represented the intention of the grantors topographically and encoded the intention of the grantees in writing. The map represents the Delaware River and two tributaries: the southerly one is labeled "Neshaminy," the creek that framed the southern and western boundary of the tract. The northern tributary, near the top of the map, appears to be the Tohickon, but it is labeled "West Branch of River Delaware," another name for the Lehigh River, some twenty miles to the north. The map would have given the Delawares the false impression that the land to be walked was the land they had already conceded, below the Tohickon, and that the Forks of Delaware, where the Lehigh meets the Delaware at present-day Easton, was not even on the table.[64]

The map did not lie. Even contemporary maps of the Delaware watershed, depending on their level of detail, do not necessarily include

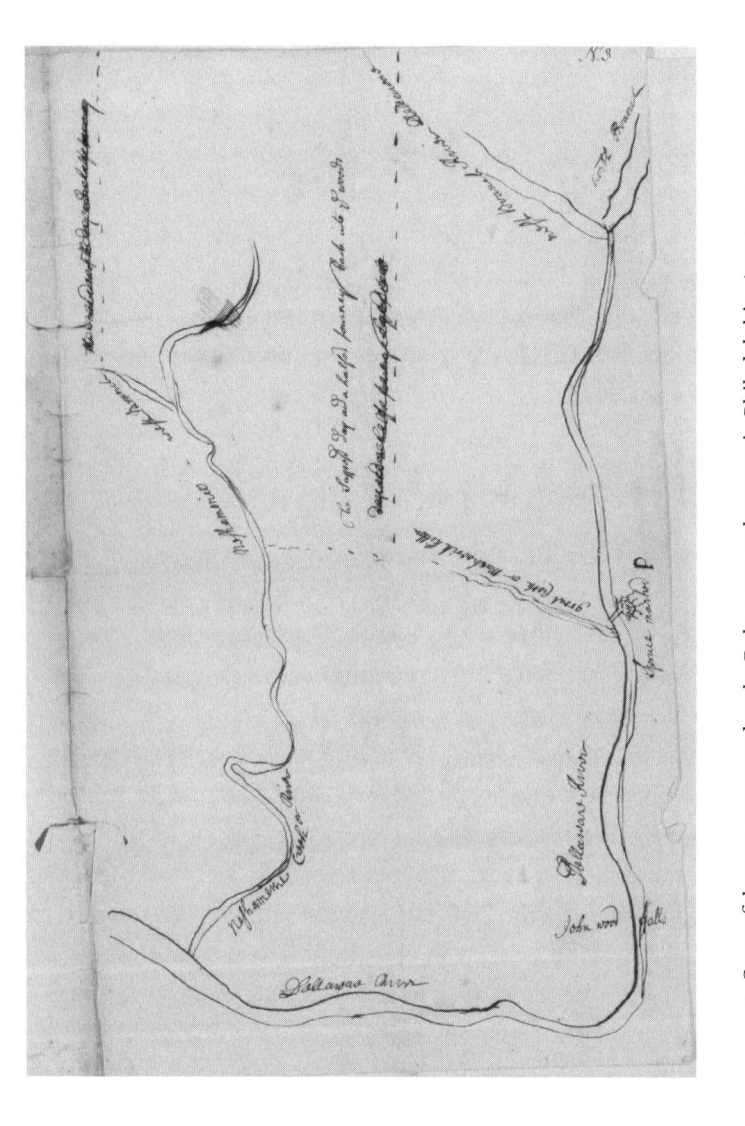

9. Copy of the map presented to the Delawares at the treaty in Philadelphia, August 24, 1737. Benjamin Chew Family Papers [2050], Box 42, Folder 4. Courtesy of the Historical Society of Pennsylvania.

Tohickon Creek. Thus the map enacted a graphic version of a type of deceit that was more commonly carried out through language. Equivocation, according to the *Oxford English Dictionary*, is "the use of words or expressions that are susceptible of a double signification, with a view to mislead; especially the expression of a virtual falsehood in the form of a proposition which (in order to satisfy one's conscience) is verbally true." Equivocation was explicitly forbidden by Quakerism: "When thou art obliged to speak," William Penn wrote in *Some Fruits of Solitude*, "be sure to speak the Truth: For Equivocation is *half way* to Lying; as Lying, the *whole way* to Hell."[65] But equivocation and other varieties of linguistic formalism were widely attributed to Quakers after Penn's generation.[66]

Benjamin Franklin provides an excellent illustration of this practice in his *Autobiography*. He observes that during his service as a clerk in the Pennsylvania Assembly, the Quaker assemblymen, in order to avoid explicit violation of their pacifist principles, employed a variety of "modes of disguising the compliance" with requests for defense appropriations. On one occasion, they appropriated money "for the purchasing of bread, flour, wheat, or *other grain*," which the governor understood to indicate "gunpowder." Franklin later applied these lessons in wordplay, joking with his friend Mr. Syng about motioning for the purchase of a "fire-engine" and then buying "'a great gun, which is certainly a *fire-engine*.' 'I see,' says [Syng], 'you have improv'd by being so long in the Assembly; your equivocal project would be just a match for their wheat or *other grain*.'"[67]

Equivocation depends on a language ideology that prioritizes the letter of an agreement over commonsense or communal understandings. In Franklin's assembly anecdotes, both parties understand the rules of the game and are complicit in the deception. Yet how did this game function when the contestants spoke different languages and represented disparate cultures? For example, in the original publication of Franklin's manuscript, in French translation, Louis Guillaume Le Veillard apparently struggled to convey the double meaning of "fire-engine": *machine a feu*, an expression sometimes used to signify a steam engine, may suggest a "cannon" but not a device for extinguishing fires. Double meanings do not usually carry from one language to another (which is one reason for the difficulty in translating jokes). Moreover, there are more subtle forms of equivocation than the one described by Franklin, and these are also challenging to translators. The practice I have in mind is parsing words, or choosing within a range of meaning. The difficulty is that supposedly equivalent terms do not have homologous ranges or linguistic values.

Ferdinand de Saussure exemplifies this principle in his *Course on General Linguistics* with his well-known example of the English word "mutton" and the French "mouton." Washington Irving gives a more pertinent example in his adaptation of the Delaware story of the founding of New Amsterdam with the bullock's hide, with his contrast between the Dutch and Indian notions of "nether garments."[68] If the Delaware hide story is read as an allegory for the Walking Purchase, the hide can be seen as a metaphor for the text of the agreement, especially the word "walk." It can be stretched to the limit; so long as it remains intact, or the strips are contiguous, the agreement is binding. Just as the Dutch colonists carefully laid out the thong, the agents of the Pennsylvania Proprietors punctiliously observed the time limit and the ostensible limitations of the word "walk." As with the grantors, the Forks Indians "had not understood it was to be done that way."[69]

If we think of the hide story as a tale about language and language ideologies, then it sounds a principle theme in Delaware oral traditions. Like Logan, Nutimus would have had culturally specific ideas about how language works. Although, unlike Logan, he left behind no "intellectual monument," these ideologies of language might be reflected in recorded Delaware oral traditions.[70] The Delaware Deborah Nichols, in the preface to a 1995 edition of the Delaware Richard C. Adams's *Legends of the Delaware Indians and Picture Writing* (1905), explains her fascination with the book by referring to the "lessons" imparted by the stories: "care in your choice of words to say what you really mean; the importance of keeping a promise; the importance of not abusing the powers you are given; and the importance of being grateful for what you are given."[71]

Implicitly, all these lessons reflect poorly on the colonists, whose words were often at variance with their intentions, and who repeatedly broke promises, abused powers, and showed outrageous ingratitude for the Indians' generosity. However, most of the stories Adams collected do not directly address colonization, and it is difficult to ascertain the degree to which the ideologies of language expressed by them were reactions to it.

Of particular relevance are the tales about the culture hero Wehixamukes. These have a complex bearing on the idea of equivocation and the distinction between literal and intended meaning. This theme occurs in other Native American traditions, but according to John Bierhorst, only "among the Lenape does it form an extended cycle."[72] Wehixamukes consistently misunderstands instructions, but his misunderstandings are literally correct, and the fault lies with the instructors. Told by his companions to mix meal when he comes to a watering hole, he mixes the meal in the hole; told during a bear hunt to look for a tree with a hole in it, he stops at a tree with a hole that is obviously too small to contain a bear; told to find a turkey to dip in the bear grease, he neglects to kill and roast the turkey before dipping it. Despite his apparent obtuseness, Wehixamukes does have magical powers: after he reveals his war party's hiding place to their enemies as a result of another failed instruction, his chief tells him to go kill the enemies by himself. The verb the chief uses, however, has the literal meaning of "throwing down," so he does just that, picking up the enemy warriors one after another and throwing them to the ground.[73]

The Wehixamukes stories are about the dangers of taking words out of an explanatory communal context. His refrain, "You should have told me so!" corresponds to the Delaware grantors' objection that "'You did not say, "I want to cut it up!"'" But while in the hide stories the grantors suffer the consequences of the grantees' deliberate ambiguity, Wehixamukes is immune to the sometimes fatal (to others) consequences of his own misunderstandings. The responsibility is on the person making the request to be clear, specific, to "talk plainly." Adams explains that the stories are "often related to the Delaware Indian children to show to little boys that they should be as careful in their selection and use of their words as they are in the selection of their arrows to shoot at a mark, for very often as much mischief is done by the wrong impression being conveyed by a sentence as there is in an arrow going astray when you most desire it to strike the mark." The hide stories, then, are about colonists who misfire purposefully, and precisely.[74]

To use another metaphor, the 1737 confirmation deed, containing the language of the supposed 1686 copy, was a verbal (and nonverbal) trap, ready to be sprung. The 1737 deed was written in the first-person plural, stating that "We, the said Monockyhickan, Lappawinzoe, Tisheekunk and Nutimus, Do, for ourselves and all other the Delaware Indians, fully, clearly, and Absolutely Remise, Release, and forever Quit claim unto the said John Penn, Thomas Penn, and Richard Penn, All our Right Title, Interest, and pretensions whatsoever of, in, or to the said Tract or Tracts of Land." The grantors agreed "that the extent of the said Tract or Tracts of Land shall be forthwith Walked, Travelled, or gone over by proper Persons to be appointed for that Purpose, According to the direction of the aforesaid Deed."[75] As noted, the wording of the "aforesaid" 1686 deed, embedded in the 1737 one, does not specify a direction: the geographic framing has the tract extend vaguely northward, "back into the Woods as far as a Man can goe in one Day and a half." Each of the key terms was specifically equivocal.

In the eighteenth century "go" connoted both locomotion at a moderate pace on foot and its modern sense of locomotion by any means.[76] *Travel* had a similar range of meaning. Even *walk*, which became the central term in the dispute, has a significant range of linguistic values, within technical limitations. The apparent rules for the Indian Walk resembled those of the modern sport of race walking, in which the competitors are disqualified if both feet leave the ground—that is, if they break into a run.[77] The translation of *walk* into Delaware, too, may have been an opportunity for an advantageous exchange. Who knows what equivalent of the English word *walk* the Delawares agreed to? The incommensurability of linguistic values across languages is amply attested to by the Moravian David Zeisberger's *Indian Dictionary*, which lists words in English, German, Onondaga, and Delaware, in four uneven columns. There are Delaware entries for "to walk" (*pómsi*), "he walks fast" (*kschoochweu*), and "to go" (*aan*); he does not list a Delaware word corresponding to "to run."⁷⁸ James Rementer, director of the Lenape Language Preservation Project for the Delaware Tribe of Indians, explains that Lenape can use compound forms to specify meaning: "he walked a certain distance" (*sakuxwe*); "he walks a long way" (*ohëlëmuxwe*); "he walks fast" (*kshuxwe*—a variant of the same word as in Zeisberger).⁷⁹ Zeisberger's colleague Heckewelder consistently argued for the copiousness and comprehensiveness of the Delaware language, which expresses "ideas, shades of ideas, and combinations of ideas"—thus, for example, the Forks Indians may have agreed to a meandering walk, exclusive of a fast walk.⁸⁰

Similarly, the two parties may have attached different values to the "day and a half's walk." According to another Moravian missionary, George Henry Loskiel, the "distance from one place to another they [the Delawares] never mark by miles, but by days journies, each comprehending about fifteen or twenty miles. These they divide into half or quarter day's journies, and mark them upon their maps will all possible accuracy. When they send parties to war or to hunt, they can describe the road, and inform them pretty exactly concerning the time required to perform the journey."⁸¹ Loskiel's use of the *journey*—which appears in the Walking Purchase agreement in the phrase "to the utmost extent of the said one day and a half's Journey"—retains the now archaic sense of "the distance usually traveled in a day," which was "usually estimated in the Middle Ages at 20 miles."⁸² Since there was precedent for using or adapting Delaware conventions of distance measurement in Pennsylvania land transfers, in 1737 the Delawares might have felt they were agreeing to a mutually understood, conventional, and determinate, if approximate, measure of distance—one day and a half's walk—which the colonists, taking the agreement out of context, could reinterpret as indeterminate—limited only by the semantic capacity of the language and the physical limitations of the walkers.

The most equivocal term of all, finally, is a blank space. The 1686 copy has treacherous lacunae that are reproduced in the 1737 deed, which fails to specify either the precise direction of the walk or the angle of the line to be surveyed from the end of the walk back to the eastern boundary of the tract, the Delaware River.[83] "Blanks were left in two of the most material Places," Thomson complained of the supposed copy, "which it cannot well be imagined a true Deed could have, or that the *Indians* would ever knowingly have executed."[84] The document that Logan walked away with on August 24, 1737, like any blank check, had the most important component in place: the signatory marks of "Manawkyhickon," "Lappawinzoe," "Teeshacomin," and "Nootamis."[85] Otherwise, the empty spaces and signifiers remained to be filled in.

The Indian Walk

In carrying out their measurements the following month, the Proprietary agents both exploited and abided by the letter of the agreement. The deposition and other reports from witnesses and participants suggest that during the Indian Walk, the sheriff Timothy Smith acted in the dual capacity (with the inherent conflict of interest) of coach and referee for the race walkers, especially since so much of the walk was conducted out of sight of the Indian observers. Smith himself testified that he relayed instructions from Thomas Penn to Solomon Jennings, James Yeates, and Edward Marshall, men who were selected for their athleticism, that "they should not overwalk themselves as he was not too anxious or covetous of so much Land . . . as that it would occasion [their] hurting themselves, but that they should walk moderately and not over hurry themselves . . . And that accordingly the said Walkers did keep constantly to a Walk and never during the said one and a half Days, whilst they were performing the same, broke into a Run or beyond the speed of a Walk."[86] (This statement appears to be a post hoc disclaimer, since the walkers did indeed overexert themselves. Smith also, reputedly, conveyed the Proprietors' incentive of five hundred acres of land to the man who walked the farthest.[87]) Another deponent testified that James Yeates did at one point run for "Five or Six steps" to catch up with the others, but one of the Delaware observers "cry'd out it was not fair"; Yeates "never went out of a walk for the rest of the way." However, Timothy Smith's nephew, who assisted him at the event, remembered the Indian observers complaining "you Run, that's not fair, you was to Walk."[88]

An 1757 examination of Edward Marshall, conducted before Governor William Denny, is especially revealing of the efforts of the Proprietors to optimize their gains without exceeding the technical limitations of the day and a half's walk. Marshall affirmed that the walk was precisely measured at eighteen hours, and that he "did not run or go out of a Walk from the Beginning to the End thereof."[89] Because the date was close to the autumnal equinox, there were almost precisely twelve hours between sunrise and sunset. On the first day, they began at 6:00 a.m. and stopped at 6:15 p.m., to compensate for the fifteen minutes spent taking lunch. (That night, the party camped outside a Delaware town, where they heard revelers staging a "cantico"; they may have been observing a harvest ceremony at the time of the equinox.[90]) On the second day, with their start delayed for two hours because the escorts' horses had strayed during the night, Marshall stopped at 2:00 p.m. instead of noon. Yet although the walk may have been technically correct, from the English perspective the pace seems to have been quite strenuous. Solomon Jennings "fell out" after only a few hours, and the Delaware observers left after the first half-day. On the second day, James Yeates collapsed while crossing a creek, and he soon died. At the "extremest point," according to Davis's *History of Bucks County*, "Marshall, who alone held out, threw himself at length on the ground, and grasped a sapling which marked the end of the line."[91]

According to Marshall, the Indians objected to the pace of the walk, and to the trajectory. He recalled that emissaries from his camp went in the morning to the nearby Indian town (presumably during the delay while others were tracking down the horses) and brought back the response from the sachem Lappawinzoe (a signatory to the 1737 confirmation deed) that "they (meaning the said Walkers) had got all the best of the Land and they might go to the Devil for the bad, and that he would send no Indians with them or to that effect."[92] Marshall reported that afterward he frequently heard Lappawinzoe say "that the said Walkers did not go the Course agreed upon between them the Indians and the Proprietors, for that they should have walked along by the River Delaware or the next Indian Path to it," and that "the Walkers should have walked for a few Miles, smoked a Pipe and now and then have shot a Squirrel and not have kept upon the Run, Run all day or to that effect."[93] At that speed (Tatamy referred to it as the "running walk," which perhaps corresponded to a single Lenape compound term) and trajectory, the walk carried well past the point where the Delaware River sweeps northeasterly.[94] Taking advantage of the other key omission in the deed, the Proprietors measured a line at a right angle from the endpoint of the walk back to the river, taking in a huge additional territory belonging to the Munsees.

The Proprietors certainly did not expect their formal adherence to the letter of the agreement to mollify the Indians, but it did provide them with a legal basis to deny wrongdoing a generation later. Thus in a 1757 letter, John Watson, the son of the Bucks County surveyor who had worked for James Logan in the 1720s, discouraged his friend Israel Pemberton, the leader of the Friendly Association for Regaining and Preserving Peace with the Indians by Pacific Means, from pursuing the case against the Proprietors. Watson "with all the Attention and Impartiality in [his] Power considered the Words of the Grant" and determined that "the Method fallen upon by the Proprietaries for ascertaining the Limits of the Grant as far as it has been carried into Execution is nearly agreeable to the Words and true Meaning of the Deed." Watson allowed that the Indian observers' inability to keep pace with the walkers might suggest that they did not anticipate the measurement would cover so much distance, but he pointed out that "in Favour to the Indians, the proprietaries have confin'd the Word go in the Grant to Walking and

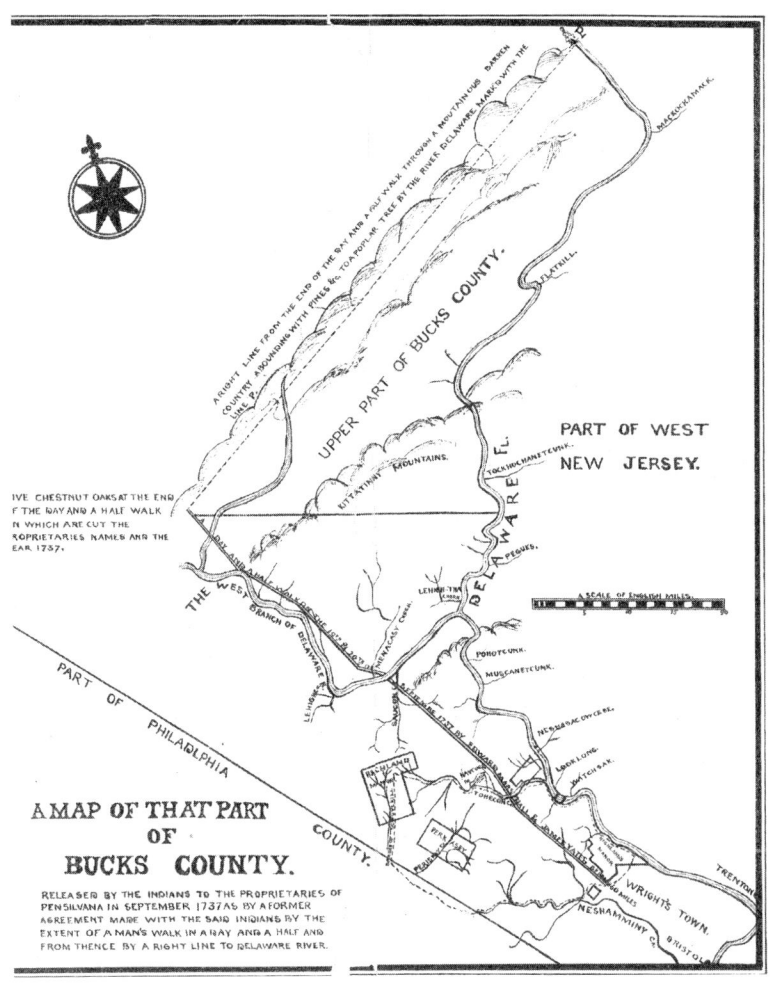

10. Map of the Walking Purchase, 1737. Source: William W. H. Davis, *History of Bucks County Pennsylvania from the Discovery of the Delaware to the Present Time*, 1:486–87.

instead of the longest Days in Sumer accepted of 18 Hours for a Day and a halfs Journey." Watson urged Pemberton to desist, "since to offer any Thing in Favour of the Indians that may be honestly refuted can do 'em little Service."[95]

However, Watson kept looking through his father's papers, and he changed his mind. He forwarded Pemberton a copy of 1727 instruction from James Logan concerning a warrant for a tract "3 or 4 Miles above Durham," which lies south of the Forks. Logan had instructed Watson's father to speak with Jeremiah Langhorne, a major landowner in Bucks County who was then on the Pennsylvania Supreme Court, "for if he has no considerable objection to it, I cannot see that we should make any other, than that it is not purchased of the Indians, which is so material an One, that without their previous Engagemt, to part with it very reasonably it cannot be Survey'd there." This document apparently persuaded Watson that Logan had known full well, in 1735, that the "Antient Deed" had not pertained to lands above the Tohickon. Although he did not want to have his name involved in the dispute, he offered to procure for Pemberton the "original" of the 1727 letter from his father's executor, if it "should be thought of any use in the Cause of Justice."[96]

Since there was no case to be made that the Walking Purchase had overreached the written agreement, the Delawares and their advocates faced the much more difficult task of establishing that the written record misrepresented the intention of the grantors. "We cannot think it necessary to make many remarks on the Extravagance of the Walk & the manner of performing it," objected a report from a committee of Quaker assemblymen in 1762. "However, we must observe that 55 Statute miles (Supposing the proprietary Account thereof to be true) never could be what the Indians in those early Times meant & understoode by a Day & an half's Journey on foot through a very mountainous Country over Creeks, Swamps, & every other Impediment to be met with in a Wilderness." Referring to the modest bounds of a deed from 1718, they claimed the tract "will be judged not too small for a Day & a half's Journey on foot in the Indian sense, if not in the sense of the other party."[97]

"We know of no other Rule for the Construction of Deeds and ascertaining the true Intention of the Grantors," the Proprietary commissioners Benjamin Chew and Richard Peters retorted, "than by takeing the natural meaning of the Words and Expressions thereof: If the Committee do, we must bow down to them and acknowledge their superior Gifts and Talents."[98] This "rule" of interpretation is an explicit statement of language ideology. It involves two related precepts. The first is that the written record of the agreement is sufficient unto itself; that an understanding of the "intention of the grantors" may be understood solely on the basis of what literary critics would call internal evidence—the wording of the deed. The second, especially disingenuous point is that words do—contrary to Locke—have "natural meaning," seemingly self-evident and not contingent on context. Peters and Chew were apparently oblivious to the contradiction posed by their use of verbal irony: they had about as much intention of bowing down to the Quakers as of eating their hats. Their rule seems willfully obtuse to the circumstances in which the deed was supposedly produced as a statement of intention. Among the words Peters and Chew propose the readers accept at face value is "we." The Proprietors wanted the first-person plural voice of the deed to be understood as something more than a legal conceit through which words written in English were attributed to Indians who did not know English and did not write.

There is truth to both sides in the philosophical debate over whether writing is benevolent or harmful, protective or treacherous. Its effects depend largely on its uses, and on relations of power. Writing is simultaneously stable and volatile: volatile *because* of its stability. Put positively, it is "autonomous" from context; put negatively, it is alienable.[99] There is truth also to Derrida's assertion that all linguistic utterances, which consist only of material "marks" or "traces," are always already alienated. Yet writing nevertheless entails a different sort of materiality than speech, one that makes it possible to bring words from one contingent context and, perhaps cynically, to apply them to another, distorting the intention of the author(s) through the very act of preserving their words verbatim. "Permanence" and "iterability" are complementary, rather than interchangeable or opposing concepts; the one renders the other more treacherous.

Of course, a definitive context is neither finite nor fixed; it can never be exhaustively described. It could never ensure successful communication. Yet it could enhance "interpretive confidence" when the communicants were acting in good faith, as William Penn and his Indian interlocutors legendarily were, and it could complicate the aims of communicants who were acting in bad faith.[100] The context for the 1686 negotiations would presumably have included the representatives of William Penn and the Delaware sachems "Mayhkeericckkishsho, Sayhoppy, and Taughhaughsey," together with an understanding about which groups they represented and where they lived; the physical position of the negotiators in relation to the cardinal points and the topographic features—mountains, rivers—which could be indicated by deictic gestures; and "oral agreements and tacit understandings."[101] The earlier negotiators may have known, as Tatamy claimed, that the walk was to follow the course of the river rather than a line drawn by compass; that the walk was to be at a middling pace; that the line drawn from the endpoint of the walk was to take the shortest distance back to the Delaware River; and even perhaps that the deal had not yet been consummated because a final agreement had not yet been reached. Two generations later all these contextual understandings could be reconstrued, because they were not set down in ink. And everything could not possibly be set down in ink. Thus, in theory, it is the unwritten context that is distorted rather than the writing itself, which is, by its vaunted characteristics, fixed and immutable.

With only the text of the agreement to rely on, the Proprietary representatives could argue that a "day and a half's walk" was open to interpretation, and that one interpretation was as valid as another: a simple matter of opinion. Teedyuscung eventually allowed as much in a formal, written retraction of his accusations: "As to the Walk, the Proprietary-Commissioners insist that it was reasonably performed; but We think otherwise: which Difference of opinion may happen without either of Us being bad men; but it is a matter that Brethren ought not to Differ about."[102] James Hamilton, then governor, agreed, adding, "Whether it was, or was not, is mere matter of Judgement and Opinion, it being an uncertain Thing, at best, how far a Man can, or shou'd go in one Day and an half's Walk."[103]

"By This Belt"

One of the issues in the wave of controversy initiated by Teedyuscung's accusations in 1756 was *when* the Delawares had first complained about the Walking Purchase. The Proprietors wished to prove that their Quaker opponents had incited him to complain about the Walking Purchase, which the Delawares had accepted at the time as a fair transaction; they collected testimony from an Indian trader who "had never heard mention of "any Wrong or Injury from the Proprietors of Pensilvania."[104] The Quakers in turn wished to demonstrate that the Proprietors had provoked the Delawares' hostility. They collected testimony from witnesses and participants in the walk, including Bucks County resident Thomas Furniss, who claimed that "the unfairness practiced in the Walk, both in Regard to the way where, and Manner how, it was performed, and the Dissatisfaction of the Indians concerning it were common Subject of Conversation in our Neighbourhood for some considerable Time—After it was Over."[105]

The Quakers present a persuasive case that the Forks Indians complained about the Walking Purchase immediately and often. However, the plaintiffs were unable to register their complaints until 1740, and then they were only partly successful in doing so. As with a modern bureaucracy, there was a protocol, involving forms and proper channels; grumblings and threatening gestures had no standing. Yet the Forks Indians were in a double bind because they were excluded from the discourse community that employed this protocol. "[W]e pray you will take Notice of the great Wrong we receive in our Land," the Forks Indians wrote in 1740 to the Chief Justice Jeremiah Langhorne and "all the magistrates of

Pennsylvania." They found it "very strange" that Thomas Penn should sell "about a hundred Families" land "that never was his to sell, for we never sold him this Land."[106] But Langhorne did not respond.

In a second letter, to Governor Thomas, they expressed increasing frustration, and invoked the articles of the Great Treaty "made between the English and our Fathers, which was, if we are Right informed, to live in brotherly Love together; but not as we live now, for we cannot enjoy our Birth-Right in Peace and Quietness, but we are abused as if we are Enemies, and not Friends, for we dare not speak for our Rights but there is an Uproar, and in Danger of being cut in Pieces and destroyed." Referring to a conflict involving Jacob Sebring, "an honest Man" who spoke up for them, and whom they had freed from the Bucks County sheriff's custody, they exclaimed that "if this Practice must hold, why then we are no more Brothers and Friends, but much more like open Enemies." They implored the governor to "assist us to settle these affairs, so that we altogether live in Peace and in brotherly Love according to our first Articles, which were made by our Forefathers." Although Langhorne did not deign to respond to their previous letter, they hoped that Thomas would, "and although we be Indians, we beg leave to subscribe ourselves, His Excellency's most humble Servants."[107] Eight Indians, including Nutimus, signed with their marks.

The "although we be Indians" phrase seems to have two applications: to the rhetorical profession of servitude to Governor Thomas, and to the oddity of Native Americans subscribing a letter. It was not unusual, however, for the Indians to compose a message in council, and to send it in expectation of acknowledgment and action. The letters paralleled the use of wampum strings and belts in treaty meetings. In his stern reply, however, Thomas suggested it was not so much the medium as the hostile tone of the letter he found incongruous: the letter was "wrote in a Manner very different from any others I have seen from the Indians to this Government, who have shewn themselves to be an honest fair People, ready to perform their Agreements, and have always been treated by us with great Tenderness and Friendship." He preferred to think that "some evil minded white Men have wrote these Letters for you without letting you know the true Contents, which I find upon a strict Examination in Presence of my Council, not to be true."[108]

He proceeded to recount the official history of the Walking Purchase—the 1686 deed, the release by the Five Nations, and the fairness of the walk: "I must acquaint you that it is you on your Part who have acted contrary to that Agreement that was made between William Penn and all the Indians, and, instead of acting like Brothers, have told me a Story which is not true, in order to break that Friendship with the White People." Observing that upon signing the release the Iroquois had urged "our Brethren Onas and James Logan never to buy any Lands of our Cousins the Delawares . . . for they have no Land remaining to them," Thomas invited the Forks Indians to come at their own expense to a meeting with the Six Nations in Philadelphia the following summer, at which the Iroquois would be apprised of their misbehavior. "You may send such as are allow'd to be of the Delaware Nation, because the Jersey or other strange Indians will not be taken any Notice of." He sent them a copy of the 1737 deed, "that all your young People, who never were here may know the Contents of it." In a written reply, the Delawares agreed to put their case before the Six Nations, "& if the Land be sold we will be easy."[109]

Nutimus and the "Delawares from the Forks," as they are listed in the minutes—distinguished from the "Delawares from Shamokin"—do not appear to have had much of a hearing at the famous treaty meetings with the Six Nations in July 1742. The Iroquois spokesman, the Onondaga Canassatego, began by addressing the English, reprising their story of the signing of the 1686 deed and the 1737 confirmation, and explaining that when the Delawares persisted in the Forks, "you requested Us to remove them, enforcing your Request with a String of Wampum." Canassatego's diction suggests that more than a material adjunct to a speech act, the wampum was itself constitutive of that act—like the wedding ring in "with this ring I thee wed." As explicated by Michael K. Foster, wampum did not simply serve mnemonic and archival functions, as it has often been understood. It also filled a "prospective" function, organizing events and eliciting responses.[110] The Indians and perhaps the English saw the wampum as containing the message, and the orator or spokesman as "reading" or enacting that message. And the wampum was productive of action and reciprocity: the acceptance of invitation wampum committed the recipient to coming to a treaty, bearing a string or belt in exchange for the one accepted. Accordingly, Canassatego implicitly acceded to the Proprietors' "request" by accepting the wampum that contained it, and he concluded his opening oration to the English by delivering "this String of Wampum in return for yours."[111]

According to the minutes, Canassatego preceded his pronunciation of banishment with an endorsement of writing, "inforced" by the authority of wampum. "Let this Belt of Wampum serve to chastise you," he told the Delawares. "You ought to be taken by the Hair of the Head and shaked severely, till you recover your Senses and become Sober. You don't know what Ground you stand on, nor what you are doing."[112] As opposed to the complaint by Moses Tatamy that "when you have got a Writing from us you lock it up in your Chest & nobody knows what you have bought or what you paid for it," Canassatego, who himself had occasion to complain of "Pen-and-Ink work," asserted that the truth of writing is self-evident because the medium is visible.[113] "We have seen with our Eyes a Deed sign'd by *Nine* of your Ancestors above *Fifty* Years ago for this very Land," he told the Forks Indians, "and a Release sign'd, not many Years since, by some of yourselves and Chiefs now living, to the Number of *Fifteen* or upwards."[114]

Canassatego's pointing to the Walking Purchase deeds as evidence of the duplicity of the Forks Delawares suggests the limitations of the common analogy between wampum and written contracts. The problem for the Delawares is that the 1737 document did indeed indicate their consent to a deal that they now seemed to be reneging on, but the devil was in the details. Wampum messages were prepared in council and repeated at treaty meetings, which, to the frustration of the European participants, were exhaustive, halting processes of repetition and deliberation.[115] The belts did contain symbolic content, but they could not be *read* in the same sense as European writing. They did not encode hidden or double meanings; there was no fine print. As Birgit Brander Rasmussen describes, the wampum did not stand alone as a static, binding contract; rather, it was the communicative nexus for "an ongoing relationship based on reciprocity and a shared world. Thus wampum did not seal an agreement so much as mark its beginning."[116]

Of course, Canassatego had not seen the 1686 deed, only perhaps the copy, and he could not read the content of the 1737 confirmation—the only legible part would have been the grantors' marks, the signatures on the blank checks. It did not matter; Canassatego was not an interpreter, but an enforcer. It may be true, as Locke wrote, that "no one hath the power to make others have the same ideas in their minds, that he has, when they use the same words that he does," but the Proprietors, using a hired henchman (Governor Thomas had just given Canassatego a present valued between three hundred and five hundred pounds), had the power to force Nutimus and the Forks Indians to abide by their interpretation.[117] They thereby exposed the power dynamics underlying the ascription of meaning in colonial transactions. "You are Women," Canassatego told the Delawares, before banishing them to live at either Wyoming or Shamokin, where they would be under Iroquois supervision. "You may go to either of these Places, and then we shall have you more under our Eye, and shall see how you behave. Don't deliberate; but remove away, and take this Belt of Wampum."[118] Canassatego added another string of wampum "to forbid you, your Children and Grand-Children, to the latest Posterity forever, medling in Land Affairs." He concluded: "For which Purpose, you are to preserve this String, in Memory of what your Uncles have this Day given you in Charge.—We have some other Business to transact with our Brethren, and therefore depart the Council, and consider what has been said to you."[119]

If the Delawares objected, the treaty minutes render them absolutely silent and passive. Decades later, in John Heckewelder's representation, the Delawares still recalled the event with bitterness. In an apparent reference to their 1741 letter to Governor Thomas, they recalled that their attempt "'to remind'" the Pennsylvania officials of the words of William Penn had backfired: "'they became angry, and sent word to our enemies the Mengwe, to meet them at a great council which they were to hold with us at *Laehauwake*, where they should take us by the hair of our heads, and shake us well. The Mengwe came, the council was held, and in the presence of the white men, who did not contradict them, they told us that we were women, and that they had made us such; that we had no right to any land, because it was all theirs, that we must be gone; and that as a great favour they permitted us to go and settle further into the country, at the place which they themselves pointed out at Wyoming."[120]

Among those "white men" who were present to see Nutimus and the Forks Indians insulted and banished was the now aged and debilitated James Logan. According to the minutes, immediately after dispatching the Delawares Canassatego turned to Logan, explaining that they had called upon their "old Friend" at Stenton "in our Way to this City, and to our Grief we found him hid in the Bushes, and retired, thro' Infirmities, from Publick Business." They "prevailed with him to assist once more on our Account at your Councils." Canassatego pronounced Logan "a wise Man, and a fast friend to the *Indians*." Canassatego concluded: "In testimony of our Gratitude for all his Services, and because he was so good as to leave his Country-House, and follow us to Town, and be at the Trouble, in this advanced Age, to attend the Council; we present him with this Bundle of Skins."[121] Logan may not have won the philosophical argument with Nutimus, but he was the victor in the war of words.

TEEDYUSCUNG AND THE FRENCH AND INDIAN WAR

In a treaty meeting in Easton, at the Forks of the Delaware, in 1756, the new governor, William Denny, asked the Delaware spokesman Teedyuscung to explain why the Delawares had sided with the French and attacked the Pennsylvania frontier. According to the minutes of the Provincial Council, Teedyuscung responded:

Brother,

You have not much knowledge of things done in this Country as others who have lived longer in it, being but lately come among us. I have not far to go for an Instance; this very Ground that is under me (striking it with his Foot) was my Land and Inheritance, and is taken from me by fraud. When I say this Ground, I mean all the Land lying between Tohiccon Creek and Wioming, on the River Susquahannah.[122]

This "bombshell" raised a number of questions.[123] Was it true? Had the Proprietors dispossessed the Delawares through fraud? Was it sincere? Had the Delawares harbored a grievance for two decades, waiting for an opportunity to exact vengeance? A preliminary question, however, is a methodological one: What did Teedyuscung actually say? Do the Provincial Council minutes provide a reliable record of his words?

In a thoughtful analysis of the multiple, variant records of "Teedyuscung's 1756 Treaty Council Speeches," Merrell points out that his words are mediated by a "chain of communication"; they pass through interpretation, transcription, and redaction before publication. As an ostensible spokesman, Teedyuscung himself was only a link in the chain, charged with conveying messages composed in tribal councils on the Susquehanna.[124] While the variations among the official and unofficial minutes show that this process necessarily distorted his messages, there is also enough concurrence to support Merrell's conclusion that the minutes do convey "genuine echoes of a long-forgotten native voice and a native sensibility."[125] This conclusion validates the historian's judicious use of treaty minutes as source materials. However, it also suggests the methodological problems facing Indians who participated in colonial-era "literacy events," or interactions involving reading or writing.[126] When they directed their words toward paper, they hoped to accomplish a great deal more than the creation of a distorted reverberation.

In 1756 the political situation provided Teedyuscung with a platform. The Quakers in the Pennsylvania Assembly stood accused of leaving the frontier vulnerable to Indian attacks through their refusal to allocate defense funding. By supporting, if not instigating, Teedyuscung's accusation, they hoped, as one Proprietary ally put it, "to throw the war on the Proprietors & shift it off themselves."[127] The charge of malfeasance was sufficiently serious that the Proprietary party went to considerable trouble to refute it.

The controversy unfolded at a series of treaty meetings in 1757–58, mostly at Easton, administered by the Provincial Council, headed by the governor, and was concluded in 1762 by the superintendent of Indian affairs Sir William Johnson under the aegis of the imperial Board of Trade. Johnson declined to come to Easton in 1757, complaining to Governor Denny that "the Delaware Indians by their Chief Teedyuscung have excepted to, and refused my Mediation" by choosing the Quaker assemblymen "for their Agents and Managers with the Crown."[128] He sent George Croghan as his deputy. Croghan and Johnson, as well as Denny and his successor James Hamilton, resented the Quakers' "meddling" in critical diplomacy.[129] Yet while they were generally able to exclude them from formal treaty meetings, they were unable to prevent the zealous Israel Pemberton and associates of his Friendly Association for Regaining and Preserving Peace with the Indians by Pacific Measures from hanging around and having contact with Teedyuscung and the other Indians.[130] Thus the Proprietors and their allies constantly suspected that the Quakers had intervened at the front end of the "chain of communication," preempting Indian diplomacy by putting words in Teedyuscung's mouth.

For their part, the Quakers and Teedyuscung raised concerns about the good faith of the Provincial Council and Board of Trade officials in construing the records of land transactions to Teedyuscung and in representing Teedyuscung's words in the treaty minutes. Accordingly, whether acting on his own initiative or otherwise, Teedyuscung suggested two innovations in the treaty protocol: the composition of his messages in writing, to be read aloud, so as to guarantee the delivery of his message, and the use of a clerk of his own as a check against the official minutes and a proxy in the examination of documents.

Yet the Proprietary faction attributed any statements from Teedyuscung in writing or about writing (or both) to those "meddling" Quakers. For instance, in July 1757 Croghan forwarded to the governor a letter Teedyuscung had submitted to him, composed in Charles Thomson's hand. The letter requested that they "produce the Writings and Deeds by which you hold the Land, and let them be read in Publick, and examined." Recognizing that the restoration of Walking Purchase lands was impossible, it demanded an inalienable tract at Wyoming, which was designated by an accompanying "draught" or map: "a certain Country fixed for our use & the use of our Children for ever." It expressed a desire for assistance in building English-style homes, and instruction in Christianity and literacy.[131] The governor decided that neither the "paper" nor the "draught" were "in the Indian Form, nor agreeable to their Notions of things"; the letter "must have been dictated by some of the People in Town or by Charles Thompson, who was known to be under the Direction of the Quakers and Commissioners."[132]

Similarly, in 1762 when Teedyuscung handed Johnson a note that contradicted the minutes by claiming that he had not understood the "many Papers *as your Clerk* was four Hours reading, in a Language I do not understand," Johnson was sure that the note could not have come from Teedyuscung's "own heart," and demanded to know "who put it in his head, or who it came from?" Pemberton answered his question by standing up to protest, with what Johnson's clerk Witham Marsh described as "great warmth and Indecency," that Teedyuscung had not pronounced himself satisfied with the presentation of the documents, "and that the Minutes were not fairly taken." Johnson thus "plainly saw thro what Channel Teedyuscung conducted his Business."[133]

The officials' skepticism may be familiar to students of mediated Native American writing, from John Eliot's missionary tracts through John Neihardt's *Black Elk Speaks*: can Indians speak through the writing of white men? Or even through writing of their own? Whether or not it was accurate, the suspicion that an "unprecedented" request for the use of a clerk could not have originated from an Indian was revealing of an stereotyped view of Indian communications: that they were confined to conventional precedent, incapable of innovation or adaptation; "that the Indians have good Memories, and can remember what was transacted twenty years ago, as if Yesterday."[134] In making his stylistic objection to Teedyuscung's "paper," it did not seem to occur to Denny that the colonists themselves did not always remain true to their own "form" and "notions of things": they used wampum, and employed Indian diplomatic rhetoric. But by meeting the Indians on their own terms, they wished to confine the Indians to those terms; they restricted their access to the English modes of communication that contained or superseded the use of wampum and oral negotiations. However compelling the use of wampum may have been in a transaction between Canassatego and Nutimus, in Indian-white negotiations it was rendered at least somewhat superfluous. The message embodied by the wampum, "read" aloud by the Indian spokesman, was reinterpreted by the translator and re-recorded for posterity in the treaty minutes; the agreement that the exchange of wampum signaled was only binding, at least in principle, to the colonists if it was ratified by signatures and marks.[135]

Teedyuscung was avowedly trying to break from precedent. "'Brother,'" Governor Denny told him when he wished to have a written message read aloud, "'you know that this is quite a new Method, and was never practiced before.'" (Denny himself had his speeches drafted in advance, in council). Teedyuscung responded: "'[Y]ou are right, this was not formerly practiced, it never used to be so. Don't you see that I am, by having a Clerk of my own, to exceed my Ancestors by having everything for the best.'" He seemed to think of writing in relation to native systems of mnemotechnics, in which each token or bead of wampum stood for an agenda item: "'I endeavor, according to my Ideas, to look to those that have the authority, for Instance, if they take up a handful of Corn or Pebbles, if they drop any, even one Grain, I will take notice, and will speak of it that they may take it up.'"[136] That is, having a clerk would allow him to make sure the officials did not misplace any grains of information. Teedyuscung excepted himself from the stereotype about Indian memories: "His Memory, he said, was weak, and as he wou'd have things done regularly, he desired he might have a Clerk to take Minutes along with the Governor's Clerk."[137] The Walking Purchase negotiations had taught that memory was "weak" in another sense—because however reliable or accurate, the English would never admit it to challenge the authority of the written word.

Denny acceded to Teedyuscung's request only after he made it an "ultimatum": he told Croghan that "the Governor had but two Choices to make, which was either to allow him a Clerk or not, and that one of his own chusing, else he would immediately set off home and hold no Treaty." Croghan averred that the idea had been "put in his Head by some ill disposed People," meaning the Quakers.[138] Denny, ironically using Indian metaphorical language, complained to Teedyuscung that "you have hearkened to idle Stories or the Singing of Birds." He was further confirmed in this opinion by Teedyuscung's choice of a clerk: Charles Thomson, identified contentiously in the Provincial Council minutes as "the Master of the Publick Quaker School in the City of Philadelphia."[139] When Johnson arrived in Easton in 1762, however, he steadfastly refused this arrangement.

Even as they raised suspicions through their strident advocacy, the Quakers denied that they had initiated Teedyuscung's request. Recorded statements by Moses Tatamy and Teedyuscung affirm an alternative attribution linking the request for a clerk to the experience with Walking Purchase. The Friendly Association recorded Tatamy's statement that *he* had proposed the idea to Teedyuscung and others "before the late disturbance," when they were in Philadelphia for a treaty with Governor Morris and were "complaining among themselves that the English cheated them. I told them in order to prevent that they should get some body to write for them as the English did & then if they kept one Copy and the English another they could never cheat them, for by comparing these Writings which must always agree they would see what was done." Subsequently, before the 1757 meeting in Easton, Tatamy "found the Indians in Council & Teedyuscung taking up a Belt told them that by that he intended to ask the Governor for leave to have a man to write for him.

This, says he, holding up the Belt shall get us a Clerk. All the Indians present approved what he said & there the matter was concluded." According to the statement, Tatamy explained as much to Conrad Weiser, and even offered to accompany him to the governor "and swear that I had heard Teedyuscung say so at Wyoming & heard the Indians there agree upon it & that I never heard the Quakers once mention it."[140]

Similarly, Teedyuscung argued that the request for a clerk was a generation in the making. According to Johnson's minutes, Teedyuscung recounted that James Logan had threatened Nutimus, declaring that he "look'd upon Him as the little Finger of his left Hand; but that He himself was a great, big man; at the same time Stretching out his Arms." Logan then claimed that "'no Body dared to write any thing wrong, for if any one writes any thing out of his own Head, We hang him.'" Teedyuscung commented, apparently suggesting that the Indian raids were a direct consequence of the use of literacy in the Walking Purchase: "Somebody must have wrote wrong, and that makes the Land all bloody."[141]

Teedyuscung also averred that he was carrying forward the complaint about the Walking Purchase directly from Nutimus, and "without the Knowledge or advice of any white man."[142] For Teedyuscung, the Walking Purchase was imposed upon Indians who were compelled to participate in literacy events on the most unequal of terms, without the knowledge or training to fend for themselves and without the presence of advocates or the safeguard of informed and independent observers. Now, in seeking redress for the theft of land, were the Delawares again expected to place their confidence in the reading and writing of colonists who had not proven their goodwill?

Johnson left Teedyuscung no alternative.[143] He refused Teedyuscung a clerk and refused his request to hand over all the records so that he could review them under the advisement of the Quaker commissioners. Instead, he offered him a session in "the Bower" at Easton, where Croghan, the interpreter Andrew Montour, and the secretary Witham Marsh would lay the records before him and interpret and explain them. The following day, Teedyuscung "delivered," in Johnson's words, "a

Easton 24 June 1762

Brother THIS IS all I have TO say to YOU, UNLES YOU will Lett me Have Copies of of the PAPERS, which YOU KNOW is MY RIGHT, AND IF I CAN HAVE THEM, I WILL WITH THE ASSISTANCE OF THE ASSEMBLY MEN WHO ARE NOW HERE GIVE YOU SUCH FURTHER ANSWER AS I MAY THINK PROPER, BUT I DO NOT THINK YOUR WANTING TO DO THINGS IN THE DARK LOOKS WELL.

Petenesgenÿ his mark
Sepasconiky his mark
Ke lupimana his mark
tunycoxcanse his mark
Muckmore his mark
Nepalawhunÿ his mark
Abramahum his mark
Joseph nulmince his mark

11. "Teedyuscung's Speech," June 24, 1762. Penn Manuscripts, Indian Affairs. Courtesy of the Historical Society of Pennsylvania.

most abusive and Scurrilous paper (which at his Desire was publickly read)."[144] The paper recounted the whole series of grievances and complained: "I cannot Trust Croghan and Montour; *and I do not know your Clerk*: So that if you will not let me have Copies of them, and time, *with the help of such men as I know*, to consider them, you cannot give the King a true state of the matter."[145] Johnson stood by his refusals, objecting that the letter calumniated "sworn Officers": "my Deputy Mr. Croghan, and the Interpreter Capt. Henry Montour; at the same time, insinuating a Suspicion of the Secretary for Indian Affairs (whom you are pleas'd to call my Clerk) and that only, *because you did not know Him*."[146]

It may be, as Anthony Wallace writes, that the offending letter was "obviously composed by a white man," but Johnson seemed especially incensed by a paragraph-long addendum in coarse print, signed with the marks of eight Delawares, including Teedyuscung and Nutimus.[147] It accused Johnson of "WANTING TO DO THENGS IN THE DARK."[148] Johnson was obtuse to the new meaning of this conventional metaphorical phrase. "To confute this malicious Aspersion," he declared, "I refer you to my message of the 23d. instant, where no mention is made that a clandestine meeting was desired by me.—I scorn so mean a Thing."[149] Yet Teedyuscung's complaint is a good deal more subtle than Johnson was willing to acknowledge: Johnson's exercise of control over the use of written language was incompatible with a policy of transparency. Yet to concede this point would likewise be to concede the unreliability of transcription, interpretation, and reporting, and the subjectivity and partisanship of the persons who participate in these processes.

According to the minutes, Johnson, however incensed at the "Diminution of the King's Authority," offered Teedyuscung the usual pretext to disavow his statements, suggesting that the offending words may have been put in his mouth without his understanding: "Sir William ask'd Teedyuscung 'if He knew the Contents of the Paper which He deliver'd to Him on Thursday last?'" Teedyuscung offered no excuse; perhaps referring specifically to the addendum, he explained that his "'Cousin wrote it.'" Yet it seems that something had happened largely off the record, if not in the dark; Johnson had brokered a deal that satisfied the Proprietary defendants, placated the Delaware plaintiffs, and left the Quaker assemblymen out in the cold. "'I did not come to have any Difference,'" Teedyuscung continued, "'but to Settle matters upon a good Footing.—I did not come to put my hand into your Purse, or to get Cloathing.—I give up the Land to you, and the white People.'"[150] The disavowal of pecuniary interest is an oblique reference to a monetary settlement; Johnson did indeed recommend that the Proprietors bestow "a Present to supply the wants of your Wives and Children."[151]

The next day, Teedyuscung delivered a paper retracting the charges of "Forgery and Fraud." It is the language of capitulation, toeing the line so completely that its authorship and sincerity are at least as questionable as those of the "papers" that had violated the officials' notions of protocol and decorum. Teedyuscung finally told Johnson and Governor Hamilton, in writing, what they wanted to hear: not only that the allegations were mistaken but that (reversing the position Nutimus had taken in 1735) "the sundry old Writings and Papers" pertaining the 1686 transaction were more authoritative and reliable than the oral "Accounts We had receiv'd from our Ancestors," and that "the Proprietary Commissioners" had been faithful intermediaries between the written word and the illiterate Indians.[152] Johnson was thus able to report to the Lords of Trade that everything had been amicably concluded, and undoubtedly to the Proprietors' delight, he recounted Teedyuscung's admission that "he never should have troubled the Proprietors about these Lands had he not been instigated to do so by the Quakers."[153]

Teedyuscung's questionable apparent retraction of a questionable apparent allegation is a poignantly fitting end to the series of communicative interactions that James Logan and Thomas Penn had initiated in 1735 with their display of the purported copy of the supposed deed from 1686. Nearly every ostensible record needs some sort of qualifier or disclaimer. Here were three generations of representations within the records, doppelgangers in a different dimension, who exerted more force on the Indians' world than the Indians did on theirs. "We,

Mayhkeerickkisho, Sayhoppy, and Taughhaughsey," agree to a day and a half's walk.[154] "We, Teeshakomen, *alias* Tisheekunk, and Nootamis, *alias* Nutimus," confirm that agreement which, illustrating Derrida's principle of iterability, was never the same agreement, only the same words.[155] So long as the colonists held the power, the representations consistently betrayed their namesakes. Nutimus had agreed, perhaps, to the transfer of a narrow parcel bounded by Neshaminy and Tohickon Creeks, his understanding of the original deal, but he soon learned that "Nutimus" had given up a tract extending into the Kittatinny Mountains. In between the accusation by one "Teedyuscung" (the nephew of "Nutimus") and the retraction by another (the "real" Teedyuscung, operating under suspicion of being an imposter himself, an unauthorized spokesman, a tool of the Quakers), seemingly tried to exercise control over his representations through his use of a clerk of his own.

It is tempting to think that the accusation is more credible than the retraction—that in 1756, with the relative suspension of power between the Quakers and the Proprietors, with Denny's apparent naivete and lack of control over the discursive situation, Teedyuscung, whether or not he was instigated by the Quakers, was able to perform a speech act that succeeded at least in initiating a process, one involving a heavy accumulation of records and representations. In any case, a retraction, a speech act whose purpose is to undo another speech act, is rarely wholly effective. It might undo the illocutionary effects—the Proprietors no longer stood accused—but not the collateral effects. The word "fraud," whatever it is that Teedyuscung said, has stuck.

It may be some indication of the sincerity of Teedyuscung's desire to gain access to literacy that after the unsatisfying close to the Walking Purchase hearings, he returned to the Pennsylvania governor, now James Hamilton, and renewed his request for a deed to the land on the Susquehanna and for literacy instruction: "for you know, according to your Custom, you hold all Lands by Deeds, and if our Uncles [the Six Nations] had given us a Deed, our Children would enjoy them after us: If they had given me a Deed, my Children and Grandchildren would live there as long as the World lasts; but as that is not done, I believe I shall leave it."[156] The English wanted Teedyuscung's band to stay within their sphere of influence, and actually to remain as an impediment to unauthorized settlement. In 1762, however, Teedyuscung reported to Governor Hamilton that he had received a wampum belt from Beaver, of the Allegheny Delawares, inviting the Indians at Wyoming to "remove thence and come and live at Allegheny." Teedyuscung wished, however, that he had ratified an agreement of friendship with Beaver in writing, whereupon the governor reminded him that "it was not the Custom for Indians to sign writings to one another." Teedyuscung continued:

> Brother,
> I have one thing more to say and then I shall have finished all I have to say at this time.
>
> Brother,
> You may remember that at the Treaty at Easton we were promised that a Schoolmaster and Ministers should be sent to instruct us in Religion and to teach us to read and write. As none have been yet provided for us, I desire to know what you intend to do in this matter. I have now done.[157]

"TATAMY'S PLACE"

In 2004 the Delaware Nation, based in Anadarko, Oklahoma, sued the Commonwealth of Pennsylvania and forty-five other defendants. Among them were Governor Ed Rendell, the Counties of Bucks and Northampton, the Township of Forks, and the present occupants of a 315-acre tract known as "Tatamy's Place," including a Crayola crayon factory and many private landowners. The complaint alleged that the chain of title to Tatamy's Place had been breached on two occasions: first, through the fraudulent arrogation of the entire region by the Pennsylvania Proprietors through the "'infamous Walking Purchase of 1737,'" and second, through an illegal appropriation of the tract from the descendants of

Moses Tatamy, the Delaware interpreter, by William Allen, in violation of the 1790 Nonintercourse Act, according to which ownership of tribal land can only be transferred through "public treaty" under the authority of the United States.[158]

The 2004 suit, which was generally understood in the media to be a gambit to leverage land for a casino elsewhere in the state, never went to trial.[159] It was successively refused by the District Court for the Eastern District of Pennsylvania and the Third Circuit Court of Appeals, and in November 2006 the Supreme Court of the United States denied the Delaware Nation's petition for a writ of certiorari.[160] All that the *Delaware Nation v. Commonwealth of Pennsylvania* accomplished was to stir up a flurry of news reports. For the current residents of the region, it momentarily reactivated a past that was represented primarily in place names and roadside markers.

The first of these markers illustrates the significance of the Indian Walk as a founding story, a counterpart to Philadelphia's Great Treaty. In 1883 the Bucks County Historical Society placed an inscribed stone at the supposed "Starting Point" of the "Indian Walk" that had opened up upper Bucks and Northampton Counties, and a "fitting monument" was erected three years later on land donated by Martha Chapman near Wrightstown. There had been "considerable controversy" as to which tree had been the "starting point," but the descendants of John Chapman, an early settler, "all unhesitantly declared the starting point was the chestnut tree that stood on the corner where the road from Pennsville joins the Durham road." The tree itself "blew down about 1765."[161]

Research on social memory has emphasized the importance of the "generational unit" and suggests that "communicative memory" does not typically carry "beyond three generations," or a span of about eighty years.[162] But traditional historians attempted to extend beyond this limit by identifying the longest interlocking links in a chain of memory. According to Davis's *History of Bucks County*, some of the Chapman children had been "old enough" in 1737 and "no doubt were present at the starting, and had a distinct recollection of it." Some of these children "lived to an advanced age, and died in the memory of persons recently living." Similarly, to support the Great Treaty tradition Roberts Vaux collected the testimony of the aged Richard Peters, who recalled childhood conversations with the aged Benjamin Lay, who remembered that it had once been common knowledge where the treaty had been held. The interval between the Indian Walk and its memorialization, 146 years, was almost precisely the same as that separating William Penn's arrival in Pennsylvania and the erection of the Penn Society Obelisk, 145 years.

While the 2004 lawsuit may have invigorated the local chain of memory, for the contemporary Delawares it may have accentuated the remoteness of the past. Their "complaint" reached back to the beginning of Pennsylvania Indian relations. It emphasized continuity between present and past, implying that Miquon's twenty-first-century avatar, Governor Ed Rendell, should be held to the terms of the Great Treaty framed by William Penn. But the changes in political regimes acted as a firewall, preventing past accountability from coming forward to the present. District Court Judge James McGirr Kelly ruled that the "sovereign"—the Pennsylvania Proprietors—had "had the power to extinguish aboriginal title." Thus, "however vile Plaintiff chooses to depict the events of the Walking Purchase, Thomas Penn's justness cannot be questioned and the outcome in this matter cannot change." The Walking Purchase was now "nonjusticiable."[163]

As for the second allegation, that there was an illegal breach in the title to Tatamy's Place, it depended on two problematic premises: first, that the tract had been "tribal land" rather than Tatamy's own private property, that he had maintained it in the capacity of "chief"; second, that the absence of a document demonstrating a legal transfer of Tatamy's Place from before 1790 meant that the Tatamy family had been illegally dispossessed at some time between the passage of the Nonintercourse Act and the transfer of the property from the estate of William Allen to Mathias Stretcher in 1803. The case illustrated that the historians' art of fashioning continuous narratives out of discontinuous documentation did not meet legal standards of probability. In principle, the chain of title is seamlessly consecutive, but the gaps in the documented ownership of Tatamy's Place were seemingly too wide to identify a specific breach. In upholding the District Court decision, Judge Jane Roth of the appellate court opined that "the Delaware Nation failed to identify a specific land conveyance that violated the Act or to allege that the gap in the chain of title post-dates the Nonintercourse Act's enactment."[164]

An irony of the case's dependence on Tatamy is that it belies his accomplishment, which was to use the colonial property system, albeit temporarily, to his own advantage, to get an Indian name on a document as an individual grantee rather than a grantor. In 1733, at a time when the Proprietors were looking acquisitively at the Forks, Tatamy applied for a land grant there. "Tattemy an Indian," the application reads, "has improved a piece of Land of about 300 acres on the forks of Delaware. He is known to William Allen & Jeremiah Langhorne. He desires a Grant for the said Land."[165] With the reference to improvement, the application indicates that Tatamy was working within the English, Lockean, system of values, that he had staked an ownership claim through his labor.[166] Being "known" to Allen and Langhorne was a big deal—these were future Pennsylvania supreme court justices. Allen, especially, became a major landowner in the Forks; these men were part of the Proprietary inner circle. The Proprietors may have been interested in cultivating the relationship with the bilingual Tatamy.[167]

The timing of his application indicates that he was aware of the imminent dispossession and displacement of the Forks Indians, which followed a pattern of encroachment he had seen unfold in New Jersey, and wished to secure his "Place." Thomas Penn issued a warrant authorizing a survey of Tatamy's Place pursuant to his application late in 1736; early in April of 1738, about half a year after the Walking Purchase, the Proprietors issued Tatamy—"one of our Indian Friends"—a patent to the tract.[168] In January 1742 "at the Instance and Request of the said Tundy Tetamy," the Proprietors issued another patent, in exchange for the surrender of the first one and the payment of "forty eight pounds, sixteen shillings and five pence lawful money."[169] Apparently, Tatamy wished to consolidate his hold on the tract through fee simple ownership; he may have been reacting to the increasing encroachment on the Forks territory in the wake of the Walking Purchase.

Later that year, after the Six Nations, represented by Canassatego, evicted the remaining Delawares from the Forks, Tatamy, along with Teedyuscung's half-brother Captain John and other Delawares, petitioned for an exemption from the banishment. They pleaded, the Provincial Council minutes report, that they had "embraced the Christian Religion" and wished to be granted land in order to live among the English "in Enjoyment of the same Religion & Laws with them." Governor George Thomas decided to catechize them to determine their "Knowledge of Christianity" and found "they had very little if any at all."[170] But because of his grant from the Proprietors, Tatamy was allowed to stay. Eventually, Tatamy, who served as an interpreter for the missionary David Brainerd, became a bona fide Presbyterian—he was baptized in 1745.[171]

Had the Delaware Nation's suit gone to trial, it might have been prejudiced by some records that were not included among their exhibits. One of these was discovered by the historian James Merrell in the Historical Society of Pennsylvania and is cited in his 1999 book, *Into the American Woods: Negotiators on the Pennsylvania Frontier*. In 1756 or 1757, around the time that the so-called King Teedyuscung was accusing the Proprietors of fraud and instigating an investigation into the Walking Purchase, the colonial secretary Richard Peters wrote to Thomas Penn identifying Tatamy as an informant for Israel Pemberton and referring to him as "the Indian to whom you granted a Tract in the Forks which afterward mortgaged and sold to Mr. Allen." Merrell speculates that Tatamy may have grown "disenchanted" with Europeans and colonial life—especially following the murder of his son, William—and sold his land.[172] Actually, a series of advertisements in the *Pennsylvania Gazette* indicates that Tatamy had lost his land a decade earlier, in 1746: these announce the public sale of "a Plantation, containing 300 Acres, situate in the Forks of Delaware, about 40 Acres clear, with some Buildings, late belonging to Moses Tatamy, taken in Execution."

> To be SOLD,
> BY Way of publick Vendue, on Saturday the 27th Day of this Inst. at one o' Clock, a Plantation, containing 300 Acres, situate in the Forks of Delaware, about 40 Acres clear, with some Buildings, late belonging to Moses Tatamy, taken in Execution. To be sold on the Premises, for ready Money, per
> JOHN HART, Sheriff.

12. Advertisement from the *Pennsylvania Gazette*, November 11, 1746, issue 930, page 3. Courtesy of the Historical Society of Pennsylvania.

Still another document, in the Historical Society, helps to fill in the gaps. In 1769 the Pennsylvania Assembly issued a resolution requesting a grant of two hundred acres to "Nicholas Tatamy an Indian taking into Consideration the Service of his Father an Interpreter, and faithful friend to this Province, and being desirous on account thereof to make some compensation to the Son." The resolution, authored by the Quakers Joseph Fox and James Pemberton, implies that Moses Tatamy had been unfairly or unscrupulously dispossessed: "they also desire that the said Warrant may be formed in such terms, as to vest the Occupation, and use of the said Lands, in the said Nicholas Tatamy, and his Descendants, in such manner and form as to prevent his, or their alienation thereof."[173]

The story these records tell is familiar enough: even Moses Tatamy, a Christian convert, with friends in the Pennsylvania government and legal title to his land, was unable to stave off dispossession. Perhaps an ultimately bitter experience motivated the "sober, honest, conscientious" Tatamy to advise his foil, Teedyuscung, to request a clerk of his own for the treaty councils during the French and Indian War.[174] Perhaps he also prompted Teedyuscung to seek to obtain a deed to lands on the Susquehanna, and to request literacy instruction. Tatamy apparently sent his own children to school in Easton; Matthew Schropp Henry, in the *History of the Lehigh Valley* (1860), reports that "an aged gentleman of Easton, still living there, says he went to school with the two sons of Tatamy, and that he had seen Tatamy's wife often, who was a white woman."[175] The idea that Tatamy had a white wife is intriguing; Tatamy's widow and son are also listed as white in the 1790 census.[176] Henry describes Tatamy as "the last remaining resident Indian south of the Blue Mountains in Northampton County," as if his descendants were not Indians.[177]

Tatamy does not correspond to the last-of-his-race stereotype, but in historical memory he was assimilated to the motif portraying "the tragic but inevitable demise of a doomed people."[178] One late nineteenth-century account, cited at length in Luke Wills Brodhead's *The Delaware Water Gap: Its Legends and Early History* (1870), is obviously derivative of Cooper: it describes "Tatamy Tunda"—Brodhead omits the English name Moses—as remaining behind when "the Mohicans set out on their pilgrimage towards the setting of the sun." It explains that "his affections were so riveted to the land of his nativity that he found it utterly impossible to abandon it. He resolved to remain: 'The last rose of summer, left blooming alone.'" This account suggests that the "proprietaries, or their agents, probably operated upon by a sense of the injustice they had done his tribe, suffered him to occupy a favorite spot on the Lehicton Creek, near the present village of Stockertown. Here he erected his wigwam, and for many years after the departure of his tribe, Tattamy Tundy might be seen stealing along the banks of the Lehicton, or sitting before his wigwam and humming the wild war-songs of his ancestors."[179] Thus, like the contemporary Delawares, the descendants of the colonists preferred to remember Tatamy as an unassimilated Indian "chief." It is probably in this sentimental spirit that residents affixed Tatamy's name to local sites: Tatamy, Pennsylvania, and the Tatamy Gap.

Until the 2004 lawsuit, such memorials were little more than local color. The suit, at least in principle, raised the prospect of the Delawares regaining their land. "'I'd like to see the Indians get their way, but not on my property,'" Paul Reese, who lives on Chief Tatamy Trail, told the *Philadelphia Inquirer*. "'The Indians could come and say that about any piece of land.'"[180] A lawyer representing Forks Township, commending the appeals court decision, agreed: "everybody's land can be traced back to some Indian tribe somewhere at some time."[181]

::::::::::::::: AFTERWORD :::::::::::::::

A Chain of Memory

In 1985 workers restoring the Great Hall on Ellis Island for the Immigration Museum, which is part of the Statue of Liberty National Monument, discovered fragments of three skeletons under a column. While they initially speculated that the remains were a vestige of the island's previous incarnation as an execution ground for criminals, a National Parks Service archeologist determined that the teeth showed a "wear pattern" typical of Native Americans. "Somehow it is very appropriate," the main architect for the restoration project commented to the *New York Times* in 1986, "that the only remains we find on Ellis Island represent the one group that was here before the waves of immigrants that came to make America."[1]

The inventory of human remains eventually included those of at least six individuals: five found on Ellis Island and one found in 1963 on nearby Liberty Island. The remains were associated with shell middens dating from the Middle or Late Woodland periods; Parks Service specialists dated their initial interment to 800 to 1600 AD. The Parks Service recognized that at the time of European colonization the "area around the Statue of Liberty National Monument was occupied by Algonquian-speaking peoples, including the Munsee Delaware peoples," and that "a continuity of material culture through time" indicated "a shared group identity between the Munsee Delaware peoples and the Middle Woodland and Late Woodland period populations of the area."[2] Accordingly, in compliance with the Native American Graves Protection and Repatriation Act, they contacted representatives of the Delaware Nation and the Delaware Tribe of Indians in Oklahoma, and the Stockbridge-Munsee Community of Mohican Indians of Wisconsin.[3]

Today, thanks to Eric Sanderson, a landscape ecologist for the Wildlife Conservation Society, we have a more vivid picture than ever of the world inhabited by the individuals whose remains were found on these islands in what is now New York Harbor. Sanderson used archival materials, including the exceptionally detailed and accurate Revolutionary War–era British Headquarters Map (1782–83), geological data, and innovative computer modeling to create a detailed digital reconstruction of the "original ecology" of Manhattan on the eve of Hudson's arrival in 1609.[4] The Mannahatta Project debuted during the Hudsonian tetracentennial as a book, an exhibit at the Museum of the City of New York, and a website featuring an interactive map with layers depicting Manhattan at various stages in its transition from "a remarkably diverse, natural landscape of hills, valleys, forests, fields, freshwater wetlands, salt marshes, beaches, springs, ponds and streams" to "one of the world's largest and most built-up cities."[5] It thus reproduces New York's civic myth, according to which the city was always already diverse.

Since the tetracentennial, the Mannahatta Project has expanded "to encompass the entire city" as the Welikia Project. Welikia is not really an indigenous toponym. It means "my good home" in Unami. A link on Welikia.org takes one to the Delaware Tribe of Indians' *Lenape Talking Dictionary*, where the late Lucy Blalock, one of the last native Unami speakers, pronounces "Welikia."[6]

On the interactive map of Mannahatta, a user can click on any "block" in Manhattan, including Liberty, Ellis, and Governors Islands, and discover what the area may have looked like upon Hudson's arrival, which plant and animal species would likely have been found there, and how it may have been used by the indigenous population, identified by Sanderson as Lenape.[7]

The map is a good metaphor for a historian's view of the past. It may be a digital reconstruction of a "forgotten landscape," but it has little resemblance to a landscape of memory, which is necessarily constituted through "vague, telescoping reminiscences."[8] When memory, as opposed to the past, is the object of study, one cannot simply peel off layers to arrive at a primeval green. With its generous harbors and its riverways into the interior of the continent, Lenapehoking (the term can only be used anachronistically) had been an important gateway for what Francis Jennings has called the "Invasion of America." Its inhabitants were among the first peoples in the Eastern Woodlands that the colonists dispossessed and displaced. Accordingly, the chain of memory connecting contemporary Delawares in Oklahoma and elsewhere to the individuals whose remains were discovered on Ellis and Liberty Islands is extremely attenuated—yet it is nevertheless discernable.

MEMORY AND NATIVE AMERICAN STUDIES

Owing to its intellectual roots and its impetus from the "memory boom" surrounding the Holocaust and the transitions from totalitarian governments, the field of memory studies has remained largely Europeanist, and predominantly concerned with memories of events that lie, albeit tenuously, within the scope of contemporary oral history, or about eighty years.[9] It has had little intersection with Native American Studies.[10] Yet there is strong relevance between these fields.

After all, Native America has experienced its own "memory boom," culminating, perhaps, with the founding of the National Museum of the American Indian, and beginning with the efflorescence of a literature that makes the transmission of memory—often designated "story"—its key concern.[11] A locus classicus for memory in Native American literature is N. Scott Momaday's *The Way to Rainy Mountain*, a lyrical representation of a landscape of memory that provides an apt if poignant comparison to memories of Lenapehoking. Momaday allows that the "fragmentary"

Kiowa "verbal tradition" ("the voice of my father, the ancestral voice") has "suffered a deterioration in time," and so he supplements it with archival memory ("the voice of historical commentary") and autobiographical memory ("personal reminiscence, my own voice") to compose a tripartite "narrative wheel."[12]

For traditionalists, the idea of the "chain of memory" can be as important as the message it carries. Its integrity facilitates a sense of continuity of group identity, of rootedness in a current locality or connectedness to a remote one; its disruption brings a sense of cultural alienation. The tradition requires faith in the process of word-of-mouth transmission. However, especially at times when what Maurice Halbwachs describes as the "frameworks for social memory"—including language, social institutions, and the natural and constructed environment—begin to crumble, the greatest weight falls on the chain's longest links: individuals who can bypass the precarious transfer of information from one generation to the next through their longevity.[13] Thus Momaday especially values his grandmother: "Although my grandmother lived out her long life in the shadow of Rainy Mountain," he wrote, "the immense landscape of the continental interior lay like memory in her blood. She could tell of the Crows, whom she had never seen, and of the Black Hills, where she had never been."[14] In Momaday's literary representation, her memory was essential, embodied, in a way his could never be.

Memory work like *The Way to Rainy Mountain* is typically occasioned by the impending dissolution of what Aleida Assmann terms "cultural working memory."[15] Momaday did not speak Kiowa, and he was two generations removed from the forced disbandment of the Kiowas "as a living Sun Dance culture."[16] Thus Momaday's memoir enacts the transfer from living "canon" to passive "archive." By writing, he was employing a resource that was neither available nor necessary to his ancestors. In this regard, his work is analogous to that of the Delaware historian Richard Calmit Adams, whose publications included *The Ancient Religion of the Delaware Indians and Observations and Reflections* (1904): "if these things are not recorded now," he wrote, "they may be lost forever." Adams observes that his ancestors "kept no written records" but instead carefully maintained the chain of traditional memory through an apprenticeship system in which ceremonial chiefs trained their successors. Adams had consulted his late elders while preparing the manuscript, to ensure its accuracy, but he laments the irreparable diminishment entailed by the transition from spoken Lenape to written English: "try as hard as I may, I feel that I can not do them justice in my effort to translate their orations and songs, for it is almost impossible for me to find words in the English language to convey to you the beautiful thoughts our orators express in their native tongue."[17] Writing over sixty years later, Momaday attempted to offset this loss through his lyricism.

While peoples everywhere have experienced the erosion of traditional knowledge in the face of the accelerated changes associated with modernity, Native Americans also experienced a catastrophic upheaval of the social frameworks for memory.[18] In some instances, European colonists and the American successors deliberately curtailed the perpetuation of native cultural traditions, such as in 1890 when "a company of soldiers rode out" to strip the Kiowas of "the essential act of their faith," breaking up their final Sun Dance gathering.[19] For Momaday, this was a culminating act, the erasure of a cultural tradition that the colonists had already made nearly impossible to maintain by exterminating the buffalo, on which it depended.

For the Delawares, the devastation had begun centuries earlier. The "earliest incident" recollected by the Lenape respondents to a survey circulated in the early 1820s by Lewis Cass was of diseases that preceded the arrival of the Europeans: "The day of a sudden turned dark and a very bad smell was smelt apparently coming from the sea shortly after they were all taken sick and a great number of them died."[20] (As the character Nanapush, an elderly Anishinaabe narrator, explains in Louise Erdrich's *Tracks*, by victimizing the most vulnerable, epidemics were particularly damaging to the continuity of communities: "Our tribe unraveled like a coarse rope, frayed at either end as the old and new among us were taken."[21]) Another early memory was of the arrival of the whites, and the trick with the bullock's hide, as discussed in chapter 2. This first encroachment was followed by others: "They say by being encroached upon by the whites they were compelled to move Westward and by farther encroachments from time to time by the whites they are still under the necessity of moving to the Westward till the present time."[22] As a rule, cultural memory is not wholly transportable; it cannot be completely disengaged from the landscape in which it is embedded.[23] Yet one of the items the Delawares carried with them is the memory of the first encroachment; they were reminded of it each time they were compelled to pick it up and move it again.

TANTAQUÉ'S TORTOISE

For Momaday, the memory of the Kiowas' ancestral homeland in the "northern Great Plains" inheres in their account of ontogeny, their "coming into the world through a hollow log."[24] Similarly, the memory of Lenapehoking is subtly intertwined with the Delaware origin myth. The earliest written record of it is in the journal of the Labadist missionary Jasper Danckaerts, which documents his travels in North America in 1679–80 with his colleague Peter Sluyter in search of a site for a colony for their Calvinistic sect. What the scholars who cite this source have not recognized is that Danckaerts's representation of the Delaware ontogeny is intended as a vindication of his Holy Scripture over their oral tradition as a medium of memory. His journal is also, simultaneously, an unintended portrait of the disintegration of traditional Lenape lifeways.

On October 16, 1679, Danckaerts and Sluyter were on Manhattan, staying in a house that would have been a short distance from the site where ferries now leave for Liberty and Ellis Islands. Danckaerts's journal entry for that day begins: "I was occupied to-day in copying my journal. In the morning there came an Indian to our house, a man about eighty years of age, whom our people called Jasper, who lived at Ahakinsack or at Ackinon" (present-day Hackensack, New Jersey).

Danckaerts and Sluyter learned that Jasper, whose Munsee name they recorded as Tantaqué, had earned the gratitude of the early Dutch colonists by supplying them with fish during a time of famine, but that now he had a drinking problem. When they opined that he should refrain from drink or suffer punishment from God, whom they styled the "Great Sakemacker," attempting to accommodate their beliefs to his understanding by using the Algonquian word for leader (more often rendered "sachem"), Tantaqué laughed at their beliefs, explaining that the Great Sakemacker did not "trouble himself with the earth or earthly things." It was "Maneto"—whom the Labadists would have understood to figure the Devil—who had forced him to feed the starving colonists and who would torment him for his drinking. The Indians had nothing to do with the Christians' God; without writing, they had no means to communicate with the beyond: "we do not know or speak to this *sakemacker*, but Maneto we know and speak to, but you people, who can read and write, know and converse with this *sakemacker*."[25]

The Labadists responded with a catechistic question about "where he believed he came from?" The question seemed intended to refute Tantaqué's metaphysics, to bring him to admit that God was the ultimate cause of his existence. Tantaqué's initial response (he came "from his father") missed the point, so they clarified: "'And where did your father come from? . . . and your grandfather and great-grandfather, and so on to the first of the race?'" Tantaqué's account of ontogeny was apparently unsatisfying:

> He was silent for a little while, either as if unable to climb up at once so high with his thoughts, or to express them without help, and then took a piece of coal out of the fire where he sat, and began to write upon the floor. He first drew a circle, a little oval, to which he made four paws or feet, a head, and a tail. "This," said he, "is a tortoise, lying in the water around it," and he moved his hand round the figure, continuing, "This was or is all water, and so at first was the world or the earth, when the tortoise gradually raised its round back up high, and the water ran off of it, and thus the

earth became dry." He then took a little straw and placed it on end in the middle of the figure, and proceeded, "The earth was now dry, and there grew a tree in the middle of the earth, and the root of this tree sent forth a sprout beside it and there grew upon it a man, who was the first male. This man was then alone, and would have remained alone; but the tree bent over until its top touched the earth, and there shot therein another root, from which came forth another sprout, and there grew upon it the woman, and from these two are all men produced."[26]

When Tantaqué had concluded his multimedia presentation on the emergence of Turtle Island and the creation of mankind, Danckaerts and Sluyter made him a present of "four fish hooks." Tantaqué, who had once succored the Dutch colonists by supplying them with fish, presumably caught through traditional means, immediately calculated the value of his present. He took leave, and returned that afternoon drunk, apparently having cashed in. In the Labadists' portrait, a man who should have been a dignified elder, a living link to the precontact period, had become degraded by the most pernicious and pervasive vice the colonists had brought with them to the New World.

From their point of view, Tantaqué's degree of revelation was sufficient to warrant eternal damnation for his continued sinfulness; he did not have the excuse of ignorance. His version of Genesis, involving a tree, a man and woman, and a flood, was evidence of the distorting effects of word-of-mouth transmission. As the Calvinist John Eliot had a fictional Algonquian missionary explain to a fictional Algonquian proselyte in a wishful scenario in his *Indian Dialogues*, "a word spoken is soon gone, and nothing retaineth it but our memory, and that impression it made upon our mind and heart. But when this word is written in a book, there it will abide, though we have forgotten it. And we may read it over a thousand times, and help our weak memories, so that it shall never be forgotten."[27]

For Danckaerts and Sluyter the Indians' ideas of creation were demonstrably distorted, and could be refuted by scripture. Outside their theological framework, however, the story of the tortoise is no more subject to falsification or scientific corroboration than is the Judeo-Christian account of creation. Yet the Lenapes' belief that they had inhabited their homeland since *time immemorial* is consistent with the "archaeological record," which suggests their ancestors had "hunted, fished, gathered and gardened" in the region "for many thousands of years in the past."[28] Archeology has turned up other attestations of the primordial turtle, including an inscribed pendant discovered in Setauket, Long Island, in the early twentieth century, and a turtle-head effigy discovered near Howland Hook, Staten Island, in the 1960s.[29] These may represent the creation myth, or the turtle phratry (clan), or both: Heckewelder learned from his Delaware informants in Ohio that the "Tortoise, or as it is commonly called, the *Turtle* tribe, among the Lenape, claims a superiority and ascendancy over the others, because their *relation*, the great Tortoise, a fabled monster, the Atlas of their mythology, bears according to their traditions this great *island* on his back, and he is amphibious, and can live both on land and in the water, which neither of the heads of the other tribes can do."[30]

A third turtle petroglyph discovered in the New York area, spotted by the archeologist Edward Lenik in 1987 on a boulder above the Bronx River, on the grounds of the New York Botanical Garden, is less likely the work of a Late Woodland–era Algonquian, as once thought, than of a twentieth-century boy scout.[31] Like the *Walam Olum*, it is a reminder of the susceptibility of fragmentary chains of memory to imposture, and of the desire for communications from the precolonial past that seem less mediated than a recorded oral tradition. Tantaqué's ephemeral illustration of the tortoise, date-stamped, made permanent, and glossed through written representation, is a counterpoint to the petroglyphs, which are permanent but undated, unattributed, and unaccompanied by any explanation. Its value as evidence rests on its earliness, on the apparent fact that it was recorded, albeit by an author who was antagonistic to its message, at a moment before the demographic and cultural changes the Delawares experienced during the eighteenth, nineteenth, and twentieth centuries, from an informant who was a living link to the period before the arrival of the colonists.

As a mediated glimpse of a living chain of memory, however, the account of Tantaqué's tortoise would be less valuable if the existence of this chain were not also attested to among subsequent generations. The parts of the chain that have become visible, so to speak, are sufficient to allow the inference that it extended deeply into the precolonial past, that the inhabitants of the region during the Middle and Late Woodland periods, including those whose remains were unearthed on Ellis and Liberty Islands, believed that the their world had come into being on the back of an enormous turtle.

As Amy Schutt points out, the creation story, with "water as a central motif," is characteristic of a people who inhabited a region that was framed by rivers and coasts and threaded with streams. In that sense, long after they departed from their ancestral homeland, the Delawares retained a deep-seated memory of a watery world. The "giant turtle" and "cedar tree" were integral to the "Gamwing" or Big House rite; the Big House, with features "such as the center pole, the double fires, and the clean, oval dance area," architecturally recreated the ontogeny described by Tantaqué.[32]

The Delaware anthropologist Jay Miller disputes the speculation that the Gamwing originated in early nineteenth-century revitalization movements. His view that present "influences were grafted onto traditions with roots in the aboriginal past" is much more consonant with current understandings of the process of cultural memory, and suggests that traditions are shaped by a "dynamic" interaction between past and present.[33] According to Miller, the Gamwing "was the Delawares' integrative rite, expressing community identity and cosmic harmony from ancient times."[34] In other words, it was a Delaware counterpart to the Kiowa Sun Dance described by Momaday, and like that rite, it had become defunct. "When elders today are asked about traditional beliefs, activities, and institutions," writes Miller, "their replies are based on memories of this ceremony, last held in 1924 near Copan, Oklahoma."[35]

"A KIND OF HOMECOMING"

By the 1980s the active memories of ceremonial culture were so tenuous that although the reinterment of the remains discovered on Ellis and Liberty Islands had to be deferred for several years to allow for the completion of the restoration and landscaping, the Delawares decided to move up the funeral ceremony to June 1987, in order to ensure the involvement of aged elders. According to the *Associated Press*, Richard Snake, the tribal president and elder of the Delaware-Munsee Nation of Ontario, Canada, Willy Snake, eighty-seven, of the Delaware Nation of Oklahoma, and Leonard Thompson, eighty-three, of the Delaware Tribe of Indians from eastern Oklahoma played key roles in the ceremony, which was performed with "modern Manhattan in the background."[36]

The participants from the Delaware Tribe of Indians in Bartlesville, Oklahoma, the largest contemporary community of Delawares, especially valued the memory of the presence in New York of their ceremonial chief, Thompson. Dee and Annette Ketchum recalled how he was able to identify regional artifacts at the Heye Museum of Natural History (then in the Bronx): "the other elders from Anadarko [Oklahoma] and Canada were not able to make these identifications because they had lost so much of the culture because of living among other tribes for so long." Thompson lived for another fifteen years after the visit to New York. In 1998, when he sat for an oral history interview, he was "still very sharp." Thompson explained that the Delawares had "first moved from where Pennsylvania is on down, [and] plumb up to New York State. And right now in New York City there is a lot of Delaware names on the streets." Dee Ketchum, Thompson's "understudy," gloomily anticipated the loss that would accompany his death: "I'm trying to squeeze from him whatever amount of information that he can give me because it's going to be a real void in my life as well as the Delaware Tribe because he's been such a mainstay."[37]

Evidently, for the participants, the experience of the visit to New York was one of renewal. Richard Snake described it "as a kind of homecoming." In the oral histories from 1998, members of the party from the

Delaware Tribe of Indians expressed their joy at being reunited with Delawares from elsewhere. "We got back there, and it was the most incredible feeling," said Annette Ketchum. "The Delawares from Canada came. The Delawares from Anadarko came, and here we are, the three tribes together for the first time in a hundred years. I had not thought about the impact of being back together. But when we got back together, it was just like we were all little kids, just standing around, just talking to each other and looking at each other. And saying how wonderful; we all had these feelings; it's almost like getting butterflies in your stomach. That's how it felt the first time we all got together." She added: "I hate to say this, but a reporter printed my picture in the New York Times in my Delaware ceremonial clothes with the Statue of Liberty in the background."[38]

The reinterment itself took place on May 1, 2003. The headstone bears the seals of the Delaware Nation, the Delaware Tribe of Indians, and the Stockbridge-Munsee Band of Mohican Indians.[39] From the tortoise traced in coal by Tantaqué in Manhattan in 1679—"a little oval, to which he made four paws or feet, a head and a tail"—to the turtle phratry symbols on the tribal seals, we see a remarkable example of cultural continuity.

::::::::::::::::::: NOTES :::::::::::::::::::

INTRODUCTION

1. On the use of "Delaware" and "Lenape" ethnonyms, see "Communities of History and Memory," this introduction.
2. Kaiser, "Munsee Social Networking," 145.
3. Heckewelder, *Account of the History, Manners, and Customs, of the Indian Nations* (1819), as seen in eHRAF World Cultures, www.yale.edu. See remarks about the text in the abstract under "Publication Information." Further citations from this text are from the edition published by the Historical Society of Pennsylvania in 1881, available through the Internet Archive, www.archive.org.
4. Heckewelder, *History, Manners, and Customs of the Indian Nations* (1881), 47, http://www.archive.org/details/histmannerscustooheckrich.
5. Heckewelder, *History, Manners, and Customs*, 75.
6. Heckewelder, *History, Manners, and Customs*, 78.
7. Heckewelder, *History, Manners, and Customs*, 78.
8. The "infamous Walking Purchase" has become a stock phrase in academic and popular history writing. For example, according to William Fenton, "the infamous 'Walking Purchase' of 1737 took a great swatch of Delaware lands." *The Great Law and the Longhouse*, 398.
9. Weeks, *American Indian Experience*.
10. Heckewelder, *History, Manners, and Customs*, 76 (emphasis original).
11. Unless otherwise indicated, I draw my definitions from OED Online (*Oxford English Dictionary*, 3rd ed.).
12. Montrose, "Work of Gender in the Discourse of Discovery," 15.
13. Montrose, "Professing the Renaissance," 20. See Brook Thomas's critique

of the New Historicists' dependence on the rhetorical figure of chiasmus: *New Historicism*, 10.
14. Greenblatt, *Marvelous Possessions*, 7.
15. Harkin, "Ethnohistory's Ethnohistory."
16. Jennings, "Brother Miquon: Good Lord!"; Jennings, "Scandalous Indian Policy"; and Jennings, *Ambiguous Iroquois Empire*.
17. Merrell, "Some Thoughts," 114.
18. Merrell, *Into the American Woods*, 37.
19. Merrell, "Revisiting Teedyuscung's 1756 Treaty Council Speeches," 819, 826.
20. Vansina, *Oral Tradition as History*, 194.
21. Provincial Council of Pennsylvania, Minutes, 7:689.
22. In his important essay on the disciplinary relations between history and literary studies (jointly published in *Early American Literature*), Eric Slauter writes: "Putting a text in a historical context can matter a great deal for literary analysis, but it can have only a minimal appeal to historians, especially when the context is stitched together from existing historiography." "History, Literature, and the Atlantic World," 159.
23. See, for example, Brooks, *Common Pot*; Cohen, *Networked Wilderness*; and Richter, *Facing East*. Two essays that establish dialogs between colonial writings and recorded oral traditions about first encounters are Haefeli, "On First Contact"; and E. White, "Invisible Tagkanysough." White's essay is an illuminating critique of New Historicist scholarship on the New World.
24. Wilkinson, "Choice of Fictions," 90.
25. I distinguish between "interdisciplinary" (involving contributions from scholars from various disciplines within a shared framework), "transdisciplinary" (involving a generative synthesis of disciplinary approaches), and "multidisciplinary" (characterized by several parallel, largely independent specialized conversations). See A. Brown et al., "Introduction: Is an Interdisciplinary Field of Memory Studies Possible?"
26. Woolard, "Introduction: Language Ideology," 3.
27. Heckewelder, "Correspondence . . . Respecting the Languages of the American Indian," 382–84.
28. Woolard, "Introduction: Language Ideology," 24. The following is a sampling of scholarship pertaining to language ideology and colonization:

Cohen, *Networked Wilderness*; Rasmussen, *Queequeg's Coffin*; Bauman and Briggs, *Voices of Modernity*; Gray and Fiering, *Language Encounter*; E. Gray, *New World Babel*; Merrell, *Into the American Woods*; Cheyfitz, *Poetics of Imperialism*; Murray, *Forked Tongues*.

29. Cohen, *Networked Wilderness*, 5–6, 182n8.
30. Wyss, *Writing Indians*; Bross and Wyss, *Early Native Literacies*; Watts, "Pictures, Gestures, Hieroglyphs," 82–83.
31. Boone, "Introduction: Writing and Recording Knowledge"; Warkentin, "In Search of 'The Word of the Other'"; Rasmussen, "Negotiating Peace." A revised version of Rasmussen's article appears as chapter 2 of *Queequeg's Coffin*, which was published too late for my use in this book.
32. Krupat, *Red Matters*, 66.
33. For an expanded version of this argument, see Newman, "Early Americanist Grammatology."
34. Heckewelder, *History, Manners, and Customs*, 131.
35. Halbwachs, *On Collective Memory*, 173.
36. Misztal, *Theories of Social Remembering*, 15–19.
37. Swales, *Genre Analysis*, 24–27.
38. Kraft states that "original people" is a mistranslation; it should be "ordinary people." *The Lenape*, 2.
39. Schutt, *Peoples of the River Valleys*, 3.
40. Herbert C. Kraft offers the following explanation of the origin of the term Lenapehoking: "Lënapehòking, meaning 'Land of the Lenape,' is a recently constructed term provided by Nora Thompson Dean at the request of the author (personal communication March 5, 1984) to obviate the need of constantly specifying 'all of New Jersey, eastern Pennsylvania, Delaware, southeastern New York State including Staten Island and parts of western Long Island, and a small portion of southwestern Connecticut.' An alternative term is Lënàpe Ëhèndawikìhtit, meaning 'where the Lenape dwell.'" *Lenape-Delaware Indian Heritage*, 9n2. After introducing the term, Kraft employs it in plain text, without the diacritical markers. Ives Goddard observes that the "groups here treated together never formed a single political unit, and the name Delaware, which was first applied only to the Indians of the middle Delaware Valley, was extended to cover all of these groups only after

they had migrated away from their eastern homelands." "Delaware," in *Handbook of North American Indians*, 213, as seen in eHRAF World Cultures.

41. For differing views on the usages of "Lenape" and "Delaware," see Schutt, *Peoples of the River Valleys*, 3; Weslager, *Delaware Indians*, 32; the Delaware Tribe's "Culture and History" website, http://www.culture.delawaretribe.org/home.htm; Becker and Beierle, "Culture Summary: Delaware." For a variant of "Lenape," see Forbes, "Renape People."
42. In New Jersey, the Nanticoke Lenni-Lenape Indians and the Ramapough Mountain Indians have state but not federal recognition.
43. For the folk etymology, see Delaware Tribe, "Frequently Asked Questions," http://culture.delawaretribe.org/faq.htm.
44. Gassaway, "Interview with Leona Parton," Western History Collections, University of Oklahoma.
45. Richter, *Facing East*, 137.
46. Rasmussen, "Negotiating Peace," 456.
47. Vansina, *Oral Tradition as History*, 27.
48. Nora, "Introduction to Realms of Memory," 2:ix; Bauman and Briggs, *Voices of Modernity*, 12.
49. Nabokov, *Forest of Time*, 59, 61; see also Nabokov, "Indian Views of History"; Lowie, "Oral Tradition and History," 598.
50. See Kammen, *Mystic Chords of Memory*, 72.
51. See Nabokov on the role of "'topographic mnemonics' for recalling place names and way stations linked . . . to early relocations of Creeks, Arikaras, Kiowas, and the Montana Crows." *Forest of Time*, 137. An influential study of the relation of Native American language, and memory, to landscape is Basso, *Wisdom Sits in Places*. More generally, the relation of memory and space has been one of the most prominent topics in memory studies. See Zelizer, "Reading the Past," 223–24.
52. Watson, *Annals of Philadelphia and Pennsylvania* (1844), 1:vii. On memory and American visual arts, see Kammen, *Meadows of Memory*.
53. W. Davis, *History of Bucks County*, 1:478.
54. Shils, *Tradition*, 55–62.
55. According to Kammen, local history associations "thrived and enjoyed greater longevity than national ones" in the period before 1870. *Mystic Chords of Memory*, 75.

56. Erll, "Cultural Memory Studies: An Introduction," 7.
57. A. Assmann, "Canon and Archive"; Vansina, Oral Tradition as History, 168–69.
58. For example, see Halbwachs, The Collective Memory, 78–83; Nora, "General Introduction: Between Memory and History"; Shils, Tradition, 55–62.
59. Klein, noting that "*Memory* is replacing old favorites—*nature, culture, language*—as the word most commonly paired with history," points out that the disavowal of a facile opposition between the two terms has become "one of the clichés of our new memory discourse. In preface after preface, an author declares that it would be simplistic to imagine memory and history as antitheses and then proceeds to use the words in antithetical ways in the body of the monograph." "On the Emergence of Memory," 128.
60. Du Ponceau and Fisher, Memoir on the History of the Celebrated Treaty, 8.
61. A. Assmann, "Canon and Archive," 105.
62. See Deborah Nichols's excellent introduction to Adams, Legends of the Delaware Indians, xv–xlv, 2.
63. Adams, Brief History of the Delaware Indians, 3. On the Dawes Act, see Banner, How the Indians Lost Their Land, 276–82.
64. Devine-Wright, "Theoretical Overview of Memory," 10.
65. Halbwachs, On Collective Memory, 173.
66. Misztal, Theories of Social Remembering, 57; see Hobsbawm and Ranger, Invention of Tradition.
67. Olick, "From Collective Memory," 159. See also B. Schwartz, "Social Context of Commemoration," 377; Misztal, Theories of Social Remembering, 67–74.
68. According to Vansina, "a tradition should be seen as a series of successive documents all lost except for the last one and usually interpreted by every link in the chain of transmission. It is therefore at second, third, or nth remove, but it is still evidence unless it be shown that a message does not finally rest on a first statement made by an observer." Oral Tradition as History, 29.
69. Misztal, Theories of Social Remembering, 92–93.
70. P. Gordon, Two Indian Treaties, 3.
71. Provincial Council of Pennsylvania, Minutes, 3:313.
72. Provincial Council of Pennsylvania, Minutes, 3:314. As A. Assmann and

other memory scholars point out, forgetting is an essential aspect of the social memory process, more the rule than the exception. Cultural forgetting is predominantly "passive" but also can take active forms, as in this instance. "Canon and Archive," 98–99.

73. Johnston, *A Narrative of the Incidents Attending the Capture, Detention and Ransom of Charles Johnston*, 262.
74. M. Austin, "Non-English Writings II," 612.
75. Oestreicher, "Unmasking the Walam Olum," 2.
76. Banner, *How the Indians Lost Their Land*, 67.
77. Summit, *Memory's Library*, 7. See also Cook, "The Archive(s) Is a Foreign Country."
78. See B. Thomas, *Civic Myths*.
79. Keyser, *Penn's Treaty with the Indians*, 13–14.
80. Vaux, "Memoir on the Locality of the Great Treaty," 90. The citation is from an editorial footnote.
81. See Lorenz, who points out that the "metaphorical turn" in theories of historiography invert "the positivism of facts." "Can Histories Be True?"
82. Vaux, "Memoir on the Locality of the Great Treaty," 91; Misztal, *Theories of Social Remembering*, 91.
83. The figure of 500,000 acres is cited by Merritt, *At the Crossroads*, 47.
84. Tatamy, "In Reference to the Walking Purchase and Teedyuscung's Request for a Clerk," 1757.
85. Boyd, "Indian Affairs in Pennsylvania," xxviii.
86. Heath, "Protean Shapes in Literacy Events," 93.
87. For illuminating discussions, see Wyss, *Writing Indians*, 8–10; Konkle, "Indian Literacy."
88. Ong, *Orality and Literacy*, 32. See Cohen's discussion of Ong in *Networked Wilderness*, 6, 182n8. As Cohen notes, scholars can benefit from Ong's "rigorous analyses of the different formal properties of mnemonic and inscriptive practices" without endorsing his "hierarchization of consciousnesses and the use of a media activity to characterize an entire culture."
89. B. Thomas, *Civic Myths*, 20.
90. Insofar as "construction" can mean "construing, explaining, or interpreting of a text or statement; explanation, interpretation; meaning, sense." *Oxford English Dictionary*.

1. LENAPE ANNALS

1. Soderlund, *William Penn and the Founding of Pennsylvania*, 317.
2. Huddleston, *Origins of the American Indians*, 14–47.
3. See Bross, *Dry Bones and Indian Sermons*, chap. 2.
4. Danckaerts, *Journal*, 150.
5. Heckewelder, *History, Manners, and Customs of the Indian Nations*, 47, 50–51, http://www.archive.org/details/histmannerscustooheckrich.
6. Deloria, *Red Earth, White Lies*, 68.
7. Mann, *Native Americans, Archaeologists, and the Mounds*, 61; Silverberg, *Mound Builders of Ancient America*.
8. "Documents and Proceedings relating to the Formation and Progress of a Board in the City of New York, for the Emigration, Preservation, and Improvement of the Aborigines of America," 79.
9. Cooper, *Last of the Mohicans*, 31.
10. Heckewelder, *History, Manners, and Customs*, 47.
11. Kraft, *The Lenape*, 7. On the chronology of oral traditions, see Vansina, *Oral Tradition as History*, 173–85.
12. Heckewelder, *History, Manners, and Customs*, 51.
13. M. Thomas et al., "Y Chromosomes Traveling South"; Wade, "DNA Backs a Tribe's Tradition of Early Descent from the Jews."
14. Oestreicher, "Unmasking the Walam Olum," 37n27.
15. Zeisberger, *David Zeisberger's History*, 32–33.
16. Calloway, *Revolution and Confederation*, 141, 573n96.
17. "Keying's function of meaning-making expresses itself by connecting events of separate periods in such a way that the events of one period are appropriated as a means of interpreting the events of the other." Misztal, *Theories of Social Remembering*, 96.
18. Vansina, *Oral Tradition as History*, 100.
19. Heckewelder, *History, Manners, and Customs*, 51.
20. Liu et al., "Social Identity and the Perception of History," 1022.
21. Cass, "Manners and Customs of Several Indian Tribes," 13 (PDF file).
22. Cass, "Manners and Customs of Several Indian Tribes," 13, 15, 17. See Rawle's 1826 rebuttal to Cass's critique: "Vindication of the Rev. Mr. Heckewelder's History."

23. Cass to Moulton, December 29, 1824.
24. Cass, "Manners and Customs of Several Indian Tribes," 13.
25. Silverberg, Mound Builders of Ancient America, 25, 56–57; see also McGuire, "Archeology and the First Americans"; Priest, American Antiquities, 37–41, 295.
26. Bryant, Poems, 148–49.
27. Priest, American Antiquities, 40–41.
28. Turner, Frontier in American History, 1.
29. McGuire, "Archeology and the First Americans," 822–23.
30. While Barton was published before Heckewelder, he refers to "a collection of valuable manuscripts, which were kindly communicated to me by . . . my worthy friend, Mr. John Heckewelder, of Bethlehem." New Views of the Origin, xxx, xci.
31. Longfellow, Song of Hiawatha, 188.
32. Longfellow, Song of Hiawatha, 282. According to Kammen, Longfellow's implication was that "[a]ll he had done was translate [the Indians'] hypnotic chant into English so that 'Americans' could make a Native American myth of origins their very own." Mystic Chords of Memory, 83.
33. Kammen notes that Cooper's motif was taken up by "Eastern artists." Mystic Chords of Memory, 87. It is equally attested to in local newspapers and histories, both before and after Cooper. For example, see my discussion of the newspaper "'reminiscences'" of Hannah Freeman, the model for Charles Brockden Brown's character Old Deb: Newman, "Edgar Huntly, Regional History, and Historicist Criticism," 335–37.
34. Heckewelder, History, Manners, and Customs, 300; Cooper, Last of the Mohicans, 350.
35. Cooper, Last of the Mohicans, 30.
36. Cooper, Last of the Mohicans, 30–31.
37. Cooper's seemingly gratuitous recourse to the sublime is actually part of a complex motif that enacts the metaphysical subtext of The Leatherstocking Tales—the exaltation of rational, civilized man over the admirable savages. See Newman, "Sublime Translation"; Cooper, Last of the Mohicans, 32–33.
38. Cooper, Last of the Mohicans, 117.
39. Cooper, Letters and Journals, 2:84.
40. Cooper, Last of the Mohicans, 32.

41. M. Austin, "Non-English Writings II," 612.
42. On Rafinesque, see Boewe, *Profiles of Rafinesque*; Boewe, "Fall from Grace"; Warren, *Constantine Samuel Rafinesque*.
43. On the *Walam Olum* and the Prix Volney Contest, see Oestreicher, "Unmasking the Walam Olum," 14–15. Oestreicher argues persuasively that the 1833 date on the manuscript is spurious; Rafinesque must have composed the *Walam Olum* in 1834, after his initial submission to the contest.
44. Rafinesque, *American Nations*, 122, 151.
45. Indiana Historical Society, *Walam Olum or Red Score*, 7.
46. Indiana Historical Society, *Walam Olum or Red Score*, 208; Rafinesque, *American Nations*, 140.
47. Indiana Historical Society, *Walam Olum or Red Score*, 69.
48. Indiana Historical Society, *Walam Olum or Red Score*, 207.
49. Oestreicher, "Unmasking the Walam Olum," 6–7.
50. Oestreicher, "Text Out of Context," 33.
51. Oestreicher, "Unmasking the Walam Olum," 16–21.
52. See Russett, *Fictions and Fakes*.
53. Oestreicher, "Unmasking the Walam Olum," 2.
54. Boewe, *Profiles of Rafinesque*, xxxiv.
55. Boewe, *Profiles of Rafinesque*, xxxv.
56. My thanks to Professor Boewe for forwarding me an excerpt from the manuscript of his authoritative biography of Rafinesque, *Life of C. S. Rafinesque*, published by the American Philosophical Society in 2011. Boewe claims that Oestreicher's "Byzantine effort has resulted in forced connections between disparate materials sometimes as improbable as those too often relied on by Rafinesque himself," 363. He suggests that Oestreicher has "made a career out of attacking Rafinesque," 363n16. Although I remain persuaded that Rafinesque is the creator of the *Walam Olum*, this point is not essential to my argument. I agree with Boewe that Oestreicher contradicts himself by characterizing the *Walam Olum* as a duplicitous "hoax" while acknowledging that "Rafinesque himself considered the *Walam Olum* 'an accurate historical reconstruction,'" 363.
57. Rafinesque, *Ancient Monuments*, 28; Oestreicher, "Unmasking the Walam Olum," 16–32.

58. Oestreicher proposes that this precedent, certainly compromising to his purported receipt of a document that happened to support his theory, induced him to invent a curious chronology according to which he received the *Walam Olum* in 1822 but only deciphered it many years later. "Unmasking the Walam Olum," 13.
59. Oestreicher, "Unraveling the Walam Olum," 19; See also Oestreicher, "Roots of the Walam Olum," 82–84.
60. Kilpatrick and Kilpatrick, *New Echota Letters*, 16.
61. Rafinesque, *American Nations*, 111.
62. Indiana Historical Society, *Walam Olum or Red Score*, 215. Oestreicher does establish that the "Fragment" is also apocryphal, and he shows how it reproduces a key historical error from his original source, Heckewelder's *History*. Oestreicher concludes, "The Burns account was intended as an additional piece of outside evidence to buttress the validity of the *Walam Olum* as a whole. . . . Its inclusion is nothing less than an audacious coda—a final flourish of the ubiquitous pen of Constantine Rafinesque." "Unmasking the Walam Olum," 12.
63. See Heckewelder, *History, Manners, and Customs*, 130–31; Hulbert and Schwarze, "David Zeisberger's History of Northern American Indians," 114; Cresswell, *Journal of Nicholas Cresswell*, 110.
64. Rafinesque, *American Nations*, 104.
65. Rafinesque, *The Good Book*, 77–78.
66. Weslager, *Delaware Indians: A History*, 91–92.
67. Squier, "Historical and Mythological Traditions of the Algonquins." Squier's biographer Terry A. Barnhart is perhaps the only scholar to cite Oestreicher without declaring the question of authenticity settled; she lists Oestreicher, without evaluating his findings, as the latest in a train of skeptics who "must continue to combat the romantic cachet and cultlike reverence that often attaches to the *Walam Olum*." *Ephraim George Squier and the Development of American Anthropology*, 142–43.
68. H. R. Schoolcraft, copy of letter to E. G. Squier, February 16, 1849.
69. D. Brinton, *The Lenâpé and Their Legends*, v–vi.
70. Harrington, *Dickon among the Lenape Indians*, ix, 202. Jay Miller describes *Dickon* as a "superb novel." "Old Religion among the Delawares," 117.
71. Harrington, *Dickon*, 202, 208, 210.

72. Oestreicher, "Unmasking the Walam Olum," 2.
73. D. Brinton, *The Lenâpé and Their Legends*, 64n1.
74. Indiana Historical Society, *Walam Olum or Red Score*, xiv.
75. See S. Williams, *Fantastic Archaeology*, 112; Darnell, *Daniel Garrison Brinton*, 28.
76. Madison, *Eli Lilly*, 135.
77. James Rementer, e-mail to Andrew Newman, March 13, 2010. See also Oestreicher, "Tale of a Hoax," 15.
78. James Rementer, e-mail to Andrew Newman, August 15, 2007. Regna Darnell suggests that Daniel Brinton could hardly be faulted for being duped when, decades later, C. F. Voegelin, "a specialist in Algonquian languages trained by Edward Sapir," vouched for the *Walam Olum* as the lead investigator of the IHS study." Darnell, *Daniel Garrison Brinton*, 28.
79. Indiana Historical Society, *Walam Olum or Red Score*, xiv.
80. Indiana Historical Society, *Walam Olum or Red Score*, x.
81. Indiana Historical Society, *Walam Olum or Red Score*, 105.
82. Indiana Historical Society, *Walam Olum or Red Score*, 105, 153.
83. Napora, *Walam Olum*, cover.
84. McCutchen, *Red Record*, x. See Newcomb, "Walum Olam of the Delaware"; Vansina, *Oral Tradition as History*, 54–55.
85. Oestreicher, "Text Out of Context," 44. After my publication of an essay on the *Walam Olum* in *American Literary History* in 2010, I received an e-mail from a reader named Vincent Barrows, containing what appeared to be a forwarded message from Joe Napora, which declared: "I never recanted anything." I e-mailed Mr. Napora but received no response. Vincent Barrows, e-mail to Andrew Newman, "FW: Walam Olum," April 5, 2010.
86. McCutchen, *Red Record*, x. The Delaware Nation Grand Council of North America was convened by Rachel Bair Redinger of Dover, Ohio, in the early 1980s to bring together representatives of the four Delaware groups in Oklahoma and Canada. James Rementer's recollection is that "it wasn't long before many people who belonged dropped out" when Redinger "kept telling them what they could or could not do." Rementer also explains that while McCutchen and his collaborator Gregory Schaaf persuaded leaders of both Delaware groups in Oklahoma that the *Walam Olum* was authentic, in Bartlesville neither the tribal chairman of the Delaware Tribe of Oklahoma

nor any of the members of the business committee that issued a resolution in support of the *Walam Olum* were Lenape speakers. After the remaining Lenape speakers, including Lucy Blalock and Nora Thompson Dean, raised serious doubts about the language of the *Walam Olum*, the Culture Committee had the tribe withdraw their support. James Rementer, e-mail to Andrew Newman, May 15, 2010. On Redinger, see Ohio Department of Job and Family Services, "Rachel Redinger," ODJFS Online. Redinger and McCutchen exemplify the hazards attending attempts by non-Indians to mediate Native American culture. Redinger apparently met resistance when she attempted to impose her notions of Delaware culture on the participants in the activities she arranged, while McCutchen was the latest to reacquaint the Delawares with their supposed sacred text. The reception of the *Walam Olum* among Delawares and other Native Americans is one of the most poignant and controversial aspects of its history.

87. Adams, Brief History, 2–4.
88. Adams, Brief History, 54–55.
89. Miller, "The Red Record," 187, 190.
90. Oestreicher, "Unmasking the Walam Olum," 2. The question of the Delawares' exposure to the *Walam Olum*, however, is convoluted. *Turtle Tales: Oral Traditions of the Delaware Tribe of Western Oklahoma*, which presents oral histories collected in 1975 and 1983 through a National Endowment for the Humanities grant and is dedicated to Poolaw, includes the story of the "Delawares Crossing the Ice," told by the elder Martha Ellis, who recalls that her "mother used to say, we came from another island (I guess I will say), not this . . . She said, 'We crossed, we had to go a way up in the North Pole, and the ocean was all frozen.'" Hale, Turtle Tales, 5. See Wallace and Reyburn, "Crossing the Ice," 45–46; Nabokov, Forest of Time, 73.
91. Oestreicher, "Unraveling the Walam Olum," 15.
92. Oestreicher, "Unraveling the Walam Olum," 21.
93. Brotherston, *Book of the Fourth World*, 191.
94. Brotherston, "Time Remembered," 333.
95. Brotherston, *Image of the New World*, 15.
96. Dennis Tedlock, e-mail to Andrew Newman, April 22, 2005.
97. Stuart, "Beginning of Maya Hieroglyphic Study."
98. Tedlock e-mail, April 22, 2005. See Tedlock, "Dialogues Between Worlds."

99. Such specialization is a typical feature of cultural memory. J. Assmann, "Communicative and Cultural Memory," 112.
100. It is understandable that Sollors, Shell, and Tedlock would have overlooked Oestreicher's articles in the Bulletin of the Archeological Society of New Jersey. Their omission of mention of the controversy and neglect of due diligence in investigating it can be attributed in part to the manner in which the Walam Olum came to their attention. Sollors, who discusses the Walam Olum briefly in the introduction, apparently was led to it (and to several other selections in the anthology) by the aforementioned 1917 edition of the Cambridge History of American Literature, in which Mary Austin makes only the most oblique mention of a controversy by asserting that the Lenape transcription had "been pronounced by Daniel Brinton to be a genuine oral tradition written down by one not very familiar with the language." (The Multilingual Anthology uses Brinton's supposedly corrected translation.) "Non-English Writings II," 619. Sollors also cites a 1948 anthology which does mention the allegations that the Walam Olum is a forgery, only to declare the matter settled. Shell and Sollors, introduction to Multilingual Anthology, 3. See Davis, Frederick, and Mott, American Literature, 1:43.
101. Sollors, introduction to Multilingual Anthology, 5.
102. Shell, afterword to Multilingual Anthology, 690.
103. Buzard, Beaten Track, 172–92.
104. Benjamin, "Task of the Translator," 70.
105. See Boone, "Introduction: Writing and Recording Knowledge," 14.
106. According to Knowlson, belief in this "original catholic tongue and . . . the primitive letters in which it was thought to have been written down . . . was both long and persistent, continuing to influence the ideas on language until very late in the eighteenth century." Universal Language Schemes), 12–13. During the early modern period, exposure to Chinese and ancient Egyptian writing systems—both source materials for the Walam Olum pictographs—fueled speculation that the original writing system must have been ideographic (or semasiographic). See Lewis, Language, Mind, and Nature, 120–21.
107. Shell and Sollors, Multilingual Anthology, 96.
108. On the Renaissance "topos of writing's exemption from the destruction of time," see A. Assmann, "Texts, Traces, Trash," 124.
109. Purchas, Hakluytus Posthumus, 1:486.
110. Indiana Historical Society, Walam Olum or Red Score, 207.

2. AN ACCOUNT OF A TRADITION

1. Livy, *The Romane historie*, supplement 6, 40.
2. Laufer, "Relations of the Chinese," 282.
3. Richter, *Facing East*, 11.
4. Mason, "Archaeology and Native North American Oral Traditions," 263. See also Lowie, "Oral Tradition and History"; Dixon, "Dr. Dixon's Reply"; Swanton, "Dr. Swanton's Reply"; Echo-Hawk, "Ancient History in the New World; Whiteley, "Archaeology and Oral Tradition."
5. Vansina, *Oral Tradition as History*, 160.
6. Lowie, "Oral Tradition and History," 598.
7. Haefeli, "On First Contact," 416.
8. Swann, *Algonquian Spirit*, 55–61; G. Williams et al., letter to Zachary Taylor, March 29, 1849.
9. According to Vansina: "The only place and date that can be given about a tradition is that of the recording of a performance." *Oral Tradition as History*, 56.
10. Van der Donck, *Description of New Netherland*, 3.
11. According to Pennebaker and Banasik, "The creation and maintenance of a collective or historical memory is a dynamic social and psychological process. It involves the ongoing talking and thinking about the event by the affected members of the society or culture. This interaction process is critical to the organization and assimilation of the event in the form of a collective narrative." "On the Creation and Maintenance of Collective Memories," 4.
12. The Hopi tradition was first recorded in 1902. The Hopi missions were established in 1630, and the Pueblo revolt took place in 1680. Wiget, "Truth and the Hopi."
13. Vansina, *Oral Tradition as History*, 82–83.
14. Heckewelder to Miller, February 26, 1801, 1.
15. Heckewelder, *History, Manners, and Customs*, 71.
16. Heckewelder, *History, Manners, and Customs*, 71–74.
17. For example, there's no mention of the tradition in Merwick's *The Shame and the Sorrow*; Jacobs relegates notice of it to a footnote: *Colony of New Netherland*, 264n7.
18. Shorto, *Island at the Center of the World*, 28; M. Hamilton, *Henry Hudson*, 23; Burrows and Wallace, *Gotham*, 15n1.
19. Shorto, *Island at the Center of the World*, 28.

20. Otto, *Dutch-Munsee Encounter*, 44; Haefeli, "On First Contact," 417.
21. Otto, *Dutch-Munsee Encounter*, 44.
22. Haefeli, "On First Contact," 435.
23. Otto, *Dutch-Munsee Encounter*, 44.
24. Burrows and Wallace, *Gotham*, 15n1.
25. Haefeli, "On First Contact," 417.
26. Haefeli observes that for the Indians "it was not until the eighteenth century that Manhattan would serve as both a mnemonic device and a symbolic claim to a territory long since lost." "On First Contact," 418.
27. Nederlandshce West-Indische compagnie, *Documents Relating to New Netherland*, 48, 260n8. Jacobs notes that there "are some indications that the first colonists arrived in 1623, but the evidence is incomplete and unreliable, so 1624 is a better choice." The colonists who arrived that year on the *Eendracht* were distributed between four locations, including "Nooten Eylandt," to shore up the West India Company's territorial claims. Jacobs, *Colony of New Netherland*, 30.
28. See Baumeister and Hastings, "Distortions of Collective Memory."
29. Heckewelder, *History, Manners, and Customs*, 73; Juet, "From 'The Third Voyage,'" 19.
30. Heider, "Universals in Color Naming and Memory." For a more recent discussion see the *Special Issue on Culture, Cognition, and Color* in the *Journal of Cognition and Culture* 5 (2005): 3–4.
31. Swann, *Algonquian Spirit*, 60. For more on the role of the color red in the accounts of the 1609 encounter, see Haefeli, "On First Contact," 424–26.
32. Heckewelder to Miller, February 26, 1801, 1; Heckewelder, *History, Manners, and Customs*, 71.
33. Juet, "From 'The Third Voyage,'" 22–23.
34. Heckewelder, *History, Manners, and Customs*, 74.
35. Bierhorst notes that the theme of the "legendary trickery of the early Dutch settlers" was first recorded in the eighteenth century and was "still being rehashed in the late 1900s." *Mythology of the Lenape*, 5.
36. Upal, "Memory, Mystery and Coherence."
37. Heckewelder, *History, Manners, and Customs*, 75.
38. "juger sa validité de representer la réalité"; "Certes non; il s'agit d'une métaphore comme nous venons de l'indiquer." Delâge, "La tradition orale," 208–10. Unless otherwise indicated, translations from French and Spanish are by the author.

39. "métaphore de la peau de bœuf transformée en fine lanière." Delâge, "La tradition orale," 209.
40. Irving, Knickerbocker's History, 54–57.
41. Irving, Knickerbocker's History, 58.
42. Nederlandshce West-Indische compagnie, Documents Relating to New Netherland, 6.
43. Van Ittersum, Profit and Principle, xxii.
44. Heckewelder, History, Manners, and Customs, 76–77.
45. My thanks to Jim Rementer for sharing the transcription and translation of the Bessie Snake story. Rementer, e-mail to Newman, March 14, 2008. Compare this translation to the one published in Swann, Algonquian Spirit, 60. See also a version of the tradition by Waubuno, or "Chief Wampum," in which the whites ask for a tract "the size of a cowhide." Waubuno, Traditions of the Delawares, 3.
46. Wagner, Yuchi Tales 158.
47. Barbeau, Huron and Wyandot Mythology, 268n3.
48. Banner, How the Indians Lost Their Land, 67. Banner's source is the ethnohistorian James Axtell, who cites a Yuchi version of the "cowhide purchase" story, explaining that "the morphology of the tales resembles European precedents." Axtell, After Columbus, 138. Axtell's source is Lankford, Native American Legends, 137–38. Lankford's source, finally, is the linguist Günter Wagner, who recorded the tradition as told by the Yuchi speaker Maxey Simms in 1928–29. Yuchi Tales, 158.
49. J. Jackson, Yuchi Ceremonial Life, 22–23.
50. J. Jackson, Yuchi Ceremonial Life, 22–23.
51. Fogelson, "Ethnohistory of Events and Nonevents," 143.
52. Subrahmanyam, Portuguese Empire, 7.
53. Barbeau, Huron and Wyandot Mythology, 270.
54. J. Jackson, Yuchi Ceremonial Life, 22.
55. Swanton does mention, using indirect speech, that one informant "had heard that the Americans were formerly out upon the ocean and at first the Muskogee would not let them land." However, it is unclear whether Swanton or the informant introduced the ethnic identification, and in any case he attributes the hide story to "another informant." Swanton, "Social Organization," 75–76.

56. Barbeau, *Huron and Wyandot Mythology*, 299–300 (for Schoolcraft version).
57. J. Jackson, *Yuchi Ceremonial Life*, 137.
58. Gerhard, "Barter through the Ages," 493.
59. For Barry Schwartz, "Keying is communicative movement—talk, writing, image- and music-making—that connects otherwise separate realms of history." *Abraham Lincoln and the Forge of National Memory*, 226.
60. Swann, *Algonquian Spirit*, 60.
61. Swann, *Algonquian Spirit*, 59.
62. G. Williams et al., letter to Taylor, 407.
63. Swann, *Algonquian Spirit*, 60.
64. Vansina, *Oral Tradition as History*, 152–55.
65. Swanton, "Social Organization," 76.
66. Abbott, "'Commendable Progress,'" 191.
67. Servius, *Servii Grammatici*, 2:124–25; Virgil, *Vergil's Aeneid*. My thanks to Lee Clyde Miller for help with the Latin.
68. Virgil, *Vergil's Aeneid*.
69. Uther, *Types of International Folktales*, 566–67.
70. Thompson, *Motif-Index of Folk-Literature*, 251.
71. For overviews, see Basset, "La Légende de Didon"; Cordier, "La Légende de Didon"; Frazer, "Hide-Measured Lands," 322; and Laufer, "Relations of the Chinese," 282–84. Primary and secondary sources for the individual accounts include: Zhang Xie, *Dong xi yang kao*, 89; Lemire, *Exposé Chronologique*, 8; Bayley, *History of India*, 395; Sikandar, *Mirati Sikandari*, 198–99; Saar, *Reise nach Java, Banda, Ceylon und Persien*, 66, 68; Reid, "Early Southeast Asian Categorizations," 291; Furnivall, "History of Syriam," 53 (Burma); Raffles, *History of Java*, 2:153–55; Bastian, *Die Volker des oestlichen Asien*, 4:367–68; *T'ai-wan fu chi* (Gazetteer of the Prefecture of T'ai-wan), cited by Laufer, "Relations of the Chinese," 282; Arboussct, *Relation d'un voyage d'exploration*, 49.
72. Lemire, *Exposé Chronologique*, 8 ("la ruse des compagnons de Didon"; "'les gens du pays de la peau qui s'étire.'").
73. Frazer, "Hide-Measured Lands," 322. In *The Golden Bough*, Frazer adds the South African example to the five he previously cited: *Adonis, Attis, Osiris*, 3:249–50.
74. Reid, "Early Southeast Asian Categorizations," 290–91. In his skeptical

discussion of the admissibility of oral traditions in archeological inquiries, Ronald Mason asks, "if more than one tradition tells the same tale, does not that agreement confer authenticity to the account and, by extension, the genre itself?" He answers this question with others: "How detailed or vague are the 'histories' with respect to actors, roles, story line, temporal perspective, place? To what degree can the independence of seemingly corroborating traditions be established? And how? How matter-of-fact as opposed to symbolically embellished are they? These are knotty questions, of course, the answers to which are contingent on the particular cases." "Archaeology and Native North American Oral Traditions," 245–46.

75. Laufer, "Relations of the Chinese," 283–84.
76. Laufer, "Relations of the Chinese," 282.
77. See Pennings, "History of the Arrangement of the VOC [Dutch East India Company] Archives."
78. Saar, *Reise nach Java, Banda, Ceylon und Persien*, 66, 68. Thanks to Martin Brückner for help with the German.
79. De Silva, *Portuguese Encounters*, 21–22.
80. De Silva, "Portugal and Sri Lanka."
81. Row, "Artifice of the Thong," 272–73.
82. A. Hamilton, *New Account of the East Indies*, 137–38.
83. Bayley, *History of India*, 395. For another version that does not voice doubts, see Sikandar, *Mirati Sikandari*, 199. For further discussion see Subrahmanyam, "On the Hat-Wearers," 50–51.
84. Hajji al-Dabir, *Zafar ul walih bi muzaffar wa alihi*, 1:215.
85. Castanheda, *História do descobrimento e conquista da Índia pelos Portugueses*, 8:242, http://hdl.handle.net/2027/nyp.33433082437751. The translated passage appears in Alam and Subrahmanyam, "Letters from a Sinking Sultan," 248–49.
86. Castanheda, *História do descobrimento*, 257.
87. Castanheda, *História do descobrimento*, 259.
88. Castanheda, *História do descobrimento*, 261.
89. "que estaua embandeyrado com bandeyras das armas de Portugal." Castanheda, *História do descobrimento e conquista da Índia pelos Portugueses*, 8:247. "Wasting no time," paraphrase Alam and Subrahmanyam, "Cunha promptly took possession of the land where the fort was to be, and placed

flags with the Portuguese arms there." "Letters from a Sinking Sultan," 251.
90. Alam and Subrahmanyam, "Letters from a Sinking Sultan," 242.
91. My thanks to Geoffrey Wade of the Asia Research Institute at the University of Singapore for locating the passages in the *Dong xi yang kao*, and the *Ming shi*, and for his translations. According to Wade, the word he translated as "buffalo" could also be rendered as "ox" or "cow."
92. Laufer, "Relations of the Chinese," 282–84; Zhang Xie, *Dong xi yang kao*, 89; Zhang Tingyu, *Ming shi*, juan 323, 8370–75.
93. Laufer, "Relations of the Chinese," 259.
94. Laufer, "Relations of the Chinese," 258–59; Morga, *Sucesos de las Islas Filipinas*, 27. "la paz, amistad y obediencia"; "tomó lo que bastó del terreno para la ciudad."
95. Cunha, *Notes on the History and Antiquities of Chaul and Bassein*, 108.
96. Gibbon, *History of the Decline and Fall of the Roman Empire*, 302n15.
97. Cantemir, *History of the Growth and Decay of the Othman Empire*, 2.
98. Cantemir, *History of the Growth and Decay of the Othman Empire*, 97n3.
99. According to Roy F. Baumeister and Stephen Hastings, the "outright fabrication of collective memory is rare. The implication may be that collective memories are to some extent constrained by the facts. Facts may be deleted, altered, shaded, reinterpreted, exaggerated, and placed in favorable contexts, but wholesale fabrication seems to lie beyond what most groups can accomplish." "Distortions of Collective Memory," 282.
100. Laufer asserts that Pu Songling's version is independent of the written versions of the Dido story, set in the Philippines and Taiwan, that first appeared in 1618 and 1694, and that "an oral popular variant must have been afloat at the same time; it is the latter which was recorded by P'u Sungling." Review of "Strange Stories from a Chinese Studio," 89–90.
101. Lowie, "Oral Tradition and History," 598. Arnold Krupat's solution to the historiographic problem of reconciling native histories to Western records and understandings of the laws of nature is to relinquish the Western "fetish of the historical fact"; to recognize that truth in history is a product of social convention. If a native group, by consensus, accepts a history as true, then it is historical. Thus if the Delawares do so, then Western readers would need to recognize as true a story that pertains to a known and

seemingly unrealistic folkloric motif, without regard for its origin. Within Krupat's anti-empirical framework, the truth of the bull's hide story is not simply allegorical. Yet, at least when applied to an account of a colonial encounter held independently by several native peoples around the world, Krupat's "cosmopolitan" conception of history is unsatisfying. Red Matters, 53.
102. Shore and Rhodes, "Princess Dido and the Ox Skin."
103. Hildebrandt and Tromba, *Parsimonious Universe*, 64–65.
104. Servius, *Servii Grammatici*, 2:124.
105. Nederlandshce West-Indische compagnie, *Documents Relating to New Netherland*, 135.
106. Frank Morgan, e-mail to Andrew Newman, August 27, 2006.
107. On early New Netherland forts, see Otto, *Dutch-Munsee Encounter*, 54–55; Nederlandshce West-Indische compagnie, *Documents Relating to New Netherland*, 260n8. For my own conversions, I used onlineconversion.com: "Convert just about anything to anything else."
108. See the Wikipedia entry on "Nora Thompson Dean/Touching Leaves Woman."
109. James Rementer, e-mail to Andrew Newman, February 25, 2007. It was Oestreicher who identified the speaker as a literature professor.
110. Vansina, *Oral Tradition as History*, 160.
111. I assume that more historians of New Netherland are aware of the tradition than have commented on it. The *Indian tradition of the first arrival of the Dutch, at Manhattan Island, now New-York, by the Rev. John Heckewelder* (an edition of his 1801 letter to Samuel Miller) is published in the collections of the New-York Historical Society; in my university library, at least, it appears on the shelf with other source materials on early New Netherland.
112. Seed, *Ceremonies of Possession*, 149.
113. Heckewelder, *History, Manners, and Customs*, 75.
114. Kottenkamp, *Die ersten Amerikaner im Westen*, 382. The translation is provided by Berthold Laufer, although he misattributes the quote to Friedrich Pott, who cites Kottenkamp. Laufer, "Relations of the Chinese," 284.
115. Vansina, *Oral Tradition as History*, 152–55.
116. Purchas, *Hakluytus Posthumus*, 19:55–56. Dido also figures prominently in an episode of Alonso de Ercilla's sixteenth-century epic about the conquest

of Chile, La Araucana. See Galperin, "Dido Episode in Ercilla's La Araucana"; Kallendorf, "Representing the Other."
117. Frazer, "Hide-Measured Lands."
118. Pott, citing Kottencamp, mentions the Dido motif and the Delaware instance in "Etymologische Legenden bei den Alten," 258–59.
119. On the relationship of the classical instance to folklore, see annotations by Arthur Stanley Pease: Virgil, Pvbli Vergili Maronis Aeneidos, 232–33.
120. MacCormack, On the Wings of Time; Waswo, Founding Legend; Lupher, Romans in a New World, 10; Elliott, Spain and Its World, 9.
121. B. Schwartz, Abraham Lincoln and the Forge of National Memory, 225–26.
122. Helgerson suggests that Dido's celebrity induced the sixteenth-century poets Henry Howard, Earl of Surrey, and Joachim du Bellay "to translate book 4 of the Aeneid as the showpieces for their new vernacular poetics." Sonnet from Carthage, 54; see also Waite, "Holy Spirit Speaks Dutch," 49.
123. Monteiro, "Camões Os Lusíadas," 109; Greenlee, "Bibliography of the History of Portugal," 515.
124. Camões, The Lusíads, 184.
125. Camões, The Lusíads, 181.
126. Grotius, Freedom of the Seas, v–vi, 8; Waswo, Founding Legend, 137–38; Virgil, Vergil's Aeneid; Van Ittersum, Profit and Principle, xix–xxiii.
127. On other uses of Aeneid I:539–40, see Waswo, Founding Legend, 137–38.
128. Davidson, Island of Formosa, 12–13.
129. Raffles, History of Java, 154.
130. Machiavelli, Discourses on Livy, 175.
131. Winterer, "Model Empire, Lost City," 4.
132. Winterer, "Model Empire, Lost City," 7–8; see also Wilson-Okamura, "Virgilian Models of Colonization," 709–37.
133. Justinus, Epitome of the Philippic History, 155–57.
134. Cited in Van Ittersum, Profit and Principle, 158–59. The 1621 West India Company charter emphasized the same priorities: see Stokes, Iconography of Manhattan Island, 1:7, Nederlandshce West-Indische compagnie, Documents Relating to New Netherland, xi.
135. Nederlandshce West-Indische compagnie, Documents Relating to New Netherland, 17.
136. Nederlandshce West-Indische compagnie, Documents Relating to New Netherland, 39.

137. Schmidt, *Innocence Abroad*, 247.
138. Janvier, *Dutch Founding of New York*, 9.
139. Merwick, *The Shame and the Sorrow*, 3, 7.

3. THE MOST VALUABLE RECORD

1. Buell, *William Penn as the Founder*, 138–39.
2. For an example of a modern textbook that presents the treaty meeting as historical fact, see Banks et al., *New Nation*, 225.
3. Abrams, "Benjamin West's Documentation," 61.
4. Vaux, "Memoir on the Locality of the Great Treaty," 89, editorial footnote.
5. See Conforti, *Imagining New England*, chapter 4.
6. Watson, *The Indian Treaty*, 131.
7. Historical Society of Pennsylvania, *Presentation . . . of the Belt of Wampum*, 207.
8. See B. Thomas, *Civic Myths:*, 4–6 et passim.
9. "William Penn and the Indians" is also one of the nineteen scenes in Constantino Brumidi's "Frieze of American History" in the rotunda. Images are available online at Architect of the Capitol, http://www.aoc.gov/cc/art/index.cfm. See Fryd, *Art and Empire*, 9–41, especially 28–31, 147. Fryd argues that "Gevelot's relief . . . derive[s] from Silvanus Bevan's William Penn Medal of 1720," but the title and the long peace pipe held by one of the Indians suggests that it is also modeled after West's painting (which, as Fryd points out, was also informed by the medal). See also Kammen, *Mystic Chords of Memory*, 86–87.
10. According to Vansina, "studies in oral history confirm that even in literate societies living memory goes no further back than eighty years." *Oral Tradition as History*, 113. See also J. Assmann, "Communicative and Cultural Memory," 112–13.
11. Voltaire, *Letters*, 29.
12. See Bauman: *Let Your Words Be Few*; "Quaker Folk-Linguistics and Folklore"; "Speaking in the Light"; *For the Reputation of Truth*. See also Barone, "Hostility and Rapprochement," 15–32.
13. Raynal, *Philosophical and Political History*, 262. On Penn, Voltaire, and the French Revolution, see Frost, "William Penn's Experiment," 577–78.
14. Sellers, "The Beginning."

15. Jennings, Ambiguous Iroquois Empire, 246. On John Hall, see Bryan, Dictionary of Painters and Engravers, 619–20.
16. Gary Nash writes that "West's treaty painting probably influenced public memory more than any artistic work except portraits of George Washington." First City, 30.
17. Pennsylvania Academy of the Fine Arts, Symbols of Peace, unpaginated.
18. John Opie, cited in Palumbo, Adverting "Present Commotions," 50–51.
19. Oldmixon, British Empire in America, 1:310.
20. Proud, History of Pennsylvania, 1:212. Proud wrote his History "principally between the years 1776 and 1780." West's painting hung in the Penn family estate, Stoke Park, until 1851, and the dissemination of the prints from John Hall's 1775 engraving would have been interrupted by the war. On the timing of the Boydell/Hall engraving, see Palumbo, Adverting "Present Commotions," 51–52.
21. On the distinction between the "Chain of Friendship" and the Iroquoian "Covenant Chain," see Jennings, Ambiguous Iroquois Empire, 247–48.
22. Clarkson, Memoirs of William Penn, 339–40.
23. Weems, Life of William Penn, 146.
24. On West's Pennsylvania roots, see Abrams, "Benjamin West's Documentation," 61.
25. Clarkson, Memoirs of William Penn, 340; Du Ponceau and Fisher, Memoir on the History of the Celebrated Treaty, 23–24; on the sash, see Watson, Annals of Philadelphia and Pennsylvania, 1:135.
26. Jennings, Ambiguous Iroquois Empire, 245; Merrell, Into the American Woods, 28–30.
27. Harper, Promised Land, 38.
28. Staley, Benjamin West, American Painter, 59–60; Sellers, "The Beginning."
29. Kammen, Meadows of Memory, 134. An exception to this trend is Jon Parmenter's argument that the painting depicts not a treaty of friendship but a 1683 land sale. "Rethinking 'William Penn's Treaty.'" I agree with the dating, but my objection to the interpretation is that West's use of the William Penn medal as a source and his comments to Clarkson and others indicate that he had the Treaty tradition in mind.
30. Rigal, "Framing the Fabric," 576n7; Palumbo, Adverting "Present Commotions," 29.

31. See Abrams, "Benjamin West's Documentationy"; Tobin, "Native Land and Foreign Desire."
32. Garvan, "The Consequence."
33. Palumbo, Adverting "Present Commotions," 36. Like Palumbo, Rigal also focuses on trade, but her fascinating "Luddite Reading" is less an interpretation than a critical response that opposes West's conquest through trade with the Indian Nativist rejection of European trade goods. "Framing the Fabric."
34. Olick, "From Collective Memory," 159.
35. Misztal, *Theories of Social Remembering*, 68.
36. Olick, "From Collective Memory," 159.
37. Abrams, "Benjamin West's Documentation," 59.
38. See Hart, "Benjamin West's Family."
39. West's 1805 letter to W. Darton is reproduced in E. S. Brinton, "Benjamin West's Painting," 114–15. It is also available in Erffa, *Paintings of Benjamin West*, 207. In Rigal's reading of the above-cited passage from West's letter, she suggests that "with the confused temporality of 'art' in this passage ('to give by that art a conquest . . . made') West conflates the consumer goods in the painting with his own work as a history painter, identifying the bolt of cloth in the painting with both the mechanical arts of British manufacturing and the representational art of history painting." "Framing the Fabric," 559–60. I do not see this conflation. West's letters show him to be a poor syntactician, but in this passage "that art" pretty clearly refers to the antecedent "composition," while the "conquest" belongs to Penn and the seventeenth century.
40. As James Spady argues, Penn's Indian policy was not really a break from precedent. "Colonialism and the Discursive Antecedents of Penn's Treaty."
41. Cited in E. S. Brinton, "Benjamin West's Painting," 114–15. On West's collection of Indian artifacts, see Einhorn and Abler, "Bonnets, Plumes, and Headbands"; King, "Woodlands Artifacts." Kammen notes that early American artists had different conceptions of "truth," including "historical veracity," "accuracy in the rendering of nature" (which would be synonymous with "likeness"), and especially "authenticity." Kammen, *Meadows of Memory*, xv.
42. Buell, *William Penn as the Founder*, 139.

43. Watson, *Annals of Philadelphia and Pennsylvania*, 1:137–38; Krause, "Penn's Elm and Edgar Huntly," 455–56. Campanella cites the 1790 travelogue of Luigi Castiglioni, who described the elm as "remarkable for the beauty of its branches, which are numerous, very wide-spreading and pendant almost like those of the African willow." *Republic of Shade*, 13–14. On "Historic American Elms in Fact, Fiction, and Art," see Kammen, *Meadows of Memory*, 134–46, especially 134–38.
44. Cited in Watson, *Annals of Philadelphia and Pennsylvania*, 1:135–36.
45. "Liberty trees" with allegorical savages, appeared, for example, in anti–Stamp Act cartoons. See Adair, "The Stamp Act in Contemporary English Cartoons"; Wolf, "Benjamin Franklin's Stamp Act Cartoon."
46. Weems, *Life of William Penn*, 146.
47. Palumbo, Adverting "Present Commotions," 31.
48. Watson, *Annals of Philadelphia and Pennsylvania*, 1:134.
49. See Nicholson, *Historic American Trees*, 11–12, 14, 22, 24–25, 28–29, 31, 38–41, 44–45, 65–66, 84–85. Alfred Fabian Young, citing a single biography of Benjamin West, claims that "the legend of the Quaker William Penn signing a humane treaty with the Lenni Lenape Indians under the 'treaty elm' was cultivated in the 1770s by the Penn family interest for political purposes." *Liberty Tree*, 347, 358.
50. Watson, *Annals of Philadelphia and Pennsylvania*, 1:134–35.
51. Cope, *Philadelphia Merchant*, 251.
52. Watson, *Annals of Philadelphia and Pennsylvania*, 1:137.
53. Vaux, "Memoir on the Locality of the Great Treaty," 91.
54. Nash, *First City*, 205.
55. Vaux, "Memoir on the Locality of the Great Treaty," 91. On Vaux, the Penn Society, and the Historical Society of Pennsylvania, see Nash, *First City*, 207.
56. Vaux, "Memoir on the Locality of the Great Treaty," 104–5.
57. Watson, *Annals of Philadelphia and Pennsylvania*, 1:135.
58. Vaux, "Memoir on the Locality of the Great Treaty," 102–3.
59. Cited in Nicholson, *Historic American Trees*, 40.
60. R. V. T. Jackson, "Family Tradition Regarding the William Penn Treaty Elm," Historical Society of Pennsylvania. For information on the relics of the Treaty Tree belonging to the Historical Society of Pennsylvania, I thank

Susan Drinan, registrar of the Atwater Kent Museum, which holds the HSP's material artifacts.
61. Nicholson, *Historic American Trees*, 40–41.
62. Watson, *Annals of Philadelphia and Pennsylvania*, 1:141.
63. Vaux, "Memoir on the Locality of the Great Treaty," 91, 106.
64. *Philadelphia Inquirer*, "Penn Treaty Park the Historic Spot to Be Preserved," October 8, 1893.
65. Vaux, "Memoir on the Locality of the Great Treaty," 89.
66. Stone, "Penn's Treaty with the Indians," 217, 237.
67. Soderlund, *William Penn and the Founding of Pennsylvania*, 88–89.
68. Craig, *The 1693 Census of the Swedes on the Delaware*, 29–30 (quote); William Penn, *Papers of William Penn*, 2:268n27.
69. Soderlund, *William Penn and the Founding of Pennsylvania*, 84, 89, 158–161. See Stone, "Penn's Treaty with the Indians," 219–24.
70. Soderlund, *William Penn and the Founding of Pennsylvania*, 160.
71. Provincial Council of Pennsylvania, Minutes, 1:64–69.
72. Watson, *Annals of Philadelphia and Pennsylvania*, 1:136.
73. T. Gordon, *History of Pennsylvania*, 603.
74. Conyngham, "Some Extracts from the Papers in the Office of the Secretary of the Commonwealth," 1:334.
75. T. Gordon, *History of Pennsylvania*, 603.
76. Scharf and Westcott, *History of Philadelphia*, 104.
77. Scharf and Westcott, *History of Philadelphia*, 104–5.
78. Nora, "Introduction to Realms of Memory," 8. Du Ponceau and Fisher observe that "the partial efforts that have been made by curious inquirers to remove the doubts, and clear up the obscurity, by means of insulated documents which have been discovered from time to time, have been attended only with partial success, and sometimes have failed of their object, by inducing erroneous notions, arising from the misapplication of those documents, or false inferences drawn from them. *Memoir on the History of the Celebrated Treaty*, iv.
79. Krause, "Penn's Elm and Edgar Huntly," 456.
80. Goddard, "Delaware," 216, as seen in eHRAF World Cultures.
81. Provincial Council of Pennsylvania, Minutes, 3:334.
82. Provincial Council of Pennsylvania, Minutes, 3:367.

83. "Indian Treaty Held at Philadelphia, August 17–18, 1731," James Steel Letterbook, 276.
84. P. Gordon, *Two Indian Treaties*, 2; Stone, "Penn's Treaty with the Indians," 224.
85. Watson, *The Indian Treaty*, 131. See also Du Ponceau and Fisher, *Memoir on the History of the Celebrated Treaty*, 34.
86. Soderlund, *William Penn and the Founding of Pennsylvania*, 59, 74, 314–16.
87. T. Gordon, *History of Pennsylvania*, 603.
88. Provincial Council of Pennsylvania, *Minutes*, 3:94.
89. Provincial Council of Pennsylvania, *Minutes*, 2:181.
90. Heckewelder, *Narrative of the Mission of the United Brethren*, 17; Merrell, *Into the American Woods*, 287–88. On the trajectory from Penn's Treaty to the Conestoga Massacre, see Richter, "Introduction: Peoples in Conversation," ix–xxi.
91. Erffa, *Paintings of Benjamin West*, 207.
92. "Substance of an Occasional Conversation with Severall Indians after dinner at Israel Pemberton's on the 19th 4 mo 1756"; Gillingham, "Indian Silver Ornaments," 104.
93. "Indian Treaty Held at Philadelphia, August 17–18, 1731," 274–76.
94. Cook, "The Archive(s) Is a Foreign Country," 527.
95. Stone, "Penn's Treaty with the Indians," 217.
96. Jennings, "Brother Miquon: Good Lord!," 200.
97. Jennings, "Brother Miquon: Good Lord!," 199–200; Stone, "Penn's Treaty with the Indians," 217; Watson, *Annals of Philadelphia and Pennsylvania*, 1:136.
98. Stone, "Penn's Treaty with the Indians," 238.
99. McPhee, "Travels of the Rock," 115–16.
100. Seelye, *Memory's Nation*, xiv.
101. McPhee, "Travels of the Rock," 116.
102. Seelye, *Memory's Nation*, 7–8.
103. Sargent Bush attributes this view to Seelye in his review of *Memory's Nation*. "America's Origin Myth: Remembering Plymouth Rock," 746.
104. Vaux, "Memoir on the Locality of the Great Treaty," 89–90.
105. Plato, *Phaedrus*, 68. According to Aleida Assmann, in "oral cultures" the "range of the cultural memory is coextensive with the embodied repertoires

that are performed in festive rites and repeated practices." There is no "passive storing memory" or "archive." "Canon and Archive," 105.
106. Du Ponceau and Fisher, *Memoir on the History of the Celebrated Treaty*, 4–5.
107. Du Ponceau and Fisher, *Memoir on the History of the Celebrated Treaty*, 7.
108. Heckewelder, *History, Manners, and Customs of the Indian Nations*, 186, http://www.archive.org/details/histmannerscustooheckrich.
109. Loskiel, *History of the Mission of the United Brethren*, 26.
110. Rasmussen, "Negotiating Peace," 457.
111. Foster, "'Another Look at the Function of Wampum in Iroquois-White Councils,'" 1:99; see also Fenton, *The Great Law and the Longhouse*, 224–39; Ceci, "Value of Wampum among the New York Iroquois"; Sayre, *Les Sauvages Américains*; Murray, *Indian Giving*, 116–40.
112. Fenton, *The Great Law and the Longhouse*, 232.
113. Heckewelder, *History, Manners, and Customs*, 107–8.
114. Heckewelder, *History, Manners, and Customs*, 108.
115. Du Ponceau and Fisher, *Memoir on the History of the Celebrated Treaty*, 8–9.
116. Loskiel, *History of the Mission of the United Brethren*, 27–28. See Becker, "Lenape Land Sales, Treaties, and Wampum Belts."
117. Historical Society of Pennsylvania, *Presentation . . . of the Belt of Wampum*, 216–17.
118. Historical Society of Pennsylvania, *Presentation . . . of the Belt of Wampum*, 212.
119. Historical Society of Pennsylvania, *Presentation . . . of the Belt of Wampum*, 237–38.
120. Historical Society of Pennsylvania, *Presentation . . . of the Belt of Wampum*, 248–50.
121. *New York Times*, "Relics of Penn at Auction," July 12, 1916.
122. *New York Times*, "Museum Here Gets Historic Wampum," November 21, 1916.
123. Speck, *Penn Wampum Belts*, 6–10.
124. Speck, *Penn Wampum Belts*, 10–13.
125. Soderlund, *William Penn and the Founding of Pennsylvania*, 160.
126. P. Gordon, *Two Indian Treaties*, 3.
127. Provincial Council of Pennsylvania, *Minutes*, 1:477.
128. Provincial Council of Pennsylvania, *Minutes*, 2:599–601.

129. According to Marshall Becker, the "well-known William Penn wampum belt, if presented to Penn or some other official by the Lenape or any other native group, may have been made and given in conjunction with any of a number of possible requests." He does not comment on the other Penn Wampum belts. "Lenape Land Sales, Treaties, and Wampum Belts," 355–56.
130. Speck, Penn Wampum Belts, 11.
131. A. Wallace, "Woman, Land, and Society," 2–6; Provincial Council of Pennsylvania, Minutes, 1:66–67.
132. Speck, Penn Wampum Belts, 12–13.
133. Speck, Penn Wampum Belts, 13.
134. Peau de Chat (Ojibwa), "Speech to Canadian Officials on Land-Purchase Policy," 161.
135. "While much of the scholarly literature emphasizes the subordination and dependence of Indians in these circumstances," writes Neal Salisbury, "Indians as much as Europeans dictated the form and content of their early exchanges and alliances." "Indians' Old World," 454. See also Kathleen Brown's analysis of the initial relations between the Powhatans and the Jamestown colony, in which the different understandings of the power differential were informed by and reflected different cultural constructions of gender. "Anglo-Algonquian Gender Frontier."
136. According to Michael S. Showalter, "There rests in the phrase Penn's Treaty with the Indians a sense of European superiority. Years after finishing the work West wrote of it as 'the picture of the Treaty between Wm. Penn and the American Indians.' Would Penn with his sense of mutual respect not have preferred the latter, more neutral and balanced—a Treaty between himself and the Indians?" An Image of Peace, 23.
137. Liu et al., "Social Identity and the Perception of History," 1032–1033.
138. Waubuno, Traditions of the Delawares, 4.
139. Heckewelder, History, Manners, and Customs, 108.
140. Swann, Algonquian Spirit, 60. Swann inserts "white people" in brackets after "our elder brother," but the apparent reference is to William Penn. Her figures of the creek, sun, and grass correspond to the references in the treaty in diplomatic records and historical accounts. James Rementer, who along with Bruce Pearson transcribed Snake's account, confirms that Snake could

not have gotten this language directly from written sources, since she could not read. Rementer, e-mail Newman, March 14, 2008.

141. Rementer adds: "Although I put that in quotes I do not have a recording of the event, but was there and recall what she said, and how you could hear a pin drop." James Rementer, e-mail to Andrew Newman, October 2, 2008.

142. Vaux, "Memoir on the Locality of the Great Treaty," 89. On Vaux's knowledge of the Walking Purchase, see "Edmund Morris to Roberts Vaux, August 27, 1826." See also Edmund Morris to Roberts Vaux, January 24, 1827.

4. WRITINGS AND DEEDS

1. "Antient Copy of Indian Purchase Deeds of 28th of August, 1686, With Confirmation, and 'Draught' Aug. 1737."
2. According to Anthony F. C. Wallace, their delay in appropriating funding was not simply principled pacifism but also an exercise in political leverage: "They would not, they insisted, vote appropriations for defense unless proprietary estates were taxed as well as citizens." *King of the Delawares*, 141.
3. Merrell, "Revisiting Teedyuscung's 1756 Treaty Council Speeches," 788.
4. Barbara A. Misztal defines countermemory as "an alternative view of the past which challenges the dominant representation of the past." *Theories of Social Remembering*, 158. Harper, *Promised Land*, 103 (quote). Harper disputes Wallace's determination that Teedyuscung was merely a "front man" for the Quakers. *Promised Land*, 122, 150n60; A. Wallace, *King of the Delawares*, 248.
5. Jennings discusses Parkman in the preface to *Invasion of America*, v.
6. Parkman, *Works of Francis Parkman*, 89.
7. Jennings, *Ambiguous Iroquois Empire*, 325; Boyd, *Indian Treaties Printed by Benjamin Franklin*, xxvii; Hunter, "Moses (Tunda) Tatamy," 73.
8. Becker, *The Forks of Delaware, Pennsylvania*, 55.
9. Shoemaker, *A Strange Likeness*, 64.
10. For example, see Fenton, *The Great Law and the Longhouse*, 398; Tobin, *Picturing Imperial Power*, 65; Krause, "Penn's Elm and Edgar Huntly," 467; Cave, *The French and Indian War*, 64.
11. Banner, *How the Indians Lost Their Land*, 67. Perhaps its closest equivalent was the "infamous Kayaderosseras Patent," which was disputed between Mo-

hawks and New York land speculators during the first half of the eighteenth century. Another controversial transaction with similarities to the Walking Purchase is the "Philipse Patent." See Nammack, *Fraud, Politics, and the Dispossession of the Indians*, 53–69, 70–85.

12. Powell, "Byrsa, the Bull's Hide, at Carthage," 311.
13. Tatamy, "Moses Tatamy's Acct of the Walking Purchase &c Taken by CT . . . 1757."
14. Boyd, *Indian Treaties Printed by Benjamin Franklin*, 157.
15. Jennings, *Ambiguous Iroquois Empire*, 325; Jennings, "Scandalous Indian Policy of William Penn's Sons."
16. "Notes About Treaty Meetings," 1757–62.
17. Novick, *That Noble Dream*.
18. Wolf, *Library of James Logan*, xviii; J. Johnson, "A Quaker Imperialist's View," 103.
19. *The Observator's trip to America*, 12; also cited in Wolf, *Library of James Logan*, xviii. Wulf, *The Brother Gardeners*, 32; Wolf, "Romance of James Logan's Books," 342.
20. Wolf, *Library of James Logan*, xviii.
21. See Lebovics, "Uses of America in Locke's Second Treatise of Government."
22. Lokken, "Social Thought of James Logan," 71.
23. Logan to Weiser, October 18, 1736.
24. Logan to Weiser, July 11, 1742.
25. "Antient Copy of Indian Purchase Deeds of 28th of August, 1686, With Confirmation, and 'Draught' Aug. 1737."
26. Hazard, *Pennsylvania Archives*, 1:541.
27. Fackenthal, "The Indian Walking Purchase of September 19 and 20, 1737," 6:14; Joseph Doan to Thomas Penn, May 29, 1735, 14, Quaker Collection; James Steel to John Chapman and Timothy Smith, April 29, 1735, 96.
28. Sullivan, *Papers of Sir William Johnson*, 3:839.
29. Sullivan, *Papers of Sir William Johnson*, 3:839–40.
30. Sullivan, *Papers of Sir William Johnson*, 3:840. "Affidavit—James Hamilton, William Allen, and Richard Peters," Philadelphia, June 12, 1762.
31. Spencer, *Early Baptists of Philadelphia*, 72; M. White, "William Biles (concluded)," 355–57.

32. Hazard, *Pennsylvania Archives*, 1:540.
33. "Affidavit—James Hamilton, William Allen, and Richard Peters."
34. Thomson, *Enquiry into the Causes of the Alienation of the Delaware and Shawanese*, 34.
35. Tatamy, "Moses Tatamy's Acct of the Walking Purchase &c Taken by CT . . . 1757."
36. "Affidavit-James Hamilton, William Allen, and Richard Peters"; Jennings, *Ambiguous Iroquois Empire*, 332.
37. Logan to Weiser, October 18, 1736.
38. Tatamy, "Moses Tatamy's Acct of the Walking Purchase &c Taken by CT . . . 1757."
39. Becker, *The Forks of Delaware, Pennsylvania*, 89.
40. Becker, *The Forks of Delaware, Pennsylvania*, 55.
41. Becker, *The Forks of Delaware, Pennsylvania*, 26. See also Schutt, *Peoples of the River Valleys*, chap. 3; A. Wallace, "Woman, Land, and Society," 12, 18.
42. [Tatamy], "Moses Tatamie's Acct. of Indian Claims, taken from his mouth at Easton by CT."
43. Tatamy, "Moses Tatamy's Acct of the Walking Purchase &c Taken by CT . . . 1757."
44. Tatamy, "Moses Tatamy's Acct of the Walking Purchase &c Taken by CT . . . 1757."
45. Soderlund, *William Penn and the Founding of Pennsylvania*, 316.
46. Tatamy, "Moses Tatamy's Acct of the Walking Purchase &c Taken by CT . . . 1757."
47. Soderlund, *William Penn and the Founding of Pennsylvania*, 59.
48. Soderlund, *William Penn and the Founding of Pennsylvania*, 74.
49. Soderlund, *William Penn and the Founding of Pennsylvania*, 84.
50. Habermas, *Communication and the Evolution of Society*, 67.
51. Fish, *Is There a Text in This Class?*
52. As M. T. Clanchy points out, in medieval England "trusting writing" was not a given. He refers to Plato in noting that "[t]hose who objected in the Middle Ages to the literate preference for the artificial memory of written record, instead of the living memory voiced by wise men of age and experience, were in a long tradition—had they known it—which extended back to myths about the origin of writing." *From Memory to Written Record*, 233.

Similarly, Mary Carruthers observes that literacy was slow to displace arts of memorization. *Book of Memory*, 195.
53. Plato, *Phaedrus*, 69–70.
54. Hazard, *Pennsylvania Archives*, 1:541.
55. On the media of speech acts, see Bach, "Speech Acts."
56. J. Austin, *How to Do Things with Words*, 60–61.
57. Derrida, *Limited Inc.*, 51–53; Searle, "Reiterating the Differences," 200. For an application of speech-act theory in a relevant communicative context, see Foster, "When Words Become Deeds," 354–67. See also Merrell, "Revisiting Teedyuscung's 1756 Treaty Council Speeches," 822.
58. Logan, "O My Soul."
59. Jennings, *Ambiguous Iroquois Empire*, 323.
60. Logan to Weiser, October 18, 1736.
61. Weiser to Logan, October 27, 1736.
62. Boyd, *Indian Treaties Printed by Benjamin Franklin*, 317.
63. Jennings, *Ambiguous Iroquois Empire*, 337; see also Harper, *Promised Land*, 119–21; A. Wallace, *King of the Delawares*.
64. This map trick may have been suggested by another boundary dispute in which Logan was heavily involved, with Maryland. See Wainwright, "Tale of a Runaway Cape."
65. Penn, *Some Fruits of Solitude*, 139.
66. See Richard Bauman, "Quaker Folk-Linguistics and Folklore," 261–62. Jennings suggests that the Quakers' midcentury investigation was hampered by awkwardness because "nearly everyone" involved in perpetrating the Walking Purchase "had been a friend." *Ambiguous Iroquois Empire*, 389.
67. Franklin, *Autobiography*, 114–15.
68. Irving, *Knickerbocker's History*, 57.
69. Wagner, *Yuchi Tales*, 158.
70. Wolf, "Romance of James Logan's Books," 342.
71. Adams, *Legends of the Delaware Indians and Picture Writing*, xi–xiv.
72. Bierhorst, *Mythology of the Lenape*, 7. See texts 23, 49, 50, 79, 97, 106, 107, 127, 149, 150, 155, 156, 167, 169. See also Adams, *A Delaware Indian Legend*, 3–9; Dean, Rementer, and Twaddle, "Delaware Indian Reminiscences [interview with Nora Thompson Dean]," 11.
73. Adams, *Legends of the Delaware Indians and Picture Writing*, 6.

74. Dean, Rementer, and Twaddle, "Delaware Indian Reminiscences [interview with Nora Thompson Dean]," 11; Adams, *Legends of the Delaware Indians and Picture Writing*, 3.
75. Hazard, *Pennsylvania Archives*, 1:542–43.
76. If the deed was framed in 1686, then it first appeared only seven years after John Bunyan's *Pilgrim's Progress*, in which "Feeble-Mind" recalls his resolution to "*run* when I can, to *go* when I cannot run, and to *creep* when I cannot go" (276).
77. Racewalk.com, "The Rules of Race Walking."
78. Zeisberger, *Zeisberger's Indian Dictionary*.
79. Rementer to Newman, October 2, 2008.
80. Heckewelder, *History, Manners, and Customs of the Indian Nations*, 384, http://www.archive.org/details/histmannerscustooheckrich.
81. Loskiel, *History of the Mission of the United Brethren*, 30.
82. *Oxford English Dictionary*.
83. "Antient Copy of Indian Purchase Deeds of 28th of August, 1686, With Confirmation, and 'Draught' Aug. 1737."
84. Thomson, *Enquiry into the Causes of Alienation of the Delaware and Shawanese*, 120.
85. Hazard, *Pennsylvania Archives*, 1:542.
86. "Copies of Depositions of Persons present at the Walk, performed in September 1737 . . . (No. 4)."
87. Watson, *Annals of Philadelphia and Pennsylvania*, 1:496.
88. "Joseph Knowles Acct of Indians Day & Half Walk," June 30, 1757.
89. "Examination of Edward Marshall," March 1, 1757.
90. "Thomas Furniss his Acct of the Walk," June 30, 1757). According to Frank Speck, the Delawares performed a "Green Corn Ceremony" in "the September phase of the new moon." It lasted "for seven days and nights" and "was a harvest ceremony in a broad sense with reference to the maturing of beans and other crops as well as corn." *Celestial Bear Comes Down to Earth*, 29. James Rementer points out, however, that September is "late in the season for green corn." James Rementer, e-mail to Andrew Newman, May 22, 2010.
91. W. Davis, *History of Bucks County*, 1:473.
92. Pennebaker and Banasik, "On the Creation and Maintenance of Collective Memories," 7–8, 14–15.
93. "Examination of Edward Marshall." This speech, usually stylized in broken

English, became one of the topoi of popular accounts of the Walking Purchase: "An old Indian said 'no sit down to smoke, no shoot a squirrel, but lun, lun, lun all day long.'" Beach, Indian Miscellany, 98.

94. Tatamy, "In Reference to the Walking Purchase and Teedyuscung's Request for a Clerk."
95. John Watson to Israel Pemberton, July 29, 1757.
96. John Watson to Israel Pemberton, August or October 19, 1757.
97. Sullivan, Johnson Papers, 3:797.
98. Sullivan, Johnson Papers, 3:809.
99. Ong, Orality and Literacy, 77.
100. Fish, "With Compliments of the Author," 71.
101. Jennings, Ambiguous Iroquois Empire, 328–29.
102. Sullivan, Johnson Papers, 3:786.
103. Sullivan, Johnson Papers, 3:788.
104. "Affidavit of John Kennedy an Indian Trader, to prove the Indians did not complain of being ill treated by the Proprietors, and people of Pensilvania, but that they had a great regard for that people and Province."
105. "Thomas Furniss his Acct of the Walk." After the walk, Furniss recalled riding with Timothy Smith, the sheriff who had supervised the walk, when they were surprised at seeing an Indian "take a gun in his hand" and assume a hostile position behind a log. Furniss emphasized that at the time of the walk, he "was a young man in the prime of life"; the remarkableness of the event "made the more strong and lasting impressions on my memory." Furniss's two observations correspond directly to research findings in the social psychology of collective memory: first, that talk—the "rehearsal" of past events, is a key factor in the retention of those events in collective memory, and second, that events from one's young adulthood are often the best remembered. See Pennebaker and Banasik, "Collective Memory of Political Events," 7–8, 14–15.
106. "Letter to Jeremiah Langhorne," Smithfield, November 21, 1740.
107. "Letter to Governor Thomas," Smithfield, January 3, 1740. On Sebring, see Jennings, Ambiguous Iroquois Empire, 342.
108. "Rough Draft of an Intended Message to the Delaware Indians 27 March 1741 sent accordingly May 1st & the answer enclosed," Philadelphia, March 27, 1741.

109. "Answer of the Chiefs of the Delaware Indians to the Governours Message of the 27th March 1741."
110. Foster, "'Another Look at the Function of Wampum in Iroquois-White Councils,'" 1:108.
111. Boyd, *Indian Treaties Printed by Benjamin Franklin*, 35.
112. Boyd, *Indian Treaties Printed by Benjamin Franklin*, 35.
113. Boyd, *Indian Treaties Printed by Benjamin Franklin*, 52; see also Rasmussen, "Negotiating Peace," 467.
114. Boyd, *Indian Treaties Printed by Benjamin Franklin*, 35.
115. Merrell, "Revisiting Teedyuscung's 1756 Treaty Council Speeches," 783.
116. Rasmussen, "Negotiating Peace," 464.
117. Locke, *Essay Concerning Human Understanding*, 318. Boyd, *Indian Treaties Printed by Benjamin Franklin*, 26–27. Thomson suggests the present was a bribe: *Enquiry into the Causes of the Alienation of the Delaware and Shawanese*, 45.
118. Boyd, *Indian Treaties Printed by Benjamin Franklin*, 36.
119. Boyd, *Indian Treaties Printed by Benjamin Franklin*, 36.
120. Heckewelder, *History, Manners, and Customs*, 78–79.
121. Boyd, *Indian Treaties Printed by Benjamin Franklin*, 36.
122. Provincial Council of Pennsylvania, Minutes, 7:324.
123. Ward, *Breaking the Backcountry*, 138.
124. Merrell, "Revisiting Teedyuscung's 1756 Treaty Council Speeches," Supplement 2. Woolard notes that "Transcription, or the written representation of speech within, for example, academic disciplines and law, is not a neutral mechanical activity, but relies on and reinforces ideological conceptions of language." "Introduction: Language Ideology as a Field of Inquiry," 23.
125. Merrell, "Revisiting Teedyuscung's 1756 Treaty Council Speeches," 819.
126. Heath, "Protean Shapes in Literacy Events," 91–117.
127. Peters, "An Account of the Conduct of the Quakers." According to Ward, the war "offered an opportunity for both the proprietors and the assembly to silence their opponents if each could convince the Board of Trade and the Privy Council that the other was responsible for the devastation of the backcountry." *Breaking the Backcountry*, 126.
128. W. Johnson, "To Governor Denny, Sept. 13, 1757."
129. A. Wallace, *King of the Delawares*, 138–39.

130. See the journal of Benjamin Chew in Boyd, *Indian Treaties Printed by Benjamin Franklin*, 313.
131. Provincial Council of Pennsylvania, Minutes, 7:681–82. Teedyuscung's "draught" is reproduced in Warhus, *Another America*, 82–83.
132. Provincial Council of Pennsylvania, Minutes, 7:683.
133. Sullivan, *Johnson Papers*, 3:771–73.
134. Provincial Council of Pennsylvania, Minutes, 7:690.
135. Provincial Council of Pennsylvania, Minutes, 7:644, 689; Merritt notes that while the "Indians invested ritual speech, oration, and memory with powers to build consensus and whites invested codified legal systems and written words with powers to enforce behavior, on some level each tried to accommodate the other's political forms." *At the Crossroads*, 213.
136. Provincial Council of Pennsylvania, Minutes, 7:689.
137. Provincial Council of Pennsylvania, Minutes, 7:651–52.
138. Croghan, "Copy of Mr. Croghan's Journal from the Close of the Treaty at Lancaster in May 1757."
139. Provincial Council of Pennsylvania, Minutes, 7:644.
140. Tatamy, "In Reference to the Walking Purchase and Teedyuscung's Request for a Clerk."
141. Sullivan, *Johnson Papers*, 3:766–67.
142. Sullivan, *Johnson Papers*, 3:778.
143. As A. Wallace writes, "this was not 1756, and Johnson was not Governor Denny." *King of the Delawares*, 246.
144. Sullivan, *Johnson Papers*, 3:783.
145. Sullivan, *Johnson Papers*, 3:777–78. The emphasis appears in the published version in the *Johnson Papers* but not in what appears to be the original in the Penn Manuscripts, nor in a manuscript copy in the Benjamin Chew Papers. A. Wallace, *King of the Delawares*, 246.
146. Sullivan, *Johnson Papers*, 3:777, 783.
147. A. Wallace was using the published version in the Johnson Papers instead of the manuscript in the HSP. *King of the Delawares*, 247, 289n18.
148. "Teedyuscung's Speech."
149. Sullivan, *Johnson Papers*, 3:784.
150. Sullivan, *Johnson Papers*, 3:784–85.
151. Sullivan, *Johnson Papers*, 789; see A. Wallace, *King of the Delawares*, 250.

152. Sullivan, *Johnson Papers*, 3:786.
153. Sullivan, *Johnson Papers*, 3:786. See also Jennings, *Ambiguous Iroquois Empire*, 388.
154. "Antient Copy of Indian Purchase Deeds of 28th of August, 1686, With Confirmation, and 'Draught' Aug. 1737."
155. Hazard, *Pennsylvania Archives*, 1:541.
156. Boyd, *Indian Treaties Printed by Benjamin Franklin*, 251.
157. Peters, "Conference at the Governor's House with Teedyuscung, November 16, 1762."
158. "The Complaint," *Delaware Nation v. Commonwealth of Pennsylvania* (U.S. District Court for the Eastern District of Pennsylvania, 2004), 12; Banner, *How the Indians Lost Their Land*, 135.
159. Associated Press, "Tribe's Bid for Casino Land to Hinge on Murky Records"; Dale, "Tribe Seeking Easton-Area Land for Casino Loses Federal Appeal," May 5, 2006; Lillian Thomas, "Delawares' Claim Goes Back to Obscure 315-Acre Grant in 1738," *Pittsburgh Post-Gazette*, May 16, 2003, http://www.post-gazette.com/localnews/20030516indiansidebarreg7p7.asp.
160. *Delaware Nation v. Commonwealth of Pennsylvania*, No. 04-4593 (U.S. Third Circuit Court of Appeals, 2006); *Delaware Nation, Petitioner, v. Pennsylvania et al.* (U.S. Supreme Court, 2006).
161. W. Davis, *History of Bucks County*, 1:476–77.
162. Mannheim, *Essays on the Sociology of Knowledge*, 304; J. Assmann, "Communicative and Cultural Memory," 112.
163. *Delaware Nation v. Commonwealth of Pennsylvania* (U.S. District Court for the Eastern District of Pennsylvania, 2004).
164. *Delaware Nation v. Commonwealth of Pennsylvania*, No. 04-4593 (U.S. Third Circuit Court of Appeals, 2006), 10.
165. Document 1-2, Exhibit A, *Delaware Nation v. Commonwealth of Pennsylvania*, (2004). Copy of original in the Pennsylvania State Archives, RG-17, Warrant Application Transcript Books, Applications, 1732–33 (Binding 123), p. 17.
166. Stuart Banner argues that Locke's references to Indians in his *Two Treatises on Government* were inconsistent with the widespread colonial recognition that Native Americans had a system of property. *How the Indians Lost Their Land*, 46–48, see also 80.
167. Schutt, *Peoples of the River Valleys*, 96.

168. Document 1-2, Exhibit C, *Delaware Nation v. Commonwealth of Pennsylvania* (2004).
169. Document 1-2, Exhibits E, F, *Delaware Nation v. Commonwealth of Pennsylvania* (2004).
170. Provincial Council of Pennsylvania, Minutes, 3:624.
171. Pointer, "'Poor Indians' and the 'Poor in Spirit,'" 141.
172. Merrell, *Into the American Woods*, 292, 429–30n152.
173. Pennsylvania Assembly, "Copy of Resolution by the Assembly, Requesting the Governor to Warrant 200 acres to One Nicholas Tatamy, an Indian."
174. "Moses Tatamy Affidavit," *New-York Mercury*, December 8, 1755. According to Merrell, "Moses Tatamy, for much of his life, was as famously sober as his fellow Delaware Teedyuscung was infamously drunk." Yet "in 1760 he was prone to 'Druncken Fitts.'" *Into the American Woods*, 100, 293.
175. Henry, *History of the Lehigh Valley*, 50.
176. Becker, *The Forks of Delaware, Pennsylvania*, 53.
177. Henry, *History of the Lehigh Valley*, 50.
178. Kammen, *Mystic Chords of Memory*, 87.
179. Brodhead, *Delaware Water Gap*, 46–47.
180. C. Gray, "Indian Claim Tests a Family's Roots." *Philadelphia Inquirer*, May 20, 2003.
181. Jordan, "Indian Tribe Loses Appeal Seeking Forks Land," May 5, 2006.

AFTERWORD

1. Brooke, "Old New York Is Being Unearthed on Ellis Island."
2. National Park Service, "NAGPRA Notices of Inventory Completion: Human Remains and Associated Funerary Objects in the Control of the U.S. Department of the Interior."
3. National Park Service, "NAGPRA Notices of Inventory Completion."
4. Wildlife Conservation Society, "Overview," http://welikia.org/about/overview/.
5. Wildlife Conservation Society, "Overview."
6. Lenape Language Preservation Project, *Lenape Talking Dictionary*, http://www.talk-lenape.org. The Indians encountered by Hudson in New York Harbor did not speak Unami, the dialect of Lenapes in southeastern Pennsylvania,

but rather the dialect now identified as Munsee. See Grumet, *Munsee Indians*, 5, 14; Grumet, *Dutch-Munsee Encounter in America*.
7. Sanderson, *Mannahatta*, 102–35.
8. Nora, "General Introduction: Between Memory and History," 1:3.
9. According to Jeffrey K. Olick, Vered Vinitzky-Seroussi, and Daniel Levy, "While the present preoccupation with memory has its origins in the Western European context and associated debates about modernity, it has since permeated political-cultural debates in other contexts as well." Introduction to *Collective Memory Reader*, 3n3. According to Jan Assmann, "studies in oral history confirm that even in literate societies living memory goes no further back than eighty years." "Communicative and Cultural Memory," 113.
10. As of 2011, searches in the Indigenous Studies Portal and the Library of Congress catalog show that "memory" has yet to emerge as a conceptual keyword in Native American Studies, despite the centrality of the transmission of cultural memory as a topic. Even studies of Native American mnemonic practices and conceptions of the past use "history" as a keyword, and do not cite research on social or collective memory. See Nabokov, *Forest of Time*; Krupat, *Red Matters*, chap. 3: "America's Histories."
11. See the critique of the National Museum of the American Indian by Carpio, "(Un)disturbing Exhibitions."
12. Momaday, *The Way to Rainy Mountain*, ix, 3.
13. Halbwachs, *On Collective Memory*, 182.
14. Momaday, *The Way to Rainy Mountain*, 7.
15. A. Assmann, "Canon and Archive," 101.
16. Momaday, *The Way to Rainy Mountain*, 10.
17. Adams, *Ancient Religion of the Delaware Indians*, 5.
18. For articulations of the opposition between traditions and modernity, see Nora, "Introduction to Realms of Memory"; Shils, *Tradition*.
19. Momaday, *The Way to Rainy Mountain*, 10.
20. Weslager, *Delaware Indian Westward Migration*, 89.
21. Erdrich, *Tracks: A Novel*, 2.
22. Weslager, *Delaware Indian Westward Migration*, 90.
23. The best exposition of this precept remains Keith Basso's *Wisdom Sits in Places*.

24. Momaday, The Way to Rainy Mountain, 16–17.
25. Danckaerts, Journal of Jasper Danckaerts, 149–50.
26. Danckaerts, Journal of Jasper Danckaerts, 150.
27. Eliot, John Eliot's Indian Dialogues, 141.
28. Kraft, The Lenape: Archaeology, History, and Ethnography, 3.
29. Lenik, Picture Rocks, 176.
30. P. Wallace, Travels of John Heckewelder, 51. Heckewelder was mistaken in understanding the Tortoise, Turkey, and Wolf designations to correspond to the Unami, Unalachtigo, and Munsee tribes. Instead, they refer to phratries that transcended other regional or political divisions. See A. Wallace, "Woman, Land, and Society," 14–15.
31. Lenik, Picture Rocks, 176. On the scientific analysis of the artifact and its possible attribution to a boy scout, see Gilbert et al., "A Turtle in the Bronx," in prep. My thanks to Dr. Gilbert for sharing the article in preparation.
32. Miller, "Old Religion among the Delawares," 114, 121.
33. Miller, "Old Religion among the Delawares," 120; Misztal, Theories of Social Remembering, 67–74.
34. Miller, "Old Religion among the Delawares," 114.
35. Miller, "Old Religion among the Delawares," 114.
36. J. Schwartz, "Indians Return to an Ancestral Home"
37. Brown and Kohn, Long Journey Home, 189, 197–210, 327–28.
38. J. Schwartz, "Indians Return to an Ancestral Home" ("homecoming"); Brown and Kohn, Long Journey Home, 189. See "Indian Ceremony on Ellis Island," New York Times, June 29, 1987, sec. B. The picture and caption (there is no article) feature Willy Snake holding a funeral pouch.
39. Pooacha, "Ancestral Delaware Remains Finally Laid to Rest."

BIBLIOGRAPHY

PUBLISHED SOURCES

Abbott, Devon. "'Commendable Progress': Acculturation at the Cherokee Female Seminary." *American Indian Quarterly* 11, no. 3 (Summer 1987): 187–201.

Abrams, Ann Uhry. "Benjamin West's Documentation of Colonial History: William Penn's Treaty with the Indians." *Art Bulletin* 64, no. 1 (March 1982): 59–75.

Adair, Douglass. "The Stamp Act in Contemporary English Cartoons." *The William and Mary Quarterly*, 3rd ser., 10, no. 4 (October 1953): 538–42.

Adams, Richard C. *The Ancient Religion of the Delaware Indians and Observations and Reflections*. Washington DC: Law Reporter Printing Co., 1904.

———. *A Brief History of the Delaware Indians*. Washington DC: Government Printing Office, 1906.

———. *A Delaware Indian Legend and the Story of Their Troubles*. Washington DC, 1899.

———. *Legends of the Delaware Indians and Picture Writing*. Edited by Deborah Nichols. Iroquois and Their Neighbors. Syracuse NY: Syracuse University Press, 1997.

Alam, Muzaffar, and Sanjay Subrahmanyam. "Letters from a Sinking Sultan." In *Aquém e além da Taprobana: Estudos Luso-Orientais à memória de Jean Aubin e Denys Lombard*, edited by Luis Filipe F. R. Thomas, 239–69. Lisbon: Universidade Nova de Lisboa, 2002.

Arbousset, Thomas. *Relation d'un voyage d'exploration au nord-est de la colonie du Cap de Bonne-Espérance : Entrepris dans les mois de mars, avril et mai 1836 par mm. T. Arbousset et F. Daumas*. Paris: A. Bertrand, 1842.

Architect of the Capitol. "Capitol Campus Art," n.d. http://www.aoc.gov/cc/art/index.cfm.

Assmann, Aleida. "Canon and Archive." In Erll and Nünning, *Companion to Cultural Memory Studies*, 97–107.

———. "Texts, Traces, Trash: The Changing Media of Cultural Memory." *Representations*, no. 56 (October 1, 1996): 123–34.

Assmann, Jan. "Communicative and Cultural Memory." In Erll and Nünning, *Companion to Cultural Memory Studies*, 108–18.

Associated Press State and Local Wire. "Tribe's Bid for Casino Land to Hinge on Murky Records." February 9, 2004. LexisNexis Academic.

Austin, J. L. *How to Do Things with Words*. Cambridge MA: Harvard University Press, 1975.

Austin, Mary. "Non-English Writings II: Aboriginal." In *The Cambridge History of American Literature*, edited by W. P. Trent, J. Erskine, S. P. Sherman, and C. Van Doren. New York: G. P. Putnam's Sons, 1921.

Axtell, James. *After Columbus: Essays in the Ethnohistory of Colonial North America*. Oxford: Oxford University Press, 1988.

Bach, Kent. "Speech Acts." In *Routledge Encyclopedia of Philosophy*, 1998. http://www.rep.routledge.com/article/U043SECT1.

Banks, J. A., B. K. Beyer, G. Contreras, J. Craven, G. Ladson-Billings, M. A. McFarland, and W. C. Parker. *A New Nation: Adventures in Time and Place*. New York: McGraw-Hill School Division, 2000.

Banner, Stuart. *How the Indians Lost Their Land: Law and Power on the Frontier*. Cambridge MA: Harvard University Press, 2005.

Barbeau, Charles Marius. *Huron and Wyandot Mythology*. Canada Geological Survey, Memoir 80. Anthropological Series 11. Ottawa: Government Printing Bureau, 1915.

Barnhart, Terry A. *Ephraim George Squier and the Development of American Anthropology*. Critical Studies in the History of Anthropology. Lincoln: University of Nebraska Press, 2005.

Barone, D. "Hostility and Rapprochement: Formal Rhetoric in Philadelphia before 1775." *Pennsylvania History* 56, no. 1 (January 1989): 15–32.

Barton, Benjamin Smith. *New Views of the Origin of the Tribes and Nations of America*. Philadelphia: Printed for the author by John Bioren, 1797.

Basset, René. "La Légende de Didon." *Revue de Traditions Populaires* 6 (1891): 335–38.

Basso, Keith H. *Wisdom Sits in Places : Landscape and Language among the Western Apache*. Albuquerque: University of New Mexico Press, 1996.

Bastian, Adolf. *Die Volker des oestlichen Asien*. Vol. 4. Jena, Germany: Hermann Costenoble, 1868.

Bauman, Richard. *For the Reputation of Truth: Politics, Religion, and Conflict among the Pennsylvania Quakers*. Baltimore: Johns Hopkins Press, 1971.

———. *Let Your Words Be Few: Symbolism of Speaking and Silence among Seventeenth-Century Quakers*. Cambridge Studies in Oral and Literate Culture. Cambridge: Cambridge University Press, 1983.

———. "Quaker Folk-Linguistics and Folklore." In *Folklore: Performance and Communication*, edited by Dan Ben-Amos and Kenneth S. Goldstein, 255–63. The Hague: Mouton, 1975.

———. "Speaking in the Light: The Role of the Quaker Minister." In *Explorations in the Ethnography of Speaking*, edited by Richard Bauman and Joel Sherzer, 144–60. London: Cambridge University Press, 1974.

Bauman, Richard, and Charles L. Briggs. *Voices of Modernity: Language Ideologies and the Politics of Inequality*. Studies in the Social and Cultural Foundations of Language 21. Cambridge: Cambridge University Press, 2003.

Baumeister, Roy F., and Stephen Hastings. "Distortions of Collective Memory: How Groups Flatter and Deceive Themselves." In *Collective Memory of Political Events: Social Psychological Perspectives*, edited by James W. Pennebaker, Darío Páez, and Bernard Rimé, 277–93. Mahwah NJ: Lawrence Erlbaum Associates, 1997.

Bayley, Edward Clive. *The History of India as Told by Its Own Historians: The Local Muhammadan Dynasties : Gujarát*. London: W. H. Allen, 1886.

Beach, William Wallace. *The Indian Miscellany*. Albany: J. Munsell, 1877.

Becker, Marshall Joseph. *The Forks of Delaware, Pennsylvania, During the First Half of the Eighteenth Century: The Migrations of Some "Jerseys" into a Former Shared Resource Area North of Lenape Territory and Its Implications for Cultural Boundaries and Identities*. Nortorf [Germany]: Völkerkundliche Arbeitsgemeinschaft, 1987.

———. "Lenape Land Sales, Treaties, and Wampum Belts." *Pennsylvania Magazine of History & Biography* 108, no. 3 (1984): 351–356.

———. "LENOPI; or, What's in a Name? Interpreting the Evidence for Cultures and Cultural Boundaries In the Lower Delaware Valley." *Bulletin of the Archeological Society of New Jersey* (n.d.).

Becker, Marshall J., and John Beierle. "Cultural Summary: Delaware." HRAF, 2002. http://www.yale.edu/hraf/.
Benjamin, Walter. "The Task of the Translator." In Illuminations, 69–82. New York: Schocken Books, 1986.
Bierhorst, John. Mythology of the Lenape: Guide and Texts. Tucson: University of Arizona Press, 1995.
Boewe, Charles. "The Fall from Grace of that 'Base Wretch' Rafinesque." The Kentucky Review (1987): 39–53.
———. The Life of C. S. Rafinesque, a Man of Uncommon Zeal. Philadelphia: American Philosophical Society, 2011.
———. Profiles of Rafinesque. Knoxville: University of Tennessee Press, 2003.
Boone, Elizabeth Hill. "Introduction: Writing and Recording Knowledge." In Writing Without words : Alternative Literacies in Mesoamerica and the Andes, edited by Elizabeth Hill Boone and Walter Mignolo, 3–16. Durham NC: Duke University Press, 1994.
Boyd, J. P. "Indian Affairs in Pennsylvania, 1736–1762." In Indian Treaties Printed by Benjamin Franklin, 1736–1762, xix–lxxxviii. Philadelphia: Historical Society of Pennsylvania, 1938.
———, ed. Indian Treaties Printed by Benjamin Franklin, 1736–1762. Philadelphia: Historical Society of Pennsylvania, 1938.
Brinton, D. G. The Lenâpé and Their Legends. New York: AMS Press, 1969.
Brinton, Ellen Starr. "Benjamin West's Painting of Penn's Treaty with the Indians." Bulletin of the Friends' Historical Association 30 (1941): 99–189.
Brodhead, Luke Wills. The Delaware Water Gap: Its Legends and Early History. Philadelphia: Sherman and Co., 1870.
Brooke, James. "Old New York Is Being Unearthed on Ellis Island." New York Times, June 16, 1986, sec. B.
Brooks, Lisa Tanya. The Common Pot: The Recovery of Native Space in the Northeast. Indigenous Americas. Minneapolis: University of Minnesota Press, 2008.
Bross, Kristina. Dry Bones and Indian Sermons: Praying Indians in Colonial America. Ithaca: Cornell University Press, 2004.
Bross, Kristina, and Hilary E. Wyss, eds. Early Native Literacies in New England: A Documentary and Critical Anthology. Native Americans of the Northeast. Amherst: University of Massachusetts Press, 2008.
Brotherston, Gordon. Book of the Fourth World : Reading the Native Americas through Their Literature. New York: Cambridge University Press, 1992.

———. *Image of the New World: The American Continent Portrayed in Native Texts*. London: Thames and Hudson, 1979.

———. "The Time Remembered in Winter Counts and the Walam Olum." In *Circumpacifica: Festschrift für Thomas S. Barthel*, 2:307–37. Frankfurt and Bern: Peter Lang, 1990.

Brown, Adam, Yifat Gutman, Lindsey Freeman, Amy Sodaro, and Alin Coman. "Introduction: Is an Interdisciplinary Field of Memory Studies Possible?," *International Journal of Politics, Culture, and Society* 22, no. 2 (June 2009): 117–24.

Brown, James W., and Rita T. Kohn, eds. *Long Journey Home: Oral Histories of Contemporary Delaware Indians*. Bloomington: Indiana University Press, 2008.

Brown, Kathleen. "The Anglo-Algonquian Gender Frontier." In *Negotiators of Change: Historical Perspectives on Native American Women*, 26–48. New York: Routledge, 1995.

Bryan, Michael. *Dictionary of Painters and Engravers: Biographical and Critical*. G. Bell and Sons, 1886.

Bryant, William Cullen. *Poems*. Philadelphia: A. Hart, 1852.

Buell, Augustus C. *William Penn as the Founder of Two Commonwealths*. New York: D. Appleton, 1904.

Bunyan, John. *Pilgrim's Progress*. New York: P. F. Collier and Son, 1909.

Burrows, Edwin G., and Mike Wallace. *Gotham: A History of New York City to 1898*. New York: Oxford University Press, 1999.

Bush, Sargent. "America's Origin Myth: Remembering Plymouth Rock." *American Literary History* 12, no. 4 (Winter 2000): 745–56.

Buzard, James. *The Beaten Track: European Tourism, Literature, and the Ways of Culture, 1800–1918*. New York: Oxford University Press, 1993.

Calloway, Colin G., ed. *Revolution and Confederation*, vol. 18 of *Early American Indian Documents: Treaties and Laws, 1607–1789*. Bethesda MD: University Publications of America, 1994.

Camões, Luís Vaz de. *The Lusíads*. Translated by Landeg White. New York: Oxford University Press, 2008.

Campanella, Thomas J. *Republic of Shade: New England and the American Elm*. New Haven CT: Yale University Press, 2003.

Cantemir, Dimitrie. *The History of the Growth and Decay of the Othman Empire*. . . . London: J. J. and P. Knapton, 1734.

Carpio, Myla Vicenti. "(Un)disturbing Exhibitions: Indigenous Historical Memory at the NMAI." *American Indian Quarterly* 30, no. 3 (2006): 619–31.

Carruthers, Mary J. *The Book of Memory : A Study of Memory in Medieval Culture*. 2nd ed. Cambridge: Cambridge University Press, 2008.

Cass, Lewis. "Manners and Customs of Several Indian Tribes." *North American Review* 22, no. 50 (January 1826): 53.

Castanheda, Fernão Lopes de. *História do descobrimento e conquista da Índia pelos Portugueses*. Nova ed. Lisboa, 1833. http://hdl.handle.net/2027/nyp.33433082437751.

Cave, Alfred A. *The French and Indian War*. Greenwood Guides to Historic Events, 1500–1900. Westport CT: Greenwood Press, 2004.

Ceci, L. "The Value of Wampum among the New York Iroquois: A Case Study in Artifact Analysis." *Journal of Anthropological Research* 38, no. 1 (1982): 97–107.

Cheyfitz, Eric. *The Poetics of Imperialism : Translation and Colonization from The Tempest to Tarzan*. New York: Oxford University Press, 1991.

Clanchy, M. T. *From Memory to Written Record: England, 1066–1307*. Cambridge MA: Harvard University Press, 1979.

Clarkson, Thomas. *Memoirs of the Private and Public Life of William Penn*. Dover NH: Samuel C. Stevens, 1827.

Cohen, Matt. *The Networked Wilderness: Communicating in Early New England*. Minneapolis: University of Minnesota Press, 2010.

Conforti, Joseph A. *Imagining New England*. Chapel Hill: University of North Carolina Press, 2001.

Conyngham, Redmond. "Some Extracts from the Papers in the Office of the Secretary of the Commonwealth, at Harrisburg, and from Other Documents. Transcribed by Redmond Conyngham, Esq. of Carlisle, and Communicated by Him to the Society. Read at a Meeting of the Council, March 15, 1826." In *Memoirs of the Historical Society of Pennsylvania*, edited by Edward Armstrong, 1:332–36. Philadelphia: J. B. Lippincott and Co., 1864.

Cook, Terry. "The Archive(s) Is a Foreign Country: Historians, Archivists, and the Changing Archival Landscape." *Canadian Historical Review* 90, no. 3 (2009): 497–534.

Cooper, James Fenimore. *The Last of the Mohicans: A Narrative of 1757*. Albany: State University of New York Press, 1983.

———. *Letters and Journals*. Edited by James Franklin Beard. Vol. 2. Belknap Press of Harvard University Press, 1960.

Cope, Thomas P. *Philadelphia Merchant: The Diary of Thomas P. Cope*. Edited by Elizabeth Cope Harrison. South Bend IN: Gateway Editions, 1978.

Cordier, Henri. "La Légende de Didon," *Revue de Traditions Populaires* 2 (1887): 295–96.

Craig, Peter Stebbins. *The 1693 Census of the Swedes on the Delaware: Family Histories of the Swedish Lutheran Church Members Residing in Pennsylvania, Delaware, West New Jersey and Cecil County, Md., 1638–1693*. Winter Park FL: SAG Publications, 1993.

Cresswell, N. *The Journal of Nicholas Cresswell, 1774–1777*. New York: Kennikat Press, 1924.

Cunha, Joseph Gerson. *Notes on the History and Antiquities of Chaul and Bassein*. Bombay: Thacker, Vining, 1876.

Dale, M. "Tribe Seeking Easton-Area Land for Casino Loses Federal Appeal." *Associated Press State and Local Wire*, May 5, 2006.

Danckaerts, Jasper. *Journal of Jasper Danckaerts, 1679–1680*. Translated by Bartlett Burleigh Murphy. Brooklyn: Long Island Historical Society, 1867.

Darnell, R. *Daniel Garrison Brinton: The "Fearless Critic" of Philadelphia*. Philadelphia: University of Pennsylvania, 1988.

Davidson, James W. *The Island of Formosa, Past and Present: History, People, Resources, and Commercial Prospects (1903)*. Oxford: Oxford University Press, 1988.

Davis, Joe Lee, John T. Frederick, and Frank Luther Mott, eds. *American Literature: An Anthology and Critical Survey*. Vol. 1. Charles Scribner's Sons, 1948.

Davis, William W. H. *History of Bucks County Pennsylvania from the Discovery of the Delaware to the Present Time*. Edited by Warren S. Ely and John W. Jordan. Vol. 1. 2nd ed. Pipersville PA: A. E. Lear, 1905.

Dean, Nora Thomson, James Rementer, and Andrew Twaddle. "Delaware Indian Reminiscences [interview with Nora Thompson Dean]." *Bulletin of the Archeological Society of New Jersey*, no. 35 (1978): 1–17.

Delâge, Denys. "La tradition orale de l'arrivée des Européens à New York." In *Culture et colonisation en Amérique du Nord: Canada, États-Unis, Mexique*, 203–14. Quebec: Les Éditions du Septentrion, 1994.

Delaware Tribe. "Frequently Asked Questions about the Lenape or Delaware Tribe." Culture and History of the Delaware Tribe. http://culture.delaware tribe.org/faq.htm.

———. "Home Page." Culture and History of the Delaware Tribe. http://culture .delawaretribe.org/home.htm.

Deloria, Vine. *Red Earth, White Lies: Native Americans and the Myth of Scientific Fact*. New York: Scribner, 1995.

Derrida, Jacques. *Limited Inc.* Evanston IL: Northwestern University Press, 1988.//
De Silva, Chandra Richard. *Portuguese Encounters with Sri Lanka and the Maldives.* Brookfield VT: Ashgate Publishing, 2006.

———. "Portugal and Sri Lanka: Recent Trends in Historiography." In *Re-exploring the Links: History and Constructed Histories between Portugal and Sri Lanka*, edited by Jorge Manuel Flores, 24–25. Otto Harrassowitz Verlag, 2007.

Devine-Wright, Patrick. "A Theoretical Overview of Memory and Conflict." In *The Role of Memory in Ethnic Conflict*, edited by Ed Cairns and Micheál D. Roe, 9–33. New York: Palgrave Macmillan, 2003.

Dixon, R. B. "Dr. Dixon's Reply." *American Anthropologist*, n.s., 17, no. 3 (September 1915): 599–600. "Documents and Proceedings relating to the Formation and Progress of a Board in the City of New York, for the Emigration, Preservation, and Improvement of the Aborigines of America. July 22, 1829." *North American Review* 30, no. 66 (January 1830): 62–121.

Du Ponceau, Peter Stephen, and Joshua Francis Fisher. *A Memoir on the History of the Celebrated Treaty Made by William Penn with the Indians: Under the Elm Tree at Shackamaxon, in the Year 1682.* Philadelphia: Printed for M'Carty and Davis, 1836.

Echo-Hawk, Roger C. "Ancient History in the New World: Integrating Oral Traditions and the Archaeological Record in Deep Time." *American Antiquity* 65, no. 2 (April 2000): 267–290.

Einhorn, Arthur, and Thomas S. Abler. "Bonnets, Plumes, and Headbands in West's Painting of Penn's Treaty." *American Indian Art Magazine*, Summer 1996, 47–50.

Eliot, John. *John Eliot's Indian Dialogues: A Study in Cultural Interaction.* Edited by H. W. Bowden and J. P. Ronda. Westport CT: Greenwood Press, 1980.

Elliott, J. H. *Spain and Its World, 1500–1700.* New Haven CT: Yale University Press, 1989.

Erdrich, Louise. *Tracks: A Novel.* New York: Harper Perennial, 1989.

Erffa, Helmut von. *The Paintings of Benjamin West.* New Haven CT: Yale University Press, 1986.

Erll, Astrid. "Cultural Memory Studies: An Introduction." In Erll and Nünning, *Companion to Cultural Memory Studies.*

Erll, Astrid, and Ansgar Nünning, eds. *A Companion to Cultural Memory Studies.* Berlin: De Gruyter, 2010.

Fackenthal, B. F. "The Indian Walking Purchase of September 19 and 20, 1737; Address of Dr. B. F. Fackenthal Jr. at the Unveiling of a Monument in Springfield Township, Bucks County, Pennsylvania, to Mark the Lunching Place of the Walkers at Noon on the First Day of the Walk." In *A Collection of Papers Read before the Bucks County Historical Society*, 6:7–24. Doylestown PA: Bucks County Historical Society, 1925.

Fenton, William N. *The Great Law and the Longhouse: A Political History of the Iroquois Confederacy*. Civilization of the American Indian, vol. 223. Norman: University of Oklahoma Press, 1998.

Fish, Stanley Eugene. *Is There a Text in This Class?: The Authority of Interpretive Communities*. Cambridge MA: Harvard University Press, 1980.

———. "With Compliments of the Author: Reflections on Austin and Derrida." In *The Stanley Fish Reader*, 55–85. Malden MA: Blackwell Publishers, 1999.

Fogelson, Raymond D. "The Ethnohistory of Events and Nonevents." *Ethnohistory* 36, no. 2 (1989): 133–47.

Forbes, Jack. "The Renape People: A Brief Survey of Relationships and Migrations." *Wicazo Sa Review* 2, no. 1 (Spring 1986): 14–20.

Foster, Michael K. "'Another Look at the Function of Wampum in Iroquois–White Councils.'" In *The History and Culture of Iroquois Diplomacy: An Interdisciplinary Guide to the Treaties of the Six Nations and Their League*, edited by F. Jennings, 99–124. Syracuse NY: Syracuse University Press, 1985.

———. "When Words Become Deeds: An Analysis of Three Iroquois Longhouse Speech Events." In *Explorations in the Ethnography of Speaking*, edited by Richard Bauman and Joel Sherzer, 354–67. Cambridge: Cambridge University Press, 1989.

Franklin, Benjamin. *The Autobiography of Benjamin Franklin*. New York: P. F. Collier and Son, 1909.

Frazer, James G. *Adonis, Attis, Osiris: Studies in the History of Oriental Religion*. Vol. 3. New Hyde Park NY: University Books, 1962.

———. "Hide-Measured Lands." *Classical Review* 2, no. 10 (December 1888): 322.

Frost, William J. "William Penn's Experiment in the Wilderness: Promise and Legend." *Pennsylvania Magazine of History and Biography* 107, no. 4 (1983): 577–606.

Fryd, Vivien Green. *Art and Empire: The Politics of Ethnicity in the United States Capitol, 1815–1860*. New Haven CT: Yale University Press, 1992.

Furnivall, J. S. "History of Syriam." *Journal of the Burma Research Society* 5 (1915): 1–11, 49–57, 129–51.

Galperin, Karina. "The Dido Episode in Ercilla's *La Araucana* and the Critique of Empire." *Hispanic Review* 77, no. 1 (2008): 31–67.

Garvan, Anthony N. B. "The Consequence: The Social Impact of Benjamin West's Painting." In Pennsylvania Academy of Fine Arts, *Symbols of Peace: William Penn's Treaty with the Indians*, unpaginated.

Gerhard, Elmer Schultz. "Barter through the Ages." *Classical Journal* 32, no. 8 (May 1937): 493–94.

Gibbon, Edward. *The History of the Decline and Fall of the Roman Empire*. New York: Printed by J. and J. Harper for Collins and Hanney, 1826.

Gilbert, Allan, Tanzhuo Liu, Jeremy Tausch, and Patrick Brock. "A Turtle in the Bronx." In *Digging the Bronx: Recent Archeology in the Borough*, edited by Allan Gilbert. New York: Bronx County Historical Society, forthcoming.

Gillingham, Harold E. "Indian Silver Ornaments." *Pennsylvania Magazine of History and Biography* 58 (1935): 97–126.

Goddard, Ives. "Delaware." In *Handbook of North American Indians*, vol. 15: *Northeast*, 213–39. Washington DC: Smithsonian Institution Press, 1978. As seen in eHRAF World Cultures, www.yale.edu.

Gordon, Patrick. *Two Indian Treaties the One Held at Conestogoe in May 1728. And the Other at Philadelphia in June Following, Between the Honourable Patrick Gordon Esq; Lieut. Governour of the Province of Pennsylvania . . . and the Chiefs of the Conestogoe, Delaware, Shawanese and Canawese Indians*. Philadelphia: Printed and sold by Andrew Bradford, printer to the province, 1728.

Gordon, Thomas Francis. *The History of Pennsylvania, from Its Discovery by Europeans to the Declaration of Independence in 1776*. Philadelphia: Carey, Lea and Carey, 1829.

Gray, Chris. "Indian Claim Tests a Family's Roots." *Philadelphia Inquirer*, May 20, 2003.

Gray, E. G. *New World Babel: Languages and Nations in Early America*. Princeton NJ: Princeton University Press, 1999.

Gray, E. G., and N. Fiering. *The Language Encounter in the Americas, 1492–1800: A Collection of Essays*. New York: Berghahn Books, 2000.

Greenblatt, Stephen. *Marvelous Possessions: The Wonder of the New World*. Chicago: University of Chicago Press, 1991.

Greenlee, William B. "A Descriptive Bibliography of the History of Portugal." *Hispanic American Historical Review* 20, no. 3 (August 1940): 491–516.

Grotius, Hugo. *The Freedom of the Seas; or, The Right Which Belongs to the Dutch to Take Part in the East Indian Trade*. Edited by James Brown Scott. New York: Oxford University Press, 1916.

Grumet, Robert S. *The Dutch-Munsee Encounter in America: The Struggle for Sovereignty in the Hudson Valley*. New York: Berghan Books, 2006.

———. *The Munsee Indians: A History*. Norman: University of Oklahoma Press, 2009.

Habermas, Jurgen. *Communication and the Evolution of Society*. Boston: Beacon Press, 1979.

Haefeli, Evan. "On First Contact and Apotheosis: Manitou and Men in North America." *Ethnohistory* 54, no. 3 (July 1, 2007): 407–43.

Hajji al-Dabir. *Zafar ul walih bi muzaffar wa alihi: An Arabic History of Gujarat*. Vol. 1. Translated by M. F. Lokhandwala. Baroda: Oriental Institute, 1970.

Halbwachs, Maurice. *The Collective Memory*. New York: Harper and Row, 1980.

———. *On Collective Memory*. Translated by Lewis A. Coser. Heritage of Sociology. Chicago: University of Chicago Press, 1992.

Hale, Duane K. *Turtle Tales: Oral Traditions of the Delaware Tribe of Western Oklahoma*. Anadarko OK: Delaware Tribe of Western Oklahoma Press, 1984.

Hamilton, Alexander. *A New Account of the East Indies*. London: Printed for C. Hitch; and A. Millar, 1744.

Hamilton, Milton W. *Henry Hudson and the Dutch in New York*. Albany: University of the State of New York, 1959.

Harkin, Michael E. "Ethnohistory's Ethnohistory: Creating a Discipline from the Ground Up." *Social Science History* 34, no. 2 (June 1, 2010): 113–28.

Harper, Steven Craig. *Promised Land : Penn's Holy Experiment, the Walking Purchase, and the Dispossession of Delawares, 1600–1763*. Bethlehem PA: Lehigh University Press, 2006.

Harrington, M. R. *Dickon among the Lenape Indians*. Philadelphia: John C. Winston, 1938.

Hart, Charles H. "Benjamin West's Family: The American President of the Royal Academy of Arts Not a Quaker." *Pennsylvania Magazine of History and Biography* 32 (1908): 1–33.

Hazard, Samuel, ed. *Pennsylvania Archives*. Vol. 1. 1st ser. Philadelphia: Printed by Joseph Severns and Co., 1852.

Heath, S. B. "Protean Shapes in Literacy Events: Ever-Shifting Oral and Literate Traditions." In *Spoken and Written Language: Exploring Orality and Literacy*, 91–117. Norwood NJ: Ablex, 1982.

Heckewelder, John Gottlieb Ernestus. *An Account of the History, Manners, and Customs, of the Indian Nations, Who Once Inhabited Pennsylvania and the Neighboring States*. Philadelphia: A. Small, 1819. eHRAF World Cultures, http://www.yale.edu.

———. "Correspondence . . . Respecting the Languages of the American Indian." In *Memoirs of the Historical Society of Pennsylvania*, 12:349–442. Rev. ed. Philadelphia: Historical Society of Pennsylvania, 1881.

———. *History, Manners, and Customs of the Indian Nations Who Once Inhabited Pennsylvania and the Neighboring States*. Edited by William Cornelius Reichel. Philadelphia: Historical Society of Pennsylvania, 1881. http://www.archive.org/details/histmannerscustooheckrich.

———. *A Narrative of the Mission of the United Brethren: Among the Delaware and Mohegan Indians, from Its Commencement, in the Year 1740, to the Close of the Year 1808. Comprising All the Remarkable Incidents Which Took Place at Their Missionary Stations During That Period. Interspersed with Anecdotes, Historical Facts, Speeches of Indians, and Other Interesting Matter*. Philadelphia: M'Carty and Davis, 1820.

Heider, Eleanor R. "Universals in Color Naming and Memory." *Journal of Experimental Psychology* 93, no. 1 (1972): 10–20.

Helgerson, Richard. *A Sonnet from Carthage: Garcilaso de la Vega and the New Poetry of Sixteenth-Century Europe*. Philadelphia: University of Pennsylvania Press, 2007.

Henry, Mathew Schropp. *History of the Lehigh Valley: Containing a Copious Selection of the Most Interesting Facts, Traditions, Biographical Sketches, Anecdotes, Etc., Etc., Relating to Its History and Antiquities. With Complete History of All Its Internal Improvements, Progress of the Coal and Iron Trade, Manufactures, Etc*. Easton PA: Bixler and Corwin, 1860.

Hildebrandt, Stefan, and Anthony Tromba. *The Parsimonious Universe : Shape and Form in the Natural World*. New York: Copernicus, 1996.

Historical Society of Pennsylvania. *Presentation to the Historical Society of Pennsylvania of the Belt of Wampum Delivered by the Indians to William Penn, at the Great Treaty Under the Elm Tree, in 1682: To Which Are Appended William Penn's Letters to the Indians, Plan for the Union of the English Colonies, and Plan for the Confederation of the States of Europe*. Philadelphia, 1858.

Hobsbawm, E. J., and T. O. Ranger, eds. *The Invention of Tradition*. Cambridge: Cambridge University Press, 1984.

Huddleston, Lee Eldridge. *Origins of the American Indians: European Concepts, 1492–1729*. Austin: Published for the Institute of Latin American Studies by the University of Texas Press, 1967.

Hulbert, Archer Butler, and William Nathaniel Schwarze, "David Zeisberger's History of Northern American Indians," *Ohio Archeological and Historical Quarterly* 19, nos. 1 and 2 (1910).

Hunter, W. A. "Moses (Tunda) Tatamy: Delaware Indian Diplomat." In *A Delaware Indian Symposium* [proceedings], 71–87. Harrisburg: Pennsylvania Historical and Museum Commission, 1974.

Indiana Historical Society. *Walam Olum or Red Score: The Migration Legend of the Lenni Lenape or Delaware Indians: A New Translation, Interpreted by Linguistic, Historical, Archaeological, Ethnological, and Physical Anthropological Studies*. Indianapolis: Indiana Historical Society, 1954.

Irving, Washington. *Knickerbocker's History of New York*. New York: Frederick Ungar Publishing Company, 1928.

Jackson, Jason Baird. *Yuchi Ceremonial Life: Performance, Meaning, and Tradition in a Contemporary American Indian Community*. Lincoln: University of Nebraska Press, 2003.

Jacobs, Jaap. *The Colony of New Netherland: A Dutch Settlement in Seventeenth-Century America*. Ithaca: Cornell University Press, 2009.

Janvier, Thomas Allibone. *The Dutch Founding of New York*. Port Washington NY: I. J. Friedman, 1967.

Jennings, Francis. *The Ambiguous Iroquois Empire: The Covenant Chain Confederation of Indian Tribes with English Colonies from Its Beginnings to the Lancaster Treaty of 1744*. New York: W. W. Norton, 1983.

———. "Brother Miquon: Good Lord!" In *The World of William Penn*, edited by Richard S. Dunn and Mary Maples Dunn, 195–214. Philadelphia: University of Pennsylvania Press, 1986.

———. *The Invasion of America: Indians, Colonialism, and the Cant of Conquest*. Chapel Hill: University of North Carolina Press, 1975.

———. "The Scandalous Indian Policy of William Penn's Sons: Deeds and Documents of the Walking Purchase." *Pennsylvania History* 37, no. 1 (1970): 19–39.

Johnson, J. E. "A Quaker Imperialist's View of the British Colonies in America." *Pennsylvania Magazine of History and Biography* 60, no. 2 (1936): 97–130.

Johnston, Charles. *A Narrative of the Incidents Attending the Capture, Detention and Ransom of Charles Johnston. To which are added, Sketches of Indian Character and Manners, with Illustrative Anecdotes*. New York: Garland, 1827.

Jordan, Tracy. "Indian Tribe Loses Appeal Seeking Forks Land." *Allentown* [PA] *Morning Call*, May 5, 2006.

Juet, Robert. "From 'The Third Voyage of Master Henry Hudson,' by Robert Juet." In *Narratives of New Netherland, 1609–1664*, edited by J. Franklin Jameson, 11–28. New York: C. Scribner's Sons, 1909.

Justinus, M. J. *Epitome of the Philippic History of Pompeius Trogus*. Atlanta: Scholars Press, 1994.

Kaiser, Siegrun. "Munsee Social Networking and Political Encounters with the Moravian Church." In *Ethnographies and Exchanges : Native Americans, Moravians, and Catholics in Early North America*, edited by A. G Roeber, 145–64. University Park: Pennsylvania State University Press, 2008.

Kallendorf, Craig. "Representing the Other: Ercilla's La Araucana, Virgil's Aeneid, and the New World Encounter." *Comparative Literature Studies* 40, no. 4 (2003): 394–414.

Kammen, Michael G. *Meadows of Memory: Images of Time and Tradition in American Art and Culture*. Austin: University of Texas Press, 1992.

———. *Mystic Chords of Memory: The Transformation of Tradition in American Culture*. New York: Knopf, 1991.

Keyser, Charles Shearer. *Penn's Treaty with the Indians*. Philadelphia: D. McKay, 1882.

Kilpatrick, J. F., and A. G. Kilpatrick. *New Echota Letters: Contributions of Samuel A. Worcester to the Cherokee Phoenix*. Dallas: SMU Press, 1968.

King, J. C. H. "Woodlands Artifacts from the Studio of Benjamin West, 1738–1820." *American Indian Art Magazine*, Winter 1991, 35–47.

Klein, Kerwin Lee. "On the Emergence of Memory in Historical Discourse." *Representations*, no. 69 (Winter 2000): 127–50.

Knowlson, James. *Universal Language Schemes in England and France, 1600–1800*. Toronto: University of Toronto Press, 1975.

Konkle, Maureen. "Indian Literacy, U.S. Colonialism, and Literary Criticism." *American Literature* 69, no. 3 (September 1997): 457–86.

Kottenkamp, F. *Die ersten Amerikaner im Westen: Daniel Boone und seine Gefährten. (Die Gründung Kentucky's) Tecumseh und dessen Bruder. Von Franz Kottenkamp*, 2. Ausgabe mit 8 colorirten Bildern ed. Stuttgart: Verlag von Schmidt and Spring, 1858.

Kraft, Herbert C. *The Lenape: Archaeology, History, and Ethnography.* Collections of the New Jersey Historical Society. Newark: New Jersey Historical Society, 1986.

———. *The Lenape-Delaware Indian Heritage: 10,000 BC–AD 2000.* Shamong NJ: Lenape Books, 2001.

Krause, Sydney J. "Penn's Elm and Edgar Huntly: Dark 'Instruction to the Heart.'" *American Literature* 66, no. 3 (September 1994): 463–84.

Krupat, Arnold. *Red Matters: Native American Studies.* Philadelphia: University of Pennsylvania Press, 2002.

Lankford, G. *Native American Legends: Southeastern Legends—Tales from the Natchez, Caddo, Biloxi, Chickasaw, and Other Nations.* Little Rock: August House, 1987.

Laufer, Berthold. "The Relations of the Chinese to the Philippine Islands." *Smithsonian Miscellaneous Collections* 50, no. 2 (1907): 248–84.

———. Review of *Strange Stories from a Chinese Studio* by Herbert A. Giles. *Journal of American Folklore* 39, no. 151 (1926): 86–90.

Lebovics, Herman. "The Uses of America in Locke's Second Treatise of Government." *Journal of the History of Ideas* 47, no. 4 (December 1986): 567–81.

Lemire, Charles. *Exposé chronologique des relations du Cambodge avec le Siam, L'Annam and La France.* Paris: Challamel Aîné, 1879.

Lenape Language Preservation Project. "Lenape Talking Dictionary," n.d. http://www.talk-lenape.org.

Lenik, Edward J. *Picture Rocks: American Indian Rock Art in the Northeast Woodlands.* Hanover NH: University Press of New England, 2002.

Lewis, Rhodri. *Language, Mind, and Nature: Artificial Languages in England from Bacon to Locke.* Ideas in Context 80. Cambridge: Cambridge University Press, 2007.

Liu, James H., Mark Stewart Wilson, John McClure, and Te Ripowai Higgins. "Social Identity and the Perception of History: Cultural Representations of Aotearoa/New Zealand." *European Journal of Social Psychology* 29 (1999): 1021–47.

Livy. *The Romane Historie Written by T. Livius of Padua Also.* Early English Books Online. London : Printed by W. Hunt, for Abel Roper, at the Sun against St Dunstans Church in Fleetstreet, 1659.

Locke, John. *An Essay Concerning Human Understanding.* London: Printed for Thomas Tegg, 1825. http://www.archive.org/stream/humanunderstandi00lockuoft.

Lokken, Roy N. "The Social Thought of James Logan." *William and Mary Quarterly,* 3rd ser., 27, no. 1 (January 1970): 68–89.

Longfellow, Henry Wadsworth. *The Song of Hiawatha*. Boston: Ticknor and Fields, 1858.

Lorenz, Chris. "Can Histories Be True? Narrativism, Positivism, and the 'Metaphorical Turn.'" *History and Theory* 37, no. 3 (October 1998): 309–29.

Loskiel, George Henry. *History of the Mission of the United Brethren among the Indians in North America, in Three Parts*. Translated by Christian Ignatius La Trobe. London: Printed for the Brethren's Society for the furtherance of the Gospel: sold at No. 10, Nevil's Court, Fetter Lane; and by John Stockdale, 1794.

Lowie, Robert H. "Oral Tradition and History." *American Anthropologist*, n.s., 17, no. 3. (September 1915): 597–99.

Lupher, Donald A. *Romans in a New World : Classical Models in Sixteenth-Century Spanish America*. Ann Arbor: University of Michigan Press, 2003.

MacCormack, Sabine. *On the Wings of Time : Rome, the Incas, Spain, and Peru*. Princeton NJ: Princeton University Press, 2007.

Machiavelli, Niccolò. *Discourses on Livy*. Translated by Julia Cona Bondanella and Peter E. Bondanella. New York: Oxford University Press, 1997.

Madison, James H. *Eli Lilly: A Life, 1885–1977*. Indianapolis: Indiana Historical Society, 1989.

Mann, Barbara A. *Native Americans, Archaeologists, and the Mounds*. New York: P. Lang, 2003.

Mannheim, Karl. *Essays on the Sociology of Knowledge*. London: Routledge and Paul, 1972.

Mason, Ronald J. "Archaeology and Native North American Oral Traditions." *American Antiquity* 65, no. 2 (April 2000): 239–66.

McCutchen, David. *The Red Record = The Wallam Olum : The Oldest Native North American History*. Garden City Park NY: Avery Publishing Group, 1993.

McGuire, Randall H. "Archeology and the First Americans." *American Anthropologist*, n.s., 94, no. 4 (December 1992): 816–36.

McPhee, John. "Travels of the Rock." *New Yorker*, February 26, 1990.

Merrell, James H. "'I desire all that I have said . . . may be taken down aright': Revisiting Teedyuscung's 1756 Treaty Council Speeches." *William and Mary Quarterly*, 3rd ser., 63, no. 4 (October 2006): 777–826.

———. *Into the American Woods: Negotiators on the American Frontier*. New York: W. W. Norton, 1999.

———. "Some Thoughts on Colonial Historians and American Indians." *William and Mary Quarterly*, 3rd ser., 46, no. 1 (1989): 94–119.

Merritt, Jane T. *At the Crossroads: Indians and Empires on a Mid-Atlantic Frontier, 1700–1763*. Chapel Hill: University of North Carolina Press, 2003.

Merwick, Donna. *The Shame and the Sorrow : Dutch-Amerindian Encounters in New Netherland*. Philadelphia: University of Pennsylvania Press, 2006.

Milano, Kenneth W. *The History of Penn Treaty Park*. Charleston SC: The History Press, 2009.

Miller, Jay. "Old Religion among the Delawares: The Gamwing (Big House Rite)." *Ethnohistory: the Bulletin of the Ohio Valley Historic Indian Conference* 44, no. 1 (1997): 113–34.

———. "The Red Record." *American Indian Culture and Research Journal* 18, no. 1 (1994): 187–90.

Misztal, Barbara A. *Theories of Social Remembering*. Theorizing Society. Maidenhead UK: Open University Press, 2003.

Momaday, N. Scott. *The Way to Rainy Mountain*. Reprint, University of New Mexico Press, 1976.

Monteiro, George. "Camões's *Os Lusíadas*: The First Modern Epic." In *The Cambridge Companion to the Epic*, edited by Catherine Bates, 119–32. Cambridge: Cambridge University Press, 2010.

Montrose, Louis A. "Professing the Renaissance: The Poetics and Politics of Culture." In *The New Historicism*, edited by H. Aram Veeser, 15–36. New York: Routledge, 1989.

———. "The Work of Gender in the Discourse of Discovery." *Representations*, no. 33 (Winter 1991): 1–41.

Morga, Antonio de. *Sucesos de las Islas Filipinas*. Edited by José Rizal and W. E. Retana. Crónicas y memorias. Madrid: Ediciones Polifemo, 1997.

Murray, David. *Forked Tongues : Speech, Writing, and Representation in North American Indian Texts*. Bloomington: Indiana University Press, 1991.

———. *Indian Giving : Economies of Power in Indian-White Exchanges*. Amherst: University of Massachusetts Press, 2000.

Nabokov, Peter. *A Forest of Time: American Indian Ways of History*. New York: Cambridge University Press, 2002.

———. "Indian Views of History." In *North America*. Vol. 1 of *Cambridge History of the Native Peoples of the Americas*, edited by B. G. Trigger and W. E. Washburn, 1–59. New York: Cambridge University Press, 1996.

Nammack, Georgiana C. *Fraud, Politics, and the Dispossession of the Indians: The*

Iroquois Land Frontier in the Colonial Period. Norman: University of Oklahoma Press, 1969.

Napora, Joe. *The Walam Olum*. Greenfield Center NY: Greenfield Review Press, 1992.

Nash, Gary B. *First City: Philadelphia and the Forging of Historical Memory*. Philadelphia: University of Pennsylvania Press, 2002.

National Park Service. "NAGPRA Notices of Inventory Completion: Human Remains and Associated Funerary Objects in the Control of the U.S. Department of the Interior, National Park Service, Statue of Liberty National Monument, New York, NY." National NAGPRA, 355579–35580. http://www.nps.gov/nagpra/fed_notices/nagpradir/nico614.html.

Nederlandshce West-Indische compagnie. *Documents Relating to New Netherland, 1624–1626, in the Henry E. Huntington Library*. Edited by Arnold J. F. Van Laer. San Marino CA: Henry E. Huntington Library and Art Gallery, 1924.

Newcomb, W. W. "The Walum Olam of the Delaware in Perspective." *Texas Journal of Science* 7 (1955): 57–63.

Newman, Andrew. "Early Americanist Grammatology: Definitions of Literacy and Writing." In *Early American Mediascapes*, edited by Matt Cohen and Jeffrey Glover. Lincoln: University of Nebraska Press, forthcoming.

———. "'Light might possibly be requisite': Edgar Huntly, Regional History, and Historicist Criticism." *Early American Studies: An Interdisciplinary Journal* 8, no. 2 (Spring 2010): 322–57.

———. "Sublime Translation in the Novels of James Fenimore Cooper and Walter Scott." *Nineteenth-Century Literature* 59, no. 1 (June 2004): 1–26.

New-York Mercury. "Moses Tatamy Affidavit." December 8, 1755.

New York Times. "Museum Here Gets Historic Wampum: Two of William Penn's Treaty Belts, Long in England, Coming to New York." November 21, 1916.

———. "Relics of Penn at Auction; Paintings, Books and Other Objects Are Sold in London." July 12, 1916.

Nicholson, Katharine Stanley. *Historic American Trees*. New York: Frye Publishing Company, 1922.

Nora, Pierre. "General Introduction: Between Memory and History." In *Conflicts and Divisions*. Vol. 1 of *Realms of Memory: Rethinking the French Past*, edited by Pierre Nora and Lawrence D. Kritzman, 1–20. European Perspectives. New York: Columbia University Press, 1996.

———. "Introduction to Realms of Memory, Volume II." In *Traditions*. In *Realms of Memory: Rethinking the French Past*, edited by Pierre Nora and Lawrence D. Kritzman, ix–xii. European Perspectives. New York: Columbia University Press, 1996.

Novick, Peter. *That Noble Dream: The "Objectivity Question" and the American Historical Profession*. Cambridge: Cambridge University Press, 1988.

The Observator's trip to America, in a dialogue between the observator and his country-man Roger. Philadelphia: Printed by Andrew Bradford, 1726.

Oestreicher, David M. "Roots of the Walam Olum: Constantine Samuel Rafinesque and the Intellectual Heritage of the Early Nineteenth Century." In *New Perspectives on the Origins of Americanist Archeology*, 60–86. Tuscaloosa: The University of Alabama Press, 2002.

———. "The Tale of a Hoax: Translating the Walam Olum." In *Algonquian Spirit: Contemporary Translations of the Algonquian Literatures of North America*, 3–41. Lincoln: University of Nebraska Press, 2005.

———. "Text Out of Context: The Arguments that Created and Sustained the Walam Olum." *Bulletin of the Archeological Society of New Jersey*, no. 50 (1995): 31–52.

———. "Unmasking the Walam Olum: A 19th-Century Hoax." *Bulletin of the Archeological Society of New Jersey*, no. 49 (1994): 1–44.

———. "Unraveling the Walam Olum," *Natural History*, October 1996, 14–21.

Ohio Department of Job and Family Services. "Rachel Redinger." ODJFS Online, Ohio Women's Hall of Fame Bio, http://www.odjfs.state.oh.us/women/hallof fame/bio.asp?ID=252.

Oldmixon, John. *The British Empire in America*. Vol. 1. London, 1741.

Olick, Jeffrey K. "From Collective Memory to the Sociology of Mnemonic Practices and Products." In Erll and Nünning, *Companion to Cultural Memory Studies*, 151–61.

Olick, Jeffrey K., Vered Vinitzky-Seroussi, and Daniel Levy. Introduction to *The Collective Memory Reader*, edited by Jeffrey K. Olick, Vered Vinitzky-Seroussi, and Daniel Levy, 3–62. New York: Oxford University Press, 2011.

Ong, Walter. *Orality and Literacy: The Technologizing of the Word*. New York: Methuen, 1982.

Otto, Paul. *The Dutch-Munsee Encounter in America: The Struggle for Sovereignty in the Hudson Valley*. New York: Berghan Books, 2006.

Palumbo, Anne Cannon. *Adverting "Present Commotions": History as Politics in Penn's Treaty.* New York: Published by Oxford University Press in association with the National Museum of American Art, Smithsonian Institution, 1995.

Parkman, Francis. *The Works of Francis Parkman.* Edited by John Fiske. Little, Brown, 1898.

Parmenter, Jon. "Rethinking 'William Penn's Treaty with the Indians': Benjamin West, Thomas Penn, and the Legacy of Native-Newcomer Relations in Colonial Pennsylvania." *Proteus* 19, no. 1 (2002): 38–44.

Peau de Chat (Ojibway). "Speech to Canadian Officials on Land-Purchase Policy, Given at a Council at the Sault Ste. Marie, August 9, 1848." In *Great Documents in American Indian History*, edited by Wayne Moquin and Charles Van Doren, 160–62. New York: Da Capo, 1995.

Penn, William. *The Papers of William Penn.* Edited by Mary Maples Dunn and Richard S. Dunn. Vol. 2. Philadelphia: University of Pennsylvania Press, 1981.

———. *Some Fruits of Solitude, in Reflections and Maxims Relating to the Conduct of Human Life.* London: Printed for Thomas Northcott, 1693.

Pennebaker, James W., and Becky L. Banasik. "On the Creation and Maintenance of Collective Memories: History as Social Psychology." In *Collective Memory of Political Events: Social Psychological Perspectives*, edited by James W. Pennebaker, Darío Páez, and Bernard Rimé, 3–19. Mahwah NJ: Lawrence Erlbaum Associates, 1997.

Pennings, J. C. M. "History of the Arrangement of the VOC Archives." TANAP, http://www.tanap.net/content/voc/history/history_ministry.htm.

Pennsylvania, Provincial Council of. *Minutes of the Provincial Council of Pennsylvania: From the Organization to the Termination of the Proprietary Government.* Colonial Records of Pennsylvania. 16 vols. Philadelphia: Printed by Jo. Severns, 1852.

Pennsylvania Academy of the Fine Arts. *Symbols of Peace: William Penn's Treaty with the Indians.* An Exhibition Sponsored by the Pennsylvania Academy of the Fine Arts and Dickinson College, Philadelphia, May 12–September 26. Philadelphia: Pennsylvania Academy of the Fine Arts, 1976.

Philadelphia Inquirer. "Penn Treaty Park the Historic Spot to Be Preserved for Future Generation." October 8, 1893.

Plato. *Phaedrus.* New York: MacMillan, 1956.

Pointer, R. W. "'Poor Indians' and the 'Poor in Spirit': The Indian Impact on David Brainerd." *New England Quarterly* 67, no. 3 (1994): 403–26.

Pooacha, Fawn Wilson. "Ancestral Delaware Remains Finally Laid to Rest—Delaware Indian News Special Report." *National Association of Tribal Historic Preservation Officers*, July 2003. http://www.nathpo.org/News/NAGPRA/News-NAGPRA31.htm#top.

Pott, Friedrich. "Etymologische Legenden bei den Alten." *Philologus*, Supplemental Band II, no. 3 (1891): [251]–348.

Powell, J. U. "Byrsa, the Bull's Hide, at Carthage, and Some Parallels." *Folklore* 44, no. 3 (September 1933): 310–15.

Priest, Josiah. *American Antiquities, and Discoveries in the West*. Albany: Printed by Hoffman and White, 1833.

Proud, R. *The History of Pennsylvania, in North America from the original institution and settlement of that province, under the first proprietor and governor William Penn, in 1681, till after the year 1742*. Vol. 1. Philadelphia: Zachariah Poulson, 1797.

Purchas, Samuel. *Hakluytus Posthumus or Purchas His Pilgrimes*. 20 vols. New York: Macmillan, 1906.

Racewalk.com. "The Rules of Race Walking," n.d. http://www.racewalk.com/HowTo/Rules01.asp.

Raffles, Thomas Stamford. *The History of Java*. Vol. 2. London: Printed for Black, Parbury, and Allen, Booksellers to the Hon. East-India Company, Leadenhall Street; and John Murray, Albemarle Street, 1817.

Rafinesque, Constantine S. *The American Nations*. Philadelphia: C. S. Rafinesque; Printed by F. Turner, 1836.

———. *The Ancient Monuments of North and South America*. 2nd ed., corrected, enlarged and with some additions. Philadelphia: Printed for the author, 1838.

———. *The Good Book, and Amenities of Nature*. Philadelphia: Printed for the Eleutherium of Knowledge, 1840.

Rasmussen, Birgit Brander. "Negotiating Peace, Negotiating Literacies: A French-Iroquois Encounter and the Making of Early American Literature." *American Literature* 79, no. 3 (2007): 445–73.

———. *Queequeg's Coffin: Indigenous Literacies and Early American Literature*. Durham NC: Duke University Press, 2012.

Rawle, William. "A Vindication of the Rev. Mr. Heckewelder's History of the Indian Nations." In *Memoirs of the Historical Society of Pennsylvania*, edited by Armstrong, 1:268–84. Philadelphia: J. B. Lippincott, 1864.

Raynal, Abbé. *A Philosophical and Political History of the Settlements and Trade of the*

Europeans in the East and West Indies. Vol. 4. Dublin: Printed for John Exshaw and William Halhead, 1776.

Reid, Anthony. "Early Southeast Asian Categorizations of Europeans." In *Implicit Understanding: Observing, Reporting, and Reflecting on the Encounters between Europeans and Other Peoples in the Early Modern Era*, edited by Stuart B. Schwartz, 268–94. Cambridge: Cambridge University Press, 1994.

Richter, Daniel K. *Facing East from Indian Country : A Native History of Early America*. Cambridge MA: Harvard University Press, 2001.

———. "Introduction: Peoples in Conversation." In *Friends and Enemies in Penn's Woods: Indians, Colonists, and the Racial Construction of Pennsylvania*, edited by William A, Pencak, ix–xxi. University Park: Pennsylvania State University Press, 2004.

Rigal, Laura. "Framing the Fabric: A Luddite Reading of Penn's Treaty with the Indians." *American Literary History* 12, no. 3 (2000): 557–84.

Row, T. "Artifice of the Thong in Founding Cities and Castles Exploded." In *A Selection of Curious Articles from the Gentleman's Magazine*, edited by John Walker, 1:271–73. London: Longman, Hurst, Rees, Orme and Brown, 1811.

Russett, Margaret. *Fictions and Fakes: Forging Romantic Authenticity, 1760–1845*. New York: Cambridge University Press, 2006.

Saar, Johann Jacobs. *Reise nach Java, Banda, Ceylon und Persien, 1644–1660. Neu herausgegeben nach der zu Nürnberg im verlag von Johann Daniel Tauber (1672) gedruckten verbesserten ausgabe des im jahre 1662 zum ersten mal ershienenen textes*. Haag: Martinus Nijhoff, 1930.

Said, Edward W. *Culture and Imperialism*. Vol. 1. New York: Vintage Books, 1994.

Salisbury, Neal. "The Indians' Old World: Native Americans and the Coming of Europeans." *William and Mary Quarterly*, 3rd ser., 53, no. 3 (July 1996): 435–58.

Sanderson, Eric W. *Mannahatta: A Natural History of New York City*. New York: Abrams, 2009.

Sayre, Gordon. *Les Sauvages Américains: Representations of Native Americans in French and English Colonial Literature*. Chapel Hill: University of North Carolina Press, 1997.

Scharf, J. Thomas, and Thompson Westcott. *History of Philadelphia, 1609–1884*. Philadelphia: L. H. Everts and Co., 1884.

Schmidt, Benjamin. *Innocence Abroad : The Dutch Imagination and the New World, 1570–1670*. New York: Cambridge University Press, 2001.

Schutt, Amy C. *Peoples of the River Valleys: The Odyssey of the Delaware Indians.* Philadelphia: University of Pennsylvania Press, 2007.

Schwartz, Barry. *Abraham Lincoln and the Forge of National Memory.* Chicago: University of Chicago Press, 2000.

———. "The Social Context of Commemoration: A Study in Collective Memory." *Social Forces* 61, no. 2 (December 1982): 374–402.

Schwartz, Jerry. "Indians Return to an Ancestral Home." *Associated Press,* June 28, 1987. LexisNexis Academic.

Searle, J. "Reiterating the Differences: A Reply to Derrida." *Glyph* 2 (1977): 198–208.

Seed, Patricia. *Ceremonies of Possession in Europe's Conquest of the New World, 1492–1640.* New York: Cambridge University Press, 1995.

Seelye, John D. *Memory's Nation: The Place of Plymouth Rock.* Chapel Hill: University of North Carolina Press, 1998.

Sellers, Charles Coleman. "The Beginning: A Monument to Probity, Candor, and Peace." In *Symbols of Peace: William Penn's Treaty with the Indians,* unpaginated. Philadelphia: Pennsylvania Academy of the Fine Arts, 1976.

Servius. *Servii Grammatici qui feruntur in Vergilii carmina commentarii.* Vol. 2. Hildesheim: G. Olms, 1961.

Shell, Marc, and Werner Sollors, eds. *The Multilingual Anthology of American Literature.* New York: New York University Press, 2000.

Shils, Edward Albert. *Tradition.* Chicago: University of Chicago Press, 1981.

Shoemaker, Nancy. *A Strange Likeness: Becoming Red and White in Eighteenth-Century North America.* New York: Oxford University Press, 2004.

Shore, C., and G. Rhodes. "Princess Dido and the Ox Skin." *Math Projects Journal,* 2003. http://www.mathprojects.com/Downloads/Geometry/PrincessDido.pdf.

Shorto, Russell. *The Island at the Center of the World: The Epic Story of Dutch Manhattan and the Forgotten Colony that Shaped America.* New York: Doubleday, 2004.

Showalter, Michael S. "An Image of Peace: Penn's Treaty with the Indians." In *An Image of Peace: The Penn Treaty Collection of Mr. and Mrs. Meyer P. Potamkin,* 20–34. Harrisburg: Commonwealth of Pennsylvania, Pennsylvania Historical and Museum Commission, 1996.

Sikandar. *Mirati Sikandari; or, The Mirror of Sikandar.* Translated by Fazlullah Lutfallah Faridi. Bombay: Education Society, 1899.

Silverberg, Robert. *Mound Builders of Ancient America: The Archaeology of a Myth.* Greenwich CT: New York Graphic Society, 1968.

Slauter, Eric. "History, Literature, and the Atlantic World." *William and Mary Quarterly,* 3rd ser., 65, no. 1 (January 2008): 135–66.

Soderlund, J. R. *William Penn and the Founding of Pennsylvania, 1680–1684 : A Documentary History.* Philadelphia: University of Pennsylvania Press and Historical Society of Pennsylvania, 1983.

Sollors, Werner. Introduction to Shell and Sollors, *Multilingual Anthology of American Literature,* 1–11.

Spady, James. "Colonialism and the Discursive Antecedents of Penn's Treaty with the Indians." In *Friends and Enemies in Penn's Woods: Indians, Colonists, and the Racial Construction of Pennsylvania,* edited by W. A. Pencak and D. K. Richter, 18–40. University Park: Pennsylvania State University Press, 2004.

Speck, Frank Gouldsmith. *The Celestial Bear Comes Down to Earth.* Reading PA: Reading Public Museum and Art Gallery, 1945.

———. *The Penn Wampum Belts.* Leaflets of the Museum of the American Indian, Heye Foundation. [New York: De Vinne Press], 1925.

Spencer, David. *The Early Baptists of Philadelphia.* Philadelphia: W. Syckelmoore, 1877.

Squier, Ephraim George. "Historical and Mythological Traditions of the Algonquins; With a Translation of the 'Walam-Olum,' or Bark Record of the Linni-Lenape." *American Review: A Whig Journal Devoted to Politics and Literature,* no. 14 (February 1849): 273–93.

Staley, Allen. *Benjamin West, American Painter at the English Court: June 4–August 20, 1989.* Baltimore: Baltimore Museum of Art, 1989.

Stokes, I. N. Phelps. *The Iconography of Manhattan Island, 1498–1909 : Compiled from Original Sources and Illustrated by Photo-Intaglio Reproductions of Important Maps, Plans, Views, and Documents in Public and Private Collections.* Vol. 1. [Mansfield Centre CT]: Martino Fine Books, 1998.

Stone, Frederick D. "Penn's Treaty with the Indians: Did It Take Place in 1682 or 1683?" *Pennsylvania Magazine of History and Biography* 6, no. 2 (1882): 217–38.

Stuart, George E. "The Beginning of Maya Hieroglyphic Study: Contributions of Constantine S. Rafinesque and James H. McCulloh." In *Profiles of Rafinesque,* edited by Charles Boewe. Knoxville: University of Tennessee Press, 2003.

Subrahmanyam, Sanjay. "On the Hat-Wearers, Their Toilet Practices, and Other

Curious Usages." In *Europe Observed: Multiple Gazes in Early Modern Encounters*, edited by Kumkum Chatterjee and Clement Hawes, 45–81. Lewisburg PA: Bucknell University Press, 2008.

———. *The Portuguese Empire in Asia, 1500–1700*. London: Longman, 1993.

Sullivan, J., ed. *The Papers of Sir William Johnson*. Vol. 3. Albany: State University of New York, 1921.

Summit, Jennifer. *Memory's Library: Medieval Books in Early Modern England*. Chicago: University of Chicago Press, 2008.

Swales, John M. *Genre Analysis: English in Academic and Research Settings*. New York: Cambridge University Press, 1990.

Swann, Brian. *Algonquian Spirit: Contemporary Translations of the Algonquian Literatures of North America*. Lincoln: University of Nebraska Press, 2005.

Swanton, John R. "Dr. Swanton's Reply." *American Anthropologist*, n.s., 17, no. 3 (September 1915): 600.

———. "Social Organization and Social Usages of the Indians of the Creek Confederacy." In *Forty-Second Annual Report of the Bureau of American Ethnology*, 23–472. Washington DC: Government Printing Office, 1928.

Tedlock, D. "Dialogues Between Worlds: Mesoamerica After and Before the European Invasion." In *Theorizing the Americanist Tradition*, edited by L. P. Valentine and R. Darnell, 163–80. Toronto: Toronto University Press, 1999.

Thomas, Brook. *Civic Myths: A Law-and-Literature Approach to Citizenship*. Chapel Hill: University of North Carolina Press, 2007.

———. *The New Historicism: And Other Old-Fashioned Topics*. Princeton NJ: Princeton University Press, 1991.

Thomas, Mark G., Tudor Parfitt, Deborah A. Weiss, Karl Skorecki, James F. Wilson, Magdel le Roux, Neil Bradman, and David B. Goldstein. "Y Chromosomes Traveling South: The Cohen Modal Haplotype and the Origins of the Lemba—the 'Black Jews of Southern Africa.'" *American Journal of Human Genetics* 66, no. 2 (February 2000): 674–86.

Thompson, Stith. *Motif-Index of Folk-Literature: A Classification of Narrative Elements in Folktales, Ballads, Myths, Fables, Mediaeval Romances, Exempla, Fabliaux, Jest-Books, and Local Legends*. Rev. ed. Bloomington: Indiana University Press, 1955.

Thomson, Charles. *An Enquiry into the Causes of Alienation of the Delaware and Shawanese Indians from the British Interest*. 1759. Reprint, St. Clair Shores MI: Scholarly Press, 1970.

Tobin, Beth Fowkes. "Native Land and Foreign Desire: William Penn's Treaty with the Indians." *American Indian Culture and Research Journal* 19, no. 3 (1995): 87–119.

———. *Picturing Imperial Power: Colonial Subjects in Eighteenth-Century British Painting.* Durham NC: Duke University Press, 1999.

Turner, Frederick Jackson. *The Frontier in American History.* New York: Holt, 1947.

Upal, M. Afzal. "Memory, Mystery and Coherence: Does the Presence of 2–3 Counterintuitive Concepts Predict Cultural Success of a Narrative?" *Journal of Cognition and Culture* 11, no. 1/2 (January 2011): 23–48.

Uther, Hans-Jörg. *The Types of International Folktales: A Classification and Bibliography, Based on the System of Antti Aarne and Stith Thompson.* FF Communications no. 284. Helsinki: Suomalainen Tiedeakatemia, Academia Scientiarum Fennica, 2004.

Van der Donck, Adriaen. *A Description of New Netherland.* Translated by Charles T. Gehring. Lincoln: University of Nebraska Press, 2008.

Van Ittersum, Martine Julia. *Profit and Principle: Hugo Grotius, Natural Rights Theories, and the Rise of Dutch Power in the East Indies, 1595–1615.* Leiden: Brill, 2006.

Vansina, Jan. *Oral Tradition as History.* Madison: University of Wisconsin Press, 1985.

Vaux, Roberts. "A Memoir on the Locality of the Great Treaty Between William Penn, and the Indian Natives in 1682." In *Memoirs of the Historical Society of Pennsylvania*, edited by Edward Armstrong, 1:87–106. Philadelphia: J. B. Lippincott, 1864.

Virgil. *Pvbli Vergili Maronis Aeneidos liber qvartvs.* Edited by Arthur Stanley Pease. Cambridge MA: Harvard University Press, 1935.

———. *Vergil's Aeneid and Fourth ("Messianic") Eclogue in the Dryden Translation.* University Park: Pennsylvania State University Press, 1989.

Voltaire. *Letters Concerning the English Nation.* London: Reprinted by and for George Faulkner, 1733.

Wade, Nicholas. "DNA Backs a Tribe's Tradition of Early Descent from the Jews." *New York Times*, May 9, 1999.

Wagner, Günter. *Yuchi Tales.* New York: G. E. Stechert, 1931.

Wainwright, Nicholas B. "Tale of a Runaway Cape: The Penn-Baltimore Agreement of 1732." *Pennsylvania Magazine of History and Biography* 87, no. 3 (1963): 251–293.

Waite, Gary K. "The Holy Spirit Speaks Dutch: David Joris and the Promotion of the Dutch Language, 1538–1545." *Church History* 61, no. 1 (March 1992): 47–59.

Wallace, Anthony F. C. *King of the Delawares: Teedyuscung, 1700–1763*. Syracuse NY: Syracuse University Press, 1990.

———. "Woman, Land, and Society: Three Aspects of Aboriginal Delaware Life." *Pennsylvania Archaeologist* 17 (1947): 1–35.

Wallace, Anthony F. C., and William D. Reyburn. "Crossing the Ice: A Migration Legend of the Tuscarora Indians." *International Journal of American Linguistics* 17, no. 1 (January 1951): 42–47.

Wallace, Paul A. W. *The Travels of John Heckewelder in Frontier America*. Pittsburgh: University of Pittsburgh Press, 1958.

Ward, Matthew C. *Breaking the Backcountry: The Seven Years' War in Virginia and Pennsylvania, 1754–1765*. Pittsburgh: University of Pittsburgh Press, 2003.

Warhus, Mark. *Another America: Native American Maps and the History of Our Land*. New York: St. Martin's Press, 1997.

Warkentin, Germaine. "In Search of 'The Word of the Other': Aboriginal Sign Systems and the History of the Book in Canada." *Book History* 2 (1999): 1–27.

Warren, Leonard. *Constantine Samuel Rafinesque: A Voice in the American Wilderness*. Lexington: University Press of Kentucky, 2004.

Waswo, Richard. *The Founding Legend of Western Civilization: From Virgil to Vietnam*. Hanover NH: University Press of New England [for] Wesleyan University Press, 1997.

Watson, John F. *Annals of Philadelphia and Pennsylvania, in the olden time; being a collection of memoirs, anecdotes, and incidents of the city and its inhabitants, and of the earliest settlements of the inland part of Pennsylvania, from the days of the founders*. Vol. 1. Philadelphia: John Pennington and Uriah Hunt, 1844.

———. *The Indian Treaty: For the Lands Now the Site of Philadelphia and the Adjacent Country*. Philadelphia: Pennsylvania Historical Society, 1836.

Watts, Pauline Moffitt. "Pictures, Gestures, Hieroglyphs: 'Mute Eloquence' in Sixteenth-Century Mexico." In *The Language Encounter in the Americas, 1492–1800: A Collection of Essays*, edited by Edward G. Gray and Norman Fiering, 81–101. New York: Berghahn Books, 2000.

Waubuno. *The Traditions of the Delawares*. 4th ed. London: Bowers Brothers, 1875.

Weeks, Philip, ed. *The American Indian Experience: A Profile, 1524 to the Present*. Arlington Heights IL: Forum Press, 1988.

Weems, M. L. *The Life of William Penn: The Settler of Pennsylvania, the Founder of Philadelphia, and One of the First Lawgivers in the Colonies, Now United States, in 1682*. Philadelphia: Uriah Hunt and Son, 1854.

Weslager, C. A. *The Delaware Indians: A History*. New Brunswick NJ: Rutgers University Press, 1972.

———, ed. *The Delaware Indian Westward Migration: With the Texts of Two Manuscripts, 1821–22, Responding to General Lewis Cass's Inquiries About Lenape Culture and Language*. Wallingford PA: Middle Atlantic Press, 1978.

White, Ed. "Invisible Tagkanysough." PMLA: *Publications of the Modern Language Association of America* 120, no. 3 (May 2005): 751–67.

White, Miles Jr. "William Biles (concluded)." *Pennsylvania Magazine of History and Biography* 26, no. 3 (1902): 348–59.

Whiteley, Peter M. "Archaeology and Oral Tradition: The Scientific Importance of Dialogue." *American Antiquity* 67, no. 3 (July 2002): 405–15.

Wiget, Andrew O. "Truth and the Hopi: An Historiographic Study of Documented Oral Tradition concerning the Coming of the Spanish." *Ethnohistory* 29, no. 3 (July 1, 1982): 183–84.

Wildlife Conservation Society. "Overview." *Beyond Mannahatta: The Welikia Project*, 2008–2009. http://welikia.org/about/overview/.

Wilkinson, James. "A Choice of Fictions: Historians, Memory, and Evidence." PMLA 111, no. 1 (January 1, 1996): 80–92.

Williams, Stephen. *Fantastic Archaeology: The Wild Side of North American Prehistory*. Philadelphia: University of Pennsylvania Press, 1991.

Wilson-Okamura, David Scott. "Virgilian Models of Colonization in Shakespeare's *Tempest*." ELH: *English Literary History* 70, no. 3 (2003): 709–37.

Winterer, Caroline. "Model Empire, Lost City: Ancient Carthage and the Science of Politics in Revolutionary America." *William and Mary Quarterly*, 3rd ser., 67, no. 1 (January 1, 2010): 3–30.

Wolf, Edwin. "Benjamin Franklin's Stamp Act Cartoon." *Proceedings of the American Philosophical Society* 99, no. 6 (December 15, 1955): 388–96.

———, ed. *The Library of James Logan of Philadelphia, 1674–1751*. Philadelphia: Library Company of Philadelphia, 1974.

———. "The Romance of James Logan's Books." *William and Mary Quarterly*, 3rd ser., 13, no. 3 (July 1956): 342–53.

Woolard, Kathryn A. "Introduction: Language Ideology as a Field of Inquiry."

In *Language Ideologies: Theory and Practice*, 3–47. New York: Oxford University Press, 1998.

Wulf, Andrea. *The Brother Gardeners: Botany, Empire, and the Birth of an Obsession*. London: William Heinemann, 2008.

Wyss, Hilary E. *Writing Indians: Literacy, Christianity, and Native Community in Early America*. Native Americans of the Northeast. Amherst: University of Massachusetts Press, 2000.

Young, Alfred Fabian. *Liberty Tree : Ordinary People and the American Revolution*. New York: New York University Press, 2006.

Zeisberger, David. *David Zeisberger's History of Northern American Indians*. [Columbus OH]: Press of F. J. Heer, 1910.

———. *Zeisberger's Indian Dictionary*. New York: AMS Press, 1982.

Zelizer, Barbie. "Reading the Past Against the Grain: The Shape of Memory Studies." *Critical Studies in Mass Communication* 12 (June 1995): 214–39.

Zhang Tingyu. *Ming shi*. Beijing: Zhonghua Shuju, 1974.

Zhang Xie. *Dong xi yang kao*. Beijing: Zhonghua Shuju, 2000.

ARCHIVAL SOURCES

"Affidavit—James Hamilton, William Allen, and Richard Peters," Philadelphia, June 12, 1762. Chew Family Papers, Benjamin Chew (1722–1810). H. Treaty at Easton, Box 42, Folder 4. Historical Society of Pennsylvania.

"Affidavit of John Kennedy an Indian Trader, to prove the Indians did not complain of being ill treated by the Proprietors, and people of Pensilvania, but that they had a great regard for that people and Province," August 18, 1757. Penn Manuscripts, Indian Affairs, 1733–1801, 3:24. Historical Society of Pennsylvania.

"The Answer of the Chiefs of the Delaware Indians to the Governours Message of the 27th March 1741," Philadelphia, May 12, 1741. Chew Family Papers, Benjamin Chew (1722–1810). H. Treaty at Easton, Box 42—Correspondence Between the Delaware Indians and Governor Thomas (1740–1741), Folder 9. Historical Society of Pennsylvania.

"Antient Copy of Indian Purchase Deeds of 28th of August, 1686, With Confirmation, and 'Draught' Aug. 1737." Penn Manuscripts, Indian Affairs, 1733–1801, 4:21. Historical Society of Pennsylvania.

Cass, Lewis. Letter to J. W. Moulton, December 29, 1824. Lewis Cass Miscellaneous Manuscripts. New-York Historical Society.

"Copies of Depositions of Persons present at the Walk, performed in September 1737 ... (No. 4)." Penn Manuscripts, Indian Affairs, 1733–1801, 4:23–5. Historical Society of Pennsylvania.

Croghan, George. "A Copy of Mr. Croghan's Journal from the Close of the Treaty at Lancaster in May 1757." Penn Manuscripts, Indian Affairs, 1757–1772, 3:13. Historical Society of Pennsylvania.

Doan, Joseph. Letter to Thomas Penn, May 29, 1735. Walking Purchase of Pennsylvania Collection, 1735–1738, Manuscript Collection 950. Quaker Collection, Haverford College Library.

"The Examination of Edward Marshall," March 1, 1757. Chew Family Papers, Benjamin Chew (1722–1810). H. Treaty at Easton, Box 42, Folder 13. Historical Society of Pennsylvania.

Gassaway, Lillian. "Interview with Leona Parton," Anadarko OK, 1937. Indian-Pioneer Papers, vol. 69. Western History Collections, University of Oklahoma, Norman OK.

Heckewelder, John. Letter to Samuel Miller, February 26, 1801. Miller Papers, 1 (BV). New-York Historical Society.

"Indian Treaty Held at Philadelphia, August 17–18, 1731." James Steel Letterbook, 1730–1741, 1731. Historical Society of Pennsylvania.

Jackson, Rosalie Vallance Tiers. "Family Tradition Regarding the William Penn Treaty Elm as Related by Rosalie Vallance Tiers Jackson to Her Nephew Clarence Van Dyke Tiers," n.d. Eyre Family Papers. Historical Society of Pennsylvania.

Johnson, William. Letter to Governor Denny, September 13, 1757. Penn Manuscripts, Indian Affairs, 1733–1801, 3:25. Historical Society of Pennsylvania.

"Joseph Knowles Acct of Indians Day & Half Walk," June 30, 1757. Etting Collection, Miscellaneous Manuscripts, I:32:95. Historical Society of Pennsylvania.

"Letter to Governor Thomas." Smithfield, January 3, 1740. Chew Family Papers, Benjamin Chew (1722–1810), H. Treaty at Easton, Box 42, Folder 9. Historical Society of Pennsylvania.

"Letter to Jeremiah Langhorne." Smithfield, November 21, 1740. Chew Family Papers, Benjamin Chew (1722–1810). H. Treaty at Easton, Box 42, Folder 9. Historical Society of Pennsylvania.

Logan, James. Letter to Conrad Weiser, October 18, 1736. Logan Collection, 4:62–63. American Philosophical Society.

———. Letter to Conrad Weiser, July 11, 1742. Logan Collection, 4:78. American Philosophical Society.

———. "O My Soul," n.d. Emily Howland Papers, 1926–1975, Manuscript Collection 1000. Quaker Collection, Haverford College Library.

Morris, Edmund. Letter, to Roberts Vaux, August 27, 1826." Vaux Family Papers, Series 1, Box 3:33. Historical Society of Pennsylvania.

Morris, Edmund. Letter to Roberts Vaux, January 24, 1827. Vaux Family Papers, 3:3. Historical Society of Pennsylvania.

"Notes About Treaty Meetings," 1757–62. Chew Family Papers, Benjamin Chew (1722–1810), H. Treaty at Easton, Box 42, Folder 26. Historical Society of Pennsylvania.

Pennsylvania Assembly. "Copy of Resolution by the Assembly, Requesting the Governor to Warrant 200 Acres to One Nicholas Tatamy, an Indian," September 30, 1769. Moore Collection FF8. Historical Society of Pennsylvania.

Peters, Richard. "An Account of the Conduct of the Quakers," July 18, 1757. Indian Missions, 1742–1898, 317.3 no. 4a. Moravian Archives.

———. "Conference at the Governor's House with Teedyuscung, November 16, 1762." Penn Manuscripts, Indian Affairs, 1733–1801, 3:106. Historical Society of Pennsylvania.

Rafinesque, Constantine S. "Wallam Olum: First and Second Parts of the Painted Engraved Traditions of the Linnilinapi," 1833 [1834?]. Rare Book and Manuscript Library, University of Pennsylvania.

"Rough Draft of an Intended Message to the Delaware Indians 27 March 1741 sent accordingly May 1st & the answer enclosed," Philadelphia, March 27, 1741. Chew Family Papers, Benjamin Chew (1722–1810). H. Treaty at Easton, Box 42, Folder 9. Historical Society of Pennsylvania.

Schoolcraft, H. R. Copy of letter to E. G. Squier, February 16, 1849. Indian Miscellaneous Manuscripts Collection, New York Public Library.

Steel, James. Letter to John Chapman and Timothy Smith, April 29, 1735. James Steel Letterbook, 1730–41. Historical Society of Pennsylvania.

"Substance of an Occasional Conversation with Severall Indians after dinner at Israel Pemberton's on the 19th 4 mo 1756." Etting Collection, Miscellaneous Manuscripts, 1:32:84. Historical Society of Pennsylvania.

Tatamy, Moses. "In Reference to the Walking Purchase and Teedyuscung's Request for a Clerk," 1757. Quaker Collection, Haverford College Library.

———. "Moses Tatamie's Acct. of Indian Claims, taken from his mouth at Easton by CT," 1757. Etting Collection, Miscellaneous Manuscripts, I:32:94. Historical Society of Pennsylvania.

———. "Moses Tatamy's Acct of the Walking Purchase &c Taken by CT . . . 1757." Society Collection. Historical Society of Pennsylvania.

"Teedyuscung's Speech," June 24, 1762. Penn Manuscripts (1733–1801), Indian Affairs, 3:105. Historical Society of Pennsylvania.

"Thomas Furniss his Acct of the Walk," June 30, 1757. Etting Collection, Miscellaneous Manuscripts, I:32:96. Historical Society of Pennsylvania.

Watson, John. Letter to Israel Pemberton, July 29, 1757. Friendly Association Manuscripts, 1:375. Friendly Association Papers, Philadelphia Yearly Meeting, Indian Committee Records, 1745–1983. Haverford College Library.

———. Letter to Israel Pemberton, 19 8 mo 1757 [sic], Etting Collection, Miscellaneous Manuscripts, I:32:92. Historical Society of Pennsylvania.

Weiser, Conrad. Letter to James Logan, October 27, 1736. Logan Collection, 4:64. American Philosophical Society.

Williams, Gideon, John Quadrobe, John Killsnake, Joseph Francis, John Wrightman, and John W. Newsom. Letter to Zachary Taylor. "To His Excellency Zachary Taylor President of the United States of America," March 29, 1849. Microfilm Publications, Microcopy No. 234. Letters Received by the Office of Indian Affairs, 1824–81, Roll 303, Fort Leavenworth Agency, 1824–1851, 1849–1851, 333–42. National Archives.

INDEX

Page numbers in italic indicate illustrations

Ab urbe condita (Livy), 88
An Account of the History, Manners, and Customs of the Indian Nations that Once Inhabited Pennsylvania and the Neighboring States (Heckewelder): bullock hide story in, 67; content of, 1–2; and memory of Great Treaty, 121; on Native Americans' origins, 27–30; and popular culture, 34; publication of, 1, 26; as source for Walam Olum, 206n62; "verbatim" account of first contact in, 60
Adams, Richard Calmit (Delaware), 15, 48–49, 150–52, 188–89
Aeneas, 87–89
Aeneid (Virgil), 67–68, 72, 87–89, 217n122
affidavits, 137, 140, 161, 231n104
Africa, 28, 72, 73, 77, 78, 87, 92
agreements: and bullock hide story, 67, 69, 77; between Delawares and colonists, 112–13; Governor Thomas on fairness in, 162–63; Teedyuscung on Beaver's, 177; use of wampum in, 11, 122, 127–28, 165; wording of, 149, 150. *See also* deed (1686); deed, confirmation (1737); deeds; Great Treaty; treaty tradition; Walking Purchase (1737)
Alam, Muzaffar, 214n89
Albany Conference (1756), 103
alcohol, 36, 60, 63–64, 70, 191, 192, 235n174
Algonquian languages, 38, 61, 191, 205n43, 207n78. *See also* Native American languages
Algonquian peoples, 10, 11, 42, 122, 185, 192, 193. *See also* Delaware Indians
Allegheny, 177
allegories, 83, 92–93, 102–5, 150, 216n101, 221n43. *See also* legends; traditions
Allen, William, 139, 140, 178–81
Alligewi. *See* Talligewi
American Philosophical Society, 205n56
Americans: and authenticity of Walam Olum, 40; and council trees, 107; curtailing of native cultural traditions, 189; and image of Great Elm, 105; and Native Americans' land

Americans (continued)
  rights, 71; oral tradition of, 12;
  preservation of native traditions
  for, 33; westward advance of,
  32. See also colonists; Europeans;
  United States; whites
Anadarko OK. See Delaware Nation
Annales school, 5
Annals of Philadelphia and Pennsylvania
  (Watson), 12–13, 105, 114
Annapolis MD, 107
anthropology, 45, 46, 122
archeological artifacts, 3, 10, 57, 195
archeological study, 185–87, 193,
  214n74. See also scholarship
archeologists, 26–27, 30–33
archival memory, 188. See also memory
archival positivism, 19–20, 118
archival research, 13, 15. See also
  scholarship
archives, 21, 134, 136, 137, 163, 186. See
  also Pennsylvania State Archives
Armstrong, Edward, 111, 120
art criticism, 102
art historians, 7, 99. See also historians
artists, 105, 204n33, 220n41. See also
  painters
art, visual, 97–104, 220n39
Asia, 69, 73–77, 87, 88, 92, 93
Assmann, Aleida, 120, 188, 201n72,
  223n105
Assmann, Jan, 236n9
Associated Press, 195
Atlanteans, 25
Austin, J. L., 145

authenticity: artists' conception of, 105,
  220n41; of first-contact accounts,
  62, 65; of Native Americans' origin
  traditions, 26, 28; of oral traditions,
  36, 214n74; of Penn's Treaty image,
  105; in records and representations,
  16; of Walam Olum, 18, 27, 40–54,
  206n58, 206n62, 206n67, 207n78,
  207n86, 209n100; of Walking Purchase
  records, 22, 132; of writing,
  36, 145, 214n74. See also truth
authority: of archival records, 118; of
  deed (1686), 147; of John Heckewelder's
  "verbatim" account, 60; of
  material forms and spoken word,
  3; of Teedyuscung, 137; of written
  records, 118, 145, 146, 171, 175,
  228n52. See also truth
autobiographical memory, 188. See also
  memory
Avery Publishing Group, 47
Axtell, James, 212n48

Bahadur, Sultan, 78, 79
Bali, 73
Banasik, Becky L., 210n11
Banner, Stuart, 68–69, 180, 212n48,
  234n166
Barbeau, Marius, 68
Barnhart, Terry A., 206n67
Barros, João de, 88
Barrows, Vincent, 207n85
Bartlesville OK, 46, 195, 207n86. See also
  Oklahoma
Barton, Benjamin Smith, 32, 204n30

Basso, Keith, 190, 236n23
Batavia. *See* Jakarta
Baumeister, Roy F., 215n99
Beaver (Allegheny Delaware), 177
Becker, Marshall, 128, 135, 141–42, 225n129
Bellay, Joachim du, 217n122
belts, wampum, 124, 126; and communities of memory, 11; function at treaty meeting (1728), 17; and Great Treaty, 121–24; offered to Six Nations, 146–47, 163–64; of Penn family, 20, 124–29; symbolic content of, 164–65; Teedyuscung's use of, 171–72; and Walking Purchase controversy, 162. *See also* Penn Wampum Belts; wampum
Benjamin, Walter, 53
Benjamin Chew Papers, 233n145
Bering Strait, 30, 31, 38–39, 42
Bevan, Silvinius, 104, 218n9
Bible, 25, 29, 87. *See also* Genesis; Holy Scripture; religion
Bierhorst, John, 151, 211n35
Big House rite, 194
Biles, William, 140
Biles, William (father), 140
Birch, William Russell, 106
bison. *See* buffalo
Black Elk Speaks (Neihardt), 53, 169
Black Fort, 77, 78
Black Hills, 188
Blalock, Lucy, 186, 208n86
Blue Mountains, 139, 182. *See also* Kittatinny Mountains

Board of Trade, 168, 232n127
Boewe, Charles, 41, 205n56
Book of Mormon (Smith), 42
books, 38, 40, 53, 192. *See also* writing
Boone, Daniel, 97
Boston MA, 107
Boyd, Julian C., 134
Boydell, John, 99
Brainerd, David, 181
Brandywine Delaware Indians, 16. *See also* Delaware Indians
Brinton, Daniel G., 44, 45, 49, 50, 207n78, 209n100
British East India Company, 89
British Headquarters Map (1782–83), 186
Brito, Felipe de, 76
Brodhead, Luke Wills, 183
Bronx NY, 195
Bronx River, 193
Brotherston, Gordon, 50
Brown, Charles Brockden, 2, 204n33
Brown, Kathleen, 225n135
Brumidi, Constantino, 218n9
Bryant, William Cullen, 30–31
Bucks County Historical Society, 13, 178
Bucks County PA, 140, 157, 158, 162, 177, 178. *See also* Walking Purchase (1737)
Buell, Augustus C., 95
buffalo, 31, 189
Bulletin of the Archaeological Society of New Jersey, 39, 209n100
bullock hide motif: ambiguity of language in, 150–52; comparison

bullock hide motif (*continued*)
   to Great Treaty, 131; comparison to Walking Purchase, 93; distribution of, 68–77, 85–86, 92, 93; Dutch colonists' request for land encircled by, 1, 55–56, 64–68; and founding of Fort Amsterdam, 62; historians' failure to mention, 61, 210n17; Indians' memory of, 189–90; records on, 20; variants of, 73, 213n71. *See also* Dido motif; land transactions; traditions
Bumppo, Natty (Hawkeye), 34–36
Bunyan, John, 230n76
Bureau of American Ethnology, 31–32
Burlington Island, 112
Burma, 73, 76, 87
Burns, John, 38, 46, 206n62
Burrows, Edwin G., 61, 62
Bush, Sargent, 120, 223n103
Byrsa, 55, 72, 83, 86–88, 90

Calcutta, India, 87. *See also* India
Calvinists, 190, 192
Cambodia, 73
Cambridge History of American Literature, 18, 38, 209n100
Camões, Luis de, 88
Campanella, Thomas J., 105, 221n43
Canada, 195, 196, 207n86. *See also* Ontario, Canada
Canassatego (Onondaga), 131, 163–66, 170, 181
Cantemir, Dimitrie, 81
cantico, 155

Captain Civility (Taquatarensaly) (Conestoga), 117
Captain John (Delaware), 181
Captain Pipe (Delaware), 71
Carruthers, Mary, 229n52
Carthage, 18–19, 55–56, 72, 82, 83, 85, 88–90, 92. *See also* Dido, Queen (Elisa)
Carthaginians, 25
Cass, Lewis, 29–30, 189
Castanheda, Fernão Lopes de, 79, 81
Castiglioni, Luigi, 221n43
Catholic mission, 73
Catskill Mountains, 10
Cayuga Indians, 127. *See also* Hill, Seneca (Cayuga)
Celtic traditions, 33. *See also* traditions
ceremonial culture, 195
Ceylon, 73, 77–78
chains of memory: of Delaware-colonist interactions, 16–17; of Great Treaty, 20, 96–98, 102–4; group identity through, 188; lengths of, 12; and New York Harbor remains, 187; reliability of spoken word in, 2; research on, 178–79; Richard Adams on, 189; of Tantaqué's tortoise, 193–94. *See also* generations
chair seat trick, 71
chants, 38, 39, 204n32
Chapman, John, 178
Chapman, Martha, 178
Chapman family, 178–79
"Charter Oak," 107
Chaul, 81

Cherokee Indians, 26, 28
Chew, Benjamin, 140, 159, 233n145
Chief Tatamy Trail, 183
Chile, 216n116
Chinese, 76, 80, 82–83
Chinese writing system, 209n106
Chingachgook, 34–35, 36
"Christian Covenanting Confession," 52
Christianity: and authenticity of *Walam Olum*, 42–43, 49; and friendship with Native Americans, 128; and Great Treaty, 98; Moses Tatamy's conversion to, 181, 182; Native Americans' attitude toward God of, 191; and Native Americans' origin, 25, 26, 193; and Penn Wampum Belt, 125; Teedyuscung's request for instruction in, 169, 177. *See also* religion; whites
Christie's of London, 126
civic centers, 107
civic myths, 95, 97, 99–100, 118, 131–32, 186. *See also* myths
civilization, 31, 32, 42–43, 146, 204n37. *See also* culture
Clanchy, M. T., 145, 228n52
Clarkson, Thomas, 101–2, 105, 106, 219n29
classical motifs: in establishment of empires, 87, 88; in Native American history, 55–56, 65–68, 70, 82, 84–85, 89–90, 92; source of, 67–68, 72; symbolism of, 68–69. *See also* Dido motif

classical philosophy, 145
Coaquanoc, 101
Cock, Lasse, 112–14
Cohen, Matt, 202n88
Colombo, 77–78
colonialism: and authenticity of *Walam Olum*, 40; and Dido motif, 73, 83, 84–93, 216n101; and Eurocentrism, 129; and Great Treaty, 96; and language ideology, 8, 151; memories of, 108; and relationship with mother country, 103. *See also* European colonization; imperialism
colonial property system, 180, 181
colonial transactions, 56, 165
colonists: bad faith of, 136, 137; on civilization of Delawares, 43; curtailing of native cultural traditions, 189; details about arrival of, 70; and documentation of Dido motif, 77; and ideal of Great Treaty, 96; interpretation of relationship with Delawares, 130–31; introduction of alcohol, 60, 63–64, 70, 192; language of, 14, 67, 151–52; memory community of, 10–11; memory of Moses Tatamy, 183; and Native Americans' origin, 32; power of, 176; trickery of, 55–56, 64, 67–69, 211n35, 212n48; truth and authenticity of stories of, 16; use of Indian methods, 170, 171; writing and oral traditions of, 6. *See also* Americans; Dutch; English; Europeans; Penn, William; United States; whites

commerce. *See* trade and trading houses
Commonwealth of Pennsylvania, Delaware Nation v., 177–78, 181, 182
communication: and authenticity of *Walam Olum*, 51; chain in Teedyuscung's speeches, 167, 168; classical philosophy on, 145; and Delaware origin myth, 191; modes of Indian and English, 142–44, 169–70, 233n135; through chains of memory, 193; and Walking Purchase controversy, 136, 160–61; of William Penn's land transactions, 143–44. *See also* oral tradition; wampum; writing
Conestoga (town), 118
Conestoga Indians, 16, 117, 128
Connecticut, 107, 199n40
Conoy Indians, 16, 117
conquest, 30–31, 34–36, 42, 104, 220n33, 220n39
Constantinople, 81
context: of bullock's hide story, 67, 86; of Indian economic transactions, 143; of memory studies, 187, 236n9; of *Penn's Treaty* image reception, 103; study of memory in, 130; of utterances, 145; of Walking Purchase, 133, 153–54, 160; of words, 151, 159, 160
Conyngham, David H., 109
Conyngham, Redmond, 114
Cooper, James Fenimore, 1, 2, 13, 27, 29, 34, 50, 183, 204n33. *See also*
The Last of the Mohicans (Cooper); *The Leatherstocking Tales* (Cooper)
Copan OK, 194
Cope, Thomas, 107
councils, 164, 167, 171–72. *See also* Provincial Council; treaty meetings
council trees, 107. *See also* trees
countermemory, 134, 226n4. *See also* memory
covenants, 101, 107. *See also* oaths; "Unbroken Faith"
Crayola crayon factory, 177
Creation stories, 23, 38, 190–94
Creek Indians, 70, 72, 200n51
Croghan, George, 168, 169, 171, 172, 174
Crow Indians, 188
cultural memory. *See* memory, collective
culture: and authenticity of *Walam Olum*, 40, 42, 45–49, 51, 52; barriers of, 86, 149–50; changes in, 96, 193–94; continuity of, 13, 196; of early modern European imperialism, 86; facts of, 99; as hazard in land transactions, 144; and memory, 201n59, 236n9; traditions of, 56, 58, 189, 190; transfer of, 34. *See also* civilization
Culture Committee (Delaware Tribe), 208n86
Cunha, Joseph Gerson, 81
Cunha, Nuno da, 79, 214n89
Cuvier, Georges, 41

al-Dabir, Hajji, 78, 80

Danckaerts, Jasper, 26, 190–94. *See also* missions and missionaries

Darnell, Regna, 207n78

Darton, W., 103–5, 220n39

Davidson, James, 89

Davis, William H., 13, 155, 178–79

Dawes Act (1887–1934), 15

day and a half's walk: direction and angle of, 152, 154–56, 160; lack of explanation of, 145; meaning of, 153, 155–58, 175; mention in "Antient Copy," 139–40; Moses Tatamy's testimony about, 141; Teedyuscung on, 160–61. *See also* deed (1686); deed, confirmation (1737); Indian Walk; Walking Purchase (1737)

Dean, Nora Thompson (Touching Leaves Woman) (Delaware), 84, 131–32, 199n40, 208n86

"Deceptive Land Purchase: Ox Hide Measure," 74–75

deed (1686): absence of, 20–21; "Antient Copy" of, 139–41; authority of, 146, 147; blank space in, 154; Canassatego's testimony about, 164, 165; date of composition, 58; as evidence against Forks Delawares, 163, 164; lack of explanation in, 145; representatives at negotiations of, 160; and Teedyuscung's retraction, 175–76; text in deed (1737), 137, 152; Thomas Penn's presentation of, 136; wording of, 152, 230n76. *See also* agreements; day and a half's walk; deeds; documentary records; land transactions

deed (1718), 158. *See also* deeds

deed, confirmation (1737): ambiguity of language in, 152; blank space in, 154; Canassatego's testimony about, 163–65; copy given to Forks Delawares, 163; on Indian Walk, 156; Nutimus's mark on, 147, 154; Proprietors' adherence to, 156–58; text of 1686 deed in, 137, 152. *See also* agreements; day and a half's walk; deeds; documentary records; land transactions

deeds, 169, 176–77, 182. *See also* agreements; deed (1686); deed (1718); deed, confirmation (1737)

defense funding, 133, 167–68, 226n2

De Halve Maen, 59

deities, 61. *See also* God; Great Spirit

Delâge, Denys, 65

Delaware (state), 10, 199n40

Delaware Bay, 44

Delaware Indians: accounts of history, 1–2; and authenticity of *Walam Olum*, 18, 49–50; battle with Talligewi, 26, 28–29; case against Proprietors' Walking Purchase, 158; in chain of memory, 187; in civic myth of Great Treaty, 97; conventions of distance measurement, 153; cultural development of, 43–44, 47–49; damage to community of, 189–90; and date of Great Treaty, 115–16; at deed (1686)

Delaware Indians (continued)
negotiations, 160; and distribution of bullock hide story, 69–72; documentary evidence of Great Treaty with, 19–20, 95; epitomizing events in history of, 69, 70; ethnographic records on, 45; on first land transaction with Europeans, 91–92; funeral ceremony for human remains, 195; geographic referents of historical traditions of, 108; at Indian Walk, 141, 155–56; interpretation of relationship with colonists, 130–31; land tenure and social structure of, 115–16, 129; land transactions with William Penn, 111–13; legend of treaty with William Penn, 107, 221n49; life in New York Harbor, 186; literal and intended meanings in traditions of, 151–52; memory of Great Treaty, 14, 15, 20, 121, 130–32, 179; memory of land transactions, 71; memory of Moses Tatamy, 183; name and ancestry of, 10–11, 199n40; name for William Penn, 143; in Ohio and Indiana, 42; origins of, 17, 25–30, 38–39, 49, 190–94, 208n90; Patrick Gordon's speech to, 16; in popular culture, 33–34; prospect of regaining land, 183; raids by, 21; role in Walking Purchase, 133–34; siding with French, 166–67; telling of bullock's hide story, 67–68; treaty customs of, 107; truth and authenticity of stories of, 16; use of pictographs, 43; use of wampum, 122, 128; verbal pledge of friendship, 116–17; "verbatim" account of Dutch colonists' arrival, 60; William Markham's land sale agreement with, 127–28; word parsing in hide story of, 150; writing and oral traditions of, 6, 36, 51–52; writing history of, 15. *See also* Algonquian peoples; Brandywine Delaware Indians; Delaware Nation; Delaware Tribe of Indians; Forks Delaware Indians; Jersey Indians; Lenape language; Munsee Delaware Indians; Native Americans

Delaware-Munsee Nation of Ontario, Canada, 195

Delaware Nation, 48, 177–78, 180, 181, 186, 195, 196, 207n86, 208n86. *See also* Delaware Indians

Delaware Nation Grand Council of North America, 48, 207n86

Delaware Nation v. Commonwealth of Pennsylvania, 177–78, 181, 182

Delaware River, 26, 36, 112, 135, 139, 146–47, 154, 156, 160. *See also* Forks territory

Delaware Tribe of Indians, 186, 195–96, 207n86. *See also* Delaware Indians

Delaware Valley, 199n40

De La Warr, Lord. *See* West, Thomas

Deloria, Vine, 26

demographic changes, 96, 193–94

Denny, William, 155, 168–72, 176
depositions, 137, 139, 154
Derrida, Jacques, 145–46, 159, 176
Dido, Queen (Elisa): acquisition of site for Carthage, 18–19, 55–56, 82, 83, 85, 88; celebrity of, 88, 217n122; and conquest of Chile, 216n116; Machiavelli's reference to, 89; William Strachey's reference to, 86–87. *See also* Carthage
Dido motif, 72–84; as "ceremony of possession," 85; classical sources of, 86–87, 89, 216n114; as descriptive and prescriptive story, 87, 91–92; historians' mention of, 61; in history of colonization, 84–93; maps of land acquired through, 74–75; scholarship on, 84, 216n111. *See also* bullock hide motif; classical motifs; land transactions; traditions
"Dido's problem," 83
diplomacy, 131–33, 136, 168–70, 225n140. *See also* friendship; hospitality; peace
discourse communities, 13
diseases, 189
displacements, territorial, 108, 180, 187. *See also* dispossession; land rights; land transactions
dispossession, 2, 48, 51, 71, 180, 182, 187. *See also* displacements, territorial; land rights
Diu, 78, 79, 81
documentary records: about Dido motif, 76–80, 82, 92, 93; authority of, 118, 145, 146, 171, 175, 228n52; copies to Indians, 117, 133, 139–41, 143–44, 171, 174; at council meetings with Teedyuscung, 169, 172; European on first contact, 61; of Great Treaty, 95–96, 108, 113–21, 222n78; of memory, 140–41; on Moses Tatamy's land, 179–82; of oral history, 140–41; and oral traditions, 57–58, 62, 64, 83, 92, 118, 215n101; on Penn Wampum Belts, 127; and Plymouth landing, 119–20; reliance on in land transactions, 172; tradition as series of, 201n68; on Walking Purchase, 132, 134, 136, 137, 143–45, 154, 158; wampum as, 122–25, 127. *See also* deed (1686); deed, confirmation (1737); records; title, chain of; writing
Dong xi yang kao (Account of the Eastern and Western Oceans), 80, 82, 215n91
Dryden, John, 72
Du Ponceau, Peter Stephen, 14, 38, 102, 115, 121, 123, 222n78
Dutch: claim of New York region, 62, 211n27; and Dido motif, 73, 76–77, 82–85, 89; establishment of empire, 87, 89; famine of, 191; first land transaction with Delawares, 91–92; fur trade of, 122; and Great Elm, 108; *History* on arrival of, 1; Indian tradition on arrival of, 56–65,

Dutch (continued)
71; in *Knickerbocker's History of New York*, 66, 150; maritime empire of, 73; records of, 77; Tantaqué's assistance to, 191, 192; trickery of, 64, 211n35; and *Walam Olum*, 44. *See also* colonists

Dutch East India Company (VOC), 77, 88, 91

Dutch Republic, 86

dynamics of memory approach, 103, 104, 194. *See also* memory

Eastern Pennsylvania, 10, 199n40. *See also* Pennsylvania

Eastern Woodlands, 122, 187

East Jersey, 115. *See also* New Jersey

Easton PA, 147, 166–68, 172, 177, 182

Eendracht, 211n27

Egyptian pictographs, 39, 209n106. *See also* pictography

ekfrasis, 101

Eliot, John, 52, 169, 192

Ellis, Martha, 208n90

Ellis Island, 185–87, 190, 194, 195

England, 96, 103

English: cultural roots of, 33; and Dido motif, 86, 87; and documentation of Great Treaty, 121; on Dutch colonization of Java, 82; and Great Elm, 108; in *Last of the Mohicans*, 34; modes of communication of, 170, 233n135; Moses Tatamy and Captain John's wish to live among, 181; Native Americans' complaint about cheating by, 171; and Native Americans' land rights, 36; system of land ownership, 180; on Teedyuscung's location, 176; treaty with Susquehannocks, 107; and Walking Purchase records, 22; and wampum belts, 128, 146–47, 163–64; way of recording land transactions, 136, 137, 143–44, 147, 171. *See also* colonists

English language, 52, 63, 150, 153, 189. *See also* language

epitomizing events, 69, 70

equinox, 155

equivocation, 147–52, 154. *See also* interpretation; language; parsing words; truth; words

Ercilla, Alonso de, 216n116

Erdrich, Louise, 189

Erll, Astrid, 13

ethnocentrism, 48, 50–52, 81

ethnography, 18, 36, 45, 49, 51, 58, 60, 93, 143. *See also* scholarship

ethnohistory, 5, 95, 115, 122

Eurocentrism, 129

Europe, 31, 40, 73, 145, 228n52

European colonization, 39, 53, 68–69, 82, 84, 86–88, 185. *See also* colonialism

European influences, 4–5, 18–19, 42, 52, 187, 212n48, 236n9

Europeans: and council trees, 107; damage to Delaware community, 189; and Dido motif, 70, 76–78, 82, 92; documents on founding of

New Netherland, 55; first contact with Native Americans, 1, 54, 56–65, 83, 108; first land transaction with Delawares, 91–92; and Native Americans' land rights, 34–36, 71; and Native Americans' origin, 25, 31, 32; relationships with native peoples, 130; speculation about Moses Tatamy's life among, 181; trade of, 103, 220n33; and wampum, 122–24, 129, 164; written records of, 54, 146. *See also* Americans; colonists; whites
Exodus, 29. *See also* Bible
Eyre, Franklin, 110

facts, 83, 99, 134, 215n99, 215n101. *See also* truth
fairness, 130, 133, 140, 143–44, 161–63. *See also* justice
faithfulness, 130, 136, 137, 160, 168, 175. *See also* Punic faith; "Unbroken Faith"
families, 15, 110. *See also* generations
Faunce, Thomas, 119
Fenton, William N., 122, 123
Ferreira, Simão, 79
firearms, 28
Fisher, Joshua Francis, 14–15, 102, 115, 121, 123, 222n78
Fishtown neighborhood, 95, 115
Five Nations, 163
flood, 38, 191–92. *See also* water
Fogelson, Raymond, 69
folkloric motif, 66, 69, 72–73, 76, 82–83, 87, 136, 216n101. *See also* stories; tales
folklorists, 7
forgetting, 17, 192, 201n72. *See also* memory
Forks Delaware Indians: complaints about Walking Purchase, 21, 161–63, 231n105; eviction of, 131, 146–47, 163–66; land of, 135; Moses Tatamy's awareness of loss of land, 180, 181; on "walk," 150, 153. *See also* Delaware Indians; Nutimus (Forks sachem)
Forks territory, 131, 136, 139–42, 180, 181. *See also* Delaware River; land; Lehigh River; Township of Forks
Formosa. *See* Taiwan
Fort Amsterdam, 62, 83–84
forts: and bullock hide tradition, 55, 66–67, 73, 76–79, 82–84, 86, 89, 214n89; and colonization formula, 91; possible ruins in Ohio, 31
Fort Zealand, 76–77
Foster, Michael K., 163–64
Fox, Joseph, 182
Franklin, Benjamin, 103, 149–50
Franks, 80. *See also* Spanish
fraud: Delawares' accusations of, 131–32; and Dido motif, 77, 91; *History* on colonists', 2; Pennsylvania Proprietors accused of, 6, 177; Teedyuscung's allegation of, 21, 134, 136–37, 142, 161, 166–77, 181; and Walking Purchase, 21, 133–37, 149, 177

Frazer, Sir James, 73, 213n73
Fredericksz, Cryn, 83
"Freedom" wampum belt, 127–28. See also belts, wampum
Freeman, Hannah, 204n33
free passage, 127–28
Free Society of Traders, 113, 117, 143. See also trade and trading houses
French, 86
French and Indian War, 21, 23, 133, 136–37, 166–77, 182, 232n127
French language, 150. See also language
French Republicanism, 99
Friendly Association for Regaining and Preserving Peace with the Indians by Pacific Means, 156, 168, 171
friendship: in colonization formula, 91; Forks Delawares' desire for, 162–63; and Great Treaty, 97, 101, 104, 107, 112, 116–18, 162–63, 219n29, 221n49; in land sale agreement, 128; Teedyuscung on Beaver's agreement of, 177; and wampum belts, 124, 126, 129; William Penn on, 113, 131. See also diplomacy; hospitality; peace
"Frieze of American History" (Brumidi), 218n9
Fryd, Vivien Green, 218n9
Furniss, Thomas, 161, 231n105
fur trade, 122. See also trade and trading houses

Galle, 78
Gamwing, 194
gender, 225n135

generations: and Great Elm, 107–8, 110; memory through oral traditions of, 188; of records and representations, 175; span of social memory through, 178–79, 188, 189; and use of wampum, 123; Walking Purchase controversy through multiple, 135–37, 160, 172. See also chains of memory; families
Genesis, 29, 38, 192. See also Bible
Gibbon, Edward, 81
gifts, 60, 64, 142–43
Gilpin, Henry, 125
Gnadenhütten OH, 121
"go," 152, 153, 156, 230n76
God, 191. See also deities; Great Spirit
Goddard, Ives, 199n40
The Golden Bough (Frazer), 73, 213n73
Gookin, Charles, 128
Gordon, Patrick, 16–17, 116, 118, 127–28
Gordon, Thomas Francis, 114–15, 117
Gottfried, Johann Ludwig, 90
Governors (Nooten or Nut) Island, 62, 186, 211n27
Great Plains, 190
Great Spirit, 29. See also deities; God
Great Treaty: absence of written records on, 95, 96, 101, 102, 113–19, 125; Bessie Snake on, 131, 225n140; as civic myth, 97; collective memory of, 179; comparison to Walking Purchase, 93, 133; date of, 97, 101, 113–16, 219n29; Delawares' memories of, 130–32; details about, 101,

113, 115; and first-contact accounts, 70; Forks Delawares' reference to, 162–63; global distribution of reputation, 99; oral tradition of, 101, 104, 108–10, 116–17, 120; popular tradition of, 14–15, 19–20, 33–34, 95–104; possible written documentation of, 121; relationship to Indian Walk, 178; report at Historical Society of Pennsylvania, 102; scholarship on, 6–7; site of, 101–2, 105–6, 108–12, 115, 120, 121, 179; and wampum, 122–25. *See also* agreements; land transactions; Penn, William; traditions; treaty tradition

Greenblatt, Stephen, 4
"Green Corn Ceremony," 155, 230n90
Grotius, Hugo, 88–89
group identity, 9, 15–16, 29, 188, 194. *See also* memory, collective
Gujarat, 78–79

Habermas, Jurgen, 144
Hackensack NJ, 190
Haefeli, Evan, 61, 62, 198n23, 211n26
Halbwachs, Maurice, 9, 15, 188
Hall, John, 99, 219n20
Hamilton, Alexander, 78
Hamilton, James, 134, 147, 161, 168, 175, 176, 177
Hamilton, Milton, 61
Harper, Steven Craig, 134, 226n4
Harrington, M. L., 44–45, 53, 206n70
Harrisburg PA, 114

harvest ceremony, 155, 230n90
Hastings, Stephen, 215n99
Head, J. Merrick, 126
Heath, Shirley Brice, 21–22
Heckewelder, John: Benjamin Smith Barton on, 204n30; and bullock hide story, 64–67, 69, 71, 72, 77, 82, 83, 85; on eviction of Forks Delaware, 165–66; fictional representation of, 36; on first contact, 61–65, 70; informants of, 63, 69, 130–31; on Lenape language, 152–53; and memory of Great Treaty, 15, 20, 121; and Native Americans' origin, 27–31; publication of *History*, 1, 26; representation of historical traditions, 6; on tortoise, 193, 237n30; and truth, 59; and *Walam Olum*, 17–18, 38–40, 48, 49, 206n62; on wampum, 121–23, 125; on writing, 9. *See also An Account of the History, Manners, and Customs of the Indian Nations that Once Inhabited Pennsylvania and the Neighboring States* (Heckewelder); missions and missionaries
Helgerson, Richard, 217n122
Henry, Matthew Schropp, 182
"hereby," 145
Heye Foundation. *See* Museum of the American Indian, Heye Foundation
Hiarbas, King, 19, 72, 86–87
Hicks, Edward, 2, 97, 98, 99, 106. *See also* painters
Hildebrandt, Stefan, 83

Hill, Seneca (Cayuga), 127–29
historians: on bullock's hide, 65;
    on chain of memory, 178–79; on
    communities of memory, 13–14;
    on Great Treaty, 96, 97, 101–3, 109,
    116, 121; Greek on Dido motif, 81;
    and map of New York Harbor, 187;
    on Plymouth landing, 119–20; on
    records and representations, 7; on
    Teedyuscung's speeches, 167; on
    transfer of Moses Tatamy's land,
    179, 181; on Walking Purchase,
    134. See also art historians; popular
    historians; scholarship
historical accuracy, 62, 67, 83, 104–5,
    108–9, 220n41. See also truth
historical events, 56, 73, 76–78, 99
historical legitimacy, 43, 46–48, 53, 54
Historical Society of Pennsylvania
    (HSP): and *Delaware Nation v. Commonwealth of Pennsylvania*, 181, 182;
    donation of wampum belt to, 20;
    and Great Treaty monument, 110–
    11; investigation of Great Treaty, 95;
    and memory of Great Treaty, 108,
    110, 132; and record of Great Treaty,
    114; report on Great Treaty at, 102;
    scholarship at, 13; wampum belt
    ("Treaty Belt") at, 124–25, 127
historical traditions, 6, 28, 97, 103,
    108, 114–15. See also traditions
historical value, 12, 56–59, 68, 76, 92,
    214n74. See also truth
historicity, 71, 92, 102, 104, 121. See also
    truth

historiography: and authenticity of
    Walam Olum, 50; and communities
    of memory, 13; of Great Treaty, 95,
    97, 113–14; and literary studies,
    198n22; on native histories and
    Western records, 83, 215n101; and
    study of Native American cultures,
    5–6; on Walking Purchase, 21, 134.
    See also scholarship; writing
history: and bullock hide motif, 65,
    66, 82, 83, 87, 92–93; as concept
    in Native American Studies, 187,
    236n10; controversy of Delawares',
    2–3; dismissal of non-Western,
    80–81; distinction from memory,
    13–14, 201n59; of Indian-European
    relations, 69; in literary context,
    7, 198n22; memory in communities of, 9–14; non-Indian scholars
    on Delaware, 15, 45, 48–51, 53;
    revisionist of Walking Purchase,
    134; truth in, 83, 137, 215n101. See
    also prehistory
history associations, 13, 200n55
History of Bucks County (Davis), 155,
    178–79
History of Pennsylvania (Gordon), 114
The History of Pennsylvania (Proud), 101,
    219n20
*History of the Decline and Fall of the Roman
    Empire* (Gibbon), 81
History of the Growth and Decay of the Othman Empire (Cantemir), 81
Hobsbawm, Eric, 103
Holocaust, 187

Holy Scripture, 190, 193. *See also* Bible
homeland (Delaware Indians), 10, 193
Homer, 47
homes, English-style, 169
Hopi Indians, 59, 210n12
hospitality, 88, 89, 129. *See also* diplomacy; friendship; peace
House of Commons, 125
Howard, Henry, Earl of Surrey, 217n122
Howland Hook, Staten Island, 193
Hudson, Henry, 18, 56, 58–63, 186, 235n6
Hudson River, 26, 35, 36, 63
Hudson Valley, 10
Hunter, William, 134
Huron Indians, 68

Ilioneus, 89
imperialism, 73, 74–75, 86, 87, 90–92. *See also* colonialism
India, 73, 80–81, 87
Indiana, 42, 70
Indiana Historical Society, 46–47, 207n78
Indian Claims Commission, 5
Indian Dialogues (Eliot), 192
Indian Dictionary (Zeisberger), 153
Indian Ocean, 55
Indian Treaties Printed by Benjamin Franklin (Boyd), 134
Indian Walk: description of, 154–61; Governor Thomas on fairness of, 163; interpretation of, 136; memorialization of, 178–79; participants in, 154, 156; starting point of, 178–79. *See also* day and a half's walk; Walking Purchase (1737)
Indigenous Studies Portal, 236n10
information flows, 71–72, 86
information preservation, 143
international law, 88–89
interpretation: of bullock's hide story, 67–68; of first-contact accounts, 61; of records and representations, 7; of Teedyuscung's speeches, 167; of Walking Purchase records, 132, 136, 137, 144, 158–59, 165; of wampum belts, 127–29. *See also* equivocation; parsing words; translation
interpretive confidence, 160–61
Iroquois Indians: and Delawares' claim to Lenapehoking, 29; and Delawares' origin, 26; history of, 46; name for William Penn, 143; at Philadelphia meeting, 163–66; representation of, 33; supervision of banished Forks Delaware, 165, 166; use of wampum, 122. *See also* Six Nations
Irving, Washington, 2, 13, 56, 65–67, 150
Israel, 29. *See also* Lost Tribes of Israel
iterability, 145–46, 160, 176

Jackson, Andrew, 29
Jackson, Jason Baird, 69
Jackson, Rosalie Vallance Tiers, 110
Jacobs, Jaap, 210n17, 211n27

Jakarta, 73, 89
Jamestown, 86, 97, 225n135
Japanese, 89
Java, 73–76, 82
Jennings, Francis, 5, 102, 119, 134, 137, 139, 141, 147, 187
Jennings, Solomon, 154, 155
Jersey Indians, 142, 163. See also Delaware Indians
Jews, 25, 29
Johnson, Sir William, 140, 141, 168, 169, 172–75
Johnson Papers, 174, 233n145
"journey," 153
Juet, Robert, 18, 56, 58, 61–64, 70
justice, 126, 144, 161–63, 183. See also fairness
Justinius, 88, 90

Kammen, Michael G., 200n55, 204nn32–33, 220n41
Kayaderosseras Patent, 135, 226n11
Kekelappan (Delaware), 115
Kelly, James McGirr, 179
Kennedy, John (Indian trader), 161, 231n104
Kensington PA, 99, 102, 107, 108, 110, 111
Ketchum, Annette, 195, 196
Ketchum, Dee, 195
keying, 28, 71, 203n17, 213n59. See also memory, collective
khipu, 8, 123
Kiowa Indians, 188–90, 194, 200n51
Kittatinny Mountains, 139, 176
Klein, Kerwin Lee, 201n59

Knickerbocker's History of New York (Irving), 56, 65–66, 77
Knowlson, James, 209n106
Kottenkamp, Franz, 85–86, 216n114
Kraft, Herbert C., 28, 84, 86, 199n40
Krupat, Arnold, 215n101

Labadists, 190–93
land: colonial acquisition through Walking Purchase, 135, 142, 226n11; Dutch colonists' request for, 1, 61; *History* on colonists' acquisition of, 1–2; as incentive to walkers, 155; prospect of Delawares' regaining, 183; Teedyuscung's request for, 176–77; transfer of tribal, 178, 179. See also Forks territory
landmarks, 3, 107, 108, 183, 195. See also memorials; monuments; place
land rights: by conquest, 34–36, 42; by discovery, 62; and Native Americans' origin, 26, 30, 31; oral traditions about loss of, 69–70; and *Penn's Treaty* image, 104; of Six Nations, 146–47. See also displacements, territorial; dispossession
landscape, 35–36, 187–88, 190, 200n51, 236n23
land transactions: accusations of fraudulent, 131, 166–67; in Benjamin West's painting, 219n29; and colonization formula, 91, 92; and communities of memory, 14; and Delaware social structure, 129;

286 ::: Index

distance measurement in, 153; English way of recording, 136, 137, 143–44, 147, 171; Forks Delawares' dispute of, 162–66; and Great Treaty, 96; "Indian Way" of recording, 21, 136, 141–47; and memory, 16; Nonintercourse Act (1970) on, 178; records at council meetings with Teedyuscung, 168; records of Moses Tatamy, 181–82; reliance on written records in, 172; representation in wampum belt, 127–29; similar to Walking Purchase, 135, 226n11; of Thomas Penn, 102–3; wampum in, 11, 165; of William Penn, 111–13, 116, 143–44. *See also* bullock hide motif; deed (1686); deed, confirmation (1737); Dido motif; displacements, territorial; dispossession; Great Treaty; patent-lands; property ownership; Tatamy's Place; title, chain of; Walking Purchase (1737)

Langhorne, Jeremiah, 158, 161–62, 180

language: fraud by, 149; Governor Denny's use of Indian metaphorical, 171; landscape bound to, 35–36; and memory, 188, 201n59; restoration of lost, 41; in Teedyuscung's papers, 174, 175; in transcription, 167, 232n124; and *Walam Olum*, 52–53, 209n106; in William Penn's land transactions, 143–44. *See also* English language; equivocation; French language; Lenape language; linguistics; Mayan language and writing; Native American languages; parsing words; speech; words; writing

language barriers, 86, 149–50

language ideology: and communities of memory, 9–10, 14; definition of, 8; in Delaware-colonist interactions, 16; and Dido motif, 19, 67–68; and equivocation, 149–54; and oral traditions, 150–52; and record of Great Treaty, 117, 118; scholarship on, 7–9; and Walking Purchase agreement, 159

Lankford, G., 212n48

Lappawinzoe (Delaware), 139, 152, 154, 156, 230n93

The Last of the Mohicans (Cooper), 27, 29, 34–36, 204n37. *See also* Mohican Indians; *The Leatherstocking Tales* (Cooper)

Laufer, Berthold, 76–77, 80, 81, 84, 86, 215n100, 216n114

Lay, Benjamin, 109, 179

The Leatherstocking Tales (Cooper), 1, 34, 50, 204n37. *See also The Last of the Mohicans* (Cooper)

Legazpi, Miguel López de, 81

legends, 102, 221n49. *See also* allegories; traditions

Legends of the Delaware Indians and Picture Writing (Adams), 150–52

Lehicton Creek, 183

Lehigh River, 135, 135, 142, 147. *See also* Forks territory

Index ::: 287

"Lekhihitin" (chief), 47, 51
Lemire, Charles, 73
Lenâpé and Their Legends (Brinton), 44
Lenapehoking, 10, 26, 29, 187–88, 190, 199n40
Lenape Indians. *See* Delaware Indians
Lenape language: bullock's hide story in, 68, 83; in *Indian Dictionary*, 153; John Heckewelder's "verbatim" account in, 60; transition to written English, 189; Unami dialect of, 186, 235n6; and *Walam Olum*, 27, 38, 39, 40, 45, 46, 48, 52, 208n86, 209n100. *See also* Delaware Indians; language; Native American languages
Lenape Language Preservation Project, 46, 84, 153
Lenape Talking Dictionary (Delaware Tribe of Indians), 186
Lenik, Edward, 193
letters: equivocation in agreement, 149; from Teedyuscung, 169–70; on Walking Purchase, 137, 140, 141, 144, 154, 158, 161–63, 165–66; to W. Darton, 103–5, 220n39
Levy, Daniel, 236n9
Liaozhai zhiyi, 83
Liberty Island, 185–87, 190, 194, 195
Liberty Tree, 107, 221n43
"Liberty Tree of Annapolis," 107
Library of Congress, 236n10
Lilly, Eli, 46
linguistics, 45. *See also* language
literacy, 8, 17, 145, 169, 172, 176–77, 182, 229n52. *See also* reading; writing
literacy events, 21–22, 167, 172
literary representation, 188
literary studies, 7, 30–31, 122, 198n22, 202n88
Liu, James H., 130
Livy, 72, 85, 86, 88
Locke, John, 138, 146, 159, 165, 180, 234n166
Logan, Deborah, 108
Logan, James: background of, 138; contest with Nutimus, 136, 138–47, 150, 166; eviction of Delawares from Forks territory, 136; on Great Treaty, 108; Iroquois on land purchases of, 163; John Watson with, 156; and knowledge of 1686 events, 146; language ideology of, 150; scheme to appropriate Forks of Delaware region, 139–40; Teedyuscung on threat by, 172; and Teedyuscung's retraction, 175; and warrant for tract above Durham, 158; written record of, 21
Loganian Library, 138
London, 99
Longfellow, Henry Wadsworth, 33, 34, 45–46, 50, 204n32
Long Island, 10, 115, 193, 199n40. *See also* New York City; New York region
Lords of Trade, 175
Loskiel, George Henry, 123–24, 153
Lost Tribes of Israel, 25, 31. *See also* Israel

Lowie, Robert, 12, 83
The Lusiads, 88
Luzon, 80

Machiavelli, Niccolò, 89
MacPherson, James, 32–33, 42
Maha Katana, 82
Mahomet II, 81
Malaysia, 69, 73–76
mammoth, 29
Monockyhickan (Delaware), 152, 154
"Maneto." See *Manitou*
Manhattan: ecology of, 186; Europeans' landing on, 62, 70, 211n26; funeral ceremony near, 195; interactive map of, 186–87; Jasper Danckaerts on, 190; *Knickerbocker's History of New York* on first Dutch settlement in, 66; tortoise drawing in, 196. See also New York City; New York region
Manhattan Project, 186–87
Manila, 73, 80, 81, 86. See also Philippine Islands
Manitou, 60, 61, 191
Mannitto. See *Manitou*
Maoris, 130
Markham, William, 112–13, 127–28
Marseilles, 89
Marsh, Witham, 169, 172
Marshall, Edward, 154–56
Maryland, 107, 115
Mason, Ronald J., 57, 214n74
Massilienses, 89
Matinicum (Burlington) Island, 112

Mayan language and writing, 51. See also language; writing
Mayflower, 119
Mayhkeericckkishsho (Delaware sachem), 160, 175
McCutchen, David, 47–49, 207n86
McGuire, Randall, 32
meaning, 138, 144, 149, 151–53, 158–60, 176
media: alternative, 96; and communities of memory, 18, 23; of history, 2–3, 14; indigenous, 8, 12, 123; and language ideology, 8, 16; of memory, 2–3, 10, 14, 16, 23, 38; news, 71, 178; of speech acts, 228n55; Walter Ong on, 202n88; Western memory, 38. See also books; communication; khipu; language; mediation; pictography; speech; wampum; writing
mediation, problems of, 53
Melaka. See Malaysia
memorials, 95, 107, 145, 229n52. See also landmarks; monuments
memory: about young adulthood, 231n105; Benjamin West's painting in public, 99, 219n16; of bullock's hide story, 68, 71, 82; of ceremonial culture, 195; of colonial era, 108; colonists' attitudes toward, 6; context of, 130; controversy of Delawares', 2–3; of Delaware ontogeny, 190–94; distinction from history, 13–14, 201n59; documentation of, 140–41; effect of writing on, 120; of encounters, 14–23; exposure to

Index ::: 289

memory (continued)
doubt, 23; of Great Treaty, 14, 15, 20, 108, 109, 113, 116, 121, 122, 131–32; in James Logan's administration of Indian affairs, 138; landscape of, 187; length of, 98, 187, 218n10; of Moses Tatamy, 183; in Native American ritual speech, 170, 233n135; and Native American Studies, 187–90, 236n10, 236nn9–10; opposition to written records, 145, 146, 228n52; and pictographs, 43; of Plymouth landing, 120; quality of Native Americans', 170–71; scholarship on, 200n51; span of communicative, 178–79; through oral tradition, 28, 58, 64, 188, 192, 193; transmission and construction of, 16–17, 115, 187, 236n10; and *Walam Olum* pictographs, 38; of Walking Purchase, 21, 71, 136, 137; and wampum, 11, 123, 129. *See also* chains of memory; countermemory; dynamics of memory approach; forgetting; national memory; popular memory; presentist memory approach

memory-keeping, 120
memory studies, field of, 187
Merian, Matthäus, 90
Merrell, James, 5–6, 102, 133, 167, 181, 182, 235n174
Merritt, Jane T., 170, 233n135
Merwick, Donna, 210n17
Mesoamerica, 40, 43

metaphor, 19, 65–66, 71, 86, 100, 151–52, 171
Mexican pictographs, 39. *See also* pictography
mid-Atlantic region, 2, 63. *See also* New England
Middle Ages, 153
Middle East, 31, 76
migration: of Delawares, 10, 200n40; and Dido motif, 80; fictional representation of, 36; forced westward, 190; in *History*, 28–30; and Native Americans' origin, 26–27, 29–32; and sharing of stories, 70; and *Walam Olum*, 17–18, 27, 38–39, 42, 49, 54, 206n58. *See also* traditions
Miller, Jay, 49, 194, 206n70
Miller, Samuel, 60, 216n111
Miner, Charles, 125
Ming Annals, 80, 81, 215n91
Miquon. *See* Penn, William
Mirror of Sikandar, 78, 80
misrepresentation, 146–47, 158–59. *See also* representation
missions and missionaries, 1, 43, 52, 73, 82, 169, 210n12. *See also* Danckaerts, Jasper; Heckewelder, John; Moravians; religion
Mississippi River, 42
Missouri River, 49
Misztal, Barbara A., 226n4
mnemonic communities, 9, 13, 21, 200n51. *See also* memory, collective
mnemonic devices, 11, 62, 123, 145, 163, 211n26

mnemonic practices, 22, 187, 202n88, 236n10
mnemotechnics, 170
modernity, 187, 189, 236n9
Mohawk Indians, 226n11
Mohican Indians, 34, 60, 63, 183, 186, 196. See also *The Last of the Mohicans* (Cooper)
Momaday, N. Scott, 187–90, 194
Montour, Andrew, 172, 174
Montrose, Louis, 3–4
monuments, 10, 109–11, 115, 179. See also landmarks; memorials; roadside markers
Moravians, 1, 18, 39, 121, 123–24, 153. See also missions and missionaries; religion
Morga, Antonio de, 80–81
Morgan, Frank, 83–84
Morison, Samuel Eliot, 120
Morris, Governor, 171
Moscow, 87
mother country, 96, 103
Moulton, Joseph W., 29–30
mound builders, 30–31, 32
multidisciplinary fields, 7, 198n25
The Multilingual Anthology of American Literature (Shell and Sollors), 50, 52, 209n100
multilingualism, 52, 53. See also language
Munsee Delaware Indians: on bullock's hide trick, 71; designation of, 237n30; dialect of, 236n6; and Ellis Island human remains, 186; first contact with, 60, 61, 63; at funeral ceremony, 195, 196; naming of Tantaqué, 190–91; territory of, 156, 185. See also Delaware Indians
Museum of the American Indian, Heye Foundation, 126, 127. See also National Museum of the American Indian
Museum of the City of New York, 186–87
Muskogee Indians, 212n55
myths, 28, 33, 40, 87, 145, 190–94, 228n52. See also civic myths

Nabokov, Peter, 12
Nanticoke Lenni-Lenape Indians, 200n42
Napora, Joe, 47–48, 207n85
narrative accounts, 59, 188
narrative paintings, 100
Nash, Gary, 219n16
National Endowment for the Humanities, 208n90
national memory, 120. See also memory
National Museum of the American Indian, 126, 187
National Parks Service, 185
national pride, 40, 95, 99
Native American Graves Protection and Repatriation Act, 186
Native American languages, 8, 200n51. See also Algonquian languages; language; Lenape language; Onondaga language
Native Americans: and affidavit on treatment by Proprietors, 161,

Native Americans (continued)
231n104; and authenticity of *Walam Olum*, 40; biannual assemblies of, 122–24; "civilization" and removal of, 17, 26–27, 42–43; classical motif in history of, 55–56, 65–68, 70, 82, 84–85, 89–90, 92; commemoration of treaty with William Penn, 110–11; complaint about past, 179; council trees of, 107; damage to communities of, 189–90; disruption of social memory frameworks, 189; and distribution of bullock hide story, 71–72; doubts about ability to write, 48, 50–52; encountered by Henry Hudson in New York Harbor, 186, 235n6; and English system of land ownership, 180, 234n166; equivocation and word choice in traditions of, 151–52; first contact with Europeans, 1, 54, 56–65, 83, 108; friendship with Quakers, 118; on Great Treaty, 101, 112, 120, 121; *History* on experience of American, 2; James Logan's attitude toward, 138; meetings with William Markham, 112–13; memory and language in colonial relations of, 14; modes of communication, 169–70, 233n135; notion of "nether garments," 150; origins of, 17, 18, 25–32, 34–35, 38–39, 42; in *Penn's Treaty* image, 102, 103, 105, 115, 220n33; as prisoners, 63; relationship with white man, 129–30, 225n135; relations with Thomas Penn, 102–3; representation in *Leatherstocking Tales*, 1; skeleton fragments at Ellis Island, 185; tradition of relations in Pennsylvania, 96; use of wampum, 122–24, 129; way of recording land transactions, 21, 136, 141–47; written agreements with one another, 177. *See also specific tribes*

Native American Studies, 187–90, 236n10

natural law, 67

Neihardt, John, 53, 169

Nepal, 87

Neshaminy Creek, 135, 139, 147, 176

Netherlands, 59

New Amsterdam, 84, 150. *See also* New York City

Newcastle PA, 112

Newcomb, William, 48

New England, 87, 96. *See also* mid-Atlantic region

"New Historicism," 4, 198n23

New Jersey, 10, 135, 138–39, 141, 143, 180, 199n40, 200n42. *See also* East Jersey

New Netherland, 55, 56, 65, 84, 91, 92, 216n111. *See also* New York region

New World, 4, 122

New York Botanical Garden, 193

New York City, 10, 186, 195. *See also* Long Island; Manhattan; New Amsterdam; Staten Island

New York Harbor, 58, 62, 69, 70, 185–87, 235n6

New-York Historical Society, 65, 216n111
New York region, 55–56, 73, 115, 126, 193–96, 227n11. *See also* Long Island; Manhattan; New Netherland; Staten Island
New York State, 195, 199n40
New York Times, 185, 196
New Zealand, 130
Nichols, Deborah (Delaware), 150
Nonintercourse Act (1970), 178, 179, 180
North Africa, 72, 78. *See also* Africa
North America, 18, 34, 58, 69, 72, 92, 190
North American Review, 29
Northampton County PA, 177, 178, 182
Nutimus (Forks sachem): appeals for justice, 162–63; claim of Forks territory, 141–42; contest with James Logan, 136, 138–47, 150, 166; control over words, 22; eviction from Forks territory, 136, 165, 166; knowledge of 1686 events, 146; language ideology of, 150; memory of land transactions, 21; and Teedyuscung, 172, 174, 175; use of wampum, 170; and Walking Purchase agreement, 147, 152, 154, 176; on writing, 143, 145, 146. *See also* Forks Delaware Indians

oaths, 97–99. *See also* covenants; "Unbroken Faith"
Oestreicher, David M.: on battle in Heckewelder tradition, 28; and bullock hide story, 84; citation in biography, 206n67; on migration theory, 42, 206n58; on *Walam Olum*, 18, 39–42, 48–50, 205n43, 205n56, 206n62, 209n100
Ohio: Delaware National Council in, 207n86; Delawares' history in, 1, 71; Delaware territory in, 42, 49, 50, 133; and Native Americans' origin, 31; persecution of Moravians in, 121; sharing of stories in, 70; tortoise in, 193
Ojibwa Indians, 46, 129
Ojibwa Midewin Birchbark scrolls, 51
Oklahoma, 10, 70, 186, 187, 195, 196, 207n86. *See also* Anadarko OK; Bartlesville OK; Copan OK
Old Deb, 204n33
Oldmixon, John, 100–101
Old Testament, 87. *See also* Bible
Olick, Jeffrey K., 236n9
Onas. *See* Penn, William
Ong, Walter, 22, 202n88
Onondaga Indians, 127, 131, 163–66
Onondaga language, 153. *See also* Native American languages
Ontario, Canada, 70, 127, 195. *See also* Canada
oral history, 11, 98, 140–41, 187, 195–96, 218n10
oral tradition: and Delaware origin myth, 192; details in, 62, 63; and Dido motif, 19, 55–56, 69, 73, 76–77, 82, 83, 86, 92–93, 214n74,

oral tradition (*continued*)
215n100; on first contact, 56–57, 59, 62–64; and Great Treaty, 101, 104, 108–10, 116–17, 120; historical value of, 12, 56–59, 76, 92, 214n74; and Holy Scripture, 190; language ideologies in, 150–52; length of memory in, 187, 236n9; location and dating of, 210n9; memory through, 28, 58, 64, 188, 192, 193; and Native Americans' origin, 25, 28, 29, 33; in Native American–white man relationship, 35, 170, 233n135; range of cultural memory in, 120, 223n105; records of, 150; as rehearsal of past events, 161, 231n105; restriction of Indians' use in negotiation, 170; scholarship on, 11–12; testing for factual accuracy, 84; transcription of, 167, 232n124; on treaty of friendship, 129; and *Walam Olum*, 18, 36, 45, 49, 208n90, 209n100; and Walking Purchase agreement, 144–45, 160; and writing, 6, 7, 36, 145, 175, 192, 193, 198n23, 228n52. *See also* communication; speech; traditions
Otto, Paul, 61, 62
oxhide. *See* bullock hide motif

Pacific Ocean, 55
pacifism, 133, 226n2. *See also* peace
painters, 2, 102, 220n39. *See also* artists; Hicks, Edward; West, Benjamin

Palumbo, Anne Cannon, 103, 220n33
parables, 68
Parkman, Francis, 134
Parliament, 125
Parmenter, Jon, 219n29
parsing words, 150. *See also* equivocation; interpretation; language
Parton, Leona, 11
Passyunk, 112
past: and collective memory, 15–16; in chains of memory, 193; creation by national memory, 120, 223n103; in dynamics of memory approach, 103, 104, 194; Great Treaty as representation of colonial, 96, 102; link to present through *Walam Olum*, 45, 54; and map of New York Harbor, 187; and Native Americans' origin, 25, 27, 28, 31; rehearsal through talk, 161, 231n105; and representation of Walking Purchase, 137; spoken word as record of, 2–3; and Tatamy's Place lawsuit, 178, 179; traditions about arrival of Europeans in, 58–59, 64; and wampum belt at treaty meeting (1728), 17
paternalism, 129
peace, 104, 112, 118, 124, 125, 128, 131, 162. *See also* diplomacy; friendship; hospitality; pacifism
peace pipe, 218n9
Pearson, Bruce, 131, 225n140
Peau de Chat (Ojibwa), 129
Pemberton, Israel, 156–58, 168, 169, 181

294 ::: Index

Pemberton, James, 182
Penn, John Granville, 20, 126, 129
Penn, Thomas: commissioning of painting, 99, 103; and Indian Walk, 154; record of 1686 land transaction, 136; relations with Indians, 102–3; sale of land, 162; scheme to appropriate Forks of Delaware region, 139–40; and Tatamy's Place lawsuit, 179–81; and Teedyuscung's retraction, 175
Penn, William: Bessie Snake's reference to, 131, 225n140; blue sash of, 101, 102; bust of, 110; commemoration of treaty by, 110–11, 179; correspondence on treaty meeting, 111–13, 115, 118; Delaware and Iroquois titles of, 143; Delawares' memories of, 17, 130–32; and Delawares' name, 11; on Delawares' origin, 25; on economic transactions, 143; on equivocation, 149; Forks Delaware on words of, 162, 166; Governor Thomas on Great Treaty made by, 163; historical records on, 101, 115; *History* on arrival in Pennsylvania, 2; image of, 100–102; Indian policy of, 104, 220n40; Indians' memory of, 120; Iroquois on land purchases of, 163; James Logan as contemporary of, 138; John Oldmixon on, 100–101; land ownership of, 139; land transaction practices, 143–44; land transactions with Delawares, 112–13; legend of treaty with Delawares, 107, 221n49; lock of hair, 126; and memory of Great Treaty, 14, 15, 121; Nutimus on land claim of, 142; pledge of friendship, 116–18, 128, 130; in popular culture, 19–20, 33–34, 95–96; portrait of, 104, 118; prospective memory of, 16; values associated with, 103, 109, 160, 225n136; and wampum, 122, 124–25. *See also* colonists; Great Treaty; *Penn's Treaty with the Indians* (Hicks); *William Penn's Treaty with the Indians When He Founded the Province of Pennsylvania in North America* (West)
Pennebaker, James W., 210n11
Penn family: and "Antient Copy," 140; Benjamin West's painting in estate of, 219n20; James Logan's relationship with, 138; and legend of treaty under elm, 107, 221n49; need to sell land, 139; *Penn's Treaty* image as heritage of, 103; and Walking Purchase map, 147; wampum belts of, 20, 124–29, 225n129
Penn Manuscripts, 233n145
Pennsbury, 139–41
Penn Society, 111
Penn Society Obelisk, 179
Penn's Treaty. *See* Great Treaty
Penn's Treaty with the Indians (Hicks), 97, 98, 99. *See also* Hicks, Edward; Penn, William
Pennsylvania: Delaware Nation's lawsuit against Commonwealth of, 177; Delawares' attack on, 133,

Pennsylvania (continued)
166–67; distance measurement in, 153; Francis Jennings on Indian relations in, 5; history of Great Treaty in, 95, 110–13, 121, 125, 131–32; History on William Penn's arrival in, 2; Indian-white man relationship in, 130; James Logan's importance in, 138; Leonard Thompson on Delawares in, 195; map of, 135; monument to founding of, 111; peace with Indians in, 118; Penn's Treaty image in, 99–100; policy of justness in, 144; popular images of, 33–34; treatment of Delawares by people of, 161, 231n104; Unami dialect in, 235n6; use of wampum by governors of, 122. See also Eastern Pennsylvania; specific places in; Western Pennsylvania

Pennsylvania, Eastern District, District Court, 178, 180

Pennsylvania Academy of Fine Arts, 102

Pennsylvania Assembly, 133, 149, 167–68, 182, 232n127

Pennsylvania Charter (1861), 97

Pennsylvania Gazette, 181, 182

Pennsylvania Hospital, 110

Pennsylvania Proprietors: accusation of fraud by, 6, 133–35, 142, 167, 181; and affidavit on treatment of Indians, 161, 231n104; and defense funding delay, 133, 226n2; and eviction of Delawares from Forks territory, 136, 147, 165–66; and Indian Walk, 154–56; interest in Forks territory, 180; interpretation of walk, 150, 160; Luke Wills Brodhead's suggestion about, 183; Moses Tatamy's testimony about, 141; offer of wampum to Six Nations, 146–47, 163–64; political agreements with Delawares, 112; Quakers' rivalry with, 133–34, 161, 168–69, 176, 232n127; scheme to appropriate Forks of Delaware region, 139–41; settlement with Teedyuscung, 175; on Teedyuscung's demands, 168–69; on terms of Walking Purchase, 21, 158–59; and title of Tatamy's Place, 179

Pennsylvania State Archives, 114, 117, 119, 128. See also archives

Pennsylvania Supreme Court, 158, 180

Penn Treaty Park, 115

Penn Wampum Belts, 20, 124–29, 225n129. See also belts, wampum

Percy, Thomas, 33

permanence, 145–46, 160

Peters, Richard, 109, 140, 159, 179, 181

"Petition from the Indians at Mashpee to the Massachusetts General Court," 52

Phaedrus (Plato), 120, 145

Philadelphia History Museum at the Atwater Kent, 124

Philadelphia Inquirer, 183

Philadelphia PA: Delaware and Schuylkil Indians in, 128; geo-

graphic referents of historical traditions in, 108; Great Elm in, 95, 106; Great Treaty in, 33–34, 99; meeting of Forks Delaware and Six Nations in, 163–66; monument to Great Treaty in, 111; and *Penn's Treaty* image, 102, 103; political treaty of Susquehannocks in, 117–18; Quaker School in, 171; treaty with Governor Morris in, 171
Philippine Islands, 76, 215n100. *See also* Manila
Philipse Patent, 135, 227n11
Phoenicians, 25
phratries, 193, 196, 237n30
pictography, 8, 27, 36–40, 37, 43, 45–47, 52–53, 209n106. *See also* writing
Pilgrims, 96, 119–20
Pilgrim's Progress (Bunyan), 230n76
place, 13, 200n51. *See also* landmarks
Plato, 120, 145, 146, 228n52
Plymouth Rock, 97, 119–20
poetry, 137
political regimes, 179
political relations, 102–3, 112, 132–34, 136, 139, 170, 226n2, 233n135, 236n9
political treaties, 107, 113, 117, 221n49
Poolaw, Linda (Delaware), 48, 49, 208n90
popular historians, 19–20, 44–45. *See also* historians
popular memory, 99, 106, 120, 121, 219n16. *See also* memory

popular traditions: and communities of memory, 12, 13; Delawares' place in, 33–34; of Dido motif, 215n100; of Great Treaty, 14–15, 19–20, 33–34, 95–104; Lappawinzoe's comment on Indian Walk in, 156, 230n93; representations of Indians in, 2; on Walking Purchase, 134, 135. *See also* traditions
portraits, 4, 104–5, 219n16
Portuguese, 69, 73–82, 85–89, 91, 92, 215n89
Potomack River, 26
Pott, Friedrich, 86, 216n114
power, 129–30, 146–47, 150–51, 159, 165, 170, 176, 225n135, 233n135
Powhatan Indians, 225n135
"The Prairies" (Bryant), 30–31
prehistory, 50, 54. *See also* history
Presbyterians, 181. *See also* religion
present, 15–16, 27, 45, 54, 179, 194
presentist memory approach, 103–5. *See also* memory
Priest, Josiah, 30, 31
Prix Volney essay contest. *See* Royal Institute of France essay contest
production: as historical moment, 22, 29, 65, 102; of *Walam Olum*, 38, 42, 43
promise keeping, 150–51
property ownership, 137, 180, 234n166. *See also* land transactions
Proud, Robert, 101, 219n20
Provincial Council, 166–68, 171, 181, 232n127. *See also* councils

public, 143, 144, 169, 174
publication, 58, 143, 144, 167
public treaties, 178
Pueblo revolt, 59, 210n12
Punic faith, 55, 72, 79, 89, 91–93. See also faithfulness; "Unbroken Faith"
Purchas, Samuel, 54
Pu Songling, 83, 215n100

Quakers: accounts of Great Treaty, 101; at council meetings with Teedyuscung, 171, 172, 175; on defense funding, 133, 167–68, 226n2; and equivocation, 149; and founding of Pennsylvania, 97, 117; on Great Elm, 109; and imperialism, 138; legend of treaty with Delawares, 107, 221n49; and Moses Tatamy's land, 182; on oaths, 98; and *Penn's Treaty* image, 99, 102; Proprietors' rivalry with, 133–34, 161, 168–69, 176, 232n127; role in Walking Purchase, 21, 93, 133, 134; and settlement with Teedyuscung, 175; as Teedyuscung's agents, 168–69; and Teedyuscung's request for clerk, 171, 172, 176; on terms of Walking Purchase, 158–59; and Thomas Penn, 103; and vulnerability of frontier to attacks, 167–68
Quipos. See khipu

Raffles, Thomas Stamford, 89
Rafinesque, Constantine S.: and authenticity of *Walam Olum*, 41, 42, 54, 206n62; background of, 38; biography of, 205n56; copy of *Walam Olum*, 18; and date of *Walam Olum*, 38, 205n43; and Native Americans' origin, 27; on "Olumapi," 47; and pictography in *Walam Olum*, 37, 39–40, 43; publication of *Walam Olum*, 39, 44, 49; on removal, 42; transcription of, 53
Rainy Mountain, 187–88
Rajamora, 81
Ralegh, Sir Walter, 3–4
Rampapough Mountain Indians, 200n42
Ranger, Terrence, 103
Rasmussen, Birgit Brander, 165
reading, 167–70. See also literacy; writing
reception: and bullock hide metaphor, 65; as historical moment, 22, 23; and Native Americans' origin, 29; of *Penn's Treaty* image, 103; of *Walam Olum*, 40, 42, 51, 52; of Walking Purchase, 93
reconstruction, 41, 53, 205n56
recorded traditions, 47, 50, 55, 56, 86. See also records; traditions
records: Bessie Snake on diplomacy, 131, 225n140; comparison to wampum, 11; of Delawares' history, 15, 16; Delawares' keeping of, 51–52; and Dido motif, 19, 20; generations of representations of, 175; of Great Treaty, 20, 99, 101; of Native American-European

encounters in writing, 35; and Native Americans' origin, 25; Native Americans' writing as, 188–89; of oral tradition, 150; scholarship on, 3–7, 11–12; spoken word as, 2–3; Tantaqué's tortoise as, 193–94; and Tatamy's Place lawsuit, 181; of Teedyuscung's speeches, 167, 168, 176; value of, 18; and *Walam Olum*, 38, 45; of Walking Purchase, 21–22; wampum as, 122, 123, 125; of William Penn's land transactions, 111–13; written by Europeans, 54. *See also* documentary records; recorded traditions; writing
recovery, agenda of, 48, 52
red, 60, 61, 63, 68
Redinger, Rachel Bair, 207n86
Reese, Paul, 183
Reid, Anthony, 73–76
relics. *See* archeological artifacts
religion, 42–43. *See also* Bible; Christianity; missions and missionaries; Moravians; Presbyterians
Rementer, James: on Bessie Snake's stories, 212n45, 225n140, 226n141; and bullock hide story, 84; on Delaware Nation Council, 207n86; on harvest ceremony, 155, 230n90; on Lenape language, 153; on memories of Great Treaty, 131, 225n140, 226n141
reminiscences, newspaper, 204n33
removal, 17, 26, 29, 30, 42–43, 131
Rendell, Ed, 177, 179

representation: and bullock hide motif, 65, 68, 69, 87, 93; of Delaware-colonist interactions, 11, 16–19, 58, 59; of Delaware ontogeny, 190, 192; of Delaware-Talligewi battle, 28–29; in generations of records, 175; of Great Treaty, 96, 97–99, 102, 104, 105, 108; as historical moment, 22, 23; and history writing, 15; of Indians by artists and writers, 1, 2, 36; John Heckewelder on, 28; and language ideology, 8; in popular culture, 33–34; of Rainy Mountain, 188; scholarship on, 3–7; Teedyuscung's attempt to control, 176; *Walam Olum* as, 49, 51; of Walking Purchase, 137; of wampum belts, 127–29. *See also* misrepresentation
Representations (journal), 4
Revadanda (Chaul), 81
revision, canon, 52
revitalization movements, 194
Revolutionary War, 101, 121, 186, 219n20
Reynal, Abbé, 99
Richardson Medal, 118
Richter, Daniel, 56–57
Rigal, Laura, 220n33, 220n39
roadside markers, 178. *See also* monuments
Roman fort, 31
Roman History (Ab urbe condita) (Livy), 88
romantic archeologists, 26–27, 30, 32. *See also* archeologists

romantic scholars, 53, 206n67. *See also* scholarship
Rome, 31, 87–89
Roth, Jane, 180
Royal Academy, 99
Royal Institute of France essay contest, 38, 41, 205n43
"run," 152–56, 230n76
"running walk," 156
Rush, Benjamin, 110
Rutgers University, 39

Saar, Johann Jacob, 77
sachem, 191
Said, Edward, 138
Salisbury, Neal, 225n135
Sanderson, Eric, 186
Sapir, Edward, 207n78
Sassoonan (Delaware), 116, 118, 128
Saussure, Ferdinand de, 150
savages, 103–5, 221n43
Sayhoppy (Delaware sachem), 160, 175
The Scarlet Letter (Hawthorne), 22–23
Scharf, J. Thomas, 115
scholarship: on collective memory, 161, 231n105; on communities of memory, 9–14; on context of historical memory, 130; on cultural forgetting, 17, 201n72; on Delaware origin myth, 190; on Dido motif, 80–81, 84, 86, 93; on first contact, 56–58; on Indian-European relations, 130, 225n135; on James Logan, 138; on memory, 187, 236n10; by non-Indians, 15, 45, 48–50, 53; on records and representations, 3–7; on span of memory, 98, 178–79, 187, 218n10, 236n9; on treaty tradition, 96; "truth" in, 59; on *Walam Olum*, 40–53, 206n67, 209n100; on Walking Purchase, 21–22, 133–35; on wampum, 122–29. *See also* archeological study; archival research; ethnography; historians; historiography; romantic scholars
Schoolcraft, Henry Rowe, 31, 33, 34, 44, 46, 70
Schutt, Amy, 194
Schuylkil Indians, 128
Schwartz, Barry, 213n59
Scull, John, 17
Scythians, 25, 26, 31
Searle, John, 145–46
Sebring, Jacob, 162
Seelye, John D., 120, 223n103
Sellers, Charles Coleman, 99
Servius, 72, 83
Setauket, Long Island, 193. *See also* Long Island
Shackamaxon, 14, 19–20, 95–96, 101, 102, 112–15, 119
Shakespeare, William, 54, 86
Shamokin, 163, 166
Shapp, Milton J., 99–100
Shawnee Indians, 9, 16, 114, 128
Shell, Marc, 50, 52, 53, 209n100
Shils, Edward, 13
Shorto, Russell, 61
Showalter, Michael S., 225n136
Siberia, 76

300 ::: Index

signatory marks, 154, 170
Sikandar. See Mirror of Sikandar
Silverberg, Robert, 30
Simms, Maxey, 212n48
Sinhalese war poem, 77
Six Nations, 127, 133, 136, 146–47, 163–66, 176, 181. See also Iroquois Indians
Sky, David (Onondaga), 127, 129
Slauter, Eric, 198n22
Sluyter, Peter, 190–94
Smith, Joseph, 42
Smith, Timothy, 154–55, 231n105
Snake, Bessie, 63, 68, 71, 131, 212n45, 225n140
Snake, Richard, 195–96
Snake, Willy, 195
social cliques, 15
social institutions, 188
social memory. See memory, collective
social order, 8, 16
social reciprocity, 61
social structure, 129–30, 225n135
Socrates, 120, 145
Sollors, Werner, 50, 52, 209n100
Song of Hiawatha (Longfellow), 33, 45–46, 50
Songs of Ossian (MacPherson), 32–33, 42
Sousa, Martim Afonso de, 79
South Africa, 73, 77. See also Africa
Southeast Asia, 73–76. See also Asia
Spady, James, 220n40
Spanish, 59, 73, 80–82, 86, 87, 89, 92
Speck, Frank, 127, 129, 155, 230n90

speech, 2–3, 5, 8, 10–12, 17, 22, 70. See also language; oral tradition
speech acts, 145–47, 163–64, 176. See also written utterances
speeches, 122–24, 156, 167, 173, 230n93
Squier, Ephraim George, 44, 206n67
Staten Island, 193, 199n40. See also New York City; New York region
State University of New York at Purchase, 84
Statue of Liberty National Monument, 185–87, 196
Stimmer, Tobias, 85
Stockbridge-Munsee Community of Mohican Indians, 186, 196
Stockertown PA, 183
Stoke Park, 219n20
Stone, Frederick, 111–12, 116–19
stories, 187. See also folkloric motif; tales
Strachey, William, 86–87
Stretcher, Mathias, 179
strings, wampum, 11, 121–24, 146–47, 162–65. See also wampum
sublime, 35, 204n37
Subrahmanyam, Sanjay, 69, 214n89
Sucesos de las Islas Filipinas (Morga), 80–81
Sun Dance, 188, 189, 194
Supreme Court. See Pennsylvania Supreme Court; U.S. Supreme Court
Susquehannah River, 26, 167, 176, 182
Susquehannock Indians, 107, 112, 117–18, 142

Swann, Brian, 131, 212n45, 225n140
Swanton, John R., 70, 72, 212n55
Swedish settlers, 108, 113
symbolization, 68–69, 164–65, 211n26
Syng, Philip, 149

Taiwan, 73, 76–77, 80, 82–84, 89, 215n100
T'ai-wan fu chi (Gazetteer of the Prefecture of Taiwan), 80
tales, 59, 76–77. *See also* folkloric motif; stories
Talligewi, 26, 28–31, 35, 36
Tamanend (Delaware sachem), 19–20, 33–34, 97, 113, 128
Tammany. *See* Tamanend (Delaware sachem)
Tammany Societies, 33–34
Tantaqué (Munsee), 190–94, 196.
Taquatarensaly. *See* Captain Civility
Tartars, 25, 31
Tatamy, Moses: application for land grant, 180–81; deposition of, 139; illegal appropriation of land of, 177–78; on James Logan and Nutimus's confrontation, 141; and lawsuit, 137, 179–81; loss of land, 181–82, 182; memory of, 183; on Nutimus's land inheritance, 142; sobriety of, 182, 235n174; on Teedyuscung's request for clerk, 171–72; on walk, 141, 156, 160; on writing, 143, 164
Tatamy, Nicholas, 182
Tatamy, William, 181

Tatamy Gap, 183
Tatamy PA, 183
Tatamy's Place, 177–83. *See also* land transactions
Taughhaughsey (Delaware sachem), 160, 175
taxation, 226n2
Taylor, Zachary, 71
Tedlock, Dennis, 50–51, 53, 209n100
Teedyuscung (Delaware): allegation of fraud, 21, 134, 136–37, 142, 161, 166–77, 181; attempt to control representations, 176; on cause for hostility, 133, 167, 172; control over words, 22; delivery of grievances, 172–74, 233n145; drunkenness of, 235n174; on own memory, 170–71; placation of, 174–75; and Quakers, 134, 168, 226n4; representation of speeches, 5–6; request for literacy instruction, 169, 176–77, 182; requests at treaty council meetings, 168–72, 174, 176, 182; retraction of fraud allegations, 160–61, 175, 176; speeches of, 167, 173; on written records of Walking Purchase, 144, 172
Teeshacomin (Teeshakomen) (Delaware), 152, 154, 176
The Tempest (Shakespeare), 86
Thomas, Brook, 22
Thomas, Cyrus, 31–32
Thomas, Governor George, 162–63, 165–66, 181
Thompson, Leonard, 195
Thomson, Charles, 134, 141, 169, 171

Tiers, Clarence Van Dyke, 110
Tischucunck (Tisheekunk) (Delaware), 140–41, 152
Tishhexkam (Tashiowycam) (Delaware), 142
title, chain of, 177, 179–80. *See also* documentary records; land transactions
Tohickon Creek, 135, 141, 142, 147–49, 158, 167, 176
tortoise, 191–94, 196, 237n30. *See also* turtles
Township of Forks, 177, 183
Tracks (Erdrich), 189
trade and trading houses: and bullock hide tradition, 66–67, 73, 76, 88; in Carthage, 89–90; and colonization formula, 91; of fur, 122; and *Penn's Treaty* image, 103, 220n33, 220n39; William Penn's letter on, 113. *See also* Free Society of Traders; wampum
traditions: accounts of, 60; and communities of memory, 11–13; cultural, 56, 58, 189, 190; dynamic view of, 16, 103, 104, 194, 201n68; erosion of knowledge of, 189; and first contact, 56–65; of hospitality, 88–89; and Native Americans' origin, 25–29, 32, 33; negative evidence against, 19, 77, 79, 82, 115; representations as historical records, 7; testing for factual accuracy, 84–85; transmission of, 16, 19, 78, 82, 201n68; value of representations of, 18; and *Walam Olum*, 40, 49. *See also* allegories; bullock hide motif; Celtic traditions; Dido motif; Great Treaty; historical traditions; legends; migration; oral tradition; popular traditions; recorded traditions
transcription: of Bessie Snake's account, 131, 225n140; and first contact, 58, 61; hazards of, 3; of native accounts, 93; of Teedyuscung's speeches, 167, 232n124; of treaty council minutes, 5–6; of *Walam Olum*, 27, 36, 52, 53, 209n100; of Walking Purchase records, 22
translatio imperii et studii, 88
translation: of bullock's hide story, 66, 80, 88, 93, 215n91; and equivocation, 150; and first contact, 58, 63; hazards of, 3, 144; of Indians' chant, 204n32; of *Penn's Treaty* image, 102; Richard Adams on, 189; of treaty council minutes, 5–6, 170; of *Walam Olum*, 27, 36, 38–40, 44, 47–49, 52–53; of Walking Purchase records, 22. *See also* interpretation
transparency, 174
"travel," 152
travel writers, 93, 221n43
"Treaty Elm." *See* tree, Great Elm
treaty meetings: and communities of memory, 14; and eviction of Delawares from Forks territory, 131, 163–66; on land purchase (1686), 140–42; map from Philadelphia

treaty meetings (continued) (1737), 148; and memory of Great Treaty, 121; in Pennsbury (1735), 139–41; repetition of wampum messages in, 164; representation of Teedyuscung's speeches at, 5–6; Teedyuscung at, 167–77, 182; on Walking Purchase, 147, 148, 162; wampum in, 11, 17, 122–24; William Penn's correspondence on, 111–13. *See also* councils

treaty minutes: petition for banishment exemption in, 181; Teedyuscung's desire for clerk to take, 169, 170–72; on Teedyuscung's list of grievances, 174; on Teedyuscung's speeches, 167, 168; on Walking Purchase, 137, 139

Treaty of Fort Stanwix (1768), 103

Treaty of Waitangi (1840), 130

treaty tradition: in Benjamin West's painting, 219n29; dynamics of memory approach to, 102, 104; between Europeans and indigenous peoples, 130; friendship in, 116; historical basis for, 112–13; and memory, 16, 17, 23, 96, 98; records of, 101–2, 111–19; trees in, 107, 109; "Unbroken Faith" in, 99, 107, 117, 125, 132; wampum in, 124. *See also* agreements; Great Treaty

tree, Great Elm: in civic myth of Great Treaty, 97; Indians' mention of, 120; loss of, 20, 23, 107–10; and memory of Great Treaty, 14, 113, 179; monument on site of, 99; in *Penn's Treaty* image, 105–10, 221n43; popular historians on, 19–20, 95–96, 101–2; records on, 114; relics from, 109–10, 119, 125; as "silent witness," 106–7, 110; symbolism of, 119

trees, 107, 178, 192, 194

Trojans, 89

Tromba, Anthony, 83

Trowbridge, C. C., 71

Trumbull, John, 13

truth: of "Antient Copy," 140; and archival positivism, 19–20; artists' conception of, 105, 220n41; and bullock hide motif, 65, 66, 77, 83, 84; cultural boundedness of, 59; and Delawares' origin, 29, 193; and Great Treaty, 98; in history, 83, 137, 215n101; of John Heckewelder's "verbatim" account, 60; in *Penn's Treaty* image, 105; in records and representations, 7, 16; of Teedyuscung's fraud allegation, 176; on value of writing, 159; in writing vs. oral tradition, 35, 57, 164. *See also* authenticity; authority; equivocation; facts; historical accuracy; historical value; historicity

turkey phratry (clan), 237n30

Turner, Frederick Jackson, 31–32

Turtle Island, 191–92

turtle phratry (clan), 193, 196, 237n30

turtles, 49, 50, 193–94, 208n90, 237n31. *See also* tortoise

Unalachtigo tribe, 237n30
Unami dialect, 186, 235n6
Unami Indians, 142, 193, 237n30
"Unbroken Faith," 99, 107, 117, 125, 132. *See also* covenants; faithfulness; oaths; Punic faith
underwear, 66, 67, 150
Unitas Fratrum (United Brotherhood). *See* Moravians
United Brotherhood. *See* Moravians
United States, 17, 32–33, 36, 40–41, 46, 50, 71, 178. *See also* Americans; colonists
U.S. Capitol, 97
U.S. Supreme Court, 178
Uther, Hans-Jörg, 72

van der Donck, Adriaen, 59, 62
Van Dusen, Mr., 110
Vansina, Jan, 11, 29, 57, 59, 84, 201n68, 210n9, 218n10
Vaux, Roberts, 13, 108–11, 120, 132, 179
Veillard, Louis Guillaume Le, 149–50
Verhoef, Willem Pieterzoon, 91
Verhulst, Willem, 91
Verrazano, Giovanni da, 62
Vietnam War, 71
Vinitzky-Seroussi, Vered, 236n9
Virgil, 65, 67–68, 72, 86–89
Voegelin, C. F., 46, 47, 207n78
Voegelin, Erminie, 47
Voltaire, 2, 97–99, 125

Wade, Jeffrey, 215n91
Wagner, Günter, 212n48

Walam Olum: absence of records on, 20; and American intellectual climate, 42; authenticity of, 18, 27, 40–54, 206n58, 206n62, 206n67, 207n78, 207n86, 209n100; and chains of memory, 193; Constantine Rafinesque as creator of, 41, 205n56; date of, 38, 58, 205n43; Delawares' exposure to, 49, 208n86, 208n90; "Fragment" of, 38–39, 42, 50, 206n62; ideological tendencies of, 40; Joe Napora on, 48, 207n85; and Native Americans' origin, 27, 28; pictography in, 36–38, 37; political tendencies of, 40, 42, 44, 50, 52; readers of, 36–38; reception of, 17–18; romantic scholars on, 53, 206n67; as sacred text, 49
"walk," 150, 152–54
Walking Purchase (1737): blank space in agreement, 154; and colonial trickery, 68–69; comparison to bullock hide motif, 93; date of, 132; Delawares' complaints about, 161–62; description of, 71; description of land tract in, 147–49, 152; as epitomizing event, 70; and Great Treaty, 96, 98, 131, 133; historical moments in, 23; historiography on, 21, 134; and "Indian Way" of land transaction, 141–47; as "infamous," 2, 133, 136, 197n8; and lawsuit, 137; maps pertaining to, 137, 147, 148, 157; memory in negotiations of, 171; and Moses

Walking Purchase (continued)
Tatamy's application for land, 180, 181; official history of, 163; patents similar to, 135, 226n11; phases of, 136–37; records on, 20–21; as scheme to appropriate Forks of Delaware region, 139–40; scholarship on, 7; and Tatamy's Place lawsuit, 177, 179, 181; Teedyuscung on lands lost in, 169, 176; and Teedyuscung's request for clerk, 171, 172; Teedyuscung's request for documentation of, 144; terms of, 136, 147–54, 156–58, 160; walkers in, 154; wording of agreement, 150, 152–54, 158–59, 176. *See also* agreements; Bucks County PA; day and a half's walk; Indian Walk; land transactions

Wallace, Anthony F. C., 129, 133, 134, 174, 226n2, 226n4

Wallace, Mike, 61, 62

Wallamâning (place-name), 39

wampum: authority in spoken recollections, 3; colonists' use of, 170; and communities of memory, 11; functions of, 17, 163–64; and Great Treaty, 15, 121–24; in Indian–white man relationship, 170; and language ideology, 8; ongoing relationships through, 163–65; preparation and repetition of, 164–65; studies of, 122; Teedyuscung's receipt from Beaver, 177; and Walking Purchase controversy, 162–65. *See also* belts, wampum; communication; strings, wampum; trade and trading houses

Wampum, Chief John. *See* Waubuno ("Chief John Wampum")

Ward, Dr. (of Indiana), 38, 46

Ward, Matthew C., 168, 232n127

warfare, 26, 28–29, 96

Washington, George, 219n16

water, 35–36, 194. *See also* flood

Watson, John (son of Bucks County surveyor), 156, 158

Watson, John Fanning, 12–13, 105–7, 109, 110, 114, 116, 117

Watson's Annals (Watson), 106–7

Waubuno ("Chief John Wampum"), 130, 212n45

Weems, Mason, 101, 102, 106

Wehixamukes (culture hero), 151

Weiser, Conrad, 139, 141, 146–47, 172

Welikia Project, 186–87

Weslager, C. A., 43, 50

the West, 103

West, Benjamin: biography of, 221n49; and communities of memory, 13; and date of Great Treaty, 97–98, 115; family of, 104–5, 108; as informant on treaty tradition, 102; letter to W. Darton, 103–4, 220n39; likenesses in paintings of, 104–5, 108–9, 113, 118; memories about, 108; painting by, 96, 99–100; in popular culture, 33–34; representation of Indians, 2, 115; reproductions and adaptations of painting of Great Treaty, 19–20; on title of painting, 225n136. *See also* painters; *William Penn's Treaty with the Indians When He Founded the Province of Pennsylvania in North America* (West)

West, Thomas, 10

West, William, 104–5

Westcott, Thompson, 115

Western Pennsylvania, 1. *See also* Pennsylvania

West India Company, 66, 77, 89, 91, 211n27, 217n134

West New Jersey, 143. *See also* New Jersey

White Eyes, 28

whites: and authenticity of *Walam Olum*, 42; and bullock hide motif, 68–70, 189–90; in *Leatherstocking Tales*, 36; and Moses Tatamy, 182; and Native Americans' origin, 30–31, 33; Native American tradition on arrival of, 71; relationship with Native Americans, 129–30, 225n135, 225n140. *See also* Americans; Christianity; colonists; Europeans

Wildlife Conservation Society, 186

Wilkinson, James, 7

William Penn Day, 131, 226n141

William Penn Medal, 118, 125, 218n9, 219n29

William Penn's Treaty with the Indians When He Founded the Province of Pennsylvania in North America (West): bolt of cloth in, 220n39; commissioning of painting, 99, 103; dissemination of, 99, 101, 219n20; in popular culture, 33–34; interpretations of, 100, 101–3, 105–6, 219n29, 220n33, 220n39; likenesses in, 104; memories about, 108; phrasing of title, 225n136; popularity of, 99–101, 219n16; as record of event, 118, 119; reproductions and adaptations of, 19–20; significance of, 96; and William Penn Medal, 218n9. *See also* Penn, William; West, Benjamin

Wisconsin, 186

witnesses, 32, 113, 140–41, 154, 161

Wolf, Edwin II, 138

wolf phratry (clan), 237n30

Wood, Joseph, 140

Woodland periods, 70, 185, 193, 194

Woolard, Kathryn, 8, 167, 232n124

words, 150–53, 156–59, 165, 166, 176, 230n76. *See also* equivocation; language

Works Progress Administration, 11

Wrightstown PA, 178

writing: absence of records in, 19–21, 95, 96, 101, 102, 113–20, 125; alphabetic, 3, 9, 123; and authenticity of *Walam Olum*, 40, 43, 44, 50–53, 209n106; authority of, 118, 145, 146, 171, 175, 228n52; Chinese symbol for, 39; and communities of memory, 10; comparison to wampum, 11, 122–23; at council meetings with Teedyuscung, 168–72; definition of, 9; and Delawares'

writing (continued)
history, 15, 191–92; dependence on, 120; and documentation of Great Treaty, 121, 125; Egyptian system of, 209n106; first-contact encounters in, 56–57; and language ideology, 8–9; in legal system, 170, 233n135; mediated Native American, 169; and Native Americans' origin, 25, 27; Native Americans' participation in colonial-era events involving, 167; and oral traditions, 6, 7, 36, 145, 175, 192, 193, 198n23, 228n52; "picture writing" as precursor to, 33, 45, 47, 48; as record, 3–4, 16–17, 188–89; records of European-Indian encounters in, 35, 54; representation in wampum belt, 127; role in Walking Purchase, 136, 145–46, 156–60, 164–65; scholarship on, 11–12, 22, 202n88; as speech act, 145–46; Teedyuscung's desire for agreement with Beaver in, 177; Teedyuscung's grievances in, 174; Teedyuscung's retraction in, 175; treachery in, 143–45, 159–60, 228n52. *See also* books; communication; documentary records; historiography; language; literacy; pictography; reading; records; written utterances

writ of certiorari, 178

written utterances, 145–46, 159. *See also* speech acts; writing

Wyandot Indians, 29, 30, 69, 70

Wyoming, 165–67, 169, 172, 177

Yeates, James, 154, 155

Young, Alfred Fabian, 221n49

Yuchi Indians, 68–69, 70, 212n48

Zeisberger, David, 27, 28, 39, 153

Zhang Xie, 80

DATE DUE

			PRINTED IN U.S.A.